Gordon Burn is the author of four acclaimed novels: *Alma Cogan* (winner of the Whitbread First Novel Prize), *Fullalove*, *The North of England Home Service* and *Born Yesterday*. He is also the author of the non-fiction titles *Somebody's Husband, Somebody's Son*, *Pocket Money*, *Happy Like Murderers*, *On the Way to Work* (with Damien Hirst) and *Best and Edwards*. Gordon Burn died in 2009.

SEX & VIOLENCE, DEATH & SILENCE

Encounters with Recent Art

GORDON BURN

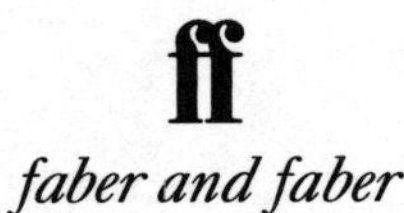

faber and faber

First published in 2009
by Faber and Faber Ltd
Bloomsbury House
74–77 Great Russell Street
London WC1B 3DA

Typeset by Ian Bahrami
Printed in England by T.J. International, Padstow, Cornwall

A CIP record for this book
is available from the British Library

ISBN 978–0–571–22929–1

10 9 8 7 6 5 4 3 2 1

CONTENTS

Contents

'A THOUSAND DEATHS
SURROUND US . . .'

FOREWORD FOR GORDON

I first met Gordon Burn twice: once on Dewsbury Market, in 1985, when I bought a second-hand copy of *Somebody's Husband, Somebody's Son*; and then in the Duke of York pub, in 2002, when we were introduced by our publisher. He was the writer I admired the most, the only one I had ever wanted to meet, and so I was tongue-tied. I was also very lucky, because Gordon became a friend.

Damien Hirst knew Gordon much better and for much longer than I did. This book, *Sex & Violence, Death & Silence*, is not only about that relationship. However, that relationship, their friendship, is at the heart of this book. And so, on Wednesday 9 September 2009, at Science in London, I met Damien to talk about that relationship, their friendship.

And to remember Gordon.

DAVID PEACE: *How did you first meet Gordon?*
DAMIEN HIRST: It was at the Saatchi Gallery. Rachel Whiteread was in a group show there and I'd gone down to see that. Gordon was writing something about Rachel. And so he just sort of turned up, and he was a Geordie and a bit of a lad. And Rachel said he was cool. Then later I think he got asked by the *Guardian* to do a follow-up piece where he wrote about me . . .

And what year was this?
I'm really crap at dates; early nineties.

But had you read Somebody's Husband, Somebody's Son *or* Alma Cogan?
No, I'd not read any of the books, not come across them. But then I met him and really liked him and I went home to my missus and said, 'I met this great guy today.' And I invited him and Carol [Gorner, Gordon's wife] over for dinner, and we all liked a bit of a booze-up. And I love snooker and I found out that he'd written that book [*Pocket Money*] about snooker. And then there was the Yorkshire Ripper book . . .

That's how I first came across Gordon's writing: Somebody's Husband, Somebody's Son, *the Yorkshire Ripper . . .*
That was when I was growing up. And I lived in Roundhay [in Leeds], so it was all around my house . . .

Wilma McCann, Irene Richardson . . .
Soldiers Fields and Canal Gardens. Two of the bodies. I cut through Canal Gardens that night, so I walked past where the body was. Without seeing the body. I used to sneak out the house at night. Nicking apples, hedge-jumping. So, on the way back home, I went through there. Canal Gardens. And then the next day it was cordoned off, police everywhere.

So once you got to know Gordon, you found out he'd written that book?
Well, he wrote about me, so I knew he was a writer, and so I sneakily went out and got the books and had a read. But then I just loved what he wrote about me. Because there's just so much shit, isn't there? With art writing. So much bollocks. People who've swallowed dictionaries. All that crap. And I just really loved Gordon, because everything he wrote, it was with real economy. But still very poetical, very lyrical.

Did he ever talk to you about how he became so fascinated with art, with writing about art?
No, not really. But I always thought Gordon was really an artist in his own right. I think anything done well is art. And Gordon took it very seriously. He dragged it out of himself, almost like fucking carving it out of marble. Really hammered it around. And it had a form. But I suppose 'economy' is the best word. It just has this wonderful economy, his writing. And then there's the cheekiness, and the humour. He has a dig at you as well . . .

I remember him telling me, 'Now your book's being made into a film, you're finished. It'll all go to your head. All over now . . .'
Like that with me. All the fucking time.

How did the cover of Happy Like Murderers *come about?*
Well, Gordon said to me that that was the kiss of death that cover. But I'd said to him, 'You want something fucking eye-catching.' And it's called *Happy Like Murderers*, and it was when it was Acid House. And so I said, 'You need a fucking smiley face on it. It'll sell loads.' And so Gordon went, 'Will you do the cover?' And he brought the ball in – he had that little ball, he found it somewhere, the dog found it – and so I just shot it in earth. But I think it was too gruesome really. I think we would have been better to have just had a yellow cover with a big fucking face on it. But then he always said to me, 'Thanks for that, kiss of death, ruined that book for me, you did, your cover.'

It is an incredible book . . .
A very dark book. He came down and played me the tapes of Fred West being interviewed by the police. Stayed up till like six in the morning listening to them. Did my head in, six hours of them. And then he showed me the videos, the videos of Rose. Porn videos. But I think it was doing his head in, that's

why he came down and showed them to me. He needed some company.

Well, he said to me he'd never write about serial killers, murderers again after that. But that book, it puts you right inside that house, right inside their minds.
Gordon always went really deep into all these things. All the things he wrote about. But I always thought art and crime were really close, too. The creative process, the creation aspect. Crime is creative.

I think that connection was always there for Gordon, from Alma Cogan *to this book [*Sex & Violence, Death & Silence*], especially in the pieces on Luc Tuymans, Gregor Schneider and, obviously, the court artists.*
And I always think you don't need explanation. There's a great thing Schnabel said in an interview once. He'd painted a leaf on a canvas. And it's huge. And they asked him, 'Why did you paint that leaf?' And he said, 'I just looked at it and I thought the veins of a leaf are like the veins of my arm.' And I think those sorts of things – to make those sorts of comparisons, but to not have an opinion either way, whether it's good or bad, but to just say, 'Hey, don't you think this is like that?' – Gordon did a lot of that where you wouldn't expect it, just to make people make connections.

Where did the idea to do On the Way to Work *come from?*
Well, we just started to do some interviews and didn't really know when to stop. I think he was fascinated with the idea of 'the artist against the world'.

Punk rock . . .
Well, you know Joe Strummer edited *On the Way to Work* for me? I was trying to edit it, go through all the stuff Gordon had

sent me. And Joe said, 'I'll read through it for you.' And he took it home that night and brought it back the next day, and he'd gone through it and corrected it all: Rizla spelt wrong/ Gary Hume won't like this bit/Is Lucian Freud a friend of yours, because he won't be after this. Joe didn't do a lot. But Gordon could put in some quite edgy stuff. So Joe just protected the innocent a bit more. And so then I gave that transcript back to Gordon and he's given it to the Tate. So they've got Gordon's transcript with Joe's corrections.

What do you think of On the Way to Work *now?*
Any time I ever do any public signings or anything like that, I always get students coming up with that book. And I love it. I just think it's really down to earth. It's honest. And that was why Gordon was brilliant. He could take something. He could rebuild it. With this economy again. But he just gets to the nub of it, without doing too much to it, without too much interference. Just occasionally, here and there, he'd make one of my answers his question, to make it flow better. To make it into this really great thing. Because you know, the truth is, when you're in those battered states, like I was in when we were doing those interviews, people run a mile. You don't really want to listen to what they have to say. So he managed to dig all that out of it. He takes out all the irrelevant stuff. Makes a very few changes. Just to make it seem real. To get to the point.

Gordon wrote a lot of Born Yesterday *in Rome, and I was over there for a couple of days and I went round to see him and Carol in this little room they had at the British School there. And he had all these notes and things spread out all over the room: there was all the Madeleine McCann stuff; the cover of* Fullalove *[Gordon's second novel]. And one of the other things was your skull –* For the Love of God. *He seemed obsessed with it . . .*

Well, I'd asked him to do some more of the interviews, but he'd said, 'We've done all that. We've said it all. You're all washed up. Fuck off.' And I know he preferred the beginning of my career. But after the Diamond Skull, he came back to me and said, 'We should do some more interviews.' And I said, 'I thought you didn't want to do any more?' And he goes, 'Well, that was before you did the Diamond Skull, you're good again now.' And I thought, 'Fuck it, let's do some then.'

And how many did you do?
Just one. About the new paintings. But it's in two halves really. First half he just came out with, 'Have you ever seen a dead body?' He just went straight in like that, and we just talked about death. About my friend who'd killed himself. About the tree he hung himself from. And then about halfway through we talk about the paintings. But it's still all about death. Very intense. Very heavy shit.

And what's happened to it?
I'm going to use it, some of it, in the catalogue for my new show [*Nothing Matters*].

But there would have been a lot more interviews then?
I don't know if there would have been a lot more. I always wanted to do more than he did. But he'd go, 'Done enough now. You're repeating yourself.'

I think it was Anselm Kiefer who said he painted because he couldn't write; did you ever think there was a part of Gordon that wrote because he couldn't paint?
I never saw him as a frustrated painter, no. But I suppose — because he created worlds that were inward, that get inside your head — I suppose there was, not an envy, but a kind of delight in seeing people who created things outside. But

xiv

Gordon was an artist. And reading anything he wrote, it was a breath of fresh air. Because he was better than anyone else.

I don't think Gordon knew how good a writer he was.
I don't either.

There's that bit, at the end of On the Way to Work, *where you say, 'Everybody wants to be remembered.' And Gordon says, 'I don't.' And you say, 'That's lucky, because you probably won't be.' But he will be, won't he? He won't get his wish . . .*
Yeah. Exactly [*laughs*].

So what do you think he'd have made of this? Us talking about him?
He'd have hated it. He'd have said, 'Shut up. Have a fucking beer.'

INTRODUCTION

I was late getting on the bandwagon. Feeling disengaged from the London art world of the late eighties and more interested in what was happening in fiction – I was writing a novel – I didn't see it coming.

I didn't know that Freeze had happened in Docklands, and I didn't see Damien Hirst's In & Out of Love show with the living and dead butterflies at Woodstock Street in central London in the dog days of Thatcherism, in 1991. The lease on The Birds, the East End shop run by Sarah Lucas and Tracey Emin, was already up by the time I read about it in an early issue of *Frieze* magazine, which launched in July 1991 with a lovely/revolting Hirst butterfly painting on the cover.

And then, in early 1992, something every home-bound writer measuring out the days in cups of tea and faraway gazes through the window hopes will happen, happened: the phone rang with a commission that was an invitation to parachute into an interesting and previously unsuspected world.

It wasn't like I was being asked to go and live with the bushmen of the Kalahari: the art world was reasonably familiar territory. I had interviewed David Hockney a handful of times, the first in 1971, at his homes in England and California; I knew some of his contemporaries – Patrick Caulfield, Peter Blake, John Hoyland – well enough to regard as friends. I had shared my life with a painter at that point for nearly twenty years.

But the London art world of those days was a village — a well-tended hamlet of a few dozen souls who, with one or two notable exceptions, kept their gardens, went to openings on Tuesdays, and did nothing to scare the horses. There was an overriding feeling that there was something vulgar about seeking success or money overtly. 'The English preferred to lose gracefully than win vulgarly,' Michael Craig-Martin, the American artist who taught many of the YBA generation at Goldsmiths, noted of the time before Hirst and his confederacy were loosed on the world. He added: 'But today they're as aggressive and outspoken as they were in the eighteenth century, and Damien is part of that.'

I remember at the photocall for Young British Artists 1 at the Saatchi Gallery that, while everybody else arrived through the street door, Hirst made his entrance from behind the door of the administration offices marked 'Private'. Peals of laughter followed him and, when the photographer had got the artists standing where he wanted them, Rachel Whiteread said to Damien: 'I'll kill you if you make me laugh.' He was wearing very expensive shoes (probably borrowed) and no socks. He had a trick of carrying a £50 note with him in those days which no taxi driver or barman ever wanted to 'break'. I grew used to seeing it appearing from and then disappearing back into his wallet, growing a waxy lustre through non-use.

The next day I was astonished when he palmed a ping-pong ball that was bobbing on a column of air in a gallery at the Institute of Contemporary Arts and stuck it in his mouth. It was part of a sculpture, but it was *his* sculpture, and he was therefore free to do with it what he liked. *I Want to Spend the Rest of My Life Everywhere, With Everyone, One to One, Always, Forever, Now*, it was called. Great title. All the titles were good, well judged without being over-poetic and unusual at a time when every painting and piece of sculpture you came across seemed to be called *Untitled*.

He liked Larkin, it turned out, and had an enviable facility with words, so that he could be funny and 'deep' and casually conversational at the same time. 'I sometimes feel I have nothing to say, I often want to communicate this,' was one of the clever things I remember him saying at the time. 'There are regular moments in the art world where something has been invented and no one knows if it's good or bad. How fantastic is that? Whenever art's been good, it's always changed the notion of what art is.'

At that second meeting I also got an inkling of how ferociously competitive he can be. As soon as I gave him a copy of my novel *Alma Cogan*, which had just been shortlisted for Whitbread Book of the Year, he hared off out of the bar at the ICA and came tearing back with a copy of the catalogue for his show – his first catalogue – and a badge which was a picture of him with a dental retractor in his mouth. 'I told him how cheeky and arrogant he was,' Rachel Whiteread said of their first meeting, in a pub in 1985, 'because he was trying to take over the world – and he hadn't made anything!'

In some respects, this book can be read as a study twice over of how artists come to prominence with their friends and contemporaries, and what happens next. The first generation is the one associated with Royal College Pop and the cool, 'uptown' Pop attitude – David Hockney, Derek Boshier and their contemporaries. The second is the group that will probably be known, even into arteriosclerotic old age, as the YBAs. In the chapter on the Brixton Breakers I quote the view of a former director of the Tate, Sir Alan Bowness, that most truly original new work is the result of group activity, and that no great art has ever emerged out of a non-competitive situation.

'On the contrary,' Bowness writes, 'it is the fiercely competitive environment in which the young artist finds himself that drives him to excel . . . Artists who emerge from such a situation do not have a consistency of style, . . . but there is a consistency of purpose. They want to get to the top.'

The YBAs were famous for their recreational excesses and unflagging high spirits; for their brash, all-out, occasionally delinquent, try-anything ambition and energy; for — it is an expression that now seems to sum up the nineties — fearlessly 'caning it'. The remarkable thing, as I discovered over time, is that they were always at work. No matter how apparently blitzed or blasted, nothing was lost on them. Wozzed or wasted, they were always in the studio. 'When they're pissed,' as the London dealer Sadie Coles told me, 'that's when they're often talking about ideas.'

Every week, it seemed, for the whole of 1992, in some pub or at some party, squeezed into a taxi or across a restaurant table, I made the acquaintance of yet another young, original intelligence whose experience of the world had just been, or was in the process of being, translated into a piece of work which — often with a minimum amount of intervention on the artist's part — seemed to suck in the psyche of the times. A rough rule seemed to be that the less the artist's hand was detectable in the finished object, the more resounding its presence in the world. This certainly seemed to me to be the case with *Ghost*, Whiteread's cast of the inside of a dismal bedsit in Muswell Hill; with the Dolphin paintings, Gary Hume's series of unnervingly blank hospital doors; Sarah Lucas's scabrous female anatomy, *Two Fried Eggs and a Kebab*; *Pimp*, Gavin Turk's hearse-like, bible-black skip; Michael Landy's *Market*; Marcus Harvey's *Myra*; Tracey Emin's *Bed*; Anya Gallaccio's *Stroke*, with its 'dirty', chocolate-coated walls.

What these works all have in common is that they convey the illusion of the visual facts of popular life passing into art without being distorted or deformed in any way. They are all tuned in to the human pulse that beats beneath urban squalor and point the way to the muted beauty that often lurks in the tawdry, vulgar and even grotesque.

Asked to describe the kind of background he came from, Damien Hirst said: 'No electricity, gas cut off, that kind of thing. Lots of police, burglaries, naughty past.' That was another thing that appealed to me about Hirst and his friends: many of them came from nothing and seemed, at the time I first met them, to be en route to a place nobody had ever quite been before. Hirst was often referred to as 'the new David Hockney', and the 'Cool Britannia' nineties have been routinely compared to the London of the Swinging Sixties, when British contemporary art appeared in a mass-cultural landscape for the first time. But Pop art was famously about 'liking things', as Warhol once said. The first American Pop artists, like their English counterparts, were looking outward at the world around them rather than focusing on their emotional reactions to it. They were among the first to understand the desire of consumers to change their lives through the purchase of clean, manufactured commodities. YBA, on the other hand, was more interested in the dirt that accrues beneath the laminate surface of shiny things. Its artists were drawn to abject and degraded materials, to the banal and dejected, to signifiers of death and decay. The trick, though, was to tell it in a jaunty, unportentous, offhand, unliterary – *anti-literary* – way.

They collectively came up with a language that was an action upon the real rather than a discourse of abstractions (taxonomies, idealisations) about it. Their special perception was that cheap language and cheap materials didn't have to equal cheap thinking, any more than a sonorous statement couched in the language of the academy made it necessarily worth hearing. And then there were the drugs.

Three days after meeting Damien Hirst for the first time, he invited us for dinner at the flat where his American girlfriend Maia was living in Waterloo. It was a small flat and a lively party. He had cooked food for about twenty people, who included several Goldsmiths contemporaries, as well as Marcus Harvey and Hugh Allan, two friends from Leeds who had also been Goldsmiths students, plus some young collectors and Richard Shone from *Burlington Magazine*. (Shone was among the rock-solid Establishment figures who, protesting that it was too far, they were *busy people*, Hirst had had taxied from Mayfair to the Freeze show in deepest Docklands in 1988.) Drugs were probably on the go – what did I know? What struck me most forcibly at the time was the music. It was the Beatles. It wasn't acid house or trance or whatever might have been fashionable just then. It was *Rubber Soul* and *Abbey Road* and everybody knew all the words. *Revolver* and the *White Album*, the mop-tops non-stop. Damien did his trick of writing all the Beatles' autographs in perfect facsimile. (A bit later, I got him to do it for Peter Blake, and watched him – as I, and so many others, had by then – fall under the Damien spell; he was hooked for life.) And then he did his other trick, which over the years I would come to recognise as a sign that the evening was moving up to another level: he put on Queen and bellowed along with Freddie Mercury the song he had chosen as a personal anthem: *Don't stop me now! Because I'm having a good time, having a good time!* ... There was a lot of kissing and group-hugging and monkeying around, but I had never heard of Es and didn't know what 'loved-up' meant. It's probably fair to say, though, that it was the key to what a lot of the art of that time was about, and the cornerstone of the artists' unquench-able self-belief and group solidarity, all linked together in friendship and rivalry.

I have a clear memory of sitting on a church step late at night and being coached by Damien Hirst, sixteen years my junior, in the dos and don'ts of drugging. He was using a credit card to chop out a quantity of cocaine on a mirror. The cocaine had been brought to our table at Green Street, a fashionable, recently opened club in Mayfair. It was in a matchbox with Craigie Aitcheson's Green Street logo of a lovely little Bedling-ton terrier on the cover. Rule one, I remember, was to always flush the toilet in a cubicle where the drug had been taken. Rule two was to check the nostrils for tell-tale deposits prior to re-entry into polite society.

Some time later his girlfriend, and my friend by then, Maia Norman, would tell me that Damien worried that I had been corrupted by him. But I hadn't. I don't think I had, not in that way. I didn't have a cocaine habit and never bought any from a dealer. I haven't been near cocaine for years.

'Hirst hagiographer' is a phrase I have seen used against me in print more than once. (The dictionary definition of hagiog-raphy is 'a book about someone that describes them as better than they really are'.) And my blood was chilled when I read Brian Sewell's review of *Visiting Picasso: The Notebooks and Letters of Roland Penrose* in the London *Evening Standard* just as I was starting to think about writing this Introduction. 'The book reveals Penrose to have been less the far-sighted hero-intellectual who introduced Picasso to a British public', Sewell concluded, 'than an unctuous, self-serving sycophant willing to endure any humiliation rather than lose his position as Picasso's lickspittle.' Did my ears burn!

But some of the best writing about British artists in recent times has been the result of fond rather than adversarial relationships: Lawrence Gowing on Lucian Freud; David Sylvester and Michel Leiris on Francis Bacon; Robert Hughes on Frank Auerbach; Marco Livingstone on Patrick Caulfield; Matthew Collings on Sarah Lucas. In a different area, it would be difficult to argue, for example, that Michael Billington's insights into Harold Pinter's preoccupations and working practices would have been sharpened by not knowing him, or that Kenneth Tynan would have written more illuminatingly about Laurence Olivier had the critic never darkened the great actor's door. Such relationships, transactional in many ways, nevertheless (as Gowing wrote about Freud) provide 'the chance to isolate and savour a sense of what is intimate and unintended in people [and become] more responsive to the genuine, unwilled oddness that human nature and capacity, left to fulfil themselves, do not conceal'.

As the first page of this Introduction makes clear, I by no means write exclusively about art. I also write about subjects such as notorious British killers (*Somebody's Husband, Somebody's Son* and *Happy Like Murderers*), snooker and football (*Pocket Money* and *Best & Edwards*), as well as many monographs and catalogue essays, plus three novels which range widely over all of these interests: *Alma Cogan*, for example, includes meditations on the role of Myra Hindley in the British psyche (Marcus Harvey acknowledges it as one of the starting points for his painting *Myra*) as well as a (made-up) catalogue entry for Peter Blake's (non-existent) portrait of the fifties singer, *Cogan*, in store at Tate Britain.

It wasn't planned, but I seem to have ended up working in that place that Robert Rauschenberg first identified more than half a century ago – 'in the gap between art and life'. My non-fiction is influenced by developments in the novel, and the same applies in reverse. More than most British writers, I think, I am open to the experience of art as an influence on what I do. My second novel, *Fullalove*, for instance, about a hack tabloid reporter, draws heavily on the 'dirty' toy pieces of Mike Kelley and Christian Boltanski's portraits of missing and murdered children, among others.

I am fortunate in that many of the artists included in this book are friends. I tend to look to shows, and art catalogues, rather than to mainstream publishing, for stimulation (direction, really) and ideas. I feel that visual artists are consistently ahead of most writers in sensing significant shifts in how we think and see.

1 BRITISH ART

from Francis Bacon *to* Gilbert and George

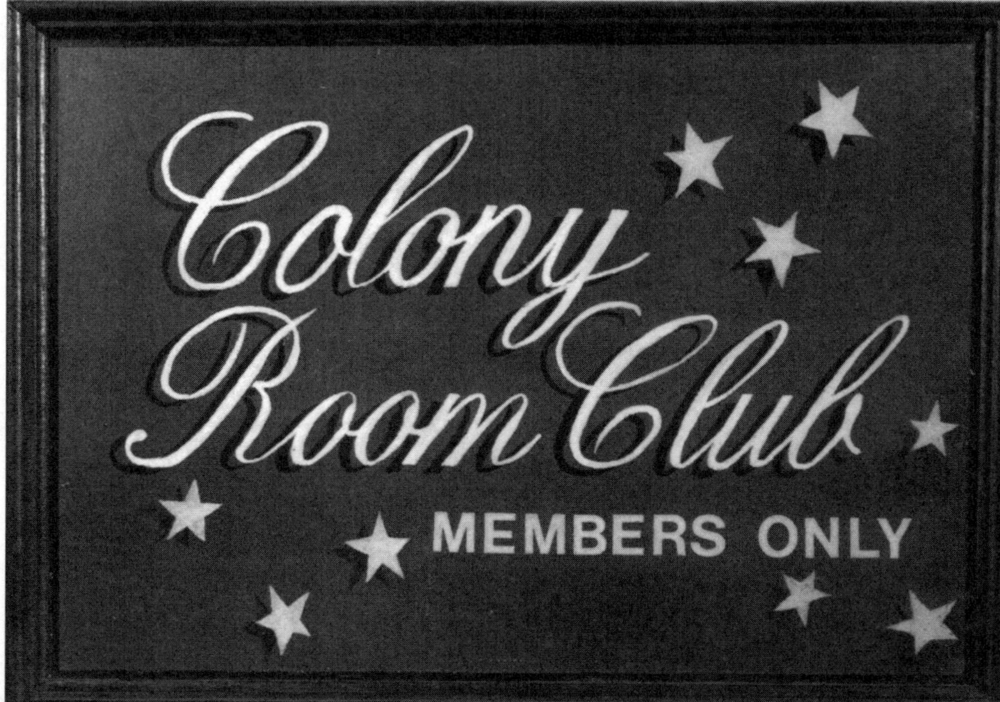

Colony
Room Club
MEMBERS ONLY

FRANCIS BACON

His subject matter is still man in the horror of his isolation — naked and obscene on a studio couch, or grinning baboon-like from behind a desk . . . But after the initial shock, one begins to feel on almost friendly terms with the creatures in his zoo. It may be an ugly, obscene and terrifying world, but it is also a deeply human one.

It is hard to read the American poet John Ashbery's review of Francis Bacon's 1963 Tate retrospective today without thinking of the menagerie currently being fed and watered in the forensically over-illuminated, bread-and-circuses *Big Brother* house. Conversely, it is impossible to watch Lea, the sex-hungry, cartoonishly enhanced, single mum from the Midlands, Pete, the Tourette's sufferer, forever rabbit-punching himself in the throat and involuntarily ejaculating the word 'wanker', or Nikki, the prating Essex diva, and not be reminded of the grotesques in a typical Bacon painting, their faces bloated with laughter or twisted into a scream.

The correspondences from time to time have been eerie. 'Devil woman' Grace flinging a glass of water in the face of 'golden girl' Suzie as she was evicted was an almost literal transcription of Bacon's 1965 painting *After Muybridge — Woman Emptying Bowl of Water and Paralytic Child on all Fours*: the ribbon of glittering water in each carries the same sting of surprise. Lea in extremis — teeth bared, nostrils flared, war-paint smeared — bears a strong resemblance to one of Bacon's (and

Lucian Freud's) favourite models, Henrietta Moraes. (From different backgrounds, and belonging to different eras, the two women have more in common than just physical appearance. Moraes once came across the photographer John Deakin selling the gynaecologically explicit pictures he had taken of her as an aide-memoire for Francis Bacon to sailors in a Soho pub. Lurid pictures taken of Lea Walker before she went into the *Big Brother* house were recently published in the *Sunday Sport*.)

The simultaneously claustrophobic and voyeuristically transparent spaces of the Channel 4 house are suggestive of the modern, vaguely threatening, cell-like rooms in which Bacon habitually isolates his figures, 'putting them before us', as a critic once noted, 'as the lepidopterist puts a new specimen on a pin'.

The diary room, where *Big Brother* contestants are encouraged to drop their game-faces and give vent to whatever extremes of rage or elation or vindictiveness the producers can coax from them, shares the mean dimensions of the cages or boxes – David Sylvester referred to them as the 'spaceframes' – which hold the screaming popes and cardinals that Bacon famously painted during the fifties. The only furniture in the diary room this time round is a ludicrously ornate, button-backed gold leather chair which (resist it or not) invites comparison with the thrones in which the snarling primate-popes of Bacon (*Study after Velázquez*, 1950; *Portrait of Pope*, 1957–8, in this current show) are trapped.

The drawing of parallels between the participants in a reality TV show and the subjects in the paintings of an artist who has been credited with 'reinventing the human head' and who, during his lifetime, prompted major works by the French structuralist thinkers Roland Barthes, Gilles Deleuze and Michel Leiris, among others, is less facetious than it might at first appear.

Bacon's overriding preoccupation was with what he liked to call 'the brutality of fact'. 'I would like my pictures to look as if a human being had passed between them, like a snail,' he once said, 'leaving a trail of the human presence and memory trace of past events, as the snail leaves its slime.'

Throughout his life, he liked to remember that Sigmund Freud kept in his possession a set of particularly horrendous photographs from the Viennese police archives; Bacon himself was welcomed as a visitor to the Black Museum at Scotland Yard on more than one occasion. His fascination with diseases of the mouth ('I like the glitter and colour that comes from the mouth, and I've always hoped in a sense to be able to paint the mouth like Monet painted a sunset') and with medical plates showing the body being positioned for X-ray are part of the foundation myth. His ambition, he said, was 'to make the animal thing come through the human'. And he did this in any number of pictures of men seated in interiors wearing City suits, as Sylvester once remarked.

It is a source of excitement to art students still that Bacon was a keen collector of photographic images that most people would turn away from, showing the inevitable course of decay and death, and that violence of subject matter was fundamental to his own art.

He spent his life tearing pictures out of newspapers and magazines — he was particularly drawn to images of predatory wildlife and sportsmen, especially boxers — and then discarding them on the studio floor where, over the decades, they turned into a sort of involuntary visual resource; a kind of painterly mulch. 'Bacon values the photograph as a source of significant falsehood, and he values it as a source of exact information about incidents to which he has not had direct access,' his friend, the former *New York Times* art critic John Russell, once wrote. 'But above all he values it as a way of breaking back into reality; or, equally, of taking reality by surprise.'

This, of course, was one of the earliest uses to which photography had been put: the camera was quickly seen as a way of creeping up on truth, catching the naked shaking animal unawares and off guard; it was seized on as a way of making statements about the fugitive nature of human beings. Fox Talbot's wife called the first cameras 'mousetraps' — little wooden boxes set down to capture flattened objects and stilled lives. 'Would Lisa please come to the diary room!'

According to Russell in his 1971 book on the artist, Bacon had to wait until he turned sixty to fulfil an ambition of several years' standing by putting a camera into a painting and characterising it as vividly as any of its human co-participants. *Triptych — Studies from the Human Body* (1970) is one of a dozen triptychs in the unprecedentedly blue-chip show which opened this week at the Gagosian Gallery. (Before it went up, there was as much excitement about how much it had cost to bring these paintings to London — they have been insured for around £400 million, it's rumoured — and the motives behind Larry Gagosian mounting what is, on paper at least, a non-selling show as there was about the opportunity of seeing the most substantial body of Bacon's work since the Hayward Gallery retrospective in 1998.)

The camera in the 1970 triptych is an old-fashioned one standing on three timber legs, with goggle-like lenses which approximate the uglified, gouged-out faces so characteristic of the people in Bacon's paintings. It has been suggested that the camera here has a symbolic role: that it stands for the faculty, much prized by Bacon, of impartial observation — it sees all, and comments on nothing. But it seems to me possible that its inclusion was intended as a rejoinder to John Berger, who, the previous year, had published an essay linking the decline of the painted portrait with the rise of photography, and in which he baldly stated that 'it seems to me unlikely that any important portraits will ever be painted again'.

'The talent once involved in portrait painting can be used in some other way to serve a more urgent, modern function,' Berger wrote. '[In all painted portraits] the sitter, somewhat like an arranged still life, becomes subservient to the painter. Finally it is not his personality or his role which impress us but the artist's vision.' Bacon, as Berger would certainly have been aware, preferred to work from photographs of friends or models rather than have the person come to the studio to sit for him. 'They inhibit me,' he once admitted. 'If I like them, I don't want to practise before them the injury that I do to them in my work. I would rather practise the injury in private by which I think I can record the fact of them more clearly.'

The Gagosian show contains at least one authentically 'important' painting: *Triptych May–June 1973* records in an austere, unflinching way the death, alone in his hotel room, of Bacon's lover and companion, George Dyer. This 'document about pain', as it has been described – the protagonist's pain, the artist's pain – is a work whose details are local and personal; it is an expression of felt, rather than operatic, grief.

However, just as the *Big Brother* contestants' tearful, disfiguring reactions are usually out of all proportion to what has caused them – Richard has eaten all the cornflakes, Lea has been bitching about Nikki behind her back – so the passages of existential angst in Bacon's painting too often can seem excessive and embarrassingly worked up – at best formulaic, at their worst merely camp.

In many ways he was a victim as well as a beneficiary of his historical moment. He had his first solo show at the Hanover Gallery in London in 1949, the year that Cyril Connolly, in the last-ever issue of *Horizon*, declared that 'it is closing time in the gardens of the West and from now on an artist will be judged only by the resonance of his solitude or the quality of his despair'.

Throughout his life, Bacon refused the interpretations of his work which imputed to it a 'message' about the Cold War atmosphere of postwar Europe, full of menace, guilt, disquiet, doubt, a sense of nearness to death. He insisted that what stirred him was the private realm, 'the vulnerability of the human situation': 'I'm just trying to make images as accurately off my nervous system as I can. I don't even know what half of them mean. I'm not *saying* anything . . . I've always been more interested in what is called "behaviour" and "life" than in art.' Nevertheless, the label of chief interpreter of the morally and spiritually bankrupt, post-atrocity universe is the one he was stuck with.

At the same time, the flamboyant figure he cut in the drinking clubs of Soho and the gambling rooms of the West End, his refusal to disguise or apologise for his homosexuality, and a commitment to living, according to the Picasso formula, like a poor man with a lot of money, gave Bacon a personal glamour, and a media presence, that no other British artist had ever had. Plus he talked a good painting. The conversations he recorded with David Sylvester between 1962 and 1986 are one of the great documents of twentieth-century art.

Some years ago the *New Yorker* writer Adam Gopnik credited Bacon with a tendency in young international art to which he gave the name the 'High Morbid Manner' — 'a detached, distanced, oddly smiling presentation of violence . . . the macabre fragment, the tortured videos, the cryptic neon signs

. . . that new kind of ghostly, frozen, remote look at death and suffering'.

The 'Conversations' are probably more greedily pored over by art students today than Bacon's work, which, far from being affectless or frozen, presently (post-Nauman, post-Hirst, post-Chapmans) seems overcooked, shouty, despairing and fetishising of death in a dated way.

2006

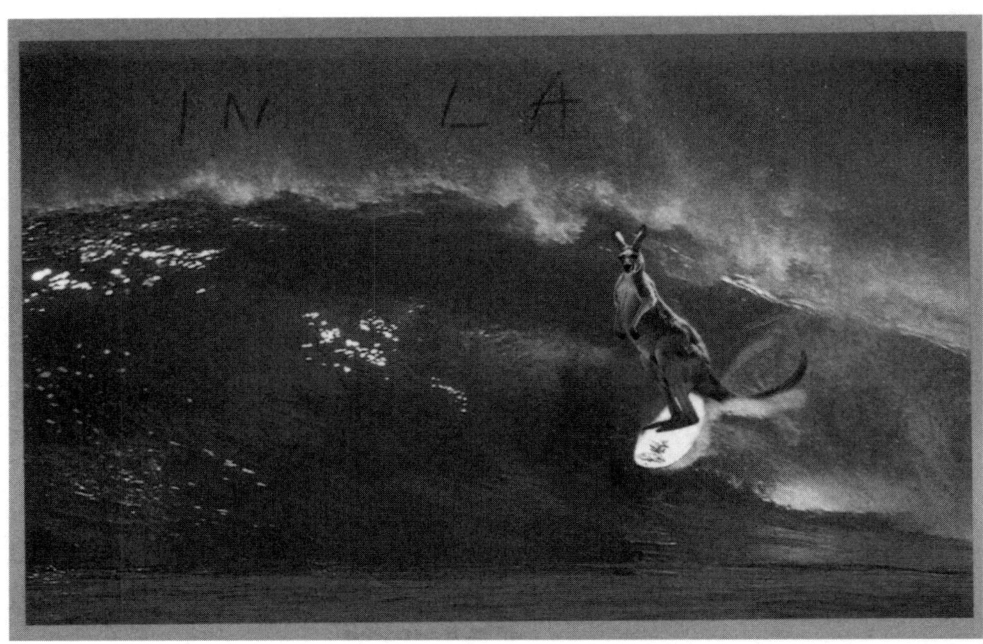

SURFING AUSTRALIA.
BACKGROUND PHOTO: KEVIN SHARLAND ©
KANGAROO PHOTO: AXEL KAYSER © NO. 360

Dear Gordon + Carol
Spent 6 weeks in Australia now in LA
with Hamish — had show in Sydney
I think it went well,
So glad to miss English
winter — still not smoking
But getting really FAT.
L.A's OK, Sunny.
For now much Love
Trace xx

Gordon + Carol
8 Beaufort Mansions
Beaufort Street
London SW3 5AG
UK

Art Mail Press, P.O. Box 809, Fremantle W.A. 6959

ART MAIL
AUSTRALIAN IMPRESSIONS

9 318586 003003

DAVID HOCKNEY

In David Hockney's living room on a Saturday afternoon, Henry Geldzahler was sleeping, slumped into the coffee-cream leather settee, his mouth sagged open and his belly rising and falling inside a tasselled and faded extra-large-size, grey and green old-time cowboy shirt.

The international edition of the *Herald Tribune* was crumpled on the floor between his stockinged feet, its centrefold sloping into the air, exactly the way it had landed as it slipped through his fingers in mid-sentence just as his eyelids dropped slowly, uncontrollably shut. Four and a half inches of cigar, the very best Havana, were smouldering into ash on a curved-edge glass tray.

Henry Geldzahler, late of Yale, the Sorbonne, the Ecole de Louvre, and Harvard Graduate School of Fine Arts, dozing on a Saturday afternoon in David Hockney's flat in a side street in Notting Hill, sweet-dreaming away the day.

Two doors away, down at street level, there's a milk machine and an accumulated stack of red plastic milk crates and a shop showing too-real rows of purple plastic grapes suspended, like the plantains, the onions and the packs of ladies' tights, from meat hooks. At the far end of the street, at the Powis Square end, where they filmed the outside shots for *Performance* and where the demonstrations take place — Women's Lib, Gay Lib, Black Power, Child Power — there's a soot-blackened line of triangular flags suspended between buildings and one slogan, sprayed bold along the length of a wall: RISING UP ANGRY.

Two blocks away, on Portobello Road, David Hockney is pushing a way through the press of people in the market, two awkward brown boxes strung together under his arm, weaving and dodging and moving too fast to notice the shrugs and nudges, the grins and the enquiring glances. Isn't he . . . *famous*?

'David's expecting you? He won't be long. He's just gone out to do some shopping.' Henry Geldzahler, an associate curator in the Department of American Painting and Sculpture at the Metropolitan Museum of Art in New York, had just finished rubbing the sleep out of his eyes when the doorbell rang. Already, though, Wagner was back on the stereo, the *Tribune* was neatly folded on the settee, his slippers were back on his feet (temporarily) and a fresh ramrod cigar was glowing red, wedged securely in his lips.

On the glass table running the length of the settee four dozen or more broken-backed tulips, drooped and fatigued, are splayed open like part of an autumn set piece for *Dr Zhivago*. Straight ahead, on the fireplace wall, a large monochrome Hockney print of irises in a slim pewter vase is hanging over a single, flaccid yolk-yellow tulip, propped up in the very same vase. Across the other side of the table and obliquely angled to it, just so, there's the tubular chair Sir David Webster nodded off to sleep in, day after day, during the sittings for his Covent Garden retirement portrait.

'Yes, he had to go out for some food. We suddenly decided to have a small luncheon party tomorrow. Ossie – Ossie Clark – phoned about an hour ago from Delhi to say that he's arriving back in London at ten-thirty tomorrow morning. We'll pick him up at the airport . . . That drawing there is one David did of Celia, Ossie's wife.'

Among the collection on the wall facing the windows there's a painting of a teenage boy by Patrick Procktor, one of Richard Hamilton's Guggenheim prints, *Two Pyramids (for David Hockney)* by Peter Blake and a drawing of Hockney with a young boy, hung high in a perfectly round frame. Otherwise the walls and the floor are flat, beige, anonymous, as they often are in the paintings.

'Some tea? In England I find tea so refreshing . . . Or take a quick nap if you like. David shouldn't be long.'

Hockney when he arrives pushes through the door suddenly in a jaunty mood, and makes straight for the bowl of tired tulips on the table. 'Come with me,' he says, consciously camping it up a bit, 'while I arrange me flowers.'

In the kitchen, he jerks the elastic bands off two boxfuls of daffodils and tulips and distributes the flowers unceremoniously around three bowls, a few dozen pushed into each. The flowers start Hockney talking about the country.

'Oh God, I don't know how Peter Blake can take it down in his signal box, never seeing strangers from one week's end to the other. I could never live in the country. Chekhov put me off that for life, didn't he you?' Henry pulls open the fridge door and extracts another ramrod Havana, chuckling.

Slumped on the drawing-room floor in odd socks, bashed-up sneakers, baggy jeans and an old washed-out yellow sweatshirt Hockney looks immediately comfortable. By propping himself up against the wall instead of positioning his body strategically in the furniture, he's ruined what he'd probably call the poetics of the room, fouled up the spatial dynamics in one move, and transformed the general air of straight-backed austerity into one of slippered, low-gear luxury. Just lying there on the floor, drawing deeply on a slim panatella, surrounded by all that not-a-thread-out-of-place order, he looks so . . . *messy*, and at ease.

It's all his, everything in the room, and, like the kid-liquorice specs and his champagne-ice hair, it's *part* of him, it fits him naturally. Even the gold toothpick dangling from the golden chain round his neck is very definitely non-chi-chi.

He owns the whole house now, but he never wanted to. It was more or less a case of buy or get kicked out, he says, so naturally he bought. He's lived up there on the second floor in the same flat for ten years, ever since he left the Royal College of Art, and through the years the place has just changed with him, become bigger, and bit by bit more sleek.

When his mother first came visiting from Bradford she thought he'd brought her to a slum, and even now the dim stone stairs leading up from the front door are only covered in bare, faded lino. They echo just like they've always done.

'Round here somehow it's — I don't know how to put it — it's a lot *nicer*. Somehow the people are a bit different. What I mean is, I *like* it. An' I'd hate the idea, as I earned more money and things like that, of actually moving out to Belgrave Square. I mean, it just wouldn't suit me at all.'

In the first few minutes, back in the kitchen, he'd let me know in a very friendly way that he'd been trying to put me off coming. What he would like now, after ten years, is a bit more peace and a measure of anonymity. Which is why he's changed his telephone number and is closing his door to the press.

'I'm always slightly taken aback if people talk to me in the street because, somehow, I always think of the audience for painting as being very small. You know, there's not all that many people interested in it, although I *am* aware that my painting has more popular appeal than say, that of Reinhardt or a rather severe abstract artist, simply because I use things that appeal to people. I mean I use happiness, sadness, things like that, which always have a broader appeal than severity or toughness. But, you see, I don't think I ever cultivated an image. I think other people did, an' that's why, at the minute, I'd like a bit of quiet . . . just so that the people would look at my work and not me.'

His face had loosened up over the last few words and he smiled. 'There's all kinds of complicated implications involved in being known as an artist, things you never think of. Like all the people on this street, little Joan across in the dry cleaners. I mean, she always knew I was an *artist* and she sees things in the newspapers, yet she'd probably never recognise a painting of mine if she saw one. She wouldn't know it. Occasionally she comes for tea so then she'll look at them, but that's all.

'Y'see, in the interests of anonymity, I *have* thought about letting me hair get back to its normal colour an' changin' me glasses an' all that, reverting, but then I thought, well, it suits me! An' somehow — it might be cowardice on my part, I don't know — it would be a tiny bit like going back to Bradford, which I couldn't do. I know that's what I looked like then.'

Henry Geldzahler had fished out a copy of the catalogue to Hockney's 1970 exhibition at the Whitechapel Gallery and it was still lying on the settee where he'd left it. Hockney scooped it up and flipped through to the back pages to a black and white reproduction less than two inches square, of a self-portrait he painted when he was sixteen and just starting out at Bradford College of Art: a grey, miserable boy, with a pudding-basin haircut and National Health specs, perched on the edge of a bed in a dingy room, staring dead ahead, straight out of the canvas. 'Oh yeah, it's accurate all right. Actually Henry there, who you were talking to before I arrived, is always trying to get me to do another one . . . I think I might do it.'

But Bradford? 'I've nothing against Bradford but I knew I wouldn't want to stay, even when I was sixteen I knew I could never live there. I only go to see my parents now, and if they weren't there I don't suppose I'd ever go.

'I suppose I was interested in art long before I went to grammar school. You know, as a child one looks at pictures in a book – in Bradford it must have been a book because there's no really good pictures to look at – and I suppose, instinctively and intuitively, you realise it's a way of communicating a feeling. And I suppose – this is my analysis of it – then you think you could do it, *you* could respond in that way and make the marks on the paper to show somebody else a feeling or an idea.

'Although maybe I was a bit different. Because when I was, say, nine and somebody asked me what I wanted to be, I would say, an artist, whereas my brothers would probably have said "I don't know". So that makes a difference if you *know* what you want to do. I mean, most people all their lives never know what they want to do really, and never ever find out, and that's life's tragedy.'

At school though they can knock feelings like that out of you; they tried and he fought back. 'A terrible, terrible school. I hated it. In my area it was sissy to go to a grammar school and I felt a bit alone. To be truthful, I think they always saw me as something of an oddity but now I suppose they think I'm very successful and if they think that they'll excuse anything – a sort of artistic Jimmy Savile.

'I remember about ten years ago in Bradford I was walking down the street and I overheard one of the neighbours saying to another, "Oo, look, 'e's back again, and 'is brothers did *so* well, you know." Idle Jack back from London. It's just, I suppose, what little people are like, who live little, ordered, quiet lives . . .

16

'I always responded to literature, it was a nice world which helped you escape; through literature you know there's another world besides Bradford, you know how people are feeling elsewhere . . . through literature and through films, mostly.'

Meanwhile, two gangling young men had arrived un-expectedly for tea and David had sent them off to look for Henry. 'I used to give great big tea parties on Saturdays, but the last one I gave I invited about . . . well I invited thirty-two, but you know, people bring other people, so about sixty turned up. Well, it was chaos! Not everybody could have a cup of tea, so I stopped giving them. Now I shall probably start again. I quite like giving teas because I don't really cook an' it's easy to make tea, isn't it?'

Glancing up from the opposite side of the street most days, you're likely to catch the thick black outline of Hockney's glasses moving behind the white slatted blinds hanging at his studio window along to the right, directly above a tobacco warehouse. He spends a lot of time there because he says it's the place he feels most at home. As you'd expect, the room is dominated by works in progress, stacked up against walls, but just inside the door, on the left, there's a large sideways-on photograph of a naked boy in a carefully lit young Adonis pose, and over by the work table in the window recess there's a dou-ble colour portrait of the same boy. In one panel he's standing in white briefs and in the other he's wearing only jeans, unbut-toned to reveal the first half-inch of pubic hair. In both pictures the boy has Hockney's gold toothpick round his neck. Peter Schlesinger was in David Hockney's drawing class three years ago at the University of California in Los Angeles (UCLA). Now he's a student at the Slade and his name's on the front door.

'The real reason I went to California at all,' Hockney said, 'was that it was sexy. It wasn't the art that attracted me. I thought it was going to be full of very beautiful boys, which it is, but they all looked alike, which is a bit of a drag when you finally view it. Which is why I'm not in California now. Believe me, it's no paradise. But for a time it was interesting. The whole world there interested me a great deal, but after a while you get bored. I mean, life wasn't quite complicated enough to keep an interest going, so really that's why I left and came back to live here.'

In the largest of the new canvases, another California swimming pool set-up, Peter is standing on the edge of the pool, fully dressed, looking down at a swimmer under the water, drifting towards him. 'When I was in Bradford,' Hockney has said, 'I was sexually naive. Now in London sex is much more important. I have a relationship with this boy that's as complete as two people could have.' Peter, he says, is indirectly responsible for another of the new paintings, the most nearly finished of a collection he's preparing for exhibition in America. It's a simple painting of a shirt on a wicker chair in a hotel room.

'I suppose it's a bit sentimental, really. I had a tiff with Peter last summer and went off to Honolulu with another boy. It turned out that the other boy had the same shirt as Peter and one morning I saw it lying there on a chair looking so pathetic that it suddenly hit me what a fool I'd been, and how miserable I really was without him. So I took a photograph of it, made some sketches and started to work when I got back.

'I showed it to little Joan from the dry cleaners the other day and asked her what she thought. "Sadness," she said, just like that. But then she knew, you see. She's seen that shirt lots of times, and she knew whose it was. But I'd hope that anyone looking at it would feel very much the same thing.'

Hockney accepted his homosexuality a long time ago. 'When I knew for sure, I decided there were only two things you could do: hide it or come right out and admit it. You've got to come to terms with yourself sooner or later and you can hardly fulfil yourself if all the time you're nervous and scared, frightened that somebody is going to find you out, so in the end I just accepted it. Why not? Of course it was a bit traumatic at first, and it's still difficult at times because of that very strong working-class puritan ethic that's still there in me somewhere, but basically I'm very content. My parents know by now of course, and I know they know, but it's just something we've never talked about. They're quite old — my mother's seventy and my father's sixty-eight — too old, I think, to understand. They're very sweet people and it's no good hurting or confusing them just for the sake of it. We get along with each other very well.

'I've more or less given up painting portraits of pairs, but the more I think about it, the more I'm sure that I'd like to paint my parents. It's a very traditional thing to do, I know, painting one's parents, but I think it could be a lot more than just that . . . their predicament, their lack of fulfilment, the desperate not-knowing what they could have had out of life. And their relationship with me . . . I think it could be OK.'

1971

It is December in Hollywood and, even in Hollywood, December means winter. A heat haze might be hovering over the pools and dissolving the outlines of cars corkscrewing up into the canyons. No matter. It is the season for log fires and bringing the sable and ranch-raised mink out of cold storage.

There's a log fire burning in David Hockney's living room

high in the Hollywood Hills this morning; and tomorrow evening, in the audience for *Tristan und Isolde* at the Dorothy Chandler Pavilion, better known for the Oscars than for opera, he will be surrounded by so much sable and mink (straight mink, cougar-trimmed mink, 'fun' mink appliquéd in gold) and celebrity chatter that he will be obliged to palm his hearing aid until Zubin Mehta taps his baton, calling the Los Angeles Philharmonic to order.

Hockney has spent twelve months working on the sets and lighting for *Tristan*, perhaps his favourite Wagner opera. And that, combined with preparations for the major retrospective of his work which opens at the Los Angeles County Museum this month, then moves to the Metropolitan in New York before finally arriving at the Tate Gallery in London in October, has left him drawn and exhausted. That *and* the forty-five-minute film he's spent weeks putting together and which the people at the Getty Museum, who put up the money for it, are now demanding be hacked to a quarter of its length.

'He's always got a bee in his bonnet, that boy,' Hockney's long-time friend and dealer, Kasmin, has cautioned in London. And the film and what it stands for turns out to be the latest of them. 'C'm 'ere,' Hockney says the minute the opening pleas-antries have been taken care of, rocking back on his heels, impatient. 'I've something I want to show you.'

A short corridor connects the big, open hub of the house in Nichols Canyon with a smaller, book-lined study that Hockney has taken to using more and more since he started losing his hearing. A giant television in one corner has its back to the wooden deck that overlooks the pool, and he immediately feeds the television with a cassette which, after a few bars of oriental music, brings up a picture of himself.

He is standing in what looks like the storeroom of a

museum, slowly unrolling an ancient Chinese scroll-painting on a velvet-covered table and talking directly to the camera. It is a simple film which cuts between scenes from the scroll (ordinary scenes of Chinese village life) and medium close-ups of the features – the peroxide hair, the glasses, the prognathous, cubistic jaw – that for twenty-five years have made Hockney Britain's most highly visible artist.

'Not exactly Kenneth Clark,' he says of his ingratiating, characteristically ramshackle screen presence. He is pacing up and down behind one of the plump pink settees that more or less fill the room. The point he seems to be making in the film is the old cubist one about there being alternative ways of seeing and depicting reality – alternative, that is, to what Hockney now believes is the almost universally accepted fixed-viewpoint, 'objective' perception of things fostered by photography and the still camera.

It is difficult to be certain what point the film is making, however, until it's over and it is possible to ask him. While it's running there are too many distractions. The phone, for instance, which, to pierce his deafness, keeps exploding in alarming yelps. And the parade of personable, unfailingly polite young men – friends, assistants – who must have David's word on this or that matter: there's a reporter on the other line; his own pictures of the *Tristan* sets should have been edited and Fed-Expressed to *Newsweek* yesterday; the plant people say there's a problem with the 'boarding-house' palms he has specified for the party.

The maid walks to a door and squirts Mr Muscle at it. The sun bounces off a life-size cut-out warthog standing outside the window. 'Just give me the facts – I can mix 'em up when I quote you,' is the inscription on an ashtray pointedly positioned on the low table. And so on.

By far the biggest distraction is Hockney himself, however. When he isn't fielding phone calls and queries he is curled up on the carpet nuzzling his constant companion, Stanley. He throws plastic waffles and squeaky toys for Stanley and holds Stanley so that his little pink tongue flickers in and out of his nostrils. Hockney is besotted with Stanley, a fourteen-month-old dachshund, and the feeling seems mutual.

Inevitably, because Hockney's concerns have always been personal and autobiographical, Stanley has found his way into the paintings — there are small, oval portraits of Stanley dotted around the house, and a Picassoid double portrait of Stanley and his master. There are even references to Stanley in the catalogue to the new exhibition. 'One of the main reasons I used to travel was to get away from all the nattering,' Hockney is quoted as saying. 'But I won't have to worry about the natterers any more. Stanley's going to growl at them when they come to the door.'

Stanley, in other words, is to become the symbol of Hockney in middle age as surely as the swimming pools, Kotah palms and exotic landscapes represented the sun-loving, boy-chasing gadabout of his younger years. The dog is part of a new stay-at-home, play-at-home, sleepy-time Hockney persona which, in addition to his hearing aid, today includes shapeless trousers and a pair of Albert Tatlock carpet slippers that his mother, who still lives there, must have had to scour the back-streets of Bradford to find for him.

It is an image that is confirmed in the final minutes of the film when, with chalk in hand and a ragged hole in the sleeve of his jumper, Hockney lectures his audience from in front of a blackboard. The catalogue to the new show is choc-a-bloc with references to learned volumes with titles like *Wholeness and the Implicate Order* and to Heisenberg's Uncertainty Principle.

Similarly, in conversation these days, it is difficult to deflect him from the formal and technical problems associated with his work.

Ask him whether, as he gets older, he finds himself becoming more like his father, a pacifist who kept his correspondence with Khrushchev, Gandhi, Nasser and other world leaders in scrapbooks made of brown wrapping paper held together with string, and Hockney looks quizzical, then, interestingly but inconsequentially, answers: 'I *like* life. I love life and I like the world. And when people tell you these are bad times, I point out, well, they're the only times we've got. There's not a lot of time. And, frankly, no matter how bad it is, there's also beauty there. Beauty's a word we don't hear much in the art world any more. They're not *concerned* about it. But I am, and I want to try and deal with it in my work. I think they're wrong and I don't mind standing on my own.'

Recent years have seen him back off from the personal and the anecdotal, which for so long was his stock in trade. A year ago the American organisers of his retrospective were jubilant when they got NBC interested in making a one-hour documentary for network television. Hockney, though, who had already seen his life and relationships stripped bare in an earlier film, refused to buy it. He made the Chinese-scroll film, setting out his thoughts on perspective, instead.

'I didn't want them to do it at all, so I put them off. The museum didn't like it, but I did. I pointed out that my work was moving towards showing that there was something wrong with the television screen. Why, therefore, should I go along with them and pretend that there wasn't? Why should I do that? In that sense I have some integrity about it. And in the end we've done this other film which, frankly, I think is far more interesting.'

A decade ago Hockney told an interviewer that 'pain and suffering' was a theme he had so far avoided tackling, but added: 'I assume it will actually become a theme as you go on through life.'

Henry Geldzahler, old friend and frequent subject of Hockney's, thinks 'the end of innocence' came in 1973 with the death of Picasso who, as his own career progressed, had become a heroic figure for Hockney. Picasso's death, Geldzahler believes, became in some indefinable way entangled with the decline and eventual death of David Hockney's own father five years later.

Howard Hodgkin was a guest of Hockney's in California at the end of 1979 and afterwards painted the first of what will eventually be three pictures commemorating the visit. *DH in Hollywood*, which has a tumescent pink phallus as its central image, has been described by one writer on art as follows: 'Hodgkin portrays Hockney in middle age, isolated in his own swimming pool and the success it represents, half-reprovingly surrounded by the high-spirited styles of his youth.'

Hodgkin himself will neither confirm nor deny that 'melancholy isolation' is the effect he set out to achieve. But, if it was, David Hockney's sister, a district nurse in Bedfordshire, would regard it as coming close to the mark. She thinks a great number of David's paintings are 'full of loneliness', as she has said in the past.

As long ago as 1965 Peter Blake started work on a portrait of Hockney (Blake still regards it as unfinished) in which bright party balloons, confetti and streamers are ironically juxtaposed with the single, seated bewildered-looking figure with the shock of 'Winsome Wheat' hair and thick Le Corbusier glasses. It is not a perception of Hockney that was common at a time when 'the golden boy' was experiencing his first rush of riches and newspaper fame.

Hockney had left the Royal College of Art just three years earlier, loudly fanfared as the brightest star in the brightest generation of students to come out of the college this century. The Sunday colour supplements were just starting, Swinging London was gearing up into overdrive and Hockney – intelligent, sexy, working-class, irreverent, the very embodiment of everything that was coming to be regarded as Pop, in other words – was instant media magic. Hot copy. To the papers he was one of the very happeningest in what at the time seemed like an avalanche of happening scenes.

He denies it all now, of course. 'The Swinging London that never was,' he calls the section dealing with this part of his life in *Hockney by Hockney*, the disarmingly candid autobiography published in 1976 when he was thirty-nine. But at the time he did little to dispel the notion that the hedonistic images he had started painting even before his first visit to California in the sixties were a true reflection of his own free-wheeling, hedonist's view of life.

'I paint what I like, when I like, and where I like with occasional nostalgic journeys,' he wrote in a catalogue note in 1962 and listed some of the occasions of his painting: 'Landscape of foreign lands, beautiful people, love, propaganda, and major incidents of my own life.'

'Given such a programme,' the man credited with coining the term 'Pop art', Lawrence Alloway, noted sourly, 'a rambling and discursive kind of art was likely to follow, and it has.'

Hockney, in the opinion of the American critic Hilton Kramer, is not only 'one of the most successful and acclaimed artists of his generation, [in demand] wherever today's western art finds a ready and eager public' but is also 'preposterously overrated . . . superficial and even reactionary . . . turning out a kind of nineteenth-century salon art refurbished from the stockroom of modernism'.

Often, as Hockney acknowledges, the bitterest criticism is directed as much at the idea of himself that he has assiduously promoted as at the work that he has produced. He acknowledges it, and yet claims not to care.

'I can't care about what I am. I can't do anything about it. I don't even *know* what the image is supposed to be now. But it's very nice if people think I just sit by the pool all day. It's OK. In fact it's a nice cover. Like when I was working on the theatre project and a guy came from Minneapolis to help me and we worked for six months solid, really very hard. And he told me afterwards, he said he thought my life . . . he didn't know I *worked*. It was just life round the pool. Drugs and boys.

'But, as I say, I'm quite unconcerned about it. I don't mind. Better not to be taken too seriously as an artist by some people. *I* think. I do. You're better off left alone.'

The English painter Lucian Freud's published comment last year that 'David Hockney would put on a green and yellow frock' in order to get his face in the papers is far from being an isolated example of the sort of comment Hockney continues to excite in Britain. Howard Hodgkin believes this kind of attitude can be explained by the well-known British distrust of success.

'It's hard to believe that any so-called serious person would think differently of David simply because his face has become famous over the years,' Hodgkin says. 'The only problem in England is that people are very jealous of anything that's remotely successful. They really hate success here.

'He's far from being a failure, but I was amazed to see it used in a catalogue introduction as an expression of approval for Frank Auerbach, that he actually still used pay-phones instead of having a telephone in his studio. This showed how "serious" he was. There's a lot of old-fashioned romantic puritanism about people's attitude to art in England that you don't find, for instance, in America.

'I mean, David's probably not nearly so successful – and this is pure speculation – as famous artists in history who were much more famous, much richer, much more public figures than he is. David is a very serious painter, and whatever variations have occurred in his work, I don't think it's because of his fame.'

'Bitchy reviews are something you come to expect in England,' Hockney himself says with resignation. 'Only in England. If they can try and knock you down they will. There's a meanness of spirit there. I know perfectly well about it. I've known about it for an *awfully* long time. I've never cared for it myself.'

Lunch is a 'winter' soup cooked by David's current companion, Ian, the owner of Stanley's brother. Hockney washes his down with a bottle of brown ale. Afterwards, still in his slippers, he follows Stanley outside and up the few stone steps to the studio.

In the past, Hockney used to get in his car and drive to a studio in west Hollywood, a short journey commemorated in a number of cubist-inflected landscapes of the late seventies. But now the west Hollywood studio is used only for the administration of the Hockney industry and for storage. He put the finishing touches to what Kasmin, only half jokingly, calls 'his ivory tower' a couple of years ago when he erected a new studio on the tennis court next to the house.

Hockney is a natural draughtsman. He is not a natural

painter. He has always found painting difficult, as he once confessed: 'It seems so sad that one has to spend a lot of time struggling just to make something if one has an idea and a vision. This is my frustration as an artist. I don't really paint very well.'

This contains an echo of something Matisse wrote in the early years of the century: 'Painting is always very hard for me – always this struggle – is it natural?' But, much in the way that Matisse found Nice and Morocco, and 'the environment', in Lawrence Gowing's words, 'took the place of style', so David Hockney found the United States of America and, in particular, southern California.

His first years in California in the mid-sixties were extraordinarily productive. They produced the images – the swimming pools, swimmers and architecture, the sprinkled lawns and 'blank allure' – on which his popularity is still based.

But from the late sixties he started to dry up. His painting became more and more naturalistic, and naturalism is a trap from which he is only now, at the age of fifty, showing signs of being able to escape.

Hockney need never paint another picture. As the style in which he lives suggests, the income generated from his drawings and etchings is more than enough to meet his needs. But it is not on his drawings or etchings, and certainly not on the Polaroids and Xeroxes and other high-tech excursions on which he has recently embarked, but on the paintings that his reputation will eventually rest.

The fact that the stage models for *Tristan* and the colour photocopying machines no longer occupy the centre of the studio suggests that the painting 'block' that has been dogging him for at least a decade may finally be at an end. But, while confirming that for the first time in a long time he is about to give himself over fully to painting again, Hockney is at pains to point out that what this does *not* mean is that he regrets any of the experiments of the past ten years.

'Kas never liked me working in the theatre,' he says, 'because I did less painting for him. But, frankly, I pursue my ideas. And if I think I can pursue some of them in the theatre, or photography or video, that's what I'll do. If the gallery doesn't like it, too bad.

'I actually found the year I spent on the Wagner was thrilling. I was able to use many of my ideas about moving focus and perspective in *Tristan*. A lot of people might have thought I was talking out the back of my hat, but I don't mind. You can't expect everybody to understand everything *immediately*. It doesn't matter if it takes time. I'm not in a rush. I've never been in a rush.

'I mean, I'm just at the point where I wish to live rather quietly, stay here and do my subversive work. I'm deeply interested in subversion. I know radical art cannot happen in an art gallery any more. It can't. It won't do anything there. It has to happen on these new surfaces, the TV screen and the pages of newspapers and magazines. I do think we're moving into a new age now. New technology's going to do far more than they think it is. Far, far more. And I intend to do my bit to push things.'

A few days earlier a 1967 painting, *The Room, Tarzana*, had gone under the hammer in London for £260,000. Hockney had been paid £250 (half the sale price) for it the year it was painted, but is unable to rise to any sense of indignation now. 'The art world,' he says, 'really doesn't interest me very much. Because it's not concerned with art at all. It's concerned with its own . . . commerce, and its own rather narrow view of things.'

As a gesture of contempt for a German collector who had refused to allow one of the earliest California pieces to return to America for the new show, Hockney was in the process of painting an exact replica.

Both this painting and *The Room, Tarzana*, as it happens, feature frankly erotic images of naked or semi-naked men. Hockney and Francis Bacon between them have been credited with liberalising attitudes towards male homosexuals in Britain through their work. And, in the case of Hockney at least, this was the result of a conscious effort 'to propagandise something I felt hadn't been propagandised as a subject. I felt it should be done.'

In the catalogue to the retrospective, Henry Geldzahler talks about 'the relentless clanging tocsin of Aids, which seems every month to toll for still another great friend or colleague'. At least ten close friends of Hockney's have died in the last few years. And this, Kasmin suggests, explains David's tendency to sidestep any discussion of the recent past these days.

Perhaps it also explains why, after working on the sets of Ravel's fairy-tale opera *L'Enfant et Les Sortilèges*, he decided to have the whole of the outside of the house repainted in playschool blues, greens and reds. Electrically patterned zebra fish have been suspended from a tree in the garden. The brilliantly clashing patterns and colours in the central living area seem to threaten to break free, the way they would in a Matisse interior, and run riot round the room.

'It's always a lovely day here,' Hockney says suddenly. 'I like that. I think there's more joy in the sun. Like van Gogh. We must understand that if we don't have joy we'll be destroyed.'

Stanley is pleading for attention round his ankles. His picks him up. 'You've heard about the stock-market crash and all these people losing their money? Well, I only paid two hundred dollars for Stanley and he's worth five million now.' Pause. 'That's just on paper of course.'

1988

30 Sunflowers, *Violets on Yellow*, *Iris with Evian Bottle*, *Gladioli with Two Oranges*. These are not titles which suggest the wildcatter tendency; art at the cutting edge. And, on the face of it, the canvases lining the gallery deliver exactly what they promise: still-lives, painted on a domestic scale, of flowers — irises, lilies, violets arranged in vases. The vases are usually standing on tables, or occasionally on plinths draped with calico or some other fabric. There are sometimes props and bits of simple set-dressing: bottles, books, lemons, oranges. You could, in other words, be looking at the output of any afternoon class in any Senior Citizens' Centre or Women's Institute in the country.

It's only the presence of David Hockney, standing in a mac in the middle of the gallery and looking chirped up, looking like somebody who feels he is at least keeping abreast of the game, that prompts you to go back and look at the paintings more closely. When you do, you realise that the colours — humming electric yellows and blues and reds — are too close to the neon end of the spectrum to be the work of learner-daubers. Then you notice that the brushwork filling the big colour areas is a conscious nod in the direction of other painters: van Gogh and Monet; the signature hatching of Jasper Johns. Then you notice other things: that the six books in the painting called *Red and Pink Ginger* are the classic Gallimard edition of Proust's *Remembrance of Things Past*; that the drop-leaf table in *White Lilies and Orchid* is wood laminate and is from the G-Plan range; that the stamens on the antirrhinums are emphatically penis-shaped.

I take it that these are postmodern? I ask.

It is well known that Hockney has been going deaf for many years. He wears a hearing aid in each ear, but still frequently cups his left ear with his hand and leans in closer, well aware of the old-gitishness of the mannerism.

'Post-what? What does "postmodern" mean?'

Er, you say. Ironic. Detached.

'I actually like flowers,' he says, grinning, vindicated. 'I mean, I have flowers in my house always. Most people like flowers. I actually did them to cheer myself up.'

Hockney turns sixty this year and, physically, there are the inevitable signs of blurring and dimming. His hair, although still thick and schoolboyish in that Alan Bennett way, has faded from the 'Winsome Wheat' of his promiscuous, media-tart years to an Audenish dishwater blond. The jutting, cubistic jaw has a deeper underbite and is becoming more jowled. The old rakishness is still somewhat in evidence but reluctantly (you feel) muted, brought down. Even stripped of all the things that make David Hockney 'David Hockney', though, including the thick liquorice glasses, which have been replaced by a simple wire pair, he still ends up seeming, somehow impregnably, himself.

Although he has now spent more than half his life living in Los Angeles, he has never 'gone Hollywood'. When I visited him in Nichols Canyon, just before the big travelling retrospective of his work arrived at the Tate Gallery in 1988, he padded around in a pair of crêpe-soled carpet slippers, and drank brown ale with his lunch. Stanley, a dachshund, was (and remains) his grand passion, and he was in the early days of trying out his new stay-at-home, play-at-home, sleepy-time persona on the world. He claims he still ignores most invitations, preferring to eat at home with a few friends. 'I am a loner, really. I've always preferred intimacy. If two or three people are speaking at the same time, it's a cacophony to me. It's a horrible noise. You want to leave it.' (A few days after telling me this, Hockney was photographed sharing a table with Sir Ian McKellen, Mick Jagger and others at the Vanity Fair Oscar-night party in Hollywood.) These days, visits to London tend to be only stopovers between LA and Bridlington in Yorkshire, where his sister and his mother, who is now in her nineties, live.

'The promotional fashioning of David Hockney was one of the key events of the early sixties,' the art historian David Mellor has written. 'He was elevated by word of mouth, a murmur spoken in the litany of success which his promotion in the new London media furthered . . . Hockney is the great exemplar, before the Beatles, of mastery over the new publicity machine by means of ironising the reporting of fame.'

History has fingered him as one of the key figures in the pantheon of Swinging London. But, conscious perhaps that the bitterest criticism in the past has been directed as much at the perceived loucheness of the way he lives as at the work he has produced, Hockney is keen to offer a revisionist version of the 'permissive' period. 'The first stage sets I ever did were for a production of Jarry's *Ubu Roi* at the Royal Court in 1966,' he says, 'and you weren't even allowed to say "shit". There was a censor, and you had to use the French word *merde*. Well, that's the Swinging Sixties. I wasn't that impressed with it really.'

'Drugs and boys,' Hockney told me once. 'That's how most people see my life. Just life round the pool. But I'm quite unconcerned about it. I don't mind. Better not to be taken too seriously as an artist by some people. I think. I do. You're better off left alone.'

His friend and former dealer, Kasmin, confirms that

Hockney has always been more comfortable with the role of observer rather than that of participant: 'David liked being around it, but he never actually got involved in the sex that much.' Hockney emits a deep belly laugh when I repeat this to him now. 'I point out that the artist himself can't be a hedonist,' he says. 'The artists are workers. Well aren't they? They are by nature workers. All artists are. I'm a worker. I just work, actually.

'It's personality. It's the only way I can make sense of anything, frankly. For myself. Otherwise I'd be too depressed.'

He has made the crossover into middle age more gracefully than many of his generation. It is interesting how he has executed the transition from golden boy to codger so seamlessly, making a pronounced stoop and encroaching deafness seem almost a style statement – the symbol of Hockney in his Old Master years as surely as the swimming pools and exotic landscapes represented the sun-loving, boy-chasing gadabout of what we are now asked to accept as myth.

'You can do an amazing lot without leaving the house,' he says. 'Vermeer never left the house, and neither do I.' It was seeing the great Vermeer exhibition at The Hague last year that in a roundabout sort of way and thanks to an associate creative process that even he can't decipher, resulted in the new flower paintings. 'I was very impressed with the colour in those paintings. Three hundred years old, and they made every other painting in the place look dull. I was very patient. I went with the crowd. It wasn't that crowded. It was the last week. But the rooms were quite small, and I was very impressed with thirty people gazing at a small picture for a long time. The most vibrant colour. And I joked when I got back to Los Angeles that Vermeer's colour will last longer than MGM's and it's three hundred and fifty years old already.

'Colour brings you a bit of joy. You see, people hate colour in some ways. They're frightened of it, aren't they? There's a colour phobia. I do know that. But I must admit I see colour everywhere. In these new paintings I wanted colour to . . . vibrate.'

Leaving formal considerations to one side, though, the flower pictures are almost parodically – certainly provocatively – maiden-auntish in their subject matter and the apparent ham-fistedness of the paint handling. Hockney kept up the pretence of them just being nice pictures of pretty flowers for quite a while, before finally conceding that perhaps they're not to be taken entirely at face value. 'My original title for the exhibition was going to be Fuck You, It's All Flowers. Then I decided I wanted the faces [portraits] in as well. I'm well aware that most people would say that paintings of flowers are absolutely banal, and so on. I know all that. On the other hand, I'm also aware that you don't remember many paintings of flowers. It's very hard. They're not specially interesting.'

Nobody could look at those paintings in 1997, knowing they're by David Hockney, I tell him, and think that they're just meant to be a celebration of flowers and colour.

'There is a quote of Stravinsky's: "Most art is sincere, and most art is bad, but some insincere art is . . ."' He forgets how it continues, but the point is made. 'These are paintings that are not about covering up. They are about laying bare. They're anti-slickness, anti-gloss, anti-everything like that. There's risk involved. Of course, it's a risk. But eventually they will be seen as mine. I know that. They always are. I see the bigger pattern, I think. "Why does he spend his own money doing those operas?" I know that's what they've been saying for years. "Why has he become obsessed with late-Picasso?" I do what I want to do, actually. I'm rich enough to do that.'

The paintings in the new show suggest those occasions when there is surfeit, a superabundance of flowers – flowers in places where, perhaps, there usually are none. Some evoke the luxe life for which Hockney has become renowned; others, though, are redolent of the living rooms of terraced houses like the one in which Hockney grew up, on those occasions when Interflora comes knocking: weddings, birthdays, anniversaries and, of course, funerals.

'Both [Hockney and Picasso] have injected into their work a powerful, ambiguous sense of death,' Richard Wollheim, professor of philosophy at the University of California, has written. 'In Hockney's art there is none of the omnipotence that Picasso's work exudes, and, instead, there is a sensibility close to Watteau's, in which the trivial suddenly, abruptly, but still abjuring solemnity, stands for the transient. But in the work of both men we find ourselves, quite unmistakably, in the presence of a sombre power from which we thought ourselves a million miles away.'

Aids is a subject which Hockney has chosen not to address directly in his work. To those, though, who believe the grief of recent years is reflected nowhere in the paintings, his advice is: look again. 'Some people have said to me, "You never dealt with Aids." Well, I thought I did. I thought there were paintings of mine full of pain, actually. But I'm not going to say to that, "You don't look hard enough." If people don't see it, it's up to them.'

At the beginning of last year, Hockney painted a series of portraits of his ninety-five-year-old mother in which she is barely recognisable as the woman in the pictures of even twenty years ago. At around the same time he painted Jonathan Silver, the director of the Hockney Gallery in Salts Mill, near Bradford, who was recovering from cancer surgery.

'David Plante was just telling me he remembers Francis

Bacon saying to him, "Give me tragedy, give me tragedy,"' Hockney says. 'For somebody who spent his whole time on uproariousness and getting drunk, gambling and fucking, it's a kind of mad remark. The tragedy's in the paintings. I'm probably the reverse. I've always said to people, "The painting might look happy, it doesn't mean to say the artist is; don't be deceived." It's a rather shallow view to think that, I always feel. Francis Bacon was probably a lot happier than I am.'

You were never happy, even in the early days in California, painting the boys and the swimming pools?

'Happiness,' he says, 'is something which seems a retrospective thing, frankly. It's only when you are firstly, deeply unhappy that you realise you were happy at some other time. But until you're absolutely unhappy, you wouldn't know that, would you?'

Ushered into a side room off the main gallery, housing a Mondrian and a Naum Gabo sculpture, Hockney had immediately produced a tiny silver box from his jacket pocket. The box's mirrored lid had me thinking for a second that something was going to happen connected to drugs. It turned out to be a portable ashtray, to collect the ash from his cigarettes. Hockney's an inveterate smoker. The no-smoking rule in almost all California's restaurants is an additional reason that he chooses not to eat in them. He had just written a letter to the *New York Times*, he said, defending the late Deng Xiaoping's right to smoke Panda cigarettes. ('Mr Deng might say, in ninety-three years of my turbulent life, thank goodness for Panda cigarettes keeping me calm. And calm to a ripe old age. Wouldn't you deduce that? I would. I think some people would be a lot better off smoking.')

Oh, it's an ashtray, I'd said when he first produced the box. I thought it was something illegal.

'Well,' he said, 'it used to be stuff like that. Now, believe it or not, it holds cigarette ash. That tells you a lot about us, doesn't it? But that's what everybody used to think.'

When did you stop doing young people's things like drugs?

He seemed slightly hurt. 'Why do you assume I've stopped? Actually, I haven't stopped, really. I'm a bit of an old . . . I like dope, actually. Smoking dope and listening to music. Wagner. Yes. Very good. Most people take drugs. They call it "medication". If you know anything about drugs, you can see what's coming, can't you? I assume we'll go from them being absolutely illegal to them pushing them down our throats. There won't be any in-between, will there? Go from one extreme to another. I won't change. I've never claimed to be a respectable person. I'm not.'

Something has changed on his visits home in just the past few years. Hockney can no longer take for granted the title of Britain's Most Famous Living Artist that he has held unchallenged since at least the mid-sixties. A rival has appeared who happens to share not only his birthplace and his initials, but also his personal charm and his appetite for life and unpredictable, restless intelligence.

'I did meet Damien Hirst once,' Hockney said. 'Actually, when he met me, d'you know what he said? I've just remembered this. It was in California. He said, "I met you when I was twelve. It was at a performance of the *Messiah* in Bradford, and I came up to you and said, 'I'm going to be an artist.'" And I then remembered. I said, "Yes, it was at the Eastbrook Hall and not at the St George's Hall," which was being repaired at the time. And I did remember all this. It came back to me.

'I'll say this about Damien: at least he's made memorable images. I think there are a lot of lively artists in London at the moment. I mean, you need all kinds of artists. You do. What's

Oscar Wilde's remark? "The only person who likes all kinds of art is an auctioneer." Another one: "It's only the shallow who do not judge by appearance."'

All the time he had been talking, Hockney had been reminding me of somebody, although I couldn't think who. And then it came to me. With his Yorkshire accent and his jutting chin and his forthrightness and sly humour he bears more than a passing resemblance to Labour's deputy leader, John Prescott.

'I don't live here. I don't follow the politics too much,' Hockney said when I mentioned this to him. 'I mean, I'm informed. I keep myself informed. I can read between the lines. I've noticed, for instance, that the weekend papers in England have started to get much fatter with advertising. That means the advertisers are using print instead of television. If you record television, you fast-forward the ads. So the only ads you're going to have on television are in disasters or sports. So that's all you'll be seeing on television soon, disasters or sports. Because you can't fast-forward them. I notice all this.

'I notice the political parties here are using whole images in newspapers. Trying to find images you remember. The mask on Mr Blair was very good. It didn't matter how long it lasted. I know how it works. That's Mr Saatchi's work – Mr Saatchi's an artist, ruthlessly using other artists. I've always thought that.'

You know him?

'No, I've never met him. I'm not [this said under his breath] that interested in art collectors.'

You're both reclusive, in a way.

'Oh I'm sure I'm more reclusive . . . I'm not involved in art politics. It doesn't interest me.'

With sunlight splashing onto the poster colours of the flower paintings, the gallery outside had taken on something of the feel of Hockney's living room in the Hollywood Hills. Looking pallid in comparison as he posed among them for a photographer, Hockney recalled a remark made by the mayor of Bridlington when he was told that the famous artist was becoming a regular visitor to the town. 'I've never heard of him,' he said, 'but he'll love it here. It's an artist's paradise.'

I think we can take it that it is in this spirit of heartfelt philistine sincerity, comical and at the same time oddly affecting, that the new work has been made.

1996

PETER BLAKE

Peter Blake, a rather short, bearded and gregarious man of fifty, used to be a very odd, lonely little boy. He was taken to the pictures from the age of two almost daily; his mother used to go to watch Shirley Temple, James Cagney, the Bowery Boys all the time in the afternoons.

When war was declared he was evacuated, with his sister, from Dartford in Kent to a Mrs Lofts in Essex, where they shared the house with a Mr Grace, who had been in the Boer War and had a leg amputated on the battlefield, and whom they could often see from the school they attended, hobbling across the horizon on his crutches, and with a farm labourer called Bill who, every morning when he got up, farted from the top of the stairs to the bottom.

Peter's parents drove up on their motorbike to see him whenever they could; there was church three times on Sunday, followed by reading in the parlour and an evening walk whose main purpose seemed to be to keep the children away from Happidrome on the wireless.

He returned to 'Bomb Alley', which is what they used to call Dartford, just in time for the Battle of Britain, which was fought above his head. Then he was evacuated again, to Worcester, this time with his granny, a dedicated hoarder with a brand-new cocktail cabinet standing in her cramped little house among all the rubbish. She was particularly well stocked up on aluminium meat mincers, and kept a trunk of tin toys waiting for her son to come home from the war. Her grandson interfered with them when she wasn't looking.

He was waylaid every night on his way from school by the bullies and, on returning to Dartford, lived through agonies of shyness.

But he did go to fairs, and to West Ham Speedway, and to the wrestling at Bexley Drill Hall with his mother and his auntie: watching them set about their least favourite fighters with handbags and umbrellas interested him at least as much as the official bouts on the programme. On his own, on Saturdays, he'd take the trolleybus to Woolwich and walk from there to Charlton Athletic's ground, where he'd melt into the regular crowd of 60,000.

He was accepted at junior art school just before the end of the war, and entered in short pants. He was a regular attender at Dartford Rhythm Club and graduated from swing to bop and from grey flannel to sharp 'hipster' suits and 'slim-Jim' ties. He took to going up to London to the 51 Club, Club 11, the Flamingo, all the modern jazz clubs, always by himself.

He was always alone, and didn't dislike it. He wasn't antisocial exactly – he had friends at the art school – but, out at the clubs, he never talked to anybody, ever.

A cycling accident when he was seventeen left him permanently scarred around the mouth and with false teeth which for four years he refused to wear. Being toothless was one of the things which set him apart in the RAF, where he did his National Service from 1951 to 1953. He was treated solicitously by the other men – almost over-sympathetically, it often seemed to him, as though he were some sort of freak.

He got his demob six days after the Coronation, which meant it was one of the few important state occasions he had

had to miss. He had watched the Victory Parade and the Queen's wedding, and he took a morning off from art school to stand outside the abbey on the day Princess Margaret married Lord Snowdon.

Back at the college, wearing the bottom half of a mutilated boiler suit, the closest approximation to the American jeans then still unavailable in London, he'd work to the accompaniment of the Four Freshmen, the Hi-Lo's, the Four Aces, the Kirby Stone Four and, later, the Four Preps, enthusiasms which none of his fellow students yet shared.

He liked Kim Novak in *Bell, Book and Candle* and Brigitte Bardot pictures snipped from *Reveille*. He amassed an enormous pin-up collection and became a fan of the nude reviews which were touring the dying Moss Empires and Stolls. He liked music hall, and especially Max Miller, and was a frequent visitor to the Chelsea Palace. He took a close interest in the exploits of the Sinatra/Dean Martin/Sammy Davis Jr 'rat-pack'.

When he left the Royal College of Art in 1956 he was awarded a Leverhulme Scholarship to study popular culture, which he interpreted as meaning touring Europe for a year, going to jazz concerts, wrestling matches and fairgrounds, getting drunk a lot and collecting 'durable expendables': cigarette packets and chip packets, plastic giveaways and badges, bus tickets, clothing labels, votive offerings, book covers, bubble-gum wrappers, fly-posters, all the kinds of things which had been silting up his modest accommodation for years.

He was, of course, an Elvis fan, although he was also unusually receptive to the 'high-school' stars – Frankie Avalon, Ricky Nelson, Fabian – who trailed in Presley's wake, and to the 'teen queens' like Tuesday Weld who appeared in their pictures with them.

In 1961, the year David Hockney and his young contemporaries at the Royal College thrust themselves into the public consciousness, Peter Blake, six years their senior and an obvious influence, won the junior prize at the John Moores Exhibition in Liverpool, and was featured in a Ken Russell TV documentary called *Pop Goes the Easel*.

He became a familiar of the Beatles and, his scars camouflaged now by a wispy beard, part of the iconography of the sixties. Quite suddenly, though, at the end of the decade, he removed himself, with his wife, the American sculptor Jann Howarth, and their daughter, Liberty, to a converted railway station in the West Country.

Here his preoccupations became his family and country living. 'Oh God,' Hockney would joke, 'I don't know how Peter Blake can take it down in his signal box, never seeing strangers from one week's end to the next. Chekhov put me off that for life.' He steeped himself in the work of Thomas Hardy, William Morris, Stanley Spencer, the Victorian children's illustrator Richard Dadd — and especially Lewis Carroll.

Blake formed the Brotherhood of Ruralists and planned an Alice in Wonderland museum, an 'Alice' garden, a Looking-Glass village school. And then, just as suddenly as it seemed to have begun, the idyll was over. His marriage fell apart and, in 1979, he suffered a short but debilitating breakdown.

All of this Blake is happy to tell you, in his quiet, thorough, rather wry way. And yet visits to the London house into which he recently moved his Tussaud's wax model of Sonny Liston, the boots belonging to Tom Thumb which he bought at auction, and his many hundreds of boxes of 'bits', are not essential to an understanding of his life: it is all in the pictures.

The paintings Peter Blake has been making since his days in short trousers reflect his interests and obsessions in the most unambiguous way. But the best of them, with their oddly mis-aligned eyes and lovingly scarred and scumbled skin, with their undertow of melancholy familiar to fans of even the Beatles' and the Beach Boys' happiest songs, reach beyond the merely autobiographical for a fusion of what T. S. Eliot once described as 'the old and the obliterated and the trite, the current and the new and surprising, the most ancient and the most civilised'.

Peter Blake will always be associated with the sixties: his *Babe Rainbow* enamel was on sale in every shop in Carnaby Street, his *Sgt Pepper* sleeve, fifteen years later, is still being picked over for 'clues'. But his Pop period, he says, was a relatively short one, as he hopes the retrospective will show.

He painted what would only later be recognised as the first Pop paintings — of ABC Minors and children reading comics — in 1954 and 1955. But the fact that they were accepted for hanging at the Royal Academy at the time emphasises the fact that Blake has always been a painter in the traditional manner. (Although he declined to be put up for selection when a young man, he finally became an RA in 1976.)

'I was really just painting what I was about, the person I was and the things I knew,' he says of his early days. 'I'd always been interested in the wrestling, the fairgrounds, the music, so I just carried on.'

From the beginning there were those who criticised his work for being knee-deep in cheap sentimentality and nostalgia, for being merely 'frivolous souvenirs of amusing times'. So when he announced his intention, at the end of 1969, of going to live in the country to paint fairies, his critics — and some of his friends — went to town.

'What was happening,' he says, 'was that the whole sixties thing had built up to such an extent that one was spending more time just being a "face" than actually working. You'd pick up the phone and it would be *London Life* wanting to know what kind of shoes you were wearing, or if they could photograph your bathroom.

'They might do a couple of actors, usually Albert Finney or Tom Courtenay, perhaps a designer like Ossie Clark, and the painters were always either David Hockney or me.

'So, really, it was quite a conscious move away from that shallow but obviously seductive media interest. What then went wrong in the country is that things went too far the other way. The seclusion became unhealthy. I became a workaholic. Plus, we had a lot of plans, crazy plans for the house and the garden and the Alice in Wonderland museum that, looking back, were overambitious.

'But the reason it caused so much antagonism, a lot of it quite vitriolic at times, is that people decided we were being exclusive and people don't like to be excluded, do they?'

Unusually for a major retrospective show, Blake will be including works by other artists: the ruralists will be represented by six large canvases, collectively called The Definitive Nude; and there will also be a 'guest slot' (just like the *Cilla Black Show*, Blake explains) for the English painter Howard Hodgkin.

When his marriage broke down in 1979 it was with Hodgkin, who at that time also happened to be picking up the pieces of his life, that Peter Blake took off for David Hockney's house in California. Such a bizarre time was had by all that on the aeroplane home Blake and Hodgkin agreed to produce three paintings each to commemorate the visit.

'There was a whole range of crazy things going on of the kind that you would expect in the house that Hockney lived in,' Peter Blake remembers. 'But when you're actually in the middle of it all, it's very strange. I was very much a kind of voyeur, really.'

Blake is currently at work on two paintings of the man whose life he seems to have just 'brushed against' every so often: the first: started in 1964, is a portrait of Hockney as a media celebrity and 'party person'. The second, started after the visit of 1979, is a triple portrait of Blake, Hodgkin and Hockney on the boardwalk at Venice, California.

'People,' Peter Blake says, 'tend to assume that I must be envious of David Hockney: I'm that much older and he's been a great deal more successful than I have, certainly in terms of finance and publicity, which is what success is often measured in.

'But I have never wanted to be Hockney. The truth is that I am actually a better painter than him and wouldn't want the kind of success he's had. I wouldn't want the pressures he has, for instance to produce, from the people around him.

'My own career has been quite a slow process. It really has built up to now. This show is what it's been about. This is the first time I'll have shown a full hand.'

1986

EXTRACT FROM *ALMA COGAN*

A story, possibly apocryphal (one of hundreds), about Mae West:

She was approached once by an intense young girl, who announced, 'I saw *Diamond Lil* last week; it was wonderful.'

'Didja, honey? Wheredja see it?'

'At the museum. The Modern Museum.'

And a dismayed Mae, seeking shelter in the sassy drawl of her film persona, inquired: 'Just whaddya mean, honey? A museum?'

*

I thought of the story this morning as I drifted through the connected but separate climate systems of the galleries at the Tate, looking for the portrait Peter Blake painted of me nearly a quarter of a century ago and that I haven't seen for almost that long.

I could have asked for directions at the information desk just as you come in, but I was hoping to come across myself without warning, to take myself unawares, even if it did mean denying a constant urge to run to the toilet and a banging in my chest like the Derry Apprentice Boys' parade.

It was early. I was among the first in. There was still the feeling of overhang from the previous day. In addition to dollars and yen and layers of small change, the glass donation boxes were choked with messages posted by school parties — 'Jo 4 Stuart', 'Sharon 4 Cookie', 'Homefucking is killing prostitution', 'What are you looking at DICKHEAD', 'If I wanted to listen to somebody talking out of his arse, I would've farted'.

There was the sound of banged metal and spilled cutlery and conversations in iron-curtain accents coming from the kitchens. The attendants were assembled in a group under the rotunda, being assigned their areas of responsibility for the shift – room 10, Rural Naturalism and Social Realism, 1870–1900; room 14, Bloomsbury and Vorticism, 1910–20 – where they would sit and watch the day stack up and listen to the humidity and temperature stabilisers ticking through their programmes.

(Room 28, the chapel-like space containing Rothko's looming soft-edged stacks of rectangles for the Seagram Building is where I would angle to get placed. It must be the equivalent of a diplomatic posting to Paris or Washington.)

In some galleries it was like being the first to walk on a new snowfall; the air hadn't been displaced. Room 23, abstract expressionism, was like this. The only sign of any life was in the paintings, which were humming with the urgency of mark-making and 'the liberated unconscious'.

I stood in front of one of de Kooning's Women for at least a minute before I got a bead on the figure embedded in the loops and slashings of paint. Before I lost it again, it reminded me of something I had seen a million times in the mirror: make-up being smeared into waxy swipes and lurid skirls of colour by the application of theatrical remover cream.

Among the information given on the card on the wall was a quotation from the artist: 'Flesh was the reason why oil painting was invented'.

A few galleries on, I stood at the edge of a tour group and listened while the guide filled them in on the background to Stanley Spencer's *The Resurrection, Cookham*. 'You can see the artist sandwiched between the two book-like tombstones at the bottom right-hand comer . . . You can also see him naked in the centre of the painting . . . "I don't want to lose sight of myself," Spencer once admitted, "for an instant."'

The students – they were a mature group – wrote this down on their pads. They kept their hands free by wearing the collapsible stools they were carrying over their shoulders or – in the case of most of the men – transversely across the chest, like armour.

The Spencer wasn't hanging on the wall. It was standing on rubber blocks on the floor, with gallery staff going backwards and forwards with ladders and lengths of wood in front of it as if they were among the resurrected and had just stepped out of the painting.

I continued wandering haphazardly, following no particular plan. Once or twice I thought I saw the picture Peter Blake did

of me in the Palaeolithic era out of the corner of my eye –
something about the scale as I remembered it, the composition, the colour. But when I edged nearer it would turn out to
be a still-life of *Shelf with Objects*, or *View of Hackney with Dalston
Lane, Evening*.

In the end I had to admit defeat and backtracked to
Information, where I asked the person on duty if she could
point me in the direction of the Peter Blake painting titled
Alma Cogan, dated, I thought, 1961–63.

She was an interesting combination of half-prim (cashmere
cardigan, pearls) and half-punkette (high-shaved side-panels,
gold wire ring in her nose). Acid-green letters started dancing
in her tiny glasses as her fingers ran over the keys. Behind and
above her, meanwhile, a second display panel spooled out slogans in liquid crystal letters of peony and tangerine.

DISGUST IS THE APPROPRIATE RESPONSE TO MOST SITUA-
TIONS . . . DYING AND COMING BACK GIVES YOU CONSIDER-
ABLE PERSPECTIVE . . . LOVING ANIMALS IS A SUBSTITUTE
ACTIVITY . . . THE HAPPINESS OF BEING ENVIED IS GLAMOUR
. . . PUBLICITY IS THE LIFE OF THIS CULTURE . . . NOSTALGIA
IS A PRODUCT OF DISSATISFACTION AND RAGE . . . On and on
they rolled. Around and around.

'I'm afraid I can't access that information,' the girl said.
'*Alma Cogan* is currently on loan to the VIP Lounge at
Heathrow.' Then a signal from the screen started throbbing in
her eye like a nerve. She keyed in another code which supplied
her with the information that the painting had recently been
returned. I could make an appointment to come in and see it
in storage at a later date.

'Name?'

It occurred to me to quickly make something up. But
'Cogan,' I said. 'A.'

There was a pause, as if the 'search' function of the console in front of her was flying through its documents and folders making another match. 'The . . . the subject of the work?' I nodded. She walked to the back of the information area and picked up a phone.

CHASING THE NEW IS DANGEROUS TO SOCIETY . . . RECLUSES GET WEAK EVEN IF STRONG ORIGINALLY . . . MURDER HAS ITS SEXUAL SIDE . . . LACK OF CHARISMA CAN BE FATAL . . . The words trickled over the jagged surface of her isolated island of hair. When she came back I half expected to see the neon colour combed in.

Somebody from conservation would be up to collect me in a few minutes, she said, if I would care to wait. And meanwhile, if I would fill in the form, taking care to make sure that the information registered on the carbon duplicates underneath . . .

The first time I met Peter Blake was when he had just stopped being a student. It was at the all-night party Mike Todd gave at the Battersea Festival Gardens after the London opening of *Around the World in 80 Days*, which would date it as 1956.

He was working on one of the amusements – rifle range, coconut shy, tombola, dodgems (they were all free that night, of course, along with everything else). He was wearing the bottom half of a boiler suit, the closest you could get at that time in England to American jeans, and a similarly improvised jean jacket.

But what I remember most vividly about him are the seams of blue puckered scars that extended from his mouth to his nose on one side of his face like a hinge and were emphasised rather than hidden by his attempt at a straggly student beard. (Since the mauling I'd witnessed just two years earlier, I had taken a more-than-usual interest in the movement of people's mouths, the wetness and glitter and the shape of the mouth and the teeth.)

He reminded me of this first meeting the second time we met, at one of my parties, when he was coming into his first fame and I was just starting to be aware of the calm that was waiting round the corner. (It was a phrase Billy Eckstine used, which had caught on. 'All of a sudden,' he said, 'it gets calm.')

It was on this occasion I think he said he would like to do a painting. I was flattered, of course, but slightly nonplussed when he said he would prefer to use a magazine picture (he seemed to already know which one) than have me come to the studio and sit for him.

But we did have lunch – at Cunningham's, the champagne and oyster bar then at the height of its fashionability, in Curzon Street. The owner Owen Cunningham's mother had been a maid in the twenties in a Shepherd Market laundry, earning a pittance from scrubbing the mountain of soiled linen sent out from the great Mayfair mansions.

Owney enjoyed a kind of social revenge by screwing the titles and blue-bloods among his regulars, who included the Gerald Legges, the Dockers, Anthony Armstrong-Jones and Olga Deterding, the Shell heiress who eventually threw it all in to go and work for Albert Schweitzer in Africa, while at the same time making sure that his show-business customers always got good value for money.

It was a lively lunch, with few of the longueurs that occur when two people are sitting alone at a table together for the first time. We were almost exactly the same age; Peter Blake had seen me perform on several occasions at the Chiswick Empire and the Chelsea Palace, and had a fan's knowledge of all departments of the wonderful business we call show.

Most of what we talked about went the way of the champagne and the oysters. The only thing that is fixed in my memory is our shared enthusiasm for fairs and in particular the way a field looks after a fair has moved on, with its circles and scars and mysterious relief patterns of raised and flattened grass.

He gave me a Betjeman quote, to the effect that there is nothing more empty than a deserted fairground, which encouraged me to try and put into words something which had been only the shadow of a notion until then.

'I love the way the wagons you see bowling along under their own steam on the road disappear inside the rides when they're set up,' I told him (as nearly as I can remember). 'The way the wheels are locked and jacked up on wooden blocks; how the overhead spokes and duckboards of the carousel are added; then the painted and mirrored panels, then the chairs or horses . . . Something in it seems to correspond to my own situation on the road, disappearing every night into the apparatus of sequins and wigs and spreading ostrich feathers . . .'

I saw him filing this away as a mental reference – the rims of his ears glowed momentarily – to use in whatever he might paint.

Some time later I received a souvenir – a small framed collaged piece, built up from that 1960 menu at Cunningham's, which would itself I suppose now be worth several thousand pounds in the salerooms. But it is gone, as far as I know, along with everything else.

'Miss Cogan?'

'Conservation' had suggested chemicals and white lab coats of the kind worn by the technicians in the EMI studios at Abbey Road as late as the mid-sixties. Facing me, though, and giving me a discreet once-over to see what twenty-five years had done to 'the subject of the work', was a person dressed in unremarkable civilian smart-casual wear – Kickers, newish jeans, cheesecloth-type shirt.

'If you'd like to come with me.'

I followed him past a piece of art splashed with whitewash on the ground like some primitive trail, and then round a tree decorated with small paintings of Christmas bells and decorations instead of the real thing, down some stairs.

At the bottom of the stairs I saw that the love notes and teenage obscenities had been removed from the donation box set into the wall and foreign notes in the higher denominations (the trick of lavatory attendants and cloakroom personnel) fluffed up on the surface like thinning hair.

We proceeded past a barrier spooled out of a plastic post and then, courtesy of a combination lock, through a door marked 'SECURE AREA — Passes must be worn'. On the other side it was like a public swimming bath — fresh after the recycled air of the gallery, with that kind of echoey no-noise and vaulted unsourced light.

A concrete ramp led down to the long sub-basement corridor, at the end of which Steenhuis, Peter, flashed his identity tag at a man sitting in an oak box of the kind cashiers sit in at the few remaining old-style butchers. 'SECURITY STATE OF VIGILANCE — BLACK SPECIAL' it said on a print-out strip inside the box where you weren't supposed to see.

Another combination lock. Another door with another message — 'Under no circumstances must this door be left open'. Another mini-climate of crackling air filtered through Mylex and Ticene gills, but with that metallic edge or imbalance that can strip the sinuses if breathed in too long.

'You can't get in here hardly in the summer,' Peter Steenhuis said in his Dutch-inflected American-English accent, 'especially in the lunch break, everybody trying to chill out.'

I went on being popular in the Netherlands and Scandinavia — also Iceland and Japan — long after my star had waned at home. I spent years singing phonetically in languages of which

I barely understood a word. Being no older than thirty, though, Peter Steenhuis was too young to remember.

'You can get all the English TV programmes in Holland now. Satellite, cable. My parents are big fans of the two Ronnies,' he said, consulting a piece of paper with the painting's acquisition number on it, as if he hadn't already sneaked a look before coming upstairs to collect me.

The pictures were hung on steel-mesh partitions which rolled soundlessly out into the sieved and bounced light like mortuary drawers. They radiated a second field of cold into the already part-refrigerated room.

When we got to the appropriate stack, he kicked a chuck which released the wheels and hauled out the frame containing a number of paintings by the British Pop artists of the early sixties.

Among them were four by Peter Blake: *The Masked Zebra Kid* of 1965; *Tuesday* (a portrait of Tuesday Weld), 1961, which prompted Peter Steenhuis to remark that he thought she was Melanie Griffith's mother ('Isn't Melanie Griffith married to that *Miami Vice* guy for the second time?'); *The Meeting, or Have A Nice Day, Mr Hockney*, 1981–5 – and T. 02285, *Alma Cogan*.

I don't know what I had been expecting. Of course I know what I had been expecting: to look down the dark tunnel of time and see myself preserved as I would choose to be in my best memory – unflawed, retouched; all minuses turned to plus, all sins forgiven, 'the fundamental rightness of the nature in question laid uppermost' (an inspiriting phrase plucked from one of the gallery walls during my morning's wandering).

But my first impression was that, unlike the elaborate gilt-wood frame, which seemed as timeless and solid as the Edwardian theatre interiors it echoed, the picture seemed to have aged with me, as if we had kept a parallel course.

It was as if the reverses of the intervening years, as well as the uncertainty of my present situation, had been able to paint themselves in; as if the pigment had been invaded by air sadness.

Its guardian and protector stepped forward and released the painting and carried it to a velvet-curtained area where he set it down carefully on a table packed and triple-packed with bubble paper whose bubbles you could burst if you pressed very hard, in the way that always drives Psyche up the wall.

'Nice painting,' Peter Steenhuis said, removing an invisible film of dust from the surface with delicate puffs of air from a rubber bulb. 'I like the restraint. None of that see-me-dance-the-polka brushwork.'

Then he withdrew to a diplomatic distance, thoughtfully removing a large-scale nude of a bodybuilder with a semi-erect penis out of my sight-line on the way.

The Tate Gallery Illustrated Catalogue of Acquisitions, 1974–76, pp. 54–6:

T.02285 Alma Cogan 1961–63
 Not inscribed
 Oil on panel, 17½ × 14½ × 1½ (44.5 × 36.8 × 3.8cm)
 Presented by E. J. Power through the Friends of the Tate Gallery
  1974

Coll: Arthur Tooth and Sons Ltd.; bt E. J. Power 1962
Lit: Robert Melville, 'The Durable Expendables of Peter Blake',
Motif, x, Winter 1962–3, pp. 20–22, repr. p. 20

Known as 'the girl with a chuckle in her voice' and for her large wardrobe of extravagant, self-designed dresses, the subject of T.02285 was one of Britain's most popular recording stars in the fifties.

Her string of twenty hits, more than any female vocalist of the era, included 'Bell Bottom Blues' (a cover of Teresa Brewer's 1953 American hit); 'I Can't Tell A Waltz From A Tango' (a cover of Patti Page's hit) in 1954; 'Dreamboat', the only No. 1 by a British female singer in the fifties; 'Twenty Tiny Fingers' (1955); a cover of Vaughn Monroe's 'In The Middle Of The House' (1956); and a cover of The Maguire Sisters' 'Sugartime' (1958). Her last hit was 'Cowboy Jimmy Joe' (1961).

Alma Cogan was one of the large generation of immediately pre-beat-boom stars whose style went out of public fashion after the emergence of the Beatles and other 'Mersey sound' groups in the sixties.

The sixties saw her moving into cabaret, overseas touring, and even a brief stint in TV commercial work – a detergent ad – while continuing to record without success for HMV, then Columbia. Her active career as a performer ceased c. 1970.

Peter Blake saw Alma Cogan on various variety bills in London in the mid-to-late fifties. He considered her to be one of the last remaining links with a music hall tradition that was on the point of disappearing (letter from the artist to the compiler, dated 11.10.74; Tate Gallery Archive TAV 503A) and that, in British art, had direct links with, inter alia, Sickert, Gore, Ginner and the painters of the Camden Town Group (see Gore T.02260; Sickert T.02039).

Peter Blake shares with Sickert an extended and profound understanding of the world of show business and a fascination with its glamour and lively vulgarity.

'Marriage did not interfere with his . . . habit of attending the halls, and he would even absent himself from a dinner party in his own home in order to go to a performance' (D. Sutton, Sickert, London, 1974, p. 235). 'His eagerness to capture the correct rendering of the tights worn by Emily Lyndale led him to follow her from hall to hall.'

Blake's interest in painting T.02285, however, was not primarily reminiscential or nostalgic, but the combination in one work of the nostalgic impulse with extreme mass-circulation-linked contemporaneity. In its transposition of pre-existing ready-made source material, the painting shares and, to some extent, pre-dates, the concerns of Lichtenstein, Warhol and other American Pop artists.

Blake started work on the painting in 1961. The source of the image was probably, though not certainly, a photograph of Alma Cogan in performance reproduced in *Fans' Library*, a monthly periodical of the fifties which featured a single entertainer in each issue and constituted a kind of early part-work.

Peter Blake purchased copies of the magazine as they were published, partly for pleasure, in his capacity as a 'fan', and partly because of his life-long interest in the images, significance and meaning of mass culture.

In his work of this period, Blake was drawn towards significant personalities as often as to the quality of the performance. Of Elvis Presley, for example, who figures in a large variety of Blakeian imagery, the artist said that he himself did not particularly respond to Presley's music: 'I have always been a fan of the legend rather than the person,' he told the compiler in a taped conversation, 3.10.74 (Archive TAV 499A).

'I wasn't ever particularly a fan of Alma Cogan, but I was very aware of her.' (Alma Cogan was the first female singer to have her own major TV series in the UK, 1959–61, ITV. Though her chart hits ceased, her chirpy personality guaranteed her regular British tours and TV appearances throughout the early sixties.) 'She was very much a presence on a national scale, and seemed to represent something – the innocence of the decade immediately following the war, old-fashioned glamour.'

Peter Blake chose the photograph of Alma Cogan on which T.02285 is based for a number of reasons. Although it was supposedly taken during a theatre performance, it looked posed. It was also printed on the same paper, in the same pocket-size format (and almost certainly by the same publisher) as *Spic*, *Span*, *Jem*, *Monsieur* and other 'girlie' magazines of the period which were later to form the basis of his Pin-Ups and Strippers series of works.

The disposition of the arms and hands seemed to echo for Blake the arms and hands in Francis Bacon's *Study after Velásquez's Portrait of Pope Innocent X* (1953); while the open mouth also recalled the human scream that has been a preoccupation of Bacon's throughout his career.

Blake also believed that Alma Cogan had lost the use of her voice for a period in the early part of her career and was attracted to this particular shot of the singer because of 'the soundless "O" of the mouth'. (She suffered hysterical aphonia, an affliction that strangles the vocal cords, in c. 1953, and was ordered not to sing for six months. It was subsequent to this illness that she developed her famous laugh-in-the-voice style.)

The curtains against which the figure is painted also invoke a device often used by Bacon in the years 1949–55. ('I've always wanted to paint curtains. I love rooms that are hung all around with just curtains hung in even folds' — David Sylvester, *Interviews With Francis Bacon*, London 1975, p. 112.)

Peter Blake's description of the colour of the curtains in T.02285 — 'spinach green' — derives from a postcard in his possession, sent to him from America by a friend and captioned, 'Alma, Alabama, Spinach capital of the world'. (He considered calling the painting *Alma Alabama* at one point.)

T.02285 evidences Blake's interest, stronger in 1961 than it has since become, in animation of surface texture. The retention of originally unintentional rough paint passages was deliberate. The most open assertion of the value of spontaneous gesture and of inflected handling is to be found, characteristically of Blake at this time, in the rendering of the diaphanous fabric of the dress, and in the areas around the eyes and mouth.

The scumbling, glazing and sgraffito techniques suggest signs of age, wear and damage and are evidence of the preoccupation running through all Blake's work with the obsolescence inherent in the popular images thrown up by a culture one of whose chief activities is producing and consuming images.

Peter Blake was completing work on *Alma Cogan* when he began his portrait *The Beatles* in 1963. One painting shows a performer approaching the end of her period of celebrity; the other shows four musicians on the threshold of overwhelming global fame.

But the emotional climate is not noticeably different: both works are equally wistful and equally solemn. He seems to see both past and present at the same nostalgic distance, so that the young Beatles seem to have as much period charm as a fading variety performer, a publicity still as an engraving. No image is so brashly contemporary that he cannot see it in this way.

This entry has been corrected and approved by the artist.

(The compiler is indebted to Miss Christine Bowles, Curator, the Pop Collection, the Victoria and Albert Museum, London, and to F. McL.)

*

Chilblains. Impetigo. It seems a world ago that people used to get chilblains, scaly red ripple marks on their legs, from sitting too close to the fire. Or went round with purple ink painted on the sores on their faces. Poverty-related ailments that you don't see now.

But chilblains and impetigo are what the fleshy parts of my body reminded me of when I studied them through a magnifying glass (actually a flexible strip of magnifying plastic, grooved like a thumb-print, made in Japan) in the meat-safe sub-basement at the Tate.

Areas of colour which in reproduction or viewed from a distance looked flat and uncorrupted, close-to turned out to be shot and broken and exquisitely damaged with legions of tiny nicks and lacerations. The flesh tones broke down into chance blots and controlled mergings which ranged in colour from oyster grey to angry red.

Passages of greasy lustre, reminiscent of real skin, were blotted up by matt or coarse passages where the trails of thin paint lost their legibility. The texture of chest and shoulder was particularly enlivened with trace lines, tones, shadows and local colour, swirling together like smoke in a bottle.

The whiteness of the scalp was visible in patches through the mass of dense dark hair, and through that, other marks — corrections, counter-images, outlines painted over, chappings and abrasions soothed with transparent glazes — could also be clearly detected.

Under magnification, the face looked like a valuable urn which had been painstakingly reconstructed. The surface had been painted in a way that seemed to contain evidence of its bloatings and shrinkages and rebloatings over the years, as well as ghostly intimations of how it was going to change with age.

Looking into the painting was like looking at a lifetime's

reflections fixed in a mirror — at bits of yourself that had found a place to go when they died.

The longer I looked, the more I saw several kinds of history smudgily superimposed; former selves which floated to the surface like memories, only to become submerged again.

The curtain behind the figure is stained with tide-lines, rejected versions, spectres of myself which are not visible on the postcard reproduction, out of print for some time, which Peter Steenhuis gave me as I was preparing to leave.

IT'S BETTER TO BE LONELY THAN TO BE WITH INFERIOR PEOPLE . . . IT'S BETTER TO BE NAIVE THAN JADED . . . MEDIA IMAGES ONLY SHOW US WHAT WE ALREADY KNOW, the sign was saying as I stepped into the damp, fungus-forming air and quickly headed off in the direction of London's rich shabbiness.

When I got back I started going through drawers and cupboards trying to find a photographic reminder of the life locked into the underlayers of the painting, but soon gave up. Everything I opened had the death smell of camphor and old clothes that have never been worn and ashy drifts of insect corpses.

Interleaved among my mother's personal belongings, her underwear and stockings and nightclothes, hidden as if in a game and never detected, was a collection of items which, as Bob Brotherhood would say, were not very eyeful.

Blown light bulbs, nibbled squares of chocolate, razor blades, a packet of CrackerBarrel, stale biscuits, a dog chew, greying dentures, sardine-tin keys, an obsessive number of Vicks inhalers, and a years-old piece of meat in a tissue were among the things I'd unearthed when I decided to stop before I came across something I would really regret finding.

The whole flat smells of neglect, decay, staleness. Dirt is ingrained in the windows, the curtains are heavy with dust, the plastic covers on the sofa where I'm sitting are scored and urine-coloured. Even after so many years, the cushions still hold the shape of my mother's broad back and tired old buttocks.

The Moors is again at the top of the news. Tuesday, December 16. Hindley has been back on the Moors, trying to help police pinpoint the graves where Pauline Reade and Keith Bennett lie buried.

The first part of the report is to camera, against an establishing backdrop of snowy moorland dotted with operations vehicles, Transit vans and police Range Rovers.

'A massive security operation involving armed policemen was mounted and the area sealed off by a cordon of roadblocks as Hindley arrived on Saddleworth Moor by helicopter shortly after dawn this morning. She spent over seven hours with senior detectives' – cut to overhead shots of vehicles speeding in convoy along the glassy ribbon of road across the Moor – 'retracing places she had visited with her former lover Ian Brady. While Hindley walked the Moor, head bowed against driving rain and heavy winds, she was watched by police marksmen.'

A red circle hovers around the head of one of a party of tadpole figures slithering across the lunar landscape of snow. It encloses a black hood worn over a black balaclava which, when they blow it up, pushing as far as it will go, hovers on the edge of disclosing who or what is in there, but in the end dissolves into dots of primary colours.

That she has an existence independent of the image that has represented her for twenty-one years – the trowel nose, the defiant eyes, the peroxide hair – is a mystery that seems hard to get to grips with. Hindley was twenty-three when she was arrested. Now she's forty-four. It is as if by changing her appearance, and keeping her current identity secret, she has effected some form of escape.

'The senior detective leading the investigation said that Hindley's recollection of bleak moorland she has not visited for over twenty years was surprisingly vivid. It had led police to a new search area where she believes more young bodies may be buried, and where digging may begin tomorrow.'

The wind-burned face of one of the searchers (filmed from above, probably from a ladder, over the heads of the other camera crews and reporters) now fills the screen. 'We will be using the new digging techniques we have been taught by experts in buried body detection, removing the topsoil and then using a trowel and a hoe to identify the different layers of soil and looking for signs that the natural layering has been disturbed,' he says.

Extract from **Tate Gallery Archive Tape TAV 499A**, recorded 3.10.74

COMPILER: I sense a certain sexual ambivalence in the figure of Alma Cogan as you have portrayed her in the painting. The hands, for instance, are very big. This could be a woman imitating a man imitating a woman.

PETER BLAKE: That was intentional. On the occasion when we met to discuss the painting, I remember her saying something along the lines of her learning all her make-up tricks from drag queens — what kind of mascara lasts longest, how to apply eyeshadow, 'all the important decisions'.

Later, some years after the portrait was finished, in the mid-sixties, I believe there was a drag act who billed himself as '. . . in the gowns of Alma Cogan', which is very strange.

1991

for Gordon

hear all, see all,

Say Nowt

Damien
xxx

RICHARD SMITH

If Richard Smith had been looking for a metaphor for how his reputation has withered and his work become discarded; for how – as he believes – he has been written out of recent British art history, he found an indelible one a couple of Thursdays ago, on a fleeting visit to London from his home in New York.

Every British artist – 'living and dead' as Smith puts it – had been invited to turn up to a picture-call to mark the relaunch of the Tate Gallery as Tate Britain. Smith had a career retrospective at the Tate in 1975, when he was still in his forties. A number of his pantechnicon-sized, three-dimensional 'constructed' canvases are in the permanent collection. And he duly took his place on the steps at Millbank alongside the great and the good, the Young and Not So Young Turks, the ennobled and bearded grandees, freighted with reputation and achievement. Present were some of the eminent Pop-ists who with Richard Smith invented Pop art in this country in the late fifties. Peter Blake was there, and so was Patrick Caulfield. Also present was Smith's old friend and former Wiltshire neighbour Sir Howard Hodgkin, who, in the years during which Richard Smith's standing has been steadily eroded, has made himself enormously famous and important.

The PR persons with the clipboards had ticked off who had turned up and who hadn't; the artists had been whipped into some sort of order; the snappers had been assembled beneath the scrubbed-up portico . . . And suddenly there was a stam-pede away from the official picture opportunity in the direc-tion of another one that had unexpectedly presented itself. Tracey Emin in a biker jacket and brassy jewellery had arrived in a taxi. Smiles freezing on the faces of the official group. 'Tracey, give us a smile, Tracey . . .' Mad Tracey from Margate, whose career still has a lot of heat under it. Our Lady of the Photo Op. 'Give me eyes, Tracey!' Smiles broadening on the faces of the PR contingent. Aluminium ladders crashing. Pandemonium.

But enough of symbolism. The reality for Richard Smith was even crueller. When he wandered inside to take a look at the radical new re-hang, it brought it home to him that, while there were Hodgkins and Peter Blakes and Hockneys – a whole roomful of Hockneys, his stablemate at the Marquess of Dufferin and Ava-backed Kasmin Gallery in New Bond Street throughout the sixties – there were no Smiths on display. No *Gift Wrap*; no *Flip Top*. None of the extraordinary, bulking, built-out paintings that he came under particularly heavy attack for in the early sixties, accused of strengthening adver-tising's success by taking it, in the form of abstracted Salem and Philip Morris cigarette packets, as his subject. His best paintings were generally large, sharing a sense of scale with cinema and billboard advertising where, as Smith said at the time, 'you could drown in a glass of beer and live in a semi-detached cigarette packet'. Twenty years later, at the main tobacco-sponsored tournaments during the heyday of tele-vised snooker, where the sets echoed the brand 'livery' and product packaging, it often looked as if the players were walk-ing around inside a Dick Smith painting.

So he was invisible in terms of his work at the Tate, and almost invisible in his person. Two recent, massively invasive operations on his heart have left him looking frail and almost transparent. He has apparently always been quiet and self-effacing. I remember seeing him many years ago at the moveable piss-up that is the Venice Biennale. Howard Hodgkin was the official British representative that year and he was being supported by a roistering group of friends who included Mick Moon, Patrick Caulfield and John Hoyland, plus a man with a rather shuffling, grey, careworn air, who turned out to be Dick Smith.

Just fourteen years earlier it had all been very different. In 1970 Richard Smith was the official British artist in Venice. Bernard Jacobson, his current London dealer, remembers being smitten at that time by the glamour surrounding Smith and his American wife, Betsy. 'I always thought of him as being like [Scott] Fitzgerald. They were the beautiful people. They had everything. I remember all the millionaires all wanting to meet Richard Smith at Venice. I mean real millionaires. Oil millionaires. Multimillionaires all over him. The party at Cipriani on Torcello was amazing: Kasmin snorting up under the trees, Robert Fraser fixing up, lakes of champagne.

'In the seventies,' Jacobson adds, 'the market was very, very strong. Stronger than the sixties. The sixties were very, very glamorous. But people were buying in the seventies, when you had the big collectors jumping on board. And Dick was part of that. He was a star.'

The world, however, moves on. Although stars may shine for ever, stardom always fades. And in an art world that has been described as being like a carnival with a casino attached, it has a tendency to fade faster than in other arenas. It can be brutal. Up like a rocket, down like a stick.

By 1984, Richard Smith's allure had dulled. The spotlight had shifted. His prices were faltering. 'It's when I took up smoking again,' he told me, 'in Venice for Howard in 1984. After that I was hooked for another many years.'

We met for lunch at the Ivy. It is a kind of shrine to the artists of Smith's generation – a Joe Tilson painting on wood is the centrepiece in the bar; paintings by Caulfield, Blake, Hodgkin and Allen Jones line the walls of the restaurant. All his friends. But no Dick Smith. Again Dick Smith was invisible. Just as you will look in vain for him in most recent books on postwar British art. He arrived before me. I couldn't help noticing that he had positioned himself in such a way that he was looking at one of the Ivy's opaque leaded windows with its shifting shadows of passing pedestrians, and not directly at any painting. Chris Corbin, who meets and greets at the Ivy at lunchtimes, pressing the flesh of the famous and familiar, schmoozing the hot and happening, failed to materialise at our table.

Smith was born in the commuter belt in Hertfordshire in 1931. His father was employed at the House of Commons as a printer on Hansard, working nights. Smith did his national service in the RAF, stationed in Hong Kong. And then, like Eduardo Paolozzi, Richard Hamilton and other members of the Independent Group at the ICA half a generation earlier, he got fired up by everything bright and synthetic and American. Living in a country still in the grip of austerity and rationing, he fell in love with the subversive glamour of America.

He was an affront to his teachers at the Royal College of Art, where he started in 1954, on two counts: his paintings were big and splashy and content-free at a time when English painting was still very pastoral, in the landscape tradition; still ruled by 'good taste' and common sense. This was especially the case after he had seen the Klines and Pollocks and other abstract expressionist pictures that came to the Tate as part of a hugely influential show of American art in 1956. And then on top of that he gave them deliberately poppy, throw-away titles like *Everly*, *Staggerly*, *Packet of Ten*, *Special Offer*. His work was hard-nosed, anti-romantic and urban. He has come to be seen as a precursor of the generation of Pop artists that included Allen Jones, Derek Boshier, Pauline Boty, Caulfield and Hockney, which emerged at the Royal College between 1959 and 1962.

He was a thinker. His work had a pronounced intellectual, as well as a purely visceral, dimension. He wrote articles for *Ark*, the RCA magazine, on men's fashion – 'The male image at mid-century' – and interior design in the movies.

Smith shared a flat-cum-studio with Peter Blake in his second year at the RCA and then again for two years after he left the College in 1957. When Terence Conran's Soup Kitchen opened on Fleet Street in the late fifties it featured a letter-collage mural by Smith and Blake. Michael Chow would later commission Richard Smith to design installations for his restaurant in Los Angeles, and Chow and Conran have remained two of his biggest supporters.

He went with Peter Blake to see Bill Haley at the Kingston Empire, and Johnnie Ray, the 'Nabob of Sob', at the London Palladium. 'It was really scraping around,' he says of their truffling for Pop culture in London in the mid-fifties. 'It seems funny now, but you really had to search it out.' In order to feel American – urban and out there and modern – Smith decided it was important to look American. 'You liked to dress in an American way, which was immensely problematical. I had a buzz cut. Gerry Mulligan. Gerry Mulligan had a great haircut. Wonderful haircut.'

Smith's lifelong subject was to be surface appearance: the resounding shallows of consumer culture; the complex sheen of advertising and packaging. The artists of the first phase of British Pop used popular material objectively. Smith and the artists of the second phase shifted their attention to the shrieking, jabbering mediated environment itself. 'I was always an abstract painter,' he says. 'So I was to do with form and mood and shape and colour. I had no icon. I wasn't into being very specific about the imagery. I didn't want to make it that explicit. Mainstream Pop was all about supermarkets and stuff. Low-grade, debased imagery. What intrigued me wasn't the nitty-gritty, down-dirty popular culture. It was the high end. These beautiful ads for Smirnoff vodka and glamorous films and store windows and CinemaScope. The upscale. It was an uptown, smart kind of culture that would drive my art.'

For the fifteen years up to his 1975 Tate retrospective, Dick Smith's life seemed charmed. A Harkness Fellowship took him to New York for two years at the beginning of the sixties. Transplanted from a bedsit studio in Turnham Green to a high-ceilinged, light-filled industrial space in Lower Manhattan, his work became correspondingly optimistic and expansive. It spread outwards across the wall, and eventually, on three-dimensional constructed canvases, out into the room. He made a series of paintings based on billboards in Times Square and gave them titles like *Chase Manhattan*, *Revlon* and *McCalls*. 'Richard's paintings had a breathiness and colour and a kind of newness absolutely separate from Pop art,' Richard Bellamy, his New York dealer in those days, has said. 'Those paintings were suffused with light, a different kind of light than I had ever seen.'

Back in London, he was visited by John Lennon at his studio in Hoxton, an area then still untouched even by beatnik bohemia; they listened to Motown, hung out. Ken Russell used the studio for the final party section in his film about the

British Pop artists, *Pop Goes the Easel*. Smith had a big show at the Whitechapel in 1966, and won the Grand Prize at the São Paolo Biennale two years later. He used the money to buy a spread in Wiltshire. 'You had that Wiltshire country life,' he says, 'with Howard [Hodgkin] twenty miles away in this stunning house. This mill. Joe Tilson, John Hoyland. Robyn Denny was living in Bath. You know, it was that. I had a big studio in a schoolhouse. I was the right kind of artist for that kind of time. I just expected to be in international group shows. Then . . . I don't know.'

In Britain, in the years after his retrospective at the Tate, it all suddenly started to go quiet. In 1978 he decided to sell up and move with his wife and son to Manhattan. There was a glamorous three-storey loft in Tribeca. A house in Telluride in Colorado for the skiing. And the other snow — the cocaine. He got heavily into it for a period following his return to America. 'There was a lot of it about. Max's Kansas City was going, and the [Warhol] Factory, and I had lots of artist friends. It was there and I started to buy it. Then I tried to turn people on. I was romantic about it, but it didn't mean being a drug-head. It was a passing phase.'

He says it was the long winters skiing and the intrusive social life that eventually started to give him the feeling that he wasn't minding the store. 'I think Dick got too close,' Bernard Jacobson says. 'Like [Scott] Fitzgerald in Antibes.' Plus Kasmin in London had shut up shop, and the Feigen Gallery in New York had gone over to Old Masters. Which meant there was nobody stoking the star-maker machinery, turning him into one of those remembered names. 'To be successful as an artist, you have to have your work shown in a good gallery for the same reason that, say, Dior never sold his originals from a counter in Woolworth's,' Andy Warhol once wrote. 'You need a good gallery so the "ruling class" will notice you and spread enough confidence in your future so collectors will buy you, whether for five hundred dollars or fifty thousand.'

Dick Smith's is no hard-luck story. He is looking forward to a show at Tate Britain next year to mark his seventieth birthday, and is still painting every day. He lives comfortably in SoHo. But in 1997 he swapped his place for Gary Hume's place in Hoxton. That was the summer of Sensation and the accompanying mania. It gave him a glimpse of what he had and how it can go.

David Bowie has Dick Smiths in his collection. The Bowie who wrote: 'Fame – what you get is no tomorrow'.

'Robyn Denny keeps saying, "Our time will come, Dick. Our time will come". And he's been saying this for years and years,' Smith says. 'Years and years and years.'

2000

PATRICK CAULFIELD

Patrick Caulfield's main subject as a painter was the blissful, occasionally transcending melancholy of human absence and solitude. The bars and restaurants and other social spaces he painted were famously devoid of people. The exit sign that is the focus of one of his later paintings called *Happy Hour* is the direction in which his fellow-drinkers have all already headed. The figure reflected in the single filled glass at the centre of the canvas is the painter pursuing his solitary practice.

It was characteristic of Caulfield that even a visit to the theatre could become a way of experiencing his separateness and enveloping aloneness even (especially) in the teeth of what, for others, was proving to be a convivial social occasion. 'The trouble with the theatre,' he liked to say, 'is that it so interferes with one's evening.' Nobody who went to the theatre with him, whether it was to see something in the West End or at Covent Garden, where he created a still talked-about set for the Royal Ballet in the early eighties, based on big, billboard-sized versions of the burgundy-shaded boudoir lights that cast their dim glow over the stalls, ever expected to see him back in his seat after the interval.

The reverie going on in his head is the one he invariably wanted to stay with. And so he would remain in the crush bar as the crowd evaporated, nursing a whisky while he watched the bar staff collecting the empties and chatting, and listened to the music and applause that was evidence of the perform-ance which was being enjoyed only a few feet away, beyond the dark oak doors and the heavy velvet curtains.

Caulfield, who died last year, was an urbanite, with no taste for the pastoral in art or in life, or for the trappings of country living. When he was invited to choose from works in the National Gallery for the Artist's Eye series in 1986, he ruled out religious pictures ('I didn't want paintings of angels') and concentrated on paintings which reflected his interest in urban imagery. Fifty per cent of his selection was drawn from the gallery's basement, the repository of paint-ings that are, on the whole, considered less remarkable than the ones in the grand rooms. The still-lives of drink and food, and scenes set in music halls and taverns, tended to be equally modest. *Lunch-time*, the painting of his own that Caulfield chose to include, was typical of his sense of humour in that there's no food to be found in it. It shows the nicotined cor-ner of a City pub decorated with a pot of geraniums and generic bric-a-brac and crowded with deep, all-too-solid shadows. If, as Grey Gowrie once maintained, 'Francis Bacon [was] unique in [the twentieth] century in his ability to render the indoor, overfed, alcohol and tobacco-lined flesh of the average urban male,' then this surely is a portrait of his comfily recessed, button-backed set and lair.

Caulfield was constantly alert to the everyday excitements of living in a major city. It is unlikely that he ever read Virginia Woolf ('It seemed to deal with a middle-to-upper-class society that I didn't know anything about and it meant nothing to me,' he once said of the mid-century English novel), but he shared with Woolf a love of urban experience, seen quite vividly, in a novel like *Mrs Dalloway*, for example, in all its hallucinatory particulars: 'In people's eyes, in the swing, tramp and trudge;

in the bellow and the uproar; the carriages, motor cars, omnibuses, vans . . . in the triumph and the jingle and the strange high singing of some aeroplane overhead was what she loved; life; London . . .'

And yet for the forty years of his career, Caulfield painted places which offered respite from the noise and sheer teeming variety of city life and the jangly rhythms of modern urban existence. These included restaurants, cafes, hotel foyers and other public places, as well as bars. For many years his first call of the day was at his local, a few minutes after the bolts had been drawn in the morning. 'Getting drunk: there was no doubt that that was always the quest,' Martin Amis once wrote of his father, Kingsley (who, as it happens, was a fellow-regular and morning tippler at the pub Caulfield used in Primrose Hill in North London). 'Being drunk had its points, but getting drunk was the good bit.'

Caulfield liked to breathe in the opening-time cellar smells and observe the shapes the slanting light cut through the fixtures and fittings; he liked to stare into the distance and listen to London. Early paintings such as *View of the Rooftops* (1965) and *Lit Window* (1969), and later ones such as *Trou Normand* (1997), *Rust Never Sleeps* (1996) and *Terrace* (2002) are proof that this was time well spent. The arrival of fellow customers he took as a sign that it was time for him to be on his way.

Because they were students together at the Royal College in the early sixties, Caulfield is often aligned with the third wave of British Pop artists which included David Hockney, Derek Boshier and Allen Jones. Caulfield (along with Hockney) always resisted the association. But among the things they had in common was a rejection of the gestural painting favoured by the abstract expressionists and other abstract painters, and the personal agonising associated with

Auerbach, Bacon and what would come to be known as the School of London.

Caulfield had a particular aversion to Richard Sickert, and the dark and damp, seedy atmospheres of his paintings. When he was at Chelsea College between 1956 and 1959, one of his tutors was Jack Smith, well known then as a kitchen-sink realist, a style that Caulfield may be thought to have simultaneously flooded with colour and stripped of emotion.

He started out in the sixties painting black-outlined objects against plain-colour fields. The paint surface was 'dumb' and uninflected, like a poster or a page in a magazine. Almost from the beginning, the pictures were pleasant, clean and bright, although Caulfield's detractors read them as bland, even blank, and devoid of conventional 'humanist' content.

'I didn't like misty brush strokes and atmospheric painting,' he once said. 'This was my reaction against the Englishness of English painting which so greatly valued a slightly understated, tentative figuration.' A turning point was his first trip abroad at the age of twenty-three, in 1960. He was in Athens, en route to Crete, and, having grown accustomed to the dull drabness of austerity Britain, was unprepared for the prewar American Cadillacs and Fleetwoods cruising the ancient streets looking for fares.

On the occasion he recounted the experience to me – in a Greek restaurant in London that he liked for its decor (he was never very interested in eating) – he still trembled, reliving the moment. The combination of the chromed and finned petal-pink Caddies against the backdrop of the Acropolis – the conjunction of the Old World with the New – was to become one of the signature ideas of his work. While many of his contemporaries and near-contemporaries – Hockney, Derek Boshier, Richard Smith – emigrated to America both actually and in the temper and content of what they produced, Caulfield, always resistant to any kind of mid-Atlanticism, no convert to the notion of 'hip', triumphantly combined European manners and conceptually complex, intellectually challenging, cutting-edge art.

His place on the fault line of European and American experience was occasionally alluded to directly in the work. From the eighties on, he started squeezing acrylic paint straight out of the bottle to jokily recreate the textures of Anaglypta and Lincrusta and other serviceable, lodging-house surfaces which were beginning to disappear. Above and alongside them Caulfield would introduce passages of photorealist painting which quoted the luridly patterned, wype-cleen Vymura wallpapers which had been imported from America and, for a time, enjoyed a brief vogue. A sly gap at floor level betrayed the fact that a Regency or art-deco column had been encased in Formica or a cheap plastic veneer. He mixed in Victorian ceiling sconces and Tiffany-style lamps with affectless contemporary prints.

A single Caulfield painting, the critic Marco Livingstone noted, could be an inventory of 'the full range of everything imaginable that painting can encompass — trompe l'oeil realism set against geometric abstraction, careful delineation abutting freely brushed areas, forceful sensations of three-dimensionality adjacent to surfaces of the most extreme flatness'.

Caulfield started off using decorator's gloss paint on hardboard because he liked the impersonal surface it produced. By the time of his major work, he had moved on to acrylic (and occasionally oil) on canvas. Where he never wavered was in his commitment to impure, industrial, non-art colour; colours that were more the colours of things than atmospheres; that referred, directly or indirectly, to the experience of modernity. In his book *Chromophobia*, the British artist David Batchelor makes the interesting distinction between what he calls 'digital colour' (commercial paints that come out of a tin) and 'analogical colour' (artists' paints that comes out of a tube).

The postwar period was the period of the digitalisation of colour in art. This, Batchelor argues persuasively, 'was an entirely new conception of colour': 'More urban colours than the colours of nature. Artificial colours, city colours, industrial colours. Colours that are consistent with the images, materials and forms of an urban, industrial art.' It was Caulfield's unabashed fondness for impure colours and sharp finishes, his determination to deal head-on with modern kitsch and artificiality, that made him an artist's artist. It seems likely, however, that it was these same qualities that throughout his life denied him the collector interest, and so the bumper pay days, that so many of his contemporaries enjoyed.

Unusually for a modern-minded visual artist, Caulfield was a voracious reader of books. He was introduced to the poems of Jules Laforgue as a student and in 1972 produced a series of twenty-two prints based on Laforgue's work. 'He is a poet of irony but not a cynic,' Caulfield said. 'He is never flowery or long winded but crisp and pungent.' Through his dealer, Leslie Waddington, he discovered the Irish poet Paul Durcan and once made me a present of several of Durcan's books. In the eighties, he started reading Raymond Carver's short stories, which also appealed to him for their refusal of floridity and windiness and for the unflinching way they addressed the problem of drink. When Carver visited England before his own premature death, Caulfield, who was unwell at the time, made a heroic effort to cross London to see him read.

Pause on the Landing, the fifteen-metre-long tapestry whose unveiling finally took place at the British Library in London this week, having originally been commissioned in 1994, grew out of Caulfield's decades-long devotion to Laurence Sterne's nine-volume novel *Tristram Shandy*. According to Caulfield's working notes, the tapestry depicts a moment when Tristram's father Walter Shandy and his uncle Toby pause on the landing as they descend from the bedroom where Mr Shandy has been bemoaning the damage done to his son's nose during birth. It can be seen as a kind of companion piece to the vast carpet Caulfield was commissioned to design for the British Council's new building in Manchester in 1991, which is a similarly uncharacteristically atemporal, abstract work.

'The most inexplicable thing about Patrick was his work,' Caulfield's lifelong friend, the painter John Hoyland, said at his funeral last October. 'It was and remains an enigma. Patrick was charming, graceful and seemingly impassive; he rarely showed his inner passions. He concealed everything that mattered to him from all but a few.'

The clues, as ever, are to be found in the work. 'We wanted to bleed the Silence', 'I've only the friendship of hotel rooms', 'And I am alone in my house' are some of the lines from Laforgue that struck a note with Caulfield as a student and became the titles of the prints he made. His place as one of the great British painters of the late twentieth century seems assured.

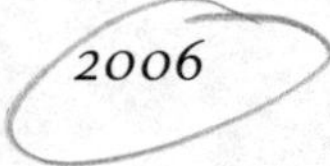

2006

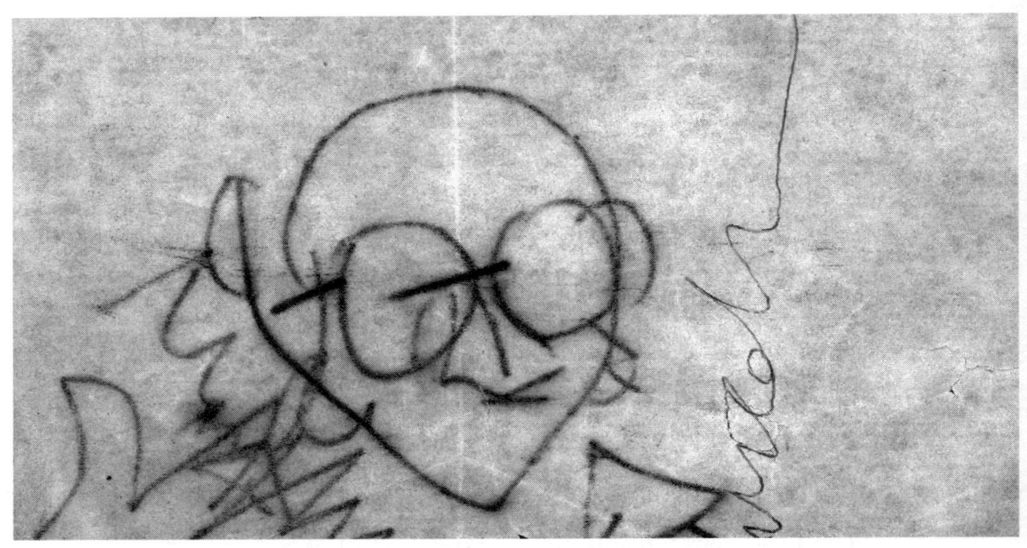

Mat Collishaw, sketch of GB

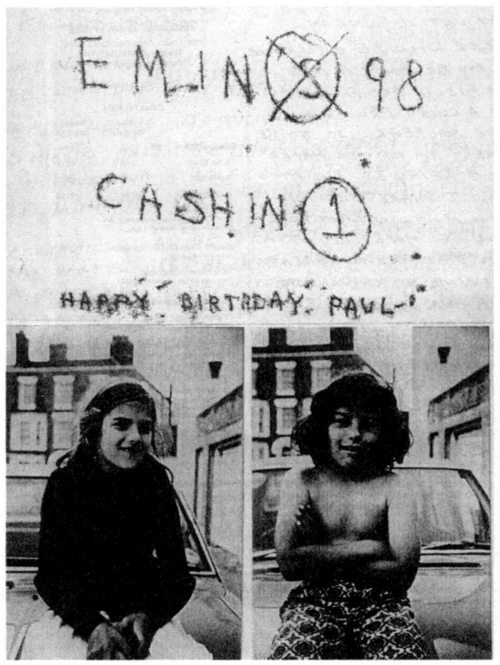

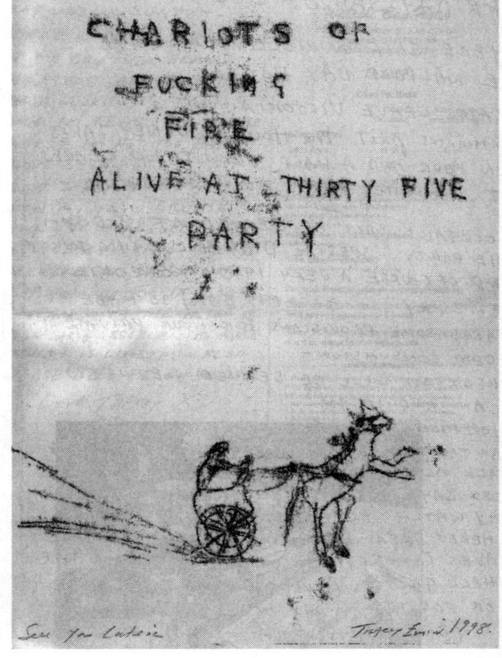

JOHN HOYLAND

'Solitary studio practice' is a term that has been bandied about a lot in recent years in connection with young British artists. Solitary studio practice is something that the hard-drinking, hard-drugging, up-all-night, who-pushed-your-button, monkey? YBAs just don't do. Angst has never been their thing. In a work mode they have a tendency to be cool, inexpressive, emotionally disengaged. Warhol's children, expressing complete boredom for aesthetics as we know it.

As the world and his granny must be aware by now, Sarah and Tracey and Abbie and Angus and Mat and Sam and the rest play and work mob-handed, giving it large in the bar at St John in Clerkenwell, pissing it up further along the street at Vic Naylor's or wherever, and staying at all times full-on. That's full-on. Yeeeeaaarrghh!

It so happens that John Hoyland lives on the other side of Charterhouse Square from the falling-down places of recent legend, and solitary studio practice is something he knows all about. Just after six most mornings, when the lights in the meat market are being diluted by the dawn and the art world's gilded girls and boys are trying to decide whether to call it a night or move it all on, Hoyland is rolling out of bed to start work.

Twenty years ago he bought a large unit in a former hat factory on the square, overlooking Bart's Hospital and tantalisingly near to the pubs that open in the middle of the night for the Smithfield butchers and market workers. He turned the back part of the space with a view of the railway lines going into the Barbican station into a studio. And it is there that most pre-dawns will find him preparing canvases or slinging the old chromatics onto monster canvases that he has laid horizontally on the floor. For years, his preferred working method has been to walk into the picture. He likes to loop and detonate paint straight out of the bottle and tube – getting the whole body behind a gesture; drawing from the shoulder. It's like Jackson Pollock made holes in cans so he could do an extended line. It's like that. He can squirt and spray, and it's like frozen energy when it dries. The speed and violence of the mark are all in there. The cult of Pollock seems to centre around photographs, not of his paintings, but of him painting. And more than fifty years later, Hoyland is still at it.

It is excessively physical. He sweats. The stretchers are big and unwieldy. The ceiling is not that high. But he is drenched most of the time in panic sweats. He takes off his shoes and steps into the canvas when he wants to paint wet on wet. He sets up breeze blocks and a plank and walks the plank over the painting, flinging dribbles and gouts of paint like a dervish. Feathering it like a parlour maid or van Gogh's *Sower*. A man in his sixties at six o'clock in the morning. Hey, geezer!

'I ought to have some sleek trolley cantilevered out, made out of core-ten steel, or bloody aluminium or something. Some hi-tech machine like a crane or something,' he says, not sounding convinced. 'A bridge. But I'm afraid it's just a plank that I got from the builders when they were doing the scaffolding that doesn't bend in the middle. You've got to be careful you don't fall into it. Trip and fall off the fucking plank.'

A pair of boots standing on a shelf in the studio tell how

long this has been Hoyland's life. A pair of sixties dandy high-zip boots from Blades, lined in leather with block toes and rock'n'roll heels, the whole encrusted in acrylic. Museumised. A museum of himself.

Painting in the studio is a job. It's different from the perfectly worthwhile jobs that people do. It's a different activity. You do your job. 'I go round picking up the canvas, so the silver iridescent's all moving around, and then I started throwing colour into it. Yellows, violets, oranges and so on, into the wet. You know you want some kind of a rhythmical break down there. And then I start picking it up and manipulating that. Letting that stuff all break up the flow. It's like trying to pull a fish. You can't just yank it out. You've got to let it run, find its own nature, and then gradually haul it in.'

He says, 'It's like being a god half of the time and a murderer the rest of the time. You're creating a universe in the studio. You're trying to make something new in the world one minute, and then you're cutting it up and lacerating it. You're tearing it. Sweating like a pig. Totally soaked. Painting is killer shit. It's kill or be killed. It is. Painting is a killer sport. That's why it's so nice to do craft kind of work sometimes. Like prints or glass or ceramics. Collaborations so you can talk and chat and have a laugh and listen to the radio. Whereas when you do painting, anybody can come along and say, "Well, you've led a completely worthless life." And hey, listen, they will. Oh, are you kidding?'

Hoyland's has been a heroic endeavour. During a thirty-year period when painting has been at an all-time critical low, supplanted by photography, video, assemblage and installation, he has never let himself be dragged down or wavered for a second in his commitment to the paint. The Academy show should establish him beyond doubt as one of the most gifted British artists of his generation and one of the best non-figurative painters still working anywhere. As Paul Moorhouse, the curator of the new retrospective, puts it, his paintings now look like irresistible icons for the cause of painting.

Hoyland's predicament is one that is common to all artists of his age. He isn't yet old enough to a be a Grand Old Man, but he is no longer young enough to be regarded as a Young Turk. He spent the early years of the nineties without a dealer. The Tate hasn't bought a picture of his for more than twenty years. Although he added the Wollaston Award for most distinguished work in last year's Royal Academy Summer Exhibition to a long list of honours and prizes, it took the intervention of a long-time supporter, Sir Anthony Caro, to secure the Academy show for Hoyland, who has been an RA since 1983. He has known a fond disregard. A stasis. He has been a dweller in Limbo Land. Hoyland decisively rejected minimalism and Duchamp-inspired conceptualism, where a favoured young painter like Gary Hume, say, many years later embraced them. The result is that a painter who was once seen to be on the cutting edge of advanced art is now, thanks to the vicissitudes of fashion, relegated against his will to the ranks of the naysayers and cultural conservatives.

These circumstances have made Hoyland, with his super-tuned bullshit detector, an uncomfortable presence. He has earned himself – unfairly, his friends would say – an abrasive reputation. He can be irascible. He can also be rib-achingly, scurrilously funny. He is to the art one-liner what Les Dawson was to the mother-in-law joke. 'They're like Sickert on Tizer', is his description of Frank Auerbach's 'exercises in suburban expressionism': 'With Frank, there's all that struggle and turmoil, and then he ends up having to put a cartoon face on top of the thick paint. A couple of dots for the eyes.'

Francis Bacon's art is 'far too illustrational. He might do a little seemingly free mark, but actually it's a little toss-off, and then a little air-brushing on it.' Bacon and Lucian Freud are merely painters of 'melodrama'. 'Drama is one thing. But melodrama is another. Like painting your mother naked with all her old veins and a rat on her tit. Or it might have been her shoulder. I mean, what kind of a life is this? People lying around with their bloody dicks hanging out.' He describes an eminent contemporary as being 'a big star of stage, screen and horseshit'. Britain is 'visually uncultivated, cultivation being fine as long as you stick to gardening, and you better keep it neat'. Hoyland didn't go to the Venice Biennale this year because he 'didn't want to see any more videos made by Uruguayan transsexuals'. 'Do you want wooden or do you want wooden?' he says, holding open a catalogue of etchings that has arrived in the post. 'Would you like it in teak or balsa?' 'Those tossers in Art and Language. You know where their headquarters is? Leamington Spa. It's not Brooklyn.' 'Have you heard about the man who once asked Picasso, "What do you do if you run out of blue?" He said, "I use red."' Boom-boom.

Hoyland's outspokenness has always got him in trouble with the members of what he calls 'the whispering classes' who are the chiefs of the art tribe. On the other hand, it was his candour and his refusal to mouth the usual pieties that brought him close to Barnett Newman and Mark Rothko and Robert Motherwell and other legends of the New York abstract expressionist scene, and made them his friends. 'When I've had a few drinks I tend to be rather honest,' Hoyland says. 'And they liked that. I think Motherwell couldn't wait to go into the studio and talk. Basically we had so much in common. He liked talking about cars and girls and art, which was the most important thing in his life. And of course when you're an intellectual, which he was, and you've got a heavy hangover and you come down to confront a blank canvas, you're no better equipped to paint than a non-intellectual who's got a hangover in front of a blank canvas. Because being an intellectual doesn't help you in painting. You can be overburdened with connoisseurship and intellectual ideas and too much exploring irrelevant things. Painting is of a different order. It's a different language.'

Hoyland grew up in Sheffield. He's Yorkshire. And he puts his outspokenness down to that. His father was a tailor. 'He never had his own business. He only worked for other people. I'm just like him, but earn more money.' In the cave-like living room in Charterhouse Square, Kenneth Hoyland's face and hands shine out of a portrait that John did of his father when he was still a teenager. Outside the bathroom is an etching of Hoyland half-dragging, half-carrying his old man home from the boozer, something he did often. He started at Sheffield Art School when he was seventeen, and arrived at the Royal Academy Schools in London five years later knowing nothing. 'Nobody taught us about modern art, because modern art was taboo in England in those days. Matisse was dismissed by everybody at Sheffield as being a purely decorative, albeit "pretty", painter. Picasso was tying a paint brush to the donkey's tail and insulting the public. It was just regarded as a complete joke. We had to draw from the cast, and from models. I mean, plenty to draw. Like, lots of veins. You used to sit there and watch flesh being heated by the radiators. I always found models a bit mad, like demented housewives. People who really wanted to be exotic dancers but didn't have the figure for it, you know. But exotic dancers who were passionate about cricket. Nutters. With nothing remotely sexual about any of them. It was just so embarrassing. I used to draw down to the knee and think, "Well, there's not much further to go; I'll be down to the ankle shortly." It was a terrible drudgery. I hated it.'

Hoyland started at the Academy Schools in 1956, the year the show Modern Painting in the United States came to the Tate. This was followed in 1959 by the landmark exhibition of abstract expressionism, The New American Painting, full of giant, heroic works by Pollock, Rothko, Motherwell, de Kooning, Kline and Gorky. 'Seeing those big Rothkos now, they're not that big. But we'd never seen anything that big. There was a kind of radiance, and the sheer inexplicable kind of mystery of them. The uncompromising nature and the scale of ambition. It wasn't a difficult choice for me. Either go towards refinement, painting debutantes' eyelashes, or shiny horses' arses, which was always a sure-fire thing. Or get involved in the revolution of twentieth-century art.'

This part of the revolution involving the painters of the New York School had an orthodoxy and a script. Both were the work of the chief theorist of the abstract expressionist movement and its most energetic promoter, Clement Greenberg. Greenberg, whom Hoyland would come to know, believed that art should be reduced to flat colour on a flat plane. The narrative or social content of the paintings should be nil. All that mattered was the surface interplay of colour and texture, space and shape, and the artist's ability to create a world instead of merely copying one. 'Paintings are there to be experienced, they are events,' Hoyland has said. 'Paintings are not to be reasoned with, they are not to be understood, they are to be recognised. They are an equivalent of nature, not an illustration of it.'

He was never part of Swinging London. He spent much of

the sixties and seventies in New York. He liked the way Rothko and Newman were sober-suited. They wore watch chains and overcoats. Newman in particular looked 'a bit like the manager of a textile company down Broadway'. They were intellectuals, but they didn't come on intellectual. Ad Reinhardt looked like a boxer. He always said, 'Art's too serious to be taken seriously.' Hoyland decided this was a good way to be. 'I rather looked down on Pop art. I was a bit more Miles Davis and classical music. James Joyce and *Murder in the Cathedral* and Auden. This kind of stuff. Duke Ellington and Stan Kenton and the blues. I thought the Beatles were rubbish. I didn't even like Elvis Presley. I was very anti all that. You've only got to see a photograph of me in those days to tell, trying to be the young professor. Professor Piffle.'

Throughout the sixties he made paintings which aimed for extremes of flatness, emptiness and bigness, as prescribed. The pigment was stained into the weave of the canvas rather than cluttering up the surface. In Greenbergian terms, they were very right-on. His main concern after 1970, though, was with building on the formal implications of his work to make it more expressive. The extremism of Newman had led to a cul-de-sac. It left nowhere for people to go except towards minimalism. Hoyland reached the point where he wanted more than formal disclosure. He wanted to let the world and emotional experience in. He wanted to recomplicate the surface of the picture without resorting to some kind of easy illustrational solution.

He started to play around with free elements. The paint handling became very loose. There was an increasing amount of dripping and dribbling and pouring until he stopped using brushes altogether. Slowness tends to be associated with seriousness. Painters like Frank Auerbach and Howard Hodgkin take years. And Hoyland was fantastically prodigious. He seemed to be knocking out works too fast. *Fried Eggs with Purple Sausages*. It was in *Private Eye*. 'There's the rather puritan idea that somehow, through struggle, and worthiness, something good will come out. Something good comes out through vision. I mean, I've always said that Auerbach was a triumph of style over vision. It's so precious, the whole thing. The sort of web that Frank has woven round himself. He's more serious about art, more serious about life, more moral . . . It just doesn't wash with me. So what?

'Picasso probably did five drawings a day. Completed works. And how long do you think some of those Matisses took? Some of them were long struggles. But you look at a Derain or a Matisse. Of course they had their scraping-down times and their throwing work away. But a lot of it is just bomp-bomp-bomp-bomp-boom. And that's it. And it retains that freshness. William Scott always said, don't fuss a painting. Never fuss a painting. This is an English disease, this fussing at work. "I don't think that passage in the nose is quite right, Hoyland. You need perhaps a touch of green . . ." It's always: "I don't think you've quite resolved that passage." They make a big virtue in England of this struggle factor.'

Struggle – the great existential dance of death – is the theme that Ron Kitaj believed linked Frank Auerbach and the other School of London painters. 'School of London' was the title Kitaj came up with in 1977 when he set out, with David Hockney, to promote a return to representations of the human figure. The campaign was mainly aimed at the conceptual work which at that time was filling the commercial galleries and art institutions. But Hoyland interpreted it as an act of general aggression.

'Calling for a return to the figure was a completely

ridiculous thing to do. I mean, if people want to paint the figure for personal reasons, that's one thing. But for a manifesto saying art's all gone wrong because it's left the figure is ridiculous. I mean, it's a real kind of Luddite thing which appeals to the most reactionary, revisionist minds. That's why it appealed in this country so powerfully. Everyone said, "Oh thank God, we're going back to real art."'

Seven years later, in 1994, Kitaj was given a retrospective at the Tate. His experience became an object lesson in the high-risk nature of the kind of enterprise John Hoyland is currently embarked on. The critical mauling he suffered caused Kitaj to return to America after thirty years living in London. He even blamed the critics for the death of his wife.

'Kitaj had always been so feather-bedded by everybody,' Hoyland says. 'The friend of the great and the good. Oxford dons. He'd always insert little meaningful passages into his work and titles that referred to literature and culture. He was always talking about Wittgenstein. A big house in Chelsea and beautiful children and a wonderful library. I mean, he lived a very privileged, cosseted kind of life. He didn't teach in art schools for years and have to go to Croydon on the train. And South Norwood, even worse. I was the original Norwood junkie. So I think he was living in a bit of a fool's paradise. Always treated different, even by the Academy. They all treated him reverentially. And when somebody suddenly comes along and says, "Hey, wait a minute – that is not all it's been cracked up to be," then it just blew him away. Andrew Graham-Dixon [of the *Independent*] was the main one. But a lot of English writers are very flaky anyway. They don't know what they think, so they'd go along with it.'

John Hoyland. Brush-cut, tinted heavy glasses and a bolo tie. A bit fly for somebody about to pick up his bus pass next month. Just because he's paranoid doesn't mean they're not out to get him. He knows a lot of people are waiting to see him take a slapping. See him place the breeze blocks. See him walk the plank. Hey, grandad! See him step lightly in the high-zip dandy boots when he reaches the other side.

1999

GILBERT   GEORGE

Art for All

'ART FOR ALL,' 12 FOURNIER STREET, LONDON, E.1, ENGLAND   Tel. 01 247 0161

Friday the 19th of April 1974 .

Dear Gordon ,

Please find enclosed the negatives you requested .

Please take good care of them for us .

We will be abroad from now until the 1st of May after which

date we look forward to seeing you again for a little chat

and a bit of a bi^{n}ge .

Lots of Love and Best Wishes to You

George and Gilbert

MALCOLM MORLEY

'Did he begin painting in borstal or was it prison?' The question was launched at the director of the Tate Gallery within minutes of the announcement that Malcolm Morley had won the inaugural Turner Prize. And so the elements of the myth began to drop conveniently into place.

'Ex-con' and 'exile' are the words that have attached themselves most persistently to Morley's name since he was formally embraced by the British art establishment at a televised ceremony last week, and it has made him all the more determined to live down what he refers to cuttingly as his 'colourful background'.

Morley took off for America twenty-six years ago when he was twenty-eight, and didn't return to England for twenty years. No more than a handful of paintings found their way back across the Atlantic during all that time and he had to wait until last year for the first major British show of his work. Not, he points out, with what is meant to pass for nonchalance, that he very much cared.

Like other expatriate artists, and most obviously Joyce and Beckett, Morley's feelings for the country he left behind are a complex mixture of loathing and longing which found some kind of focus in the Turner Prize. 'The London art world's a bunch of losers,' he can say, slapping a faux naif hand over his mouth. And he can talk dismissively of big fish in little ponds while simultaneously confessing that he experienced a sort of epiphany when the telephone rang in his Bowery studio at lunchtime on Tuesday, 6 November, and it was Alan Bowness telling him he'd won the Turner Prize.

'I got all emotional . . . I felt like a little boy.

'As he said it there was a sudden sound of angels in Heaven and in the middle of them was my grandmother, and she smiled. And it was such a euphoric sensation. It was far out. I mean, it was a real vision.

'Somebody told me that when you have a great moment in your life you share it with your ancestors. So, although I despised the way they turned this prize into a blood sport, and I despised the part of me that wanted to win it, I was very moved. I got all emotional. Disgusting. I said to Alan Bowness — I felt like a little boy. I said, "I never became an American citizen, you know."'

Morley has never thought of himself as an American or a European but always as an 'English' painter. He was born in Highgate, North London, where he narrowly missed being killed when the house was hit by a bomb during the war. He never knew his father and on several occasions as a child ran away from home with the intention of going to sea. Over the last twenty years, his work has evolved from meticulous, super-realist renderings of photographic images to messier, more painterly, less controlled canvases, both styles presaging popular movements. But the same autobiographical elements have remained consistent throughout: big ships, toy trains, violent death, uneasy sex, the English countryside viewed from a prison cell.

Morley can be a difficult customer, unyielding, aggressive, truculent, and he makes no apologies for it. Once, when he was still far from rich, he slashed a painting to pieces in front of its new owner and handed back the cheque worth $40,000. On another occasion, he turned up with a water pistol loaded with red paint to squirt at one of his own paintings in an auction room in Paris.

He chose to be interviewed on neutral territory, in an apartment abutting the Whitney Museum belonging to his New York dealer, in order to give his interviewer as little purchase as possible. And he had been going through his life, dutifully perhaps, but amiably, when a question touching on why he had chosen housebreaking (for which he served a three-year prison sentence) over any other sort of crime caused him to suddenly bridle.

'I don't like that train of thought at all,' he said. 'Not at all. I think the question is real bad. It feels really wrong. It feels an invasion of something very personal. Then I've got nothing personal left. I feel goosebumps coming right now.'

Well, perhaps we could talk about why he had left England straight from the Royal College? 'I don't think there's any whys in it.'

But it was significant. He'd chosen America. He could have gone anywhere.

'It comes back to "colourful background" again. I don't really want to go over any of that ground at all. You get fed up talking about yourself. After a while it feels like a terrible bore.'

Did he want to talk about how his style developed?

'I don't want to talk about that.'

What was he painting now?

'I don't want to talk about that either.'

Was there anything he did want to talk about?

'Well, if I hear it, I'll let you know.'

He had said he felt 'homeless' rather than 'exiled'. Did he still feel more English than American?

'I don't feel anything.' Morley has a curious Australian-sounding accent. 'I don't feel anything about anything. Except maybe terror of some kind. Some kind of psychic pain which is overwhelming. Most of the time. Every day of the week goes like a nightmare.'

'You've always thought like that?'

'To a greater or lesser degree. I take pills to try to help me over it. But there's no answer. It's occupying space, really. Occupying a vacuum. A void.

'I suppose you could call it being alive . . . if you're unemployed like I am – I'm really not employed – you drift. In a way, the very thing you've got, which is the luxury of time, is also the most dangerous element for evolving tendencies that you'd never have a chance to find out about if you had a job. I have all the freedom that anybody wants, and to me it's pure terror.'

The obvious answer would be to get a job. He could go back to doing what he used to do, waiting on tables.

'That's not a bad idea. There's some interesting people who have renounced whatever it was they had, Wittgenstein became a hospital orderly or something . . . I remember Malevich once said the artist should renounce one thing a day. The point is, I never wanted to be a painter. I hate it. I'd prefer to make films. But you know behaviourist theory, B. F. Skinner's idea that one tends to do what one gets reinforcement for. And when I came out of jail I guess the first thing I showed was that I could do paintings and the probation officers live on that . . .

'But really I felt that doing painting was like being banished from the world. The moment you leave the herd, you take on an anxiety that the herd doesn't have. And then the herd wants to destroy anybody who breaks away, because it threatens them. You can go crazy if you're not careful.'

Morley said he felt pleased he had not turned up for the prize-giving. He would have felt guilty surrounded by his 'brother' artists. He said he felt a weird guilt about his success in life, and that he had done his best to destroy it. 'Drugs, heavy stuff. Coke. All the stuff that will stop you achieving more than you've already done. I keep thinking about all those guys I was in jail with. They're still in the nick.'

Next week Malcolm Morley will be in London and he will be fêted at the Tate. The Tate, however, still has not bought a single picture. Of the two Morley paintings presently hanging in the gallery, one is owned by Charles Saatchi, who has the biggest holding of Morley's work of anybody in the world. The other was offered to the Tate by Morley's dealer two years ago and turned down. 'It made me realise,' he said in New York the other day, 'that I have more reasons for staying here.'

1984

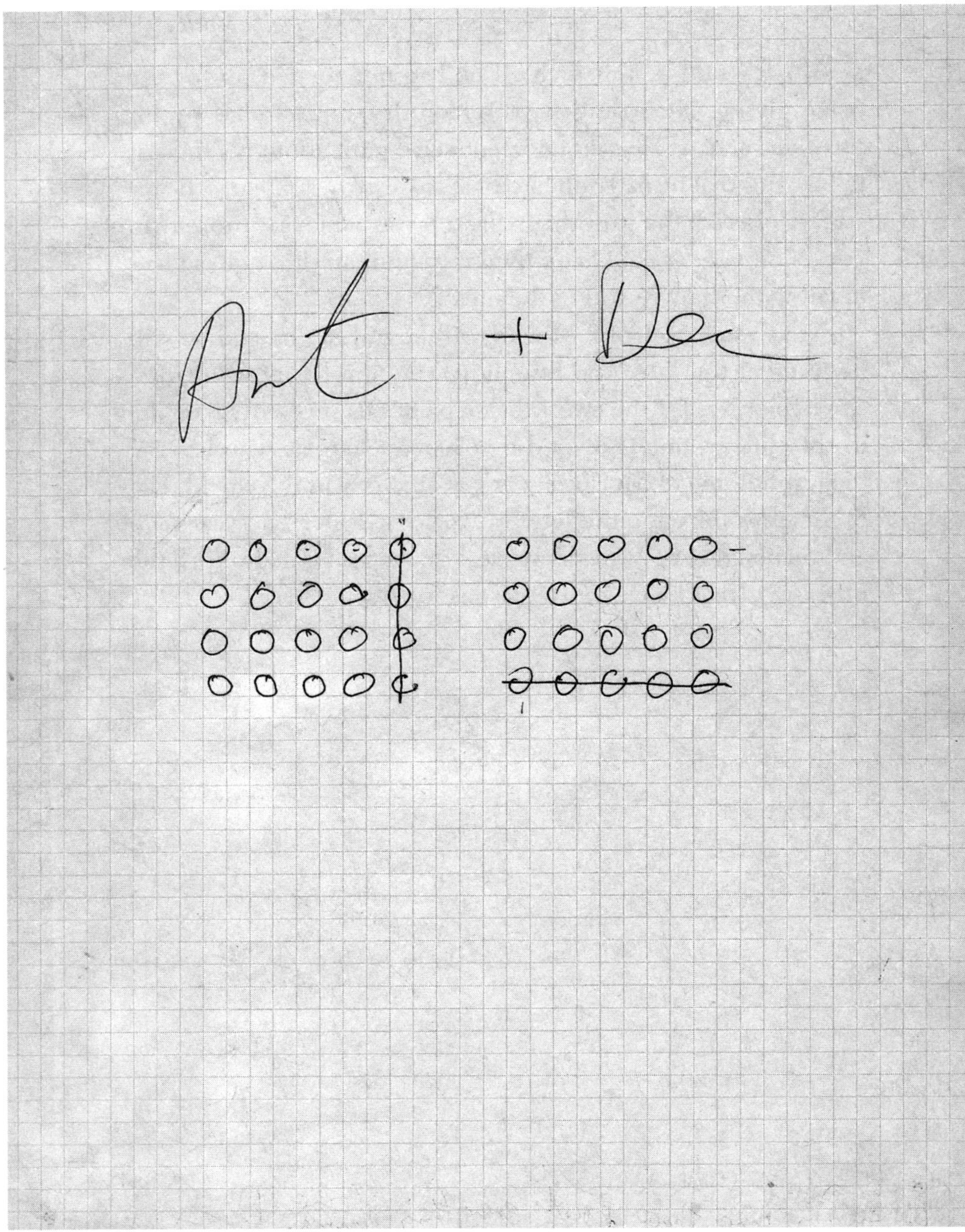

Damien Hirst

IAN HAMILTON FINLAY

Ian Hamilton Finlay's home and neoclassical garden at Little Sparta is a long haul from the Bond Street galleries where he shows his work but whose doors he never darkens: one tube ride, one in-flight breakfast, one fifty-minute taxi ride with Mr Dick.

The journey ends with a slow bounce along a farm track with three gates, which explains the copies of the *Glasgow Herald* that Mr Dick, an experienced Little Sparta hand, keeps spread out under the pedals for the mire. 'They're certainly cut off up here right enough,' he says as he climbs back in for the third and final time, dislodging a clod the size of a cairn terrier from his right boot.

The part of Lanarkshire where Ian Hamilton Finlay has lived with his wife and two children for the past twenty or so years is rugged rather than Arcadian. The garden, a modern version of the poetic gardens of the eighteenth century, complete with ponds, statuary and classically pilastered temple dedicated to Apollo ('His music, his missiles, his muses'), was hacked out of the moorland by the Finlays by hand.

Little Sparta (or Stonypath, as it was then) was an abandoned hillside croft belonging to Sue Finlay's father when they moved into it in 1966. It is in such an unprotected position that the bigger pieces of inscribed stonework in the garden – the principal reason visitors travel there from all over the world –

have to be lagged like outdoor plumbing throughout the winter; the smaller pieces are taken inside.

'We get such fierce frosts that they will actually split stone. Spring here is like Russia or something: a great burst of green suddenly, because the winter goes right on into the spring. We don't really have your spring.'

Finlay is an ascetic. 'Opulence is Infamy' is one of his favourite epigrams by one of his favourite epigrammatists, Saint-Just, Robespierre's chief lieutenant in the French Revolution. A related saying, by Epictetus, is something else Finlay can readily quote: 'There is a difference between living well and living profusely. The one arises from contentment and order, and decency and frugality: the other from dissoluteness and luxury, and disorder and indecency.' Finlay's study, like the rest of the house, is a model of peasant simplicity: a wood-burning stove, a day-bed, an untamed accretion of books. I assumed it would be a house without a television, but I was wrong: there is an old model standing on the draining board in the kitchen. And it is there, at this time on a Saturday, he would normally be watching *Saint and Greavsie*.

'A great sacrifice,' Finlay said, and then proceeded to compare Greavsie to 'a character from classic mythology called Silenus — a slightly fat fawn wandering around the woods. A very jocular, affable attitude to everything, smiling, beaming . . . it's Greavsie exactly. He seems so genuinely like a benign quaffer of pints, even though I know he's a teetotaller. Anyway, I've given all that up for you.'

Little Sparta, hailed by one architectural critic as 'a visual and intellectual masterpiece', is prominently featured in *The Oxford Companion to Gardens*. Ian Hamilton Finlay merits his own entry in the latest edition of *The Oxford Companion to English Literature* for his involvement with concrete poetry in the early sixties. He is now best known (throughout America and the rest of Europe, if not in this country) for public land-scaping projects which engage all his talents and which, in the past, have involved a variety of collaborators, ranging from traditional craftsmen to architects and other contemporary artists.

The Finlays were poor and Little Sparta, he says, started as a potato patch and evolved from there. 'As you know, when you begin an activity, the activity itself generates a sort of momentum. So after a bit we found we were making a garden. And then a garden that people began to call a garden. And then, very surprising to us, a garden that people actually came to see and even wrote about. Then, at a certain point, I began to think about working in the garden as a poet, renewing this whole tradition of the garden inscription, sculpture in the garden, and so on, until eventually my main concern became what could be done through the garden, outside in the world.'

He has completed large landscape-and-sculpture ('garden-esque') commissions in San Diego, Vienna, Eindhoven, Brittany, Otterlo, and Celle, near Florence. Unlike other artists who work in the environment, however, Finlay opts for an almost conceptual approach, and does not immerse himself in the local setting. Mr Dick, the taxi driver, for example, expressed some astonishment that Mr Finlay had not accompanied his wife to inspect their installation at last year's Glasgow Garden Festival. Part of the reason, although not the main one, is that Finlay saw the Garden Festival, like so many things today, as having more to do with tourism and 'society which never reflects on itself' than with art.

'We have seen the demotion — the degradation — of the arts in our time so that they are now merely an adjunct to tourism. And the tourist, by definition, is a person who looks but doesn't feel. The essence of tourism is something superficial. So when the arts are presented in that context, we have to recognise that some fundamental change has occurred. And what I am here to do is bring this change into consciousness.

'There is no seriousness in Britain any more. Freedom of speech is fine, but freedom of thought is absolutely forbidden. Stand a wee bit outside it the way we do and you see how pathetic it all is. There's nothing there. No rigour, no standards, nothing.'

Finlay has an aversion to most aspects of the late twentieth century and suffers from a kind of agoraphobia into the bargain.

He also has a heart condition which has prevented him leaving Little Sparta for many years. Sue Finlay, his collaborator on their home garden, does the necessary travelling: she visits sites, brings back plans, reports and pictures, and supervises all on-site installations.

Finlay rejects any notion that his confinement to Strathclyde could be seen as inhibiting: 'The idea that I don't see the works is ludicrous. I see them absolutely clearly before anybody else. If I didn't, the works wouldn't come to exist. D'you follow? It's like saying that Kafka would have understood the situation of Europe better if he'd been a commercial traveller. One has got to allow that vision and response don't have to be purely material things.'

He laughs off suggestions that he has chosen to lead a reclusive existence. Given the constant stream of visitors to the garden, interviewers, collaborators in his work and the controversy that seems constantly to engulf him, he says that he has to fight to get a day free of the world.

'For example, I was rung up in the middle of the night by a man who was obviously an Arab or something. He said to me,

"I hear you've been treated unfairly by the Minister of Culture in France." I said, "Yes, but you do realise it's almost half-past two in the morning? Could you not ring again in seven hours?" And he said – I'm sure he said – "It depends on the camels." He was obviously in the desert or something. "We know these things in the Middle East," he said, and hung up.'

'Have you ever,' I asked Finlay at one point, 'been into a modern shopping precinct?'

'No, no,' he said. 'Oh no.'

'Don't you think you should, just once, to see what one's like?'

'I know what they're like.'

'Perhaps they're even worse than you think.'

'I'm sure they are.'

'Have you ever experienced Muzak?'

'Yes, in my day they had that.' He is sixty-three. 'But I should take you up on the moor where I go for my walks. Then you could experience what real epic purity is like.'

What sets Ian Hamilton Finlay apart from most contemporary artists is that his art is explicitly and unapologetically linked with a defence of the cultural, ethical and spiritual values that he believes are in danger of being wiped out by what he calls, with reference to his beloved French Revolution, the 'secular Terror'.

The events of 200 years ago in France have for many years provided Finlay with a model of how to proceed in his life and his work. Essentially, this has meant one thing: 'To think is to act.'

Something else that has set him apart has been his willingness to hit out whenever he has felt his position to be under attack.

If this has earned him a reputation as a pedagogue and a

zealot, then his answer is simple: the same was said about Robespierre and Saint-Just. 'What's wrong with a zealot? I mean, when I began to read Robespierre's speeches, these were really some of the most wonderful speeches I'd ever read in my life.

'The result is that I don't see the Revolution in the way it's fashionable to see the Revolution, as blood and the blade. I mean, I'm not loath to invoke the blade, because there's a lot of people I'd like to . . .' Here he draws a finger across his throat. 'But I do see the Revolution as essentially pastoral. The kind of society propounded by Saint-Just is really a kind of Jacobin vision of the golden age.'

It was these convictions that, in 1986, helped Finlay win the most prestigious commission of his long career. In collaboration with the landscape architect Alexandre Chemetoff, he was invited by the French Ministry of Culture to produce a permanent memorial to the Declaration of the Rights of Man.

The memorial was to be part of the town of Versailles' celebration of the bicentenary of the Revolution. It was to be erected on the site of the National Assembly, where the Declaration was signed in 1789, and would be unveiled at a ceremony attended by the President of the Republic.

The first rumblings of opposition to Finlay's prestigious French commission were heard in 1987. He has a well-documented history of skirmishes and of longer, more embittered battles which he has been able to incorporate into his work. Even the early signs, however, were that the row over the bicentenary garden was to be something more than just another localised feud.

The campaign against Finlay was led by the magazine *Art Press*, which claimed that his stone carving *Osso*, exhibited in Paris in 1987, used the double-lightning flash of the Waffen-SS without explanation, and that this showed he had Nazi sympathies.

The accusations were without foundation. Both the catalogue and a note on the gallery wall explained that in *Osso* (Italian for 'bone') Finlay wished 'to point out the element of terror and disquiet which is inseparable from nature in its pure state, devoid of any redemption'.

But the accusations were reiterated in a radio broadcast in March last year, in which it was also claimed that Finlay's work was inspired by Nazism and that he was fascinated by Nazi violence. The 'almost comically specious grounds' for this, as the writer Patrick Marnham claimed in Finlay's defence, was that his garden in Lanarkshire was divided into 'war zones' (it is not), and that the Finlay washing line there is labelled the 'Siegfried Line' (a joke).

The fact that none of his accusers had ever visited Little Sparta hardly seemed to matter. A few hours after the programme went out, François Léotard, the Minister of Culture, cancelled Finlay's commission. The reasons were simple and purely political: Léotard was playing a prominent role in the presidential election and was anxious to avoid any last-minute embarrassment.

Finlay now has multiple lawsuits running in Paris, in which he is represented by the same lawyer who represented the victims of Klaus Barbie. What distresses him most, however, is that two Ian Hamilton Finlays now exist in the world. There is the one he knows as himself, who exists in Little Sparta, and there is the one that is a sort of hologram of lies, smears and innuendo who is alive in the world's art press and more generally in the media in France.

His task, as of course he recognises, is to bring the two together. 'What I've learned is two things: one, that the facts have no power over the mythology. Two, that if you're going to stand up for things, you've got to accept that you're going to be reviled for it. At least while you're alive. You've just got to accept that as a fact.'

It was only as I was leaving that I read the badge he had been wearing all day. It was another quotation from Saint-Just: 'Too Many Laws, Too Few Examples', it said.

1984

LONDON DEALERS

Andy Warhol probably said it best: 'To be successful as an artist, you have to have your work shown in a good gallery for the same reason that, say, Dior never sold his originals from a counter at Woolworth's. You need a good gallery so the "ruling class" will notice you and spread enough confidence in your future so collectors will buy you, whether for $500 or $50,000. No matter how good you are, if you're not promoted right, then you won't be one of those remembered names.' Whenever he visited London and somebody else was paying (as they invariably were), Warhol stayed at the Ritz. It followed, therefore, that when Julian Schnabel, Warhol's successor as international cover boy and hot paparazzi favourite, visited London for his first commercial show with Leslie Waddington in the early eighties, he stayed at the Ritz.

On a previous visit, a rival London dealer sent the limousine to collect Schnabel at the airport and, like an Edwardian dandy making his play for a Gaiety girl, kept his suite filled with flowers for the length of his stay. Every timid tap at the door meant another crinoline basket spilling lilies, roses, imported Japanese almond blossom. But it was to no avail. Schnabel was promised to another.

Leslie Waddington is pre-eminent among London's dealers in twentieth-century art. What he wants, he tends to get. Waddington Galleries is second only to Spink (coins, medals,

Chinese art) in the league table of British dealers in all areas. No other gallery specialising in the work of living or modern (i.e. recently dead) artists features in the top ten.

In 1988, Waddington paid himself a salary of £756,000. The gallery's pre-tax profits for that year were £6.5 million on a turnover of £26 million. Last year profits leapt to £22 million on a turnover of £74 million, boosted in large part by the Swedish dealer Bo Alveryd, who, in one week last October, blew $70 million with Waddington and two other London dealers – the once-mighty Marlborough and Bernard Jacobson, a recent convert to Academy-style British figurative painting.

The crude rule of thumb for dealers specialising in contemporary artists has always been: find them when they're young and cheap and sell them when they're older and much more expensive. In return for supporting an artist, showing his work and fostering his reputation among museum curators, important collectors and in the press, a dealer expects a 40–60 per cent commission. If we exclude David Hockney, Leslie Waddington represents the best of the sixties generation of British painters, including Peter Blake, Patrick Caulfield, John Hoyland, Allen Jones and Joe Tilson.

The vast bulk of the gallery's profits, however, comes from the sale of works by Picasso, Matisse, Dubuffet, Ben Nicholson and other gilt-edged modern masters, which Waddington has either stockpiled over the years or bought more recently for resale at auction. So it came as a surprise when Waddington and not one of his younger rivals laid on the liveried chauffeur and the ivory-coloured Daimler, the champagne and flowers, when Julian Schnabel and his beautiful wife, Jacqueline, descended on London in 1983.

Schnabel was a prestige acquisition – a clever card to play at that point. No less crucially, he was money in the bank.

Unlike many dealers who have come and gone during his thirty years in the business, dealers whose galleries performed a mainly social function — as drinking clubs, knocking shops, interior-decoration agencies — Waddington has always treated his business as a business. By 1983, it was clear that the art market was enjoying a boom of the kind it hadn't seen since the early sixties. The undisputed market leader was Schnabel, who, in the space of four years, had gone from washing dishes in a New York restaurant to being, in the words of American *Vogue*, 'the hottest young artist on two continents'.

From $3,000 in 1978, prices of Schnabel's hefty horsehair- and crockery-covered canvases had soared to $60,000 in 1983. The phenomenon could be partly explained by the fact that Charles Saatchi, the most active collector of new art in the eighties, was known to be buying Schnabels on an industrial scale. By the time of his second one-man show with Leslie Waddington in 1985, Schnabels were selling for upwards of $125,000. By then Schnabel had dumped his original American dealer, Mary Boone, in favour of the staider, richer Pace Gallery. The move was reputedly lubricated by a 'sweetener' worth $1 million — not a vast amount of money in a market where a painting by Jasper Johns, only twenty years Schnabel's senior, would soon be bringing $17 million at auction.

Peter Blake made no attempt to hide his displeasure at having to share a gallery with 'the art equivalent of Bruce Springsteen . . . both of them far too successful on the basis of far too little talent'. The analogy was taken up by Paul Maenz, who runs a prominent gallery in Cologne. 'These flashy new artists grew up with rock. For them the issues are one-night stands, hit-and-run events. They think in terms of charts, the Top 10 . . . Nowadays, at twenty-two someone expects to be packaged as the latest promising new superstar.'

Art history these days is measured not in decades but in years and months. By 1985, Schnabel was already in the dying seconds of his fifteen minutes centre-stage. Glittering and mascaraed, a successor was ready waiting in the wings. Jeff Koons's first New York show in 1986 was a sell-out. Last December, when he showed in galleries in New York, Cologne and Chicago, Koons and his dealers realised \$5 million on his factory-made porcelain figures of, among others, a kitsch John the Baptist and a super-kitsch albino Michael Jackson cuddling his pet chimp Bubbles.

The first person to give Koons space to show his work was the New York dealer Meyer Vaisman. Now, at thirty, Vaisman is himself an artist. His best-known piece features four white lavatory seats set out on a raised canvas-covered base like a field toilet. In giving Vaisman his first solo show in Britain at the end of October, Waddington knows he is likely to enrage all the artists connected with his gallery who were enraged by Schnabel. He accepts this but says that one of the strengths of the gallery is that disagreements are allowed. 'Why should we agree and be a pack, like a lot of the culture vultures?'

The interesting thing is that, unlike Kasmin and Robert Fraser in the sixties, Nigel Greenwood and Anthony d'Offay in the seventies, and Nicholas Logsdail in the eighties, Waddington has never had a reputation for being in the spearhead of contemporary culture. He can be scathing on the subject of the 'in-crowd' of faddists and slaves to fashion who, he believes, have held sway in institutions like the Tate Gallery and the British Council in recent years. He is most comfortable with the generation of artists his own age, some of whom he has supported to a degree that most dealers would consider suicidal. There is a roster of twenty artists who receive a guaranteed income of around £25,000 a year from the gallery, as an advance against sales. In a few cases this has meant paying artists even in years when they were not only not selling but not producing work at all.

'I'm not there for two years,' is Waddington's position. 'I'm there for twenty or thirty years. And if I don't make money out of one artist, I'll make it out of another. For instance, I recently gave John Hoyland three galleries for a show. Now I can't make money out of a John Hoyland show even if I sell everything. But I do it. Not to be nice, but because it gives me pleasure. I think my basic activity is to provide space where the artists' works can be seen and not discard them when they go out of fashion. It's a view I've got.'

Next Wednesday, for the first time in many years, a new young British painter is being given a solo show at Waddington Galleries. Leslie Waddington saw Ian Davenport's work at his degree show at Goldsmiths two years ago, when he was just twenty-three, and signed him up. This show, like the Vaisman show which immediately follows it, confirms that, behind the detached, dry, Jesuitical demeanour, and despite the half-days he is obliged to work since he had heart-bypass surgery several years ago, Waddington's competitive edge is as sharp as it has ever been. Invigorated no doubt by the fact that more money has been spent on contemporary art over the past three years than ever before in history, he appears to be as wholeheartedly in the game now as at any time in his career. The object is still to outwit, outmanoeuvre, demoralise and generally outplay the opposition.

His domination of Cork Street, the focus of the commercial art world in London, is obvious at a glance. Four of the biggest, whitest, most sumptuously ascetic galleries bear his name, and there is a vast new print gallery nearby in Clifford Street.

Waddington was the only one of the dealers invited who declined to travel to the studio to sit for Timothy Greenfield-Sanders's large-format camera. The reason offered was as succinct as it was truthful: 'I'm rich enough to do what I want.' 'Waddington and Marlborough are the Gucci and Pucci,' in the words of Anne Berthoud, one of several dealers whose boutique-sized businesses cluster close to the Waddington empire. 'They can virtually name their own prices; people are happy to buy the name.'

Nicola Jacobs absorbed this important lesson during the two years she spent working at Waddington in the seventies. When she set up on her own at 9 Cork Street, sponsored by her father, owner of the British School of Motoring, she took full-page advertisements in *Harpers & Queen* and *Interiors*. 'Have you ever bought an original painting? It says an awful lot more about you than any furnishings ever will,' Nicola cooed from behind a bowl of Hockneyesque tulips. 'You too can attend a private view! It's a very nice way to spend an evening.'

'New money buys new art,' the saying goes. 'Old money supports country houses and horses.' In a letter to potential first-time buyers earlier this year, the veteran New York dealer Ben Heller spelled out some of art's 'peculiar advantages' as an investment medium: 'It is highly mobile, readily transferable into any currency, is a true mark of status, a truly desired expression of the good, the wealthy life,' Heller enthused. 'It is easier to handle than multiple homes and servants . . . it opens doors to new status and new friends, to new contacts and places to visit all over the world . . . It is my absolutely firm position that art, properly bought, can be viewed as a transfer of assets from one column to another.'

A radical breakthrough in British art in the eighties was that British artists, for the first time, established an international profile. By showing them as part of an exhibition programme that has included Warhol, de Kooning, Jasper Johns and Joseph Beuys, as well as most of the leading painters of the European avant-garde, Anthony d'Offay has ensured that Gilbert and George, Richard Long and Bruce McLean are better known in Düsseldorf, Chicago and other world art centres than they are at home.

In a world whose traditions of confidentiality between dealer and client conspire to keep it a hotbed of gossip, rumour and speculation, d'Offay is the object of more curiosity and the source of more speculation than any other individual. This is because his manner manages to suggest both flaccidness and blind ambition, both the chapel of rest and the private vault. 'Anthony d'Offay smiles,' the writer Brian Sewell has said, 'but always makes me feel like a rabbit.'

It is also the hangover from a past which included estate chasing (finding elderly artists, their widows or descendants, and helping to clear out the attics) and being unwittingly roped in on an art-forgery racket. Shortly after paying £109,000 for what turned out to be a number of fake Wyndham Lewis paintings in 1980, d'Offay decided to get out of early-twentieth-century British painting and mount a direct challenge to Leslie Waddington by moving into the international avant-garde. D'Offay has carved out his own territory at the opposite end of Bond Street from the Waddington hegemony, where he has recently been joined by the Anthony Reynolds and Annely Juda galleries.

Nicholas Logsdail, whose gallery, the Lisson, fostered the

dominant British school of the eighties known as the New British Sculpture, has put an even greater distance between himself and Cork Street. The Lisson operates from a lofted, tailor-made space in a resolutely unchic enclave off the Edgware Road. (Kasmin, for one, says he has never been there and wouldn't know how to find it.) The maverick address of the Lisson has come to symbolise Logsdail's relations with an art establishment he characterises as 'cups of tea and cucumber sandwiches – a bit smug and local and pleased with itself'.

It is an extraordinary fact that only three British artists – Henry Moore, Francis Bacon and David Hockney – have meant anything outside Britain in the past forty years. America only discovered Lucian Freud, Frank Auerbach and the 'School of London' painters in the late eighties. Logsdail determined at the outset that his strategy would be international. The measure of his success is that almost all the holdings in the Saatchi collection of British artists aged forty or under are from the Lisson. Three Lisson artists have won the Turner Prize presented by the Tate Gallery, and Lisson artists have represented Britain at the last two Venice Biennali.

Logsdail's success is the result of the stubborn and uncompromising exhibitions policy he has pursued since he opened his gallery as a student fresh out of the Slade more than twenty years ago. Nevertheless there have been charges of slick marketing, of manufacturing reputations to create an exportable commodity – what the late Peter Fuller derided as 'Biennale International Club Class Art'. When Leslie Waddington talks about an 'in-crowd' he means, with one or two exceptions, Logsdail and his sculptors. 'What I want to know is this,' says Waddington. 'Is Mr Logsdail going to be able to do the same thing with his artists in ten years' time, when fashions have moved on?'

Logsdail, for his part, believes Waddington is the textbook example of a dealer who has failed to promote his artists' reputations internationally with the necessary vigour.

Dealers have never been popular with the people who depend on them for their living. Marcel Duchamp called them 'lice on the backs of artists'. 'The people who make art their business,' Picasso once declared, 'are mostly impostors.'

'People always regard you as an exploiter,' said Robert Fraser, owner of London's most exciting gallery in the sixties. 'Artists don't like dealers. They are egoists and don't see you do anything for them besides providing them with bread and butter. If you don't accept that from the word go, you are likely to end up feeling very sore.'

Apart from two traumatic months with Nicholas Logsdail, the Scottish sculptor David Mach has managed his affairs successfully without having a regular London gallery. 'They want to nail your foot to the floor so you walk around in a tiny little circle. It actually quite upsets them if you try and break out and do something new.'

In the speculative fever that has fuelled the contemporary art boom of the past few years, dealers have had the squeeze put on them by Sotheby's and Christie's and by the new breed of collector who is buying only for resale at a profit. In the cases of Schnabel and Koons, the two most conspicuous examples, art prospectors were on the scene before any dealer got near them.

The young Scottish painter Stephen Conroy sold his entire degree show at Glasgow College of Art overnight in 1986. (The school's head of fine art has since barred the doors to visitors.) John Greenwood, who graduated from the Royal College of Art this year, has been commissioned by Charles Saatchi to paint six pictures. Bob and Susan Summers, two

American collectors of contemporary British painting, snapped up the work of another 1990 RCA graduate.

There is a growing number of art arbitrageurs who function without a gallery. They put together specific clients and paintings (often the property of owners who initially have no intention of selling) and, once a successful match has been made, cream off a large commission.

Charles Saatchi, in the opinion of the New York-based British painter Sean Scully, several of whose paintings Saatchi recently unloaded, is only 'a superdealer'. 'These guys create price levels for themselves. They put one painting in a sale and bid it up to huge levels. And the artist loses control of his work, while his relations with the dealer he has worked with so long go for nothing. We are just pawns.'

It would appear from all this that the traditional functions of the dealer are being steadily eroded. Is the day approaching when a Filofax, a calculator and a folio of laminated transparencies for laser mailing around the globe will constitute the basic requirements for anybody wanting to operate in the superheated art industry? Leslie Waddington thinks not. 'What all this ignores,' he says, 'is that most people who buy art buy it because they like it. There is an awful lot of buying going on in this country at the moment by people who are not in it to make a quick profit. It's distorting to talk only about money. Art has become a very interesting, active part of our culture. If you go to the Tate on a Sunday afternoon, which I often do instead of on a snobby evening, it's crowded with people from the age of eighteen to thirty. Mobbed. The contagion is there, and the fabulous collections being formed here now reflect that excitement.

'Saatchi is not my biggest collector by a very long way and he's not the biggest spender in this country. The kind of buying that is going on here now is amazing. As for dealers having lost the initiative, I gave you my profit figures for last year. That's the answer to that.'

1993

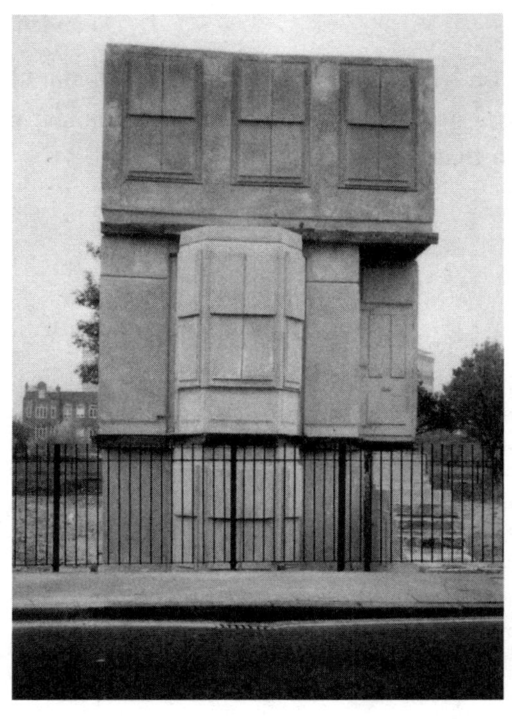

Rachel Whiteread b.1963
Untitled (House) 1993
commissioned by Artangel
Photo: Sue Ormerod
Courtesy Karsten Schubert, London
© The artist 1996

Rachel Whiteread: Shedding Life
Tate Gallery, Liverpool, Autumn 1996
Museo Nacional Centro de Arte Reina Sofía, Madrid, Spring 1997
MU 2312   Muse Productions, Stroud, GL5 3EH, GB
Tel: 44 (0)1453 767222   Printed in England

GILBERT AND GEORGE

It was a Friday. They had risen, with some difficulty, shortly before nine and, leaving behind them a room as tidy and silent and in every way as unmoving as a department store window after dark, by twenty-past they were enjoying a breakfast of cabbage-and-something in the meat-porters' cafe a brisk two minutes' walk from their front door.

Stepping out in their usual fashion, sharp left past the furrier and the church and the importer of bananas, they had nodded their good-mornings and, looking about them as they went, had noted the changes that a night can bring. As always, the high point of breakfast was the ending: fruit dumplings, hot custard, that sort of thing. 'Often,' George says, 'I have a second and still I have a struggle not to ask for more.' 'The chef,' Gilbert says, 'he is brilliant. A brilliant man. A genius. Also he works so hard, all through the night.'

'An absolute marvel,' George concurs. 'Outrageous, absolutely.'

Eleven o'clock found them at home drinking, George over by the window, tippling on a bottle of Walnut Brown, a sweet sherry, his left hand at his waist and his other settled by the glass and the bottle on the sill. Gilbert was taking the weight of his body on one arm against the fireplace wall, one foot crooked over the other and a sherry lighter and drier than George's in his free hand.

In appearance they were, as they always are, immaculate: white shirts and dark ties, toe-capped black Oxfords and tailored brown suits — three buttons, single-vented, and with a faint over-check. Both identical. There are dissimilarities, of course. The gold motif on George's tie is 'Two chaps', and on Gilbert's 'Pink elephants'; Gilbert has left one button undone and his trousers are hitched a fraction above the ankle, permitting a glimpse of socks several shades pinker than George's brassy red (socks are something they have a common fund of).

And then there are the obvious. George is the one who wears glasses, he is English, he smokes and his complexion is fair. Gilbert is shorter, darker, Italian. Art for All, where they live, is a sparsely furnished, almost bare room with tarnished, high-gloss walls and a dusty wood floor, at the same time sinister, refined and, were it not for its impeccable order, vaguely squalid. A hanging bare light bulb, square-shaped in an incongruously modern way, provides the only lighting. There are two straight-backed and stern, hard green chairs, a table/stool of raw wood and one large piece of furniture: a desk/blackboard. And that is all. A place for everything and everything in its place. Two glasses, two bottles, one ashtray, a telephone, a pack of Gold Flake and Gilbert and George.

Quite suddenly then the doorbell rang and their visitor was upon them. As always, George played host. 'May I take your coat?' And then: 'A drink perhaps? What will it be? A sherry? Gin and tonic?' The visitor backed up to the blackboard/desk with a glass and a bottle and, standing too, couldn't help but fall into the rhythm of the room.

'Do you have many callers?'

'Not a lot, no.'

'It's very difficult to reach us because we really are never here.'

'We're not very often here. Most mornings when we're in London.'

'We're here then.'

'Are those your original suits?'

'Oh no. They're new. We're always changing tailors. We're never satisfied.'

'The last one was Burtons.'

'We like clothes so that we can just fling them on every day rather than to have to think a lot about it.'

'We like them because they are just some boring suits. Ordinary, boring suits.'

'What was your first conversation?'

'It was when we were at college. You're better at remembering, Gilbert.'

'I remember only he used to call me Gilbert-the-filbert. There was a language problem. I didn't understand one single word.'

'He soon picked it up though, didn't you, Gilb?'

In the silences, often and long, the only sounds were of three people drinking. Corks out of bottles, drinks into glasses, and glasses meeting hard surfaces. Today, they would get sedately drunk.

> Went up to the bar and ordered
> these drinks, lost those
> somewhere ordered a couple more,
> found that we had forgotten the others so we had another
> round, found some and tended
> to lose track a shade (Wonderful stuff!)
>
> *Bristol Cream*, a Greeting Card
> sculpture, Gilbert and George (1973)

At one point George excused himself and returned with a

stem glass, which he stood in the window. It was clean and clear but broken so that the ragged points and splinters caught the light, like a piece of meticulously rinsed debris from a pub brawl. A new sculpture. He turned it this way and that, held aloft in one hand. 'Terrific, yes? Don't you think that's shocking, absolutely?'

Later, photographs would be produced: Gilbert and George formally posed in Art for All and at pubs, and then Gilbert and George in progressive states of headlong drunkenness, until at last they are paralytic and spreadeagled on the floor in a slop of spilled drink, cigarette ends, broken glass and spent matches. The photographs are to be blown up and turned into a series of seven-feet-high swastikas, nine portraits to each.

'Do you remember when they broke my nose?' Gilbert had asked.

'They were the skinhead types,' George said. 'Such a marvellous style of dress they have. Lovely, really. We were their greatest supporters, you know. Everyone thinking about this great wave of skinhead violence, and there we are, walking around the streets admiring this amazing style. It's rather unfair they attacked us.'

'You never see it any more,' Gilbert said. 'Not in the East End.'

'It's still a style supported rather heavily by male prostitutes. I think that's the last stronghold of skinheads in London. I don't know why. "Gentlemen Prefer Skinheads" or something.'

'It was the time of queer-bashing when they kicked us in.'

'Absolutely. There was a time when you couldn't walk across to Liverpool Street from here without all the groups, or two or three young men, shouting or making some fresh remark. Homosexual jokes or something, yes? Amazing. We never used to understand it. And now they wouldn't do it in a hundred years. They're all dressed up like swans or something. Just so dyed-up and . . . Silver underwear. So fancy. We never understand why they were so funny then.'

'Fighting is rather nice,' Gilbert said.

> There were two young men who were covered with blood,
> They are wounded and slashed and covered with mud.
> They battle along singing a song
> Straining to be jolly though the journey's long
> They think nothing of health or worry or care
> Because their job is to do their share
> So left leg out and away it goes
> And where they go to nobody knows.

'Manliness', from *Limericks*, Gilbert and George (1971)

Long gone are the days when the choice before a visitor to Art for All would be tea or milk and the works were a reflection of that simpler life – singing sculptures and eating sculptures, poignant domestic scenes and humble pastoral pieces featuring the sculptors 'gazing after Art in the Nature'. All of it desperately innocent and not darkened by even a hint of impropriety.

But George and Gilbert have become drinkers and the drinking has nudged them towards a flirtation with violence, beauty and squalor. 'We didn't,' George explained, '. . . neither of us used to drink at all, you know. We never went to pubs or anything.'

'And we still don't like it, to drink. It's completely artistic, the whole thing,' said Gilbert.

Outside, the grey morning had become a grey afternoon, but their visitor, standing all the while, obviously was still puzzled. 'Nerves,' Gilbert said. 'Meeting people and so on. Especially in the art world. We dislike always the normality of meeting people. They talk the most boring subjects. Awful! So if you get completely smashed, you really are free.'

'At the same time it brings you very close,' George added. 'You can literally do anything to anyone if you're completely drunk. You don't mind who you grab or anything. On the other hand, it creates an amazing distance. I mean, if you feel quite secure in your drunkenness you don't feel anyone can really come close.'

'Every time when you are out and you meet some people, drinking is the only way. You don't even think what you are doing. You are just carried away.'

'It's not very often that you can taste what you're drinking anyway. It's just a part of the evening, like eating or smoking cigarettes. Because the first drink just knocks us out completely.'

'Completely! The first one. I think nerves make a person completely drunk.'

'But a lot of the time we were drinking,' George said, 'we weren't using it in our work, d'you see? We were still using images of nature and the more homely life, and then we felt brave enough to introduce it into the work.'

'Nearly all the artists, they are nearly all drunks. The whole art world, they all get drunk all the time. It's amazing.'

'We think it's very honest of us to realise that it can be a subject. You get really smashed and the next day you paint a beautiful picture, pretty stripes or something, and then you get drunk again, and it's absolutely nothing to do with your way of life, really. And we like to be very lifelike, in a way, not to be too artistic. So we thought we'd use drink as a subject. As an aesthetic. We'd have to anyway, because we don't have any artistic interests, as such. We're not interested in painting or in any technical aspect of art at all.'

'It means we're not invited to a lot of things now because people expect a disaster to happen. Sometimes you can see them: "Oh my God," they're saying. "Here they come again." We don't mind what they think.'

Soon after one o'clock, as the first bottles of the day were being drained, it started to rain and the room was abruptly thrown into darkness. High up on a building opposite a sign started to lift on the wind, causing its hinges to creak. 'Rather eerie,' George said, 'to see a sign swinging. It always reminds me of things like *Kidnapped*. The sign creaking, then someone comes along. It always begins with something very abstract like that. Even *Treasure Island* has a swinging inn sign, I think.'

When it's this dark, standing behind the half net at the windows, it is possible to see out onto the street without being seen, and to clearly overhear conversations on the pavement. There are regular fights and squabbles among the groups of tramps and homeless people who roam the area and, in the later winter afternoons, George and Gilbert will sometimes stand silently and unobserved by their window, listening in. Mostly though, between bouts of drinking, they spend their afternoons at the cinema.

'Nothing breathtaking will occur here,' they wrote in 1971, 'but in the darkness of a picture house, where time is killed, the world explodes realistically into giant action stories, men are killed, women are loved, mountains are blown up, night falls, volcanoes erupt, John Wayne rides again and Caesar speaks anew to the people. All this until the reel is done and viewers drift blinking and reeling out into the bright city.'

When night-time came and the blind came down, George helped Gilbert and the visitor into their coats and made

certain before leaving that the fire was on one bar. He carried
a tumbler of gin and tonic with him out onto the street and
staggered only slightly. They would return home too late
tonight to catch the old lady with her wad of newspaper on her
knees scrubbing the street, the same one who can never let
Gilbert pass without crying out to him, 'Johnny! Johnny!'

For Gilbert and George, the sculptors, another day.

1973

GILBERT: We never say no. We try never to . . .

GEORGE: We don't like to polish up. It's not ever good if you
polish something up.

GILBERT: We never examine ourselves in that way. We just
accept it . . . We have our ideas that we are interested in. And
that's our art. Our new thoughts that we get from the street
or wherever we go. Art we have no interest in whatsoever.

GEORGE: Our inspiration is not to be found in that world anyway. Our inspiration is outside of galleries and museums.
Absolutely. I mean, if we went to a museum, we are more
likely to be inspired by the doorman or something, rather
than what's inside. We've never been inspired by other people's art.

GB: When did you begin to steer away from drink?

GILBERT: We never did drink a lot. Only when we meet people. But if we're alone we never drink.

GEORGE: We never go to pubs.

GILBERT: Never! Not once.

GEORGE: Only with people. Alone we never even have half a
pint of bitter. We've no interest really in that.

GILBERT: We used to go out with people. But never alone.
Never. We don't have any time left.

GEORGE: Absolutely.

GILBERT: The actual people who are important are very, very few.

GB: You don't go dancing any more?

GEORGE: Hardly ever. I can't think of the last time we danced. We hardly go out even to walk, many days.

GILBERT: We are completely isolated.

GEORGE: A normal Sunday we would be working . . . And the amount of inspiration one needs is very, very little, in fact. One doesn't have to scout around for three weeks. One second's looking out the window is enough to . . .

GILBERT: The main thing is, we don't have time to do the pieces any more.

GEORGE: We like to say what we want to say to the world as much as we can, for as long as we can . . . Carry On Screaming.

GILBERT: We are very interested in that. In messages.

GEORGE: After all, we only have eighty more years or whatever it is. It's not a lot. More tea?

GB: People get in the way of the work. Unannounced guests are not welcome?

GEORGE: We always look out of the window first to see it isn't somebody we're not expecting. We have one very quiet window we can lift.

GB: Tell me about the Pugin and the Christopher Dresser – the vases and furniture you've started collecting.

GEORGE: They came from pieces more. We always find things that agree with us. We like to buy things that support what we already think.

GILBERT: We like very much recently symbolic art. Symbolic. That's why we started to collect furniture with symbolic . . .

GEORGE: Yes, we're more and more and more interested in

meaning. That's our biggest interest, really. As opposed to form.

GILBERT: Even the colours are always used symbolic.

GEORGE: We were more involved with form in earlier times, to a certain extent. Now the form is less dominant.

GILBERT: Everybody just mentions how powerful our shows are. Visually. They are frightened. It's true. All over.

GEORGE: It's important that they feel affected, that it means something to them. Not just that they liked the colours or liked the show . . . That's why we're so interested in this film [Philip Haas]. Because that is an amazing form. More and more bombastic, fascistic . . .

GILBERT: Overpowering . . . We like to affect people with our art. Recently we manage to get through much more. Especially to the young people.

GEORGE: The galleries always remark that.

GILBERT: Our form is a more direct language to people. They can understand it. We always wanted to do that. Have a simple language that everybody can understand.

GEORGE: A piece like *Speaking Youth* doesn't depend on a knowledge of cubism or vorticism or anything else. It doesn't require any specialised knowledge.

GILBERT: Nothing.

GEORGE: We wouldn't like that . . . You always have wankers. But you can always convert them. We do. Professional people in the art world are only interested in the public reaction anyway. Never in their own. They don't have a reaction of their own.

GILBERT: They never know.

GEORGE: Museum curators only know what the show means to them after the opening of the show when the people start coming. When you get fifty thousand road sweepers coming in who are crazy about it, then they're keen all right. Amazing good toffee-nosed theories immediately. They can see that, independent of them, the show works. Without their permission.

GILBERT: We have always been based on that. We never need any art person.

GEORGE: A lot of art absolutely needs specialised professional people to say that it's good in order that it can exist, because nobody else would know.

GB: You have talked in the past about the growing tendency for you not to be invited to art-world dos.

GILBERT: We never go . . . We dislike that stuff. It has nothing to do with art.

GEORGE: It's not we who are badly behaved anyway. It's just that they don't understand alcohol, that's all. They think alcohol's for standing around and behaving as though it's water. Alcohol is for getting drunk. That's what it's for. It's silly if you just stand there all evening, all elegant. You might as well not be drinking.

GB: People are frightened of you?

GILBERT: We do have a wall around ourselves. We have to protect ourselves.

GEORGE: Even we have stuff within ourselves that does disturb people, I would say. Very much.

GILBERT: Oh yes.

GEORGE: From seeing us, or hearing a snippet of conversation or something. Many times when we're in restaurants or in public places, very anonymously dressed, very plainly dressed, we always realise that people are talking about us, or that there's some nonsense going on about us.

GILBERT: Always. We always disturb people. It doesn't matter where we go.

GEORGE: What we represent is disturbing to a lot of people. [Giggles from Gilbert] They're not used to that. We are not grey anonymous liberal softies.

GILBERT: A lot of people don't like us because we are very clear in what we accept and don't accept. Our views are very strict.

GEORGE: On the whole, people like easy-going people, don't they? That's more acceptable.

GB: Tell me about the fascistic element.

GEORGE: It's a life force. It's a life force that we accept and honour very much.

GILBERT: You could say that goodness is fascistic. What people used to believe was good – religion – you could say that is fascistic.

GEORGE: I mean, we're only here because of the force of fascism, anyway. Life doesn't exist without it . . . Without the good works of fascism there wouldn't even be a civilisation. An anti-fascist never built anything. Anti-fascism never created anything. It is to do with destroying the other stuff. It is not a living force in itself. It's a negative, anti thing. That's all.

GILBERT: People who run the world are all fascist.

GEORGE: Western power. So-called Western power . . . Extermination camps have nothing to do with fascism.

GILBERT: They have to do with the left, in fact. Because fascism in Germany was a left-wing party.

GEORGE: The most famous extermination camp was in fact socialist. Not right-wing . . . That's why it's called right. Because it's the right side. That's where it gets its name from.

GB: Perhaps we should talk about 'the knights'.

GILBERT: We like the idea, to lift up completely normal people.

GEORGE: Higher spirits. Timeless. That is what man really is, and always will be like that . . . It's very old-fashioned to oppose that in a way. The power that is in young people like that is fantastic. Amazing. We like to honour that in our work.

GB: You have inevitably been accused of being pro-National Front.

GEORGE: We're not against people saying that. We wouldn't go out of our way to decry the National Front. It's just a political party.

GB: But they are advocating violence against your Asian neighbours here.

GEORGE: Pakistanis lead fuller lives than anybody else. My God, they're all going to public schools. They're the richest people in the whole of the street here. They drive off in cars to the beautiful suburbs. Absolutely. They earn super-money.

GILBERT: They are the most brutal people that we ever met.

GEORGE: 'Is it to my advantage?' they ask themselves every single second. They're not like us, thinking these kind, Christian, historical things. Courteous and polite . . .

GILBERT: More timeless. More to do with the spirit . . .

GEORGE: We're not based anyway just on the moment. We're based on everything so far, plus the moment. We don't think just exactly in this . . . day.

GB: Do you still think of what you do as sculpture?

GEORGE: We're not so interested in definitions any more.

GB: When did that start to disappear?

GEORGE: I suppose in the mid-seventies probably. Seventy-four, seventy-five. People got too interested in that. 'What is sculpture?' They don't even see what's in the picture any more. They don't even see what's there.

GILBERT: Even the public are mystified if we say, 'These photo-pieces are sculpture.' We don't like that. We hate all these academics in art, and aesthetics and so on . . .

GEORGE: We gave a lot of people freedom to make art with meaning, because that was away completely in the early seventies. You could only concentrate on form. The meaning had to be removed totally – minimal, conceptual . . .

GILBERT: That's why we had a very difficult time.

GEORGE: We emerged at a time when 'meaning' was virtually a dirty word. The picture or the sculpture had to be totally devoid of meaning. We were consciously fighting back against that. We had to. To establish our freedom to do that.

GB: I notice that you now own a television.

GEORGE: We restrict ourselves to half an hour in the evenings. *Coronation Street* we watch. That is our favourite. *Songs of Praise.*

[The doorbell rings. It is Danny, the drunk from the film.]

GILBERT: 'But I'm a happy drunk. I'm an honest drunk. And I'll be drunk the day I die.' That's what he said. 'I am the madman who nobody loves – but I'm quite intelligent.'

GEORGE: 'Happiness – now tell me if I'm right; you're quite bright – happiness is misery, isn't it?' Amazing stuff, yes? Completely serious.

GB: Why do you like people like him? You clearly do.

GEORGE: It's not a question of 'liking'. We can tailor it all into our message.

GILBERT: I think there is much bigger philosophy in people like that. There is more life in them. They are outside. Outside the system. We like all the people that are outside the system, we realised.

GEORGE: All these physically inferior, mentally retarded,

splendid people – all perfectly all right. No problem at all. Then we've got this one educated one, with a woolly hair-style, yes? And he said, 'My life so far? Quite interesting. Met a lot of interesting people, been to a lot of interesting places, but in general I don't describe my life so far to a camera.' Amazing. And the others did it so splendidly.

GILBERT: We are outside the system, like the drunks. And the ones who are not, they are bad artists.

GEORGE: Certainly . . . We're not anti-establishment or anything like that.

GB: Have you always been incapable of having what you call 'normal' relationships?

GILBERT: I never want that. I never had that before, even . . . I don't want to be normal with normal relationships. I have absolutely no interest in people in that way.

GEORGE: The gulf between people is very important. They would be telling us everything. We have to keep completely free brains. Independent. One way, completely. We like to look at them under our microscope and say what we want to say. Wicked scientists, if you like, hmmm?

GILBERT: We are not interested in other people's views. We never have. Not for one second, in fact. Nobody . . . For many years they thought we had to do with nothing.

GEORGE: They thought our art had no connection with anything. They didn't know what it meant or what it was about or anything. Now they all fight amongst each other with more and more elaborate theories.

GILBERT: We hate that generation [of Lawrence Gowing]. Hate it. They never did anything.

GEORGE: So patronising. Nationalistic their whole life. They're civil servants, all sitting on committees together. Comfortable lives.

GILBERT: First, they are foreign wankers. Every one of that generation. Totally.

GEORGE: They all talk about Monet or Manet or . . . These lockjaw names. Disgusting. Art from wine-growing countries. It's true. That's all they support.

GILBERT: That was the biggest mistake of English artists. And even the Pop generation had a lot to do with that, looking towards America.

GEORGE: New York – it's an English city anyway. It's part of England's heritage. But these other people, they go over and they are just overwhelmed by it in a completely idiotic way.

GILBERT: And they are overwhelmed without knowing. Without knowing. It's incredible. Amazing big disease.

GEORGE: 'It's a very nice place.' The Americans think that's the most offensive thing you can say about it. They hate it. They ask you if you've seen the latest Terry-Thomas film. It's just a charming, old-fashioned English place.

GB: But what about the [New York] club you used to like to visit called The Toilet? And the fist-fucking magazines that you can get there but that you can't get here?

GEORGE: We had an interest in that side of life and so found things to help us follow our interests. Everything is part of our art anyway. We exclude nothing. Just at that time we were more centred on that.

GILBERT: We still drink. Every time we go out we are completely smashed. We get drunk when we drink. Immediately. But we don't drink – whatyoucallit – to have a nice time. Wine with luncheon or something . . . That is why the old generation we dislike very much. That is why we don't ever want to meet them. We are much more famous in other countries than in England. In America we are very, very famous; in New York. They are the biggest buyers of our art. Young people we love. But the old queens in museums . . .

GEORGE: If no one can understand it except them and their friends, then they think it's superior. And better, therefore.

GILBERT: We would like to do plays.

GEORGE: We'd do good ones. Very good ones, I'm sure.

[A man appears on the upper ledge of a house opposite.]

GEORGE: He's dicing with life. D'you see? It's very dangerous. He might fall off before we finish our tea . . .

People are very embarrassing. Some people are proud. Some people are proud and shy. We're the proud and shy ones . . . We normally reserve our social life for when we have to go to an opening of some sort. A social obligation to go to an opening. We save it all up and channel all our bad behaviour into that one evening, and contain it, yes? Get drunk, mess the trousers, and go home.

GILBERT: It's exactly that.

GB: The influence of your work is becoming increasingly obvious in commercial art, album covers and so on.

GEORGE: The metallised heads. That was unbelievable for that time. I mean, we did the pieces in the pop world, with the Who and people . . . pop festivals, the Lyceum, the Marquee . . . It's not so obvious in England, the effect we had on popular culture. But on the Continent people are very aware of that.

GILBERT: Every artist tries to put together different subjects; they never know how to do it. And we know exactly, because square-by-square we can do it.

GEORGE: It's the standard largest-size cut of photographic paper. But we found we can use that combination to do an endless piece. A 150-part piece, or a two-part piece. Endless combination. Much more graphic and direct and powerful.

GILBERT: And the transport is absolutely nothing. Nobody has such a big show, so many pieces. Our drawing pieces even used to be done like that. In a sheet.

GEORGE: Everything else is like that anyway. A house is just built up out of bricks. One's life is just built up of days and minutes and stuff.

GB: Was it Wittgenstein who . . .

GEORGE: Don't mention foreigners in this house!

GILBERT: It is amazing, the disease of English people to mention foreigners all the time. It makes me mad. It is so destructive to the English.

GEORGE: To destroy Britain. That is the only intention.

GILBERT: In art, just every writing is only to do with mentioning foreign names. Every single piece of writing. Just incredible. Even in Victorian times they had so many artists who were so brilliant. That era hasn't been discovered yet. But it was just so rich. That has been completely forgotten because of stupid . . . The Bloomsbury Group. They were the first foreign wankers.

GEORGE: *Since Cézanne*. Bell's most famous book. It is the most poisonous title. You should go to prison for that in a good country. Absolutely.

GILBERT: That was our biggest success. To become completely independent of every other artist.

GEORGE: Even Leslie Waddington refers to all his English artists as 'the English Picabia' or 'the English something-else'. Every time. Terrible.

GILBERT: That we feel is the biggest disease here. We could smash him in his face for saying that. We would, if he would say that of us. Absolutely.

GEORGE: Artists on the whole are very shy to say something. We answer as straight as we can. They're all protecting the reputation of their intellect, they feel. That's the idea. People think they are very intelligent artists, and they must not destroy that. If somebody thinks we're idiotic, they can think we're idiotic, certainly. What we will not tolerate is people saying that they don't like our work. We don't tolerate that at all. We don't allow people to say that to us. Absolutely not. Most people know that they shouldn't say that to us.

GILBERT: We cut them off totally.

GEORGE: It's completely uninteresting that somebody doesn't like our work. It's a completely stupid idea anyway.

GILBERT: They have stupid heads.

GEORGE: I can't think of the last time somebody said that. I'm very good at replying. I just say, 'Well, you're an old pig, aren't you?' That's a good reply. It scares the knickers off them immediately.

GILBERT: They don't know what they think. That's the amazing thing. They don't know. They're pretending. They have opinions from other people.

GEORGE: They're protecting themselves, usually. They're afraid that they'll appear a stupid person if they say that they do like your work.

GILBERT: Especially here in England, they never want to have a view, straight out. If you are friends with, like, people at the Tate, that's finished. You have to be outside attacking them, in a way. Every second.

GEORGE: We're very discriminated against there. From beginning to end. To this day. What was it they said? We were taking the mickey out of English manners. Incredible, hmmm? Such a lower-class idiotic thing to say . . . They like to like it, and they don't like to like us in that way. Our art is not for the liking classes to like. We don't do it for that. It's not the reason. Our pieces aren't even likeable in that way.

GILBERT: Boy Scout art.

GEORGE: Druid art . . . It's quite wrong that they don't have a very, very good representation of our work [at the Tate].

GILBERT: Nationalised idiots! They are just that. Just trying to make a living out of it.

GEORGE: Cosy lives they want. No trouble.

GILBERT: They always water it down. From the first day that we did art here they try to water us down . . . They're ashamed of life. I come from a very artistic family. They accept all art.

GB: Have you ever seriously considered having a different base from which to work?

GEORGE: We've never thought of living somewhere else, no. It's the most realistic place to live, isn't it, really? It's the best place to see the world from. Whatever happens in London is the same as the world is. Whereas whatever happens in Zurich is just to do with Zurich. London is the world in that way. Every rotten corner, every person in the street is a world statement. 'All right, boys!' they say to us. Amazing nice.

A country house in Bulawayo would be all right. Really. That would be exciting, I must say. Certainly. That would be quite inspiring. In the Sudan or somewhere. I thought you knew we were Africa crazy. Downtown Johannesburg would be lovely. We're more interested in the white man's African culture in a way. Africa's the garden of England. England's allotment. Unfortunately we have no time to travel. We only go where we have exhibitions, really.

GILBERT: I would like to go to Khartoum as a visitor. Stay in a nice hotel. Comfortable. I don't like uncomfortable places.

GEORGE: Amazing dreary . . . But we've become more worldly wise, you could say.

GILBERT: And patriotism. I think that was one of the best things. We managed to crystallise that. We managed to kill off a lot of clichés, for us, in art. For instance, that always everything in art has to be related to some other art.

GEORGE: Even artists on television have to say they're influenced by some foreigner. Shows they're good if they say that. Monet: some stupid old French tart having a picnic on a bit of rotten grass beside some foreign dirty river. And they say that is better than Bacon? That is amazing. Shocking, really. Some disgusting French bread sticking out of some horrible basket . . . They don't even know an English name, half of them.

GILBERT: Landseer. It was so heavy with meaning. Very artistic. But at the moment they just laugh at him.

GEORGE: Now if they think about Landseer, they just think he's some nonsense old bourgeois capitalist nineteenth-century imperialist rubbish.

GILBERT: We want to be completely outside with — whatyoucall — hooligans and tramps. We don't want to be put inside. Not at all. I always felt that they are not radical enough here.

GEORGE: They're nice artists, people like that. That's exactly what they are. Limited down to doing the right stuff.

GILBERT: We know so well that we have nothing to lose. It was very good, because we had so many enemies in the seventies that it made us very, very strong. We could see much more clearly in our heads what we wanted to do because of that.

GEORGE: We have to be on the top of the bus, with the skinheads.

1978

'What did you think of the match the other night?' We were meeting a few days after Liverpool's glorious Champions League victory over Milan in Istanbul. Gilbert looked disbelieving, then blank. 'Are you mad?' George arched an eyebrow and took a deep drag on his cigarette. The message was clear: such a shoddy beginning.

But it didn't seem such a stupid question: a young artist of their acquaintance had told me a couple of nights earlier that Liverpool's fightback had reduced him to tears. Plus, the spectacle of intense patriotic feeling and tribal bunting, the rough energy and close male association, all of it suffused in a vivid lionheart red, bore all the hallmarks of Gilbert and George's radical, and sometimes reckless-seeming, work of the seventies and eighties. Pieces with titles such as *Cocky Patriot*, *Britisher* and *Boot*, showing a big Doc Marten stomping into a puddle and splashing up what can be read as either swags of bright cherry blossom or blood. (That ambiguity is at the heart of all G&G's work. One of its salient features, as the critic David Sylvester remarked several years ago, is that it is double-edged.) One thing, though, they have always been clear on: their art, they say, deals with life, not art.

'What you call this winning or losing is nothing,' Gilbert said. He is no longer young. He's sixty-three now. He had a pair of glasses dangling from a cord round his neck. 'It's just pure luck.'

'Pure luck!' George agreed. 'It has seventy pages of every newspaper. It's extraordinary, the sports coverage. It's appalling.'

'Appalling!'

'We always think it's horrible on the news when you're told how many people have died in an aeroplane crash, and all the horrible things happening – "and now over to the sports desk".

Only death and sport. What a diet! They never use the fact that an amazing book has been published today as the main news item, do they?'

I say that in an age of the faked event and synthetic emotion, Liverpool winning stood out as an authentic experience — something real happening as you're watching on television, which hardly ever happens any more.

'Trooping the colour,' Gilbert said. 'The wedding of Diana. The death of Diana. The funeral of the Pope. Mass hysteria.' He was still tetchy. 'Art is not based on that.'

'We read a report years ago,' George said, 'that watching sport is bad for the brain, because the expectation is so limited. It can only be nil–nil, one–nil, two–one . . . It's never eighty-two–one, is it? If the support from the newspapers and the television was withdrawn, within two or three years football would just be like tiddlywinks, I suspect. Also it had a very ugly beginning, just kicking Turkish heads around in sacks, that's how it started. I'm serious. They'd bring them back to show that they'd killed an infidel. That's why all the pubs in England are named the Turk's Head and the Saracen's Head. Then they kicked it round the village square to celebrate. What a beginning.'

George is full of slightly sarcastic, arcane information like this. He can tell you what the street names around the Spitalfields area of East London reveal about the history of the workers' movements and social reformers, as well as the fact that the boys hustling for customers outside the Brick Lane Balti restaurants are known locally as 'tikka touts'. Gilbert is his best audience. They have been together for almost forty years. They are like a settled married couple. They love each other. But, even though they own a number of prime properties in the new, gentrified East End, they are far from slipping into a comfortable and cushioned old age. As *Hooded*, one of their pieces for Venice, which was picked up by a number of news sources, including the *Guardian*, to illustrate the recent shopping-centre ban on hoodies, suggests, they are still effortlessly channelling the Zeitgeist; still tuned into their times.

In practical terms, this means they have to be up early to beat the council cleaners power-blasting the latest tags and graffiti off the nearby walls and buildings. Starting with the Dirty Words pictures of 1977 – *Smash the Reds, Prostitute Poof, Cunt Scum* – the marks by which unaligned or alienated people claim the streets have always found their way into the work. Some of their most recent pieces incorporate lamp-post stickers – 'Homes not hotels', 'Say fuck off to rich bastards' – and flyers put out by fundamentalist Muslim groups.

But being on the front line between militant Islam and the 'yupper classes' carries with it certain perils. I had assumed their front door looked the way it did in order to spite the neighbours, whose houses have all been beautifully painted with colours from the National Trust 'Heritage' range. It turns out, though, that it was recently booted down by a gang of Muslim youths while they were out. The shutters on the upper windows stay closed since a brick was lobbed through one of them, damaging many of the thousands of nineteenth-century Christopher Dresser vases they have amassed. The doorstep most mornings is fouled with human piss or shit.

The consolation, as always, is the work. 'Look at this!' George said excitedly, flipping through a catalogue to a recent piece. '*White Bastards*. And this one. *Chichiman*. You don't know what a chichiman is? It's what they call you just before they kill you in the West Indies for being queer. And in the rap songs. "Kill the chichiman".'

Their aim, they say, is to be mature and young at the same time. 'Young people don't consider, say, the New Horny Pictures to be typical of sixty-year-old artists. They're up to date, on account of their subject, their form, their meaning, the feelings they arouse. It's not a pensioner's art.'

Usually when I think of Gilbert and George, I think of drink, and being drunk. This also holds true of any number of other artists you could mention, particularly those belonging to the generation who could be thought of as G&G's stroppy children. Sarah Lucas and Tracey Emin's short-lived double act as The Birds, complete with 'I feel fucky' T-shirts and shop in Bethnal Green Road, was a conscious homage to G&G. The Chapman brothers apprenticed themselves for a brief period to Gilbert and George.

But booze was only the condition in which the YBAs made their work. For Gilbert and George, for a period in the seventies, leglessness was their subject, getting righteously hammered their vocation. 'Nearly all the artists, they are nearly all drunks,' I remember Gilbert telling me merrily around this time, about an hour into a mid-morning session. 'The whole art world, they all get drunk. It's amazing.' Visitors to Fournier Street in those days were likely to be handed the familiar green bottle of Gordon's; the artists would already have one each, and be swigging it neat. The living sculptures drank as they strode through Liverpool Street station, drank in taxis, glugged from tumblers of gin and tonic in the bright afternoon streets and went home to take pictures of each other sprawling bladdered among the dregs and the empties and the dark shadows and puddles.

So that was the first surprise of our recent meeting: no drink. No alcoholic refreshment was offered. This is partly because they are no longer as young as they were, partly because, after thirty years of printing and inking by hand, they have recently gone digital. The first fruits of their computer literacy started to appear — to ream out of them — last year. Their vast image bank has been downloaded onto a network of nine computers, and for twelve months they have been producing urgent, teeming, fractured work which embraces the whole modern urban berserk.

The thirteen Hooligan Pictures led to the thirty-eight Perversive Pictures which have mutated into the more opaque iconography of the twenty-five Ginkgo Pictures for the British Pavilion in Venice. The ginkgo tree grows a bifurcated leaf whose one side exactly mirrors the other and which smells, as G&G discovered to their tremendous pleasure, 'of shit'. They made an associative connection between the ginkgo leaf and the pubic lice which had been a leitmotif of their twenty London E1 Pictures of 2003. 'Nobody has a good word to say for pubic lice,' George said. 'They don't appear in art galleries or museums anywhere. They are very discriminated against. So we determined to tidy some of them up and make them look very grand and heraldic — a coat of arms. Some are used in the natural state, and some we mirrored and used as our heads.'

And the hooded figures, computer-mutated Asians and West Indians that recur repeatedly in the new work? 'They are there because we felt it. We saw it,' Gilbert said. 'We saw them every night that we go to dinner.' They have dinner at the same time every night in the same Kurdish restaurant that for George is a brisk ninety-minute walk, and for Gilbert a short taxi ride, from their home. 'A fascinating garment, yes?' George remarked of the common-or-garden hood. 'The only garment, we feel, which combines the qualities of the foreskin and the condom in one piece . . . There's no reason for honkies to do honky art.'

'You see all these Arab newspapers, you don't understand one single word, and that creates some kind of . . . tension,' Gilbert said, referring to the Arab calligraphy that swarms over the mural-like Ginkgo works. 'Don't you think? So we thought it interesting to combine typesettings that are similar to that, but in Western styles. "Ishmael". "Mohammed". But the date is in Gothic.'

They claim to have sold only two pieces to British collectors in the past fifteen years. Saatchi wasn't having any. They complain that the Tate won't hang the little they've got. But in Venice one of the most important Italian collectors will be hosting a dinner in his palazzo in honour of the dirty duo. 'And this will be hanging in the room where we are to eat,' George proudly declared. *Spit On Shit* is one of the Fundamental Pictures of 1996 and depicts no more and no less than what it says – a gob of spit sliding down two monumental turds. 'Very few art works are called *Spit On Shit*. It's about being alive in the Western world,' George said. 'What else?'

2005

21st Century
life
(in 20 stages)

see boards for
todays
puddings

BORN DEAD
CANCER
GO OUT WITH STYLE
COME AGAIN
MICGAINE
I'LL GET THESE
FUCK OFF
YOUR MUM'S DEAD
YEAH YEAH YEAH
3rD BIRTHDAY
TORTURED
FOR FUN
LOVE TAD
LIGHTS OUT
LAST ORDERS
COTTAGE PIE
PUDDINGS BY
ART FLIRT
CUNT
GOODBYE
NICE TIGHTS

THE FIRKIN BREWERY™

NIGEL GREENWOOD

The art dealer Nigel Greenwood never achieved the renown of his near-contemporaries Robert Fraser and John Kasmin. Fraser and Kasmin, who had the support of wealthy backers, a luxury that Greenwood never enjoyed, allied themselves with the second wave of British Pop artists in the early sixties and quickly found themselves bathed in the same kind of media glamour which attached itself to Patrick Caulfield, Bridget Riley, Derek Boshier and David Hockney, an artist who ascended to previously unimagined heights of fame shared only by pop stars such as the Rolling Stones and the Beatles.

Greenwood was closer in age to Hockney and his contemporaries than to the fashionable dealers who represented them. But, in art terms, he was temperamentally out of sympathy with the brasher forms of popular culture from which Pop emerged and which it, in turn, bled back into. Pop art was about 'liking things', as its avatar Andy Warhol once said. It was about surface appearance – the resounding shallows of consumer culture; the complex sheen of advertising and packaging; it was about everything bright and synthetic and American. The American Pop artists in particular were not much interested in ideas.

Nigel Greenwood's was a cooler, cleaner, more rigorous and more cerebral, even monkish, aesthetic. He was stimulated by ideas and instinctively drawn to the 'idea art' –

minimalism, conceptualism, installation, performance, and site-specific art – which he started to show at his Chelsea gallery in London from around 1970. In the commercial sector, Greenwood stood bravely alone at that time in fostering the climate for difficult, advanced art in Britain. It was rewarding but not remunerative. The Saatchi era of getting and spending, of 'I want it all and I want it now', was many years in the future. There were perhaps two serious collectors of new art in the whole country. It was an uphill struggle. To his immense credit, Greenwood never bent with the winds of fashion; he never compromised and never wavered in his commitment to work which was frequently intractable and occasionally even virtually invisible.

Conceptualism was famously about the 'withdrawal of visuality', and visitors to the Nigel Greenwood Gallery were sometimes unclear about what it was they were meant to be seeing. But the 'gallerist' (a term not invented in those days) was always discreetly on hand to point out the quiet interventions of a David Tremlett or a Richard Tuttle, or the almost imperceptible inflections in a grey monochrome Alan Charlton painting. Shows such as the grids of austere black and white photographs of pit-head winding gear and industrial cooling towers taken by the German husband-and-wife team Bernd and Hilla Becher, then unknowns, now stars of the international art firmament, were either ignored or routinely rubbished by the critics.

'I'm just used to everyone bitching about everyone,' Greenwood once said, 'treating you like an old doormat over which they want to walk. They've made their mind up in advance. Generosity is not a quality for which the British art world is renowned. Britain manages to sell itself on negativity. If I was on Broadway, I'd have to close every show immediately.

Thank God one isn't entirely dependent on the idiosyncrasies of the English press.' Greenwood had an infectious, instantly recognisable laugh and it was frequently to be heard echoing around the tall, elegant rooms of the gallery off Sloane Square.

Nigel Greenwood was born in Plymouth and grew up in the village of Noss Mayo in South Devon. He attended a prep school in Elstree, Herts, and then Sherborne School in Dorset, which he hated. He went to Christchurch, Oxford, but left after a year for a spell in Rome, during which, when he wasn't teaching geography and Latin at St George's English School, he was earning pocket money as a background extra in the Burton–Taylor *Cleopatra* and Visconti's *The Leopard*.

He was a student of Anthony Blunt's and John Golding's at the Courtauld Institute in London from 1962 to 1965 and was then taken on as manager of the Axiom Gallery in Duke Street, a few doors from where, two years earlier, Robert Fraser had opened what soon became the most fashionable gallery showing contemporary art in Europe. Kasmin was nearby, and between them they formed a key axis of a London whose new mood the poet Christopher Logue described in his autobiography as 'friendly, self-centred, improvisatory, carefree, and frivolous': 'Sexiness was flaunted and prized. There was a hint of freebooting, of danger . . . An act of will was evident: this party is going to last.'

It was a party at which Nigel Greenwood, ascetic only in his taste in art, was a welcome and enthusiastic guest. When he held his first exhibition, at a studio in Glebe Place in Chelsea in 1969, it was in a building where the Beatles had posed for the 1967 cover of *Sgt Pepper* and where the album's photographer, Michael Cooper, was still a neighbour.

In 1971 he found the space, further down the King's Road, that he would turn into London's least parochial, most independent-minded gallery and his home for the next thirty-three years. 'Downstairs I could make storage for the art and myself with even a spare room for visiting artists,' Greenwood recalled recently. 'Once the doors and radiators were removed and a coat of white paint covered all the walls, part of this unremarkable Chelsea house was ready to sail into the uncharted waters of the seventies avant-garde with what was to prove a riotously diverse crew.'

Within a few months of opening he had discovered the gallery's first art stars in the 'living sculptures', Gilbert and George. *Reclining Drunk* was a display of 200 Gordon's Gin bottles flattened as ashtrays and arranged on the gallery floor. *Underneath the Arches* featured the artists miming for hours to the old Flanagan and Allen song, standing on a canteen table. In 1974, Greenwood published *Dark Shadow*, a beautifully hand-finished book version of Gilbert and George's 'drinking sculptures', many of which had been rehearsed on a now folkloric tour to the Far East and Australia in the company of the dealer the year before.

Greenwood's involvement with artists' books continued as an integral part of the activities of the gallery. When he eventually bowed to the inevitable and transferred his business to the West End in 1985 ('some of the artists wanted the surroundings of success'), Nigel Greenwood Books expanded to sell books and catalogues to libraries and collectors all over the world, as well as publish a book list of 200 current titles three times a year.

He continued to work as an adviser and private dealer after the gallery was forced to close in 1992, but there was a sense that his huge reserves of knowledge and experience, as well as an undiminished passion for art and a rare talent for making and sustaining friendships, were senselessly underused by a public sector which would have done well to harness them.

After his cancer was diagnosed, he showed an unsettling awareness of the scandal of death, and its finality. But he continued to talk about art and artists, pumping friends for news of shows they had seen, to the end. The Donald Judd retrospective at Tate Modern was one of the last exhibitions he visited and he reported that he found its plainness and authority – its puritan spirituality – comforting. It made him feel alive.

Nigel Greenwood, art dealer, was born on 28 May 1941. He died on 14 April 2004, aged sixty-two.

2004

2 THE AMERICANS

from Willem de Kooning *to* Matthew Barney

Gordon

Warhol

Andy Warhol

1975

Gordon

WILLEM DE KOONING

Willem de Kooning's needs have always been simple. When at the age of sixty-four he visited London for the first and only time, many years ago, and was asked what he most wanted to do or see, he requested just one thing: to meet Francis Bacon. Bacon by that time, like de Kooning himself, was numbered among the select group of twentieth-century revolutionaries – including Matisse, Picasso, Léger, Klee, Soutine and Miro – whose ambition had been to achieve images of the human figure that would bear no reference to outworn art-historical conventions.

From the early fifties on, this had meant screaming, writhing, purgatorial male specimens in Bacon's case, and fierce, fleshy, no less alarming images of women in de Kooning's. The London meeting, potentially tricky, passed off amicably, with de Kooning resisting the temptation to keep up with Bacon to demonstrate his own near-legendary capacity for drinking. But arguments continue to rage in Soho and SoHo watering holes to this day as to which of the two can most justly claim the title of the world's greatest living painter.

The encounter with Bacon, at the tail-end of the sixties, was arranged by de Kooning's friend and dealer of many years, Xavier Fourcade, who attends to every detail of his existence.

It is almost entirely due to his dealer that 'Bill' de Kooning, at the age of eighty, finds himself an immensely wealthy man.

Three days before our visit, a 1953 painting of his called *Two Women*, measuring only twenty-two by twenty-eight inches, had sold for $1,980,000 at Christie's in New York, setting a new record for postwar art. Only the day before, a private collector had paid $1 million for three of his most recent paintings, sight unseen.

In the last eight years, during which he has forsworn the two-week 'benders' which have punctuated his adult life, de Kooning has enjoyed one of the most productive periods of his career. One of the things which gradually came to Fourcade's attention after he assumed control of de Kooning's affairs was the way in which, between visits to the studio, paintings which he considered 'masterpieces' perpetually disappeared. In common with most of his contemporaries who came to be grouped under the abstract expressionist banner, de Kooning has always had difficulty deciding when a painting is finished: it was his practice to repeatedly, almost ritualistically, scrape canvases down and begin all over again, layering paint on paint. Fourcade, however, by stocking the studio with a never-ending supply of canvas, has weaned him away from this wasteful habit.

The results, currently on view in London, have not met with unanimous approval. 'The largely incoherent work of a talent in decline,' was *Time* magazine's verdict on the paintings of the seventies. But these paintings, recognisably from the same hand which produced the Women series and the other masterpieces of the late forties and fifties, have already given way to those of the eighties, which history may come to regard as some of the most important work de Kooning has ever done.

It was on de Kooning's early work that the critic Harold Rosenberg based his idea of 'action painting'. The paintings on which de Kooning's reputation presently rests are characterised by muscular stabs and virtuoso slashes and spatters of paint. But even within the orthodoxies of 'action painting' he was unpredictable, suddenly abandoning abstraction in 1951 for the Women paintings which have since been described as 'unequalled in the history of art in fierceness, garishness, and hysteria'.

'You never know what to expect when you come in here,' Elaine de Kooning, his wife, said somewhat maternally. 'You never know what he's going to be up to next.' De Kooning married Elaine Fried in 1943 and separated from her in 1956. Now she is back looking after him. Another woman, the mother of his daughter, lives a short ride away from the house in East Hampton which he designed himself in the fifties, and there are childhood photographs and drawings of Jane, now twenty-eight, scattered throughout the studio and the living area.

De Kooning's Women drew their inspiration from the glossy smiles of the models in the famous 'T-zone' advertisements for Camel cigarettes (which has led Robert Hughes to describe them as looking like 'Doris Day with shark teeth . . . one of the most memorable images of sexual insecurity in American culture'). Magazine advertising still provides de Kooning with much of the raw material for his painting. This intelligence has to be gleaned from Tom, his young assistant, however, because de Kooning guards his privacy jealously. The day before he had refused to address a word to what Elaine described as a 'darling, very sweet, super-smart', but unannounced, elderly male visitor.

'I love to go out in a car. I'm crazy about weekend drives even if I drive in the middle of the week,' he once said, explaining the voluptuous landscape paintings which succeeded the

Women in the second half of the fifties. 'I love to be on those highways, you know; and they are really not very pretty . . . All those different big billboards . . . I love those grotesque signs . . . Content (in a painting), if you want to say, is a glimpse of something, an encounter, you know, like a flash.'

'The Worship of Art: Notes on the New God' was the title of an article by Tom Wolfe in last month's issue of *Harper's* magazine, and evidence of the trend is everywhere apparent in New York. The van Gogh show at the Metropolitan is sold out weeks in advance; queues start forming for Primitivism at the revamped Museum of Modern Art hours before the turnstiles open, and the new Julian Schnabel show at the Pace Gallery is as crowded as the bargain basement at Macy's.

It is easy, swept up in the hysteria, to forget that it wasn't always like this, that New York wasn't always the capital of modern art. Just thirty years ago, there were only about fifty modern artists living in New York City, compared with today's estimated 14,000, and fewer than twenty galleries. Willem de Kooning was forty-four when he was given his first one-man show in 1948 and almost sixty before he could make a decent living.

De Kooning never liked the country when he lived in Manhattan, where he settled soon after his arrival from the Netherlands in 1926. But now that he lives in the country he rarely travels into the city any more. 'He likes to be where he is. He likes to be settled,' Elaine de Kooning said, and he nodded silently in agreement. Xavier Fourcade had to hire a helicopter to get him from the house to the airport when he made what was only his second visit to Holland in fifty years, in 1976. And then he wanted to turn round and fly straight home the minute the plane touched down in Amsterdam. 'They'll take my papers away,' he protested. 'They won't let me out.'

It was the pressures of celebrity that finally drove de Kooning to East Hampton, although he had become adept at ignoring letters, the telephone, the doorbell, and refusing all invitations. He still throws all his mail away unopened unless it is intercepted and says he has never felt any sense of guilt. 'Why should I? I have time only for my work.'

He works seven days a week and had been working until shortly before our arrival on what, in the half-light, looked like a set of nine or ten fresh canvases.

Did he always work on several paintings at once? 'But they are finished!' The triumph in his voice was unmistakable. The surfaces of the new paintings are fragile and airy and predominantly white and it pleases de Kooning that visitors, more attuned to the violence and edginess of his best-known work, don't immediately 'see' them.

'Art never seems to make me peaceful or pure,' de Kooning wrote in 1951, but his art – and his person – seem to have undergone a transformation. Standing in front of the camera for almost an hour, moving only when asked to move and deploying his limbs precisely as instructed, he seemed possessed of the same serenity and lack of self-consciousness as the blooming near-white paintings ranged behind him.

Unshaven, hair dishevelled, wearing dungarees and decomposing moccasins, he was barely recognisable as the dapper, trilby-toting young immigrant. His handshake, though, is like a vice, and he prolongs it, clamping tighter, until it elicits a smile of submission.

1984

THE **Philosophy of Andy Warhol**

ELLSWORTH KELLY

Art world joke: Why are conceptual artists painting again? Answer: Because they think it's a good idea.

I tell it to Ellsworth Kelly in the hope that his reaction might throw some light on where he stands. Is he a painter of retinal pictures – that is, art designed to please the eye? Or is he at the other pole, and part of the tribe of heavy thinkers? After half a century in the top rank of international artists, it's still not that clear.

'Why are conceptual artists painting again? Hmmm . . .' He links his hands behind his head and stares hard at a piece of corner architectural detailing which he had informed me earlier was called a 'squince'. ('You need it where a square meets a dome. Helps keep the building up.') 'What is a good idea in painting?' He keeps on staring. 'Let me get it . . . Oh, yeah, I forgot, it's a joke. So tell me.' So I tell him. He's very good about it. 'That's very good!' It's the way you tell 'em. He laughs obligingly.

We are in the Serpentine Gallery in London, where Kelly's new show opens at the weekend. Although he is now in his eighties, he is still working with undiminished vigour and a firm commitment to a kind of unsentimental, anti-heroic rhetoric which several decades ago was given the name 'hard-edge' abstraction. Many of the new paintings are reliefs – monochrome canvas on monochrome canvas, yellow on red, red on blue. Others are stacked up in narrow hyperchromatic bands of colour, like billboards from which the text has been excised. 'Bright, vulgar, modern colours', as David Batchelor has written, 'in bright, vulgar, modern collisions with other bright, vulgar, modern colours.'

The colour is applied by hand, by Kelly himself, not studio assistants, but it looks machine-sprayed, mechanical; there's no sign of human intervention, just the calm, laboriously executed uniformity – 'a stunning emptiness' as it was described when it was new, in the late fifties.

Kelly belongs to the half-generation who came after the abstract expressionists and made their name for being cool, systematic and anti-gestural. He was never the type to mouth off himself, but his young friend and ally, Frank Stella, delighted in rattling the cages of Franz Kline, de Kooning (Pollock was recently dead) and the other 'painterly painters' of the New York School for him.

Stella attacked the 'transcendental nonsense' of the by-then legendary splashers and drippers. 'If you pin them down, the people who want to retain the old humanistic values in painting always end up asserting that there is something there besides the paint on the canvas,' Stella said. 'My painting is based on the fact that only what can be seen is there . . . I try to keep the paint as good as it was in the can.' Philip Leider, editor and founder of *Art Forum* magazine, famously said the new artists felt that 'anything less than the most compressed statement is fat, sloppy and boring'.

Kelly and Stella met when they were both selected to be in the landmark Sixteen Americans show at the Museum of Modern Art in New York in 1959. Kelly showed his joiner-panels of bright percussive monochromes, Stella his black bitumen paintings of monotonous, parallel 'pinstripes'. 'I felt he knew what I knew,' Kelly says. 'Right away. I got his phone number and went to see him next day.'

Kelly has always liked the colours used by Mark Rothko and intended to tell him this when they were introduced at a private view of Rothko's work in the fifties. 'But he just said, "Don't you think I need a rest?" and walked away from me. He was rather irascible.'

There is a painting in the Serpentine show which is based on colours from the less doomy part of Rothko's palette: a large rectangle of orange is combined with smaller rectangles of pale green and yellow. The crucial point for Kelly — it is the one he established his reputation making — is that the three colours are contained within their own, discrete panels and not painted onto a single canvas. The hard edges which separate them preserve the integrity of each colour. 'There's no dominance here,' Kelly says. 'It's like the relationship between the two of us: I'm a body, you're a body. If I did it as a single painting, the orange would be the main colour and the others its satellites. By doing it in panels, each has its own uniqueness. It's the difference between depicted space — a painted image — and literal space. I feel my paintings are fragments of the world and I'm simply digging them up and presenting them. I want to get more into the real world.'

He was still jet-lagged. He wasn't long off a plane from New York, where he lives in a small town in upper New York State. He was also still slightly reeling from a television programme he had turned on after checking into his hotel the night before. 'It was about these, I guess, artist brothers in London,' he says. 'A lot of pornography, and a lot of violence. I said to my friend, "I've never seen anything in America like this." I began thinking, What am I doing?'

It seems strange now, at a distance of more than forty years, to think that his own work was the cause of controversies every bit as strident as those surrounding the Chapmans. Painting was a high-stakes business in New York in those years, with reputations rising and crashing overnight. The big two warring critics, Clement Greenberg and Harold Rosenberg, were constantly carving out and shifting territories. It was ideologies at dawn. A friend of de Kooning's took issue with him when he saw he had a 'banal' Ellsworth Kelly print in his studio. 'Kelly names the colours,' de Kooning said, and Kelly still looks gratified as he repeats this. The cool style might be 'just' style, just surface, but, as John Cage pointed out, the surface was part of the depth.

Kelly had met Cage in Paris in the late forties. 'He happened to be in the same hotel I was in. This was my studio. I didn't really know who he was, but he made me feel like he liked what I was beginning to do. After he went home, he sent me a letter saying, "Oh you better come back to America." There were interesting artists coming up like Rauschenberg. He was doing the combines. I walked in on those. And I was very impressed. They were just the opposite of me. This was the heart of everything.'

Temperamentally, and in the lowered temperature which was common to their work, Kelly was more in tune with Rauschenberg's friend Jasper Johns. The three of them were contemporaries. Rauschenberg's and Johns's careers took off like rockets. Kelly's was a slower burn; his work sold sporadically at first, maybe because, at the very time New York was becoming the art capital of the world, he had gone to live in Europe, the centre from where energy had so recently leaked away. He did all the traditional European fine-art things: painted landscapes like Bonnard; hired models and drew from the nude. 'And all of a sudden,' he says, 'I started to think, I'm not

European. It was so boring to have to paint like someone else. I wanted to be a modern artist. I've always wanted to see something that hasn't been done, that you don't find anywhere else. I went to see Brancusi in his studio. I think he was an influence.'

He tells a parable-like tale about the day he nearly met one of his heroes, Picasso. 'I was walking past his Paris studio when a big car with a chauffeur pulled right up on the sidewalk. I don't think the driver saw me. I was pressed against the wall. I looked in and smiled in recognition. It was Picasso. "Do I know you?" He opened the door. If I'd got in that car my whole life could have been different.'

Kelly had said he didn't want a tape recorder used for the interview. I'd attributed that to high aesthetic reasons along the lines of Yves Klein's belief that 'colour is enslaved by the line that becomes writing' (or something). But it turned out to be more personal. 'I used to have a speech impediment when I was young,' Kelly explains. 'I'm not a quick thinker. There's always been a gap between what I'm saying and what I'm thinking. I hate to read what I've said written down. I'm slow. So I find it difficult watching films, for example. The TV. Everything's so fast. I want to look. I want time. Time to me is very important. Watching the light change in that doorway over there in the past hour, for instance. I want my painting to be like that. In the realness of it. The shadow along the top is very beautiful.'

Is he a Buddhist? 'I'm not a believer. I used to meditate when I was a kid. I met a woman right after I got out of the army. She was quite a woman. She was a faith healer, and I believed in her. She cured my terrible impediment in a week.'

'We are ghosts,' the British abstract painter John Hoyland remembers Kelly telling him once. 'Artists are ghosts. We're there, but nobody knows where we are.'

'I said that?' Kelly says. 'Did I say that?'

In the failing light, four identically shaped kite-like canvases painted blue, red, green and black have started to flicker or shimmer against the high white wall where they are hung. Prompted by the twin strands of ghosts and the army, perhaps, a memory comes to him from his days serving in Europe during the war. 'I was with a camouflage regiment. We had just found an abandoned truck full of bottles of white wine. I had set my tent up a little distance away from where the others had theirs and I was headed back to it with a book and one of these bottles of wine when this car came by. It stopped, and it was Hemingway. We registered each other. But nothing,' Kelly says. 'No words.'

Silence again. 'A painting is like a life,' he says at length, making an arc in the air with his hand. 'I like to leave it here — a little unfinished. Half open or maybe a quarter open. And not exactly about something. It's mostly about perception. I guess I have to satisfy my eyes. A [Donald] Judd was finished. It was a box.'

2005

LEO CASTELLI

As usual, Mr Castelli's appointments arranged for the afternoon had got seriously 'stacked up', and his client, a woman of mature years who had come down into the bowels of Manhattan especially, was starting to look unloved.

Her paper-thin Seiko told her that she'd been kept waiting almost thirty minutes and still Castelli, talking now in English, now in German, now in his native Italian, was phone-hopping, effortlessly suave, unflaggingly charming and apparently oblivious.

Ascending from the street in her Porsche-designed spectacles and her tailored two-piece from the Country Room at Lord & Taylor, she had stepped out of the lift into the long, blond-floored main gallery at Leo Castelli, passed through a blacked-out room in which words like 'inevitable' and 'astonish' and pictures of seagulls and children playing were being flashed on to a wall, and arrived finally, through heavy felt curtains, in the inner sanctum.

Although there was a long white counter and a battalion of pleasant young people behind it manning the weapons of modern commerce, this room, too, was hushed and seemingly roofless and in fact conformed most closely to her idea of a conventional art gallery.

The white walls were hung with the works of Castelli's most famous artists, who between them had succeeded in changing the face of modern art in the previous quarter-century: Jasper Johns, Robert Rauschenberg, Frank Stella and Roy Lichtenstein were all represented by major works; a cube of compressed metal, one of John Chamberlain's junked-car sculptures, was mounted on a plinth, while a telephone rested on one of Andy Warhol's Brillo boxes from the sixties, its front panel crazily blinking.

For a first-time buyer, which is what the lady in the Lord & Taylor suit was hoping to become, they presented a dazzling prospect.

None of the pieces in the room had sold for more than a few hundred dollars when they were first shown, and some hadn't sold at all. Now, though, if she wanted to buy one – Rauschenberg's *Bed*, say, or *Target with Plaster Casts* by Jasper Johns (neither of which happened to be for sale, being the personal trophies of Leo Castelli) – it would cost her upwards of $250,000.

It was way beyond her pocket, she confided to another 'stacked up' Castelli visitor. But after years of holes in the ground and bleeding bodies and other unembraceable forms of avant-garde art, all the talk was that the painters had once again stolen the initiative, and the thing was to get in at the basement, as it were.

Her life, so far, hadn't been without art: she had a few 'middle-range' Impressionists that had been handed down. But with dead painters – painters whose reputations were already made – collecting didn't carry the same thrill.

'This is a whole different game,' she said, unselfconsciously nursing a pamphlet titled 'Three Ways to Catch the New Wave', which indicated how seriously she was taking the whole business. 'They're not all going to come up, of course. Nothing's certain. Which makes it that much more exciting.'

At last, having patted the heads and pecked the cheeks of what seemed an endless stream of expensively beautiful young women, a pastime he fitted in between taking his international calls, Mr Castelli approached and informed the lady without ceremony that, no, he didn't yet have the right picture for her.

He said it so charmingly, though, retaining her age-dappled hand in both of his, that it came out sounding like 'yes'.

'Leo is the eternal Continental diplomat,' the American writer Tom Wolfe once wrote of Castelli, after the dealer had chastised his most *arriviste* collector for being vulgar (Robert Scull, a taxicab mogul, had wanted to buy up an entire Jasper Johns exhibition).

'His voice is soft, suave and slightly humid,' Wolfe continued. 'Every word he utters slips through a small velvet Mediterranean smile. Nobody says "No" like Castelli.'

And, true to form, the lady in the Lord & Taylor floated out of the gallery as if she'd just acquired a bullish modern master instead of being denied the opportunity of spending $25,000, the price of a David Salle, part of the New Wave and therefore 'hot' in New York — the more so for being Castelli's latest signing.

It is his ability (some have called it genius) for placing works where they will do an artist's career most good, combined with an unerring eye and a lifelong commitment to 'vanguard' art, that has kept Leo Castelli taking chances when he no longer needed to, that very quickly established him as the world's most influential dealer in contemporary art.

When Castelli arrived there from Italy at the beginning of the Second World War, New York was far from being the hub of avant-garde art that it would become only a decade and a half later.

In 1947 the art critic Clement Greenberg, a friend of

Castelli's, could still bemoan the fact that, out of a population of 140 million, the audience for the epoch-making work being done in America by the likes of Jackson Pollock, Willem de Kooning and other 'action painters' was perhaps fifty: 'a small circle of fanatics, art-fixated misfits who are as isolated in the United States as if they were living in Paleolithic Europe'.

And yet by the early sixties it was all a social chronicler of even Tom Wolfe's stamina could do to keep up with the fads and fashions and status battles raging within what he had identified as 'The New Art Gallery Society' – 'this promenade of socialites, stars, literati, culturati . . . press agents, gossip columnists, fashion designers, interior decorators, and other hierophants' who had become disciples of 'the new religion: Art!' What happened?

What mainly happened was Pop, the first genuinely popular movement in all modern art. And Pop was first sprung on the world from the house at 4 East 77th Street in Manhattan where Leo Castelli both lived and showed off the Young Turks who were dedicated to what then looked like an outrageous proposition: that making art didn't have to be an exercise in anguish and agony, as Pollock and the abstract expressionists seemed to believe. It could also be *fun*.

Pop art (and, therefore, in the opinion of many, the art business) is usually thought to have been born on 20 January 1958, the day Jasper Johns's first one-man show, featuring paintings of archery targets, letters of the alphabet and the Stars and Stripes, opened at the one-year-old Castelli Gallery, causing a sensation.

Neither Johns nor his friend and co-activist Robert Rauschenberg were themselves 'Pop artists'. But together, by breaking the spell cast by the first generation of deeply serious, heavily angst-ridden New York painters, they prepared the ground for Roy Lichtenstein, Claes Oldenburg, James Rosenquist, Andy Warhol and other, later stars of the Castelli roster, and ensured that the gallery's history became synonymous with the history of art in the third quarter of the twentieth century.

Leo Castelli was fifty when he started selling paintings from his apartment on East 77th Street, and none of his numerous friends in the New York art world could understand why it had taken him so long.

Born in Trieste, of wealthy parents, Castelli had frittered away his early years and had then been corralled into insurance and banking before following his father-in-law to the United States in 1941.

After a spell in US army intelligence he again found himself in a job that bored him, overseeing the knitted-goods division of the family textile business.

Both Castelli and his wife Ileana, however, were lifelong devotees of avant-garde literature and art; he'd part-financed a gallery in Paris (sandwiched between the Ritz and Schiaparelli) just before the war, and their Upper Fifth Avenue apartment (owned by his father-in-law) had become a place where the abstract expressionists and their circle tended to congregate.

The Castellis had the basis of a strong art collection as a result of the Paris enterprise – Léger, Kandinsky, 'lots of Dubuffets', sculpture by Antoine Pevsner.

And under the tutelage of Sidney Janis the dealer, Clement Greenberg the critic and Alfred Burr the curator of the Museum of Modern Art, Castelli spent money he says he couldn't afford, 'just out of pure love', on works by Mondrian, Gorky, Pollock, de Kooning.

'It was not at all my intention,' he says, 'to buy and sell.

Unfortunately, little by little as time went on, I sold everything. I just had to have some capital.'

Castelli had been dealing successfully but unspectacularly from his living room for several months before confirmation finally came that he was in the right business: visiting an exhibition of young unknowns at the Jewish Museum in New York at the end of 1957, he found himself confronted by an all-green painting (of a target, although he didn't realise it at the time) that picked him up and shook him and changed his life.

'It hit me in a fantastic way,' he remembers, 'so much so that I felt I must see the artist who had done a thing like that *immediately*. There was nothing like that before in my life.'

Jasper Johns's show with Castelli was an almost immediate sell-out (the Museum of Modern Art bought four pictures), a fact that prompted the now famous jibe from Willem de Kooning, that his friend Leo could sell beer cans as art if he put his mind to it.

(Leo, of course, did: Johns's bronze Ballantine Ale cans fetched $90,000 at auction in 1973 and are among the most highly prized art objects of the past thirty years.)

Robert Rauschenberg, on the other hand, was not an instant seller: only one canvas from his first show found a buyer – and she asked for a refund soon afterwards.

Castelli, though, never faltered in his commitment, as he has never failed to support any artist he has shown, sometimes to the tune of tens of thousands of dollars. Donald Judd, for instance, a now highly successful minimal sculptor, was kept on the payroll through all the years that he wasn't selling; and Dan Flavin, whose fluorescent light pieces remain difficult to place, is still guaranteed his monthly cheque.

More often, though, with Frank Stella, Kenneth Roland, Cy Twombly and Robert Morris as well as those already men-

tioned on the books, it has been a case of placating the collectors, among whom rivalry can become intense. (One regular
buyer from the gallery, learning that a Lichtenstein he had set
his heart on was already sold, snatched the painting from the
wall and made off with it down the street.)

Castelli, however, prefers to think that money is the least
part of this kind of zeal. 'I don't know anybody that buys for
investment here,' he said rather sharply. 'They may sell later on
because of the problems of insuring a painting that cost $1,200
and is now worth half a million.

'But generally speaking the people I sell to are genuine collectors, or museums, or other galleries, and I can't think of
anybody who ever bought a painting here for speculation. I
wouldn't know those people.'

In the early seventies, Leo Castelli pioneered the colonising
of the old warehouse district of Lower Manhattan known as
SoHo (south of Houston Street), where he now runs — and
personally supervises — two enormous spaces.

The traffic, from artists' 'loft' to gallery, bar to boutique, is
every bit as hectic as in the uptown, culture-rush days of the
sixties; but Castelli is no longer part of it. 'My lifestyle,' he
says, perhaps with relief, 'doesn't go in that direction any
more.'

At seventy-six, his appetite for all things new, though,
remains undiminished. 'Of course,' is his astonished reply
when asked if he has read a novel that is only beginning to be
reviewed. And after a 'dreary decade' when he took on no new
artists, he is starting to sit up and take notice again.

In a clever manoeuvre he has recently secured half shares in
the two most 'bankable' exponents of the 'New Painting' in
America: David Salle and Julian Schnabel.

The fact that it is not a move that all his established artists have found to their liking seems to have been as important as the pacemaker embedded in his heart in making him feel young again.

'The fact is, nobody expected me to get involved in this movement,' Castelli said. 'And I am glad that people are surprised. There is something there, obviously.'

1983

ANDY WARHOL

The artist as box office. 'Andy!' the hand-painted signs in the window say. 'In person! Today!' There isn't about to be a repeat of last night, when they rioted in Oxford Street – this is, after all, Mayfair; this is the Arts Council shop – but the queue started to form an hour ago and now, under barked instruction from a commissionaire, it's straggling in an orderly fashion down the street. Andy Warhol is about to autograph copies of his latest book, a 'non-fiction' called *From A to B and Back Again*.

He slips in, Viyella encasing putty. He sits where he is directed, at a bare table, and his arrival, although keenly anticipated, goes unnoticed by a large part of the shop. The Nothingness Himself. It's a description Warhol likes, and an idea it has become his life's work to promote. He's a vacuum, he has said. A mirror. He wishes he could be a machine. He would like to be plastic. 'I think everybody should be a machine. I think everybody should be like everybody. I think it would be terrific if everybody was alike.' Perhaps the best known of his sayings is the one that goes, 'In the future, everybody will be famous for fifteen minutes.' Or was it five, Andy will wonder, or perhaps thirty? He says he can't remember.

Andy Warhol has a sense of celebrity rivalled only by Muhammad Ali's. Only Warhol says next to nothing. He moves hardly at all (the muscles in his jaws are his most active part); his latex features register a permanent blank. But he is efficient. A woman from the publisher's marvels at his signing average and it's not as if he's just scribbling his name: everybody gets a version of the famous soup can, a bit sloppy in the execution, but inscribed personally and with the date.

Part of the Warhol entourage – there always is one – is a New York woman whose Jackie wig and dark glasses and make-up, spectral with a slash of crimson, make her age impossible to guess at. Roz Cole is Warhol's literary agent and, because they know all about her client's public reticence, the desperate press have descended on her. They want to know about the engagement, rumoured to be imminent, between Andy and Lord Lambton's daughter, Anne. Miss Cole appears genuinely incredulous; she waves a hand dismissively and the charms on her bracelet clang. Anne Lambton, she says, is a bright, hard-working girl and, in the months she has been employed there, she has been an absolute treasure at the Factory. It's a popular myth, she adds, that the Warhol studio on New York's Lower East Side is the hang-out of what-you-call-them . . . *freaks*, drag queens and drug addicts, that type. 'The Factory,' she says, 'is a place of work. They won't have people around who don't carry their weight. Andy's very hot on that.'

'This factory,' says an agency man, 'what is it they call it, exactly?'

Miss Cole tugs violently at her black cape and says brightly that Andy has been very active of late. There's a new film, to be called *Bad*, and two more books are on the way: a collaboration with Paulette Goddard, 'you know Paulette, the glamorous movie star', called, tentatively, *Movie Star*, and *Popism*, Warhol's proposed version of the sixties. 'Andy Warhol's,' Miss Cole says, 'is a very special talent. And he really can draw, you know. He does portraits all the time. John Richards, the director of

Knedlar's, says that Andy is just about the greatest painter there is. It's not a flash-in-the-pan thing. He's very solid.' He'd written one book, a 'novel' titled *a*, before Roz Cole persuaded him into *From A to B*, his philosophy. No, it wasn't hard, she said; once he was in possession of the first cheque, there wasn't any problem getting Andy to meet his deadlines.

Warhol is forty-five. Or forty-eight. His brothers are manual labourers in Pittsburgh, where he comes from, or else they are priests. He lives with his mother, or he lives alone. His hair he always claims to be a wig, but it's probably real. As Paul Morrissey, director of the later Warhol films, has said, Andy is a promoter who also creates, and his greatest creation is himself. This much, though, is known: the middle son of Czech parents, he was a sickly child. He suffered three nervous collapses by the time he was ten, and fell victim to St Vitus's dance; he spent his childhood in bed eating chocolate bars and playing with a doll, while his mother read Dick Tracy to him in an accent he could barely understand.

He studied to be a commercial artist at the Carnegie Institute of Technology and in 1952 moved to New York, where he took a job with a shoe company drawing shoes. As early as 1955 he had an exhibition of shoe 'portraits' painted in gold, with each shoe named after a film star, and *Life* magazine reproduced them over two pages. He drew butterflies on personal greetings cards and inscribed them 'Happy Butterflyday'. He hand-illustrated books on cats and fairies fluttering at the bottom of his garden. He dressed tastefully and was very shy.

In 1961 the large paintings he had started to make out of comic strips were exhibited in a department-store window, and within a year he had made the breakthrough. Pop art became the biggest thing to hit New York since the twist, and art openings started to take over from first nights at the theatre as 'musts' for the chic, the ambitious and the rich. Warhol was painting dollar bills, Coca-Cola bottles and Campbell's soup tins, the most commonplace images he could find, and fashionable society wasn't alone in adoring them. The critics raved. They interpreted them as being ironic, as somehow being an indictment of consumer culture, and they were entirely wrong. There was no attempt to make the objects symbolic of something else, Warhol said, to show emotion, to enlighten or create. 'I don't care. I don't care about anything, that's what my work is all about.'

He adopted the principles of the assembly line to produce 'consumer art' and turned out paintings en masse. It was easy: a photographic image – the electric chair, a race riot, a soup can, Liz Taylor – was silk-screened on to canvas, and it was a completely mechanical process that any 'assistant' could carry through as efficiently as Warhol himself. 'I tried doing them by hand,' he said, 'but I find this way it's easier. This way I don't have to work on my objects at all.'

There was nobody more famous in New York by 1963, nobody whose presence was more feverishly sought, but by then Warhol had already started to interest himself in film. His techniques in this area were to prove just as simple: a camera would be set up and things allowed – or, more often, not allowed – to happen in front of it. *Empire* was the same view for eight hours of the Empire State Building, *Kiss* was a kiss slowed down to fill eight hours. *Sleep* (six hours) was a man sleeping, *Eat* (six hours) was a man eating, and *Haircut* (eight hours) was a man having his hair cut. Predictably, perhaps, Warhol said that he liked boring things. 'My films,' he said, 'are just a way of taking up time.'

Sound came next, and primitive scenarios, and with them the Factory school of 'superstars' – Baby Jane Holtzer, Edie

Sedgwick, Viva, Ultra Violet, Candy Darling and Holly Wood-lawn, the last two being men. The transvestism and the sex apart, though, Warhol films were slowly starting to look more 'conventional'. Colour and proper scripts were experimented with, the running time was cut, and by the time they started to be distributed commercially – *Heat*, *Flesh*, *Trash* etc. – they were being directed for him by somebody else. 'I didn't expect the movies we were doing to be commercial,' Warhol said. 'It was very heady to be able to look and see our movie out there in the real world on a marquee, instead of in there in the art world.'

Again, he was successful critically as well as commercially. *Chelsea Girls*, which cost $10,000 to make, was reported to have grossed $100,000 at the box office. He was called an innovator, one of the true originals. Ultimately, though, it's the earliest work, the Campbell's soup cans, the Elvis Presleys and the Day-Glo Marilyns, that Warhol's reputation rests on. He became the highest-priced living American painter when a piece called *Campbell's Soup Can With Peeling Label* (1964) changed hands recently for £40,000.

'If Warhol had been merely the courier of images startling for their familiarity, he would have sunk out of sight in a season,' John Russell, the *Sunday Times* art critic, wrote on the occasion of the Tate retrospective in 1971. 'If he had been merely a discerning analyst of the State of the Nation in high art, he could have become a quietly hermetic figure, known mainly to specialists. But he interlocked the two in ways which ensured the widest possible publicity on the one hand, and a genuine historical importance on the other. Timing counted,' Mr Russell added, 'but pertinacity counted too. And when it comes to pertinacity, Warhol is in the class, appearances not withstanding, of Bismarck and Mao Tse-tung.'

The doors of the Ritz revolved slowly and, looking lost, Andy Warhol stepped out of them. The interview was for five o'clock, and it was ten to. He hung back while the friend he was with collected his room key for him, and he concentrated hard on the floor. Being touched is one of the phobias Andy admits to and so he was reluctant to shake hands, but he submitted. He was wearing exactly what he'd been wearing earlier at the signing: a well-worn jacket of printed velvet, a tie with dachshunds on and the button-fly jeans that seemed to be de rigueur throughout his camp. He had his tape recorder, of course (his wife, he calls it), and he was carrying the catalogue of an exhibition he'd just been to. Had he enjoyed it? 'Well . . . yes,' he said. 'Such an, ahhh, big gallery.' Silence. 'So many paintings.'

'The interviewer should just tell me the words he wants me to say and I'll repeat them,' Warhol has always said. 'I'm so empty I can't think of anything to say. I'm not more intelligent than I appear. If you want to know all about Andy Warhol, just look at the surface of my films and my paintings and me, and there I am. There's nothing behind it.' Valerie Solanas, who shot and nearly killed him in 1968, claimed afterwards that she was motivated only by frustration; talking to Warhol, she said, was like talking to a chair.

Because the lift was small, it afforded the opportunity on the way up of studying Warhol's face at close quarters. His nose, which is something else he's got a thing about, was red and veinous blue, the only touch of colour in a mask that looked as though it might be as collapsible, and as rubbery-smelling, as any joke-shop purchase. The natural pallor was exaggerated by an all-over foundation of pimple cream.

'The albino-chalk skin. Parchment like. Reptilian. Almost blue. The greying lips. The pin-head eyes. The bored languor.

The shadowy, voyeuristic, vaguely sinister aura. The skin and bones . . .' It's no accident that Warhol knows his press clippings by heart, or that, if the book is to be believed, he can sometimes be found in the mornings reciting them to his second-best friend, his mirror.

A human skull, which Warhol had picked up in Paris, was the single sign that suite 108 was being lived in. Warhol settled himself on an upright chair, but his companion, after removing a jacket to reveal scarlet braces, picked up the telephone. 'Could I have the *service d'étage?*' he said. Roz Cole had talked a lot about somebody called Bob Colacello, the executive editor of Warhol's magazine *Interview* and, apparently, Andy's amanuensis. 'He's very intelligent,' she'd said. 'Very smart. Bob takes charge of everything. He'll answer for Andy. I wouldn't advise ignoring him.' So was it Bob in the braces?

Warhol chuckled, briefly. No, he said, this was Fred, his business manager, Fred Hughes. The name seemed familiar and I asked wasn't he the sound man on some of the early pictures? 'He thinks you were a sound person, Fred.' Warhol laughed again. Fred, still on the phone, cupped his hand over the receiver. 'I was, Andy. *Lonesome Cowboys*. And on *L'Amour, Naked Restaurant* . . .'

'You used to do sound? You did not!' Warhol seemed honestly to have forgotten. '. . . and on *Blue Movie*,' Fred said. 'I ran the whole thing. I was doing the business then, too. I just did the sound so badly in the end they hired somebody else. The next sound man became a director.' Andy was still saying 'gee' when I wondered whether he still lived with his mother. 'Ahh,' he said, 'she's, ah, still around.'

She used to do paintings and sign them 'Andy Warhol's Mother'. Was she still doing that? 'No,' he said. 'No, not too much. Gee, though, we went to dinner last night, I can't remember where, and we met some playwright. We met that really great playwright. What's his name, Fred? Harold Pinter!'

'Did you get into conversation?'

'Just hello,' Andy said. 'And goodbye.'

'With a long gap in between.'

'About three hours.'

I asked him about the book he was planning on the sixties. 'I don't think it's going to be interesting unless I get some sex into it,' he said. 'I don't know about sex though, so I don't know how I'm going to do it. I'll have to go back and ask people if they had sex in the sixties, what the intrigue was.'

The door opened and a man came in carrying a small package. This one was Bob Colacello. 'Bob Bowlacherries,' Andy said. 'What you got there? What'd you buy me, Bob? What'd you buy me?'

'I just had my hair cut,' Bob said. 'Just across the hall. The old man was so sweet. He said I had beautiful hair but that it would be 30 per cent better if I massaged it every day with this brush.'

Andy pointed out that Colacello's 'champagne chin' was noticeable now, and decided he was hungry. 'How about some sandwiches, Bob? Or some cookies. Oh, and petits fours. They're colourful. We didn't have any lunch. We had leftovers.' Roz Cole arrived then, and then a photographer and his assistant. Fred Hughes's room service was admitted and two minutes later there was another knock. 'These two boys are models,' Andy said. 'From Paris. Tom and Jerry. Did you work today, Tom?' Tom said he was trying to contact Bianca Jagger who was on the loose in the hotel, but that she kept pretending to be her maid. He made Andy a present of a box of shortbread. Bob Colacello, meanwhile, had been called to the telephone. 'The contracts,' he was saying, 'are all wrong. We want to be paid immediately, up front . . . That's ridiculous. Every foreign publisher does . . . Well, tell them we're not usual . . . And we're not giving them the magazine rights before publication . . .'

'I started as a commercial artist, and I want to finish as a business artist,' Andy Warhol has written in his book. 'After I did the thing called "art", or whatever it's called, I went into business art. During the hippy era people put down the idea of business – they said "money is bad" and "working is bad", but making money is art and working is art and good business is the best art.

'It's just turning out a product and you have to worry about it, so that's why it becomes business,' he said. 'The painting's the only thing that keeps our office running, so you work to turn out a few just once in a while. *Chelsea Girls*. That movie made ten dollars.' Fred and Bob between them had been over-anxious and new orders of tea and biscuits kept arriving. Several dozen books were delivered. Warhol's British publisher breezed in.

'Did you see the Andy Warhol lookalike who turned up this morning?' the publisher said. 'Wasn't that sinister? What d'you think he's up to, that guy? Where d'you think his head's at, as you say in your country? He was obviously a deliberate imitation of Andy. He had a gold chain round his neck with an "A" on it. Did you see?'

Two years ago the American magazine *Esquire* set out to examine the paradox that is Andy's Warhol teen appeal. In an article called 'Andy's Children: They Die Young', it catalogued the deaths of several of those directly connected with the Factory or with Warhol's films: Andrea Feldman jumped from the eighteenth floor of an apartment building shortly before the release of *Heat*, in which she starred; Edie Sedgwick, an early superstar, died of a drug overdose; Jeremy Dixon, who used to help edit *Interview*, died the same way; Bruce Pecheur, part of the Andy repertory, was stabbed to death at home; Candy Darling was at the time dying of cancer.

'Warhol,' the article said, 'passes through life surrounded by the young. Kids run away and wander into his studio, into his life, or he finds them at parties or in the streets, or they are brought to him by his friends much as people give each other gifts . . . Warhol likes to look at them. He is observant. He listens and condones. And from them he learns so much about American experience that his work always reflects trends in the culture long before the rest of us catch on.'

In a room that by now was in turmoil, in which the extravagances of room service had pushed the occupants to the walls, Warhol was the peaceful centre, silently sipping tea and nibbling on dry toast. There was nothing he wanted to say, he said, about the *Esquire* article. 'You talk about it, Bob. The guy who wrote it was your friend.'

'It was just so many lies,' Colacello said. 'For example, saying that Candy Darling refused all cancer treatment because she wanted to die. He knows we sent the best doctors to Candy, she was in the best hospital, she got every possible treatment, you know. From way back, because of his reputation more than the reality, Andy has tended to attract some nutty types. But that article was just all lies. The same writer, he did a piece on Jim Bailey, the female impersonator, which was so vicious and pathetic.'

'I like Jim Bailey,' Andy said. 'He's just a hard-working person. He's an entertainer. He tries to entertain people. Like us.'

Somebody asked about the wounds from the time of the Solanis shooting and Andy undid his shirt to show that he was still wearing a corset. The actual scars were currently on show

at the Museum of Modern Art in New York, he said, photographed by Richard Avedon.

1975

'Natural death seems far less natural than unnatural death,'
Rebecca West once wrote. 'It is much more difficult to understand than somebody dying because they have been stabbed or
shot or poisoned by somebody that hates them.'

Nineteen years ago, Andy Warhol was shot by somebody
who hated him – Valerie Solanas, a bit-part player in one of the
early Warhol underground movies, *I, A Man*, and a founder
member of SCUM, the Society for Cutting Up Men. Many
people would have considered it less shocking for Warhol to
have died in those circumstances – violently, at the hands of
somebody who felt that her life was being 'controlled' by him
– than in his sleep after a routine gall-bladder operation in a
New York hospital.

An unnatural death would, in many ways, have seemed the
logical outcome of the unnatural existence he sustained
throughout the sixties, surrounded by what the British artist
Richard Hamilton has recently described as 'the dregs of
humanity in New York – transvestites, homosexuals, drug
addicts; every kind of extrovert personality in this field who
became part of his circus'.

It would have been a prototypical, late-twentieth-century
American death for a – possibly *the* – prototypically late-
twentieth-century American. Famously obsessed with
celebrity, sex, trivia, trash, flash and money, Warhol, especially in the early work for which he is most likely to be
remembered, also betrayed a fascination with the tragically
dead – Marilyn Monroe, the graveside Jackie Kennedy – and

peculiarly twentieth-century ways of dying: car smashes, assassination and the electric chair.

It is evidence of the ambiguity of the messages that he was constantly sending out – some of his electric chairs, for example, were in go-go yellows and purples – that a number of commentators in America refused to take the attempt on his life seriously. 'If he recovers, we'll find out it was one big Pop art joke, and Andy'll be laughing all the way to the bank,' a New York television station reassured its viewers. In the sort of double bluff that was characteristic of him, Warhol's wounds went on show in the Museum of Modern Art a few months later, photographed by the super-chic Richard Avedon.

'Andy liked to make you believe he was without depth or substance. He was flippant,' says his friend Bianca Jagger. 'It was his talent to make it all seem easy and superficial.'

A whole generation before 'the blank generation' of Johnny Rotten and alienated youths for whom he was both a role model and a trailblazer, Warhol was glorying in the title of The Nothingness Himself. Asked to express an opinion, he would invariably reply, 'I, um, ahh, gee . . . I dunno.' The paintings were often executed by one of his battalion of assistants. The films that went out under the brand name Warhol were usually directed by somebody else. He sent a stand-in on a lecture tour of America, and audiences were convinced by the putty-like complexion and silver-white synthetic wig. In public at least, everything and everybody was indiscriminately 'ahh, great'.

'He had this obsession with indifference,' Richard Hamilton has said. 'A total unwillingness to be committed to any kind of social attitude or morality or image or aesthetics.' For Hamilton, Warhol's epic neutrality and passivity constituted 'a kind of saintly presence'. To Peter Blake, on the other hand, who, with Hamilton, was the pioneer of Pop art in

Britain, it showed itself as an almost criminal self-centredness and disregard.

'The one thing you can't forgive him,' Blake says, 'is the litter of broken lives. A bit like Muhammad Ali, he left a trail of dereliction. Ali did it by torturing people in the ring. Andy Warhol . . . well, it was a very odd set-up, wasn't it?'

'Voyeur-in-chief to the marginal and the rich' is what he was dubbed by Robert Hughes, the art critic of *Time* magazine. 'Warhol's insight was that you do not have to act crazy; you can let others do that for you.'

This view of him as a kind of malign Pied Piper is one which is strenuously resisted by Warhol's friends.

Bianca Jagger: 'He was an observer. All right, at the worst he could be called a voyeur. But he was an observer of *everything*. He had collections of tapes of people talking, photographs — he wanted to leave behind a documentary of his times.'

Lou Reed, frontman of Warhol's group the Velvet Underground: 'He had a very strong work ethic; he was very exciting to be around. This talk of decadence and ruined lives is absurd.'

Nick Rhodes, of Duran Duran: 'He had a great spirit. Even at dull parties, he *always* made it fun. He looked for the interesting element. If I thought somebody was interesting, I'd always take them to meet Andy.'

Anthony d'Offay, who gave Warhol his last show in Britain, in July 1986: 'All other Pop-art figures pale in comparison with him. His genius was to stay in touch with very young people, and to live in the present.'

At the time of his death, aged anything between fifty-five and fifty-nine, Warhol was still keeping abreast of the times. He had conferred his blessing on the new 'delinquent aesthetic', which much of his own work prefigured, by collaborating with two of the leading young exponents of graffiti art. He had acquired the film rights to Tama Janowitz's *Slaves of New York*, the 'hot' new book by the 'hot' young writer in town. He had directed a promotional video for Curiosity Killed the Cat, the pretty young British group who were on the cover of *Smash Hits* the week he died.

He had renounced junk food for health foods. He had hired an exercise instructor and, his body concealed by a black T-shirt at all times, had started to work out and jog. 'The silver-haired idol of the jet-set', 'the worst but most importantly influential artist alive' (Norman Mailer), was clearly not contemplating his demise. The excitement of being a modern person was still coursing through his veins.

'I just thought that things were magic,' Warhol once said, 'and that you would never die.'

1987

JAMES TURRELL

James Turrell — burly, bearded, with a taste in clothes that might best be described as tall-in-the-saddle professorial (tweed jackets, bolo ties) — doesn't immediately strike you as somebody who has spent his life working in a medium as flimsy and evanescent and, well, lightweight as light.

But Turrell uses light the way other artists use paint and canvas and wood and stone. He projects it undiluted onto walls and colours it up and floods or filters it into rooms to create environments that to some are simply pretty, trippy spaces, but which, to a growing number of others, represent the most important spiritual art currently being made in America.

Turrell grew up in California and is one of a line of West Coast artists, dating back to Richard Diebenkorn and forward to John McCracken, who have made the high, clear, tonal light of southern California into a subject.

His father was an aeronautical engineer and amateur ornithologist, and Turrell himself, who is now fifty, has been flying for more than thirty years. Throughout the sixties and seventies he held himself aloof from the New York-dominated gallery-dealer system and subsidised his work as an artist by renovating antique aircraft, running an air-messenger service and working as an aerial cartographer.

'I think the art world does work a lot with art as treasure,' he says, 'and this certainly is not my major interest. I try to retain the quality of the knowing naive. This is difficult to do. And it also involves the protection of oneself from, you know, art-world cynicism. I think what's been distasteful in recent years is for the yuppie, or whatever it is, to see art looked upon as just a career.'

The writings of Saint-Exupéry were an early influence, and many of Turrell's light installations are poetic evocations of weather phenomena encountered while flying – squall lines, thunderstorms, foggy scrims, dense curtains of rain and stacking cloud layers. He says that flying for him has always been like being in the studio. 'It's a front seat. Definitely for looking at atmosphere and things that occupy this ocean of air. We do tend to perceive the sky as always being out there, away from us. So although we're living at the bottom of an ocean of air, we don't feel to be immersed in it.' He wants the spaces he creates to be an expression in light of what is outside. 'My desire,' he says, 'is to set up a situation to which I take you and let you see. It becomes your experience.'

Wedgework and *Trace Elements*, two of the pieces Turrell showed at the Hayward Gallery in the summer, were large, adjacent rooms connected by a blacked-out corridor. *Wedgework* consisted of a walk-in box with one side pushed back to admit an expansive, hot-red, translucent atmosphere that seemed to billow portentously, like dry ice floating in behind Arthur ('I am the god of hellfire') Brown on a *This is Cilla* set of the sixties.

In *Trace Elements*, a dim, purple-grey, Rothko-like rectangle hovered at the end of an only slightly less tenebrous room. After five or ten minutes, the centre of the rectangle (actually a shallow recess side-lit with ambient halogen light) seemed to resonate slightly, while the edges blurred into a pale violet ether. If you willed it to happen very hard, the surface seemed to hover outward or marginally recede, but in truth there was very little in the way of visual incident.

The lack of substance in Turrell's work, its dependence on light and the property of light to define space, volume and colour, has led inevitably to comparisons not only with Mark Rothko but also with Barnett Newman and Ad Reinhardt. Turrell accepts these: part of the legend that is fast attaching itself to him is that as a young art student he had fallen in love with the American abstract paintings that were projected on the wall day after day, only to discover that he was disappointed by the comparative deadness of the originals. He realised that what really interested him wasn't painting but the numinousness of projected light, and he started to use light as his material.

'Visionary', 'messianic', 'apparitional', 'transcendental' are words that are frequently used in connection with James Turrell's work. Several critics have credited them with ecstatic revelation and with metaphysical intimations. 'Sublime, sublime, sublime, sublime: the reflexes go clickety-clack,' the critic Robert Hughes once scoffed at the Rothko idolaters. But Hughes gave an ecstatic review to Turrell's first museum show, at the Whitney in New York in 1981: 'In contemplating these peaceful and august light chambers, one is confronted – perhaps more vividly than by any current painting – with the reflection of one's own mind creating its illusions and orientations, and this becomes the "subject" of the work. The art, it transpires, is not in front of your eyes. It is behind them.'

In 1977, Turrell acquired an extinct volcano called Roden Crater in the Painted Desert in Arizona. Here, at a cost of several million dollars, he is making a series of spaces 'that will engage celestial events' – dawn, sunset ('nightrise'), the moon and the stars. Lying at the bottom of the crater, looking up, visitors will be able to experience 'celestial vaulting' – the tendency of the eye to see the sky as a curved, finite dome rather than as a vast, shapeless expanse.

'The crater is bigger and higher than the Pyramids,' Turrell says, 'but, in this instance, the pyramid is already made – you just have to put the chambers in. There are ten, each about the cost of an American middle-class home – under $300,000. So there you have the basic price of it. It's not that bad. It's just taken a little while to get it done, y'know. It's a long-term goal.'

Turrell's first British show, at the Anthony d'Offay Gallery in 1991, was seen as heralding the end of eighties rapaciousness and crassitude. To the *Daily Telegraph*, he was 'the greatest artist of the twenty-first century'. Other reviewers, not noted for their receptiveness to preternatural experience, let out a unanimous 'Oh wow!'

'Epiphanies' in the Joycean sense – moments in which 'the soul of the commonest object seems to us radiant' – are what Turrell's work is about: 'disciplined presentation of the lush sublime', in his own words. But James Joyce also differentiated between sentiment and sentimentality, likening sentimentality to 'unearned emotion'.

The work Turrell showed in London this year (early, hard-edged light projections ran at d'Offay to coincide with the Hayward show) seemed unwilling to earn the aimed-for complexity of response in the viewer and to want to achieve their effects shorthand. Coming to *Wedgework* and *Trace Elements* and the projector pieces was like reading the celebrated close of Joyce's *The Dead* in isolation from the story's preceding fifty pages.

This, as it happens, is how the youthful Joyce intended his epiphanies to be read. Experience taught him that they would have to give up their disembodied existence to become part of a narrative; that he would have to form these isolated spasms of insight into a linked chain of moments in which 'the soul is born'.

Air Mass, Turrell's most successful piece at the Hayward, was also the one that most effectively incorporated the idea of time; of change and experience, and of narrative, though not necessarily linear, development. In other words: something happened. And that something was the changing colour of the sky, as seen through the cutaway roof of a tall temporary structure on the Hayward balcony, and modified – to a deep velvety blue on clear evenings – by hidden fluorescent uplighters. Come dusk, the benches were lined with grey-faced city dwellers, trying to be put in touch with their other, 'cosmic' selves.

'From the period of Giotto on,' Turrell says, 'there's been a look at things beyond this life with art. And the fact that artists engage in this activity when they could be doing other things which might perhaps actually earn them a more decent living is certainly a sign of optimism and hope.

'I was a Quaker. I'm no longer a go-to-meetings Quaker. I have fallen away a bit. I found perhaps more of what I was interested in in this kind of work than I did in these other religious forms. I honour where I came from; I feel fine about it. It's not a bad experience at all. But I'm not interested in brand names.'

1993

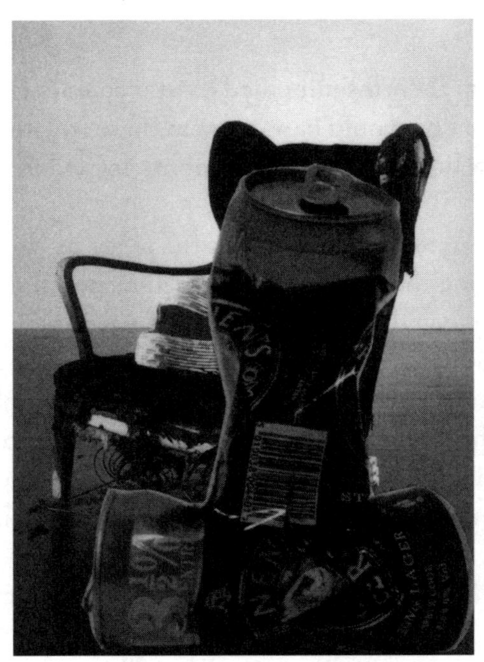

Gordon & Carol.
I'm off to Japan on thursday.
I don't know if you're going
away for the summer. I'm
back 11th July. It would be
good catch up with you in
July or August if at all
possible — otherwise it's going
be October. Sorry again
for fucking it up.
love
Sarah.

Sarah Lucas
Is Suicide Genetic?   1996
Mixed media, 100 x 85 x 65 cm
Collection Gabriela and Thomas Pitrowski-Rönitz
Courtesy Contemporary Fine Arts, Berlin
© The Artist
Published by the Hayward Gallery, SBC, London 1997
Printed by Expression Printers Ltd

JULIAN SCHNABEL

Julian Schnabel has been compared by his harsher critics to a baby hippo, beef-on-the-hoof and a Strasbourg goose. The hottest young artist on two continents, in other words, and whichever way you look at it, he's big.

The great new genius of American painting also goes in for Rocky Balboa singlets and *On the Waterfront* T-shirts rolled back to his armpits, which doesn't help. Julian's been lifting a few weights this year because he wasn't doing anything and his wife thought he was getting kinda fat, but the evidence of a Brooklyn-Jewish childhood and an adult passion for Tex-Mex cooking hasn't nearly been worked off.

If Schnabel is big, however, Schnabels are bigger, and made of even tougher stuff: oil on linoleum, aluminium, elk horn, buffalo hide and timber; and, most notoriously, oil, in the form of mythical and pseudo-religious imagery, crudely splashed on to plaster and a scabby surface of broken plates.

Six years ago, examples of Schnabel's bombastic, heavy-duty painting could be picked up for $3,000. Charles Saatchi, who owns more Schnabels than any other private collector, started buying when they cost even less. The paintings currently on show at the Waddington Gallery in London are priced at between $55,000 and $125,000 each.

Agony, Schnabel once wrote, was the reason he started painting. 'Maybe I make paintings larger than I am so that I can step into them and they can massage me into a state of unspeakableness,' he has said. He is as garrulous as his friend Andy Warhol is ungiving in the presence of strangers and, having committed a new Christian name to memory, instantly goes into his rap.

It is a rap full of words like 'imagistic' and 'deconstruction' and sentences which seem to have no beginning and no end. 'Even in these paintings that are completely embedded in their own materialism in order to exist,' he begins, setting off up Cork Street, and continues in the gallery, in the basement library, in the back of the Daimler and in the lift at Claridge's, as he walks through the door of his suite.

He has transferred his patronage from the Ritz to Claridge's, he says, ever since the Ritz misplaced a smoked salmon that his father-in-law had given to his wife. His wife, it appears, is in Belgium with their two daughters, Lola Montes and Stella, recuperating from the trip to India they have just made.

'Let me read something I wrote just the other day in the airplane,' he says, opening an exercise book and beginning to pick his way through the notes for an essay to be called – he announces the title with all the earnestness of a fourth-former called out before the school – 'The Performance of Making a Painting'.

The hottest painter on two continents, it's becoming obvious by now, is intent on talking himself out of the 'Lifestyle' ghetto and on to the heavyweight pages further on in the 'Review'. But just how important this is to him only becomes apparent when the photographer arrives.

'Why is there a picture of me?' he wants to know. 'This notion of the art star, the superstar . . . What I'm saying is, the function of just emanating information is innately embedded in . . . I mean, if there's this picture of me here, that just feeds the fuel for the existence of this figure in the landscape. You know what I'm saying?'

Well, no, not really. Not quite. In the selected bibliography published in the latest catalogue of his work, he has, after all, included a profile of his wife in American *Vogue*. In March Jacqueline and Julian Schnabel – 'If you want to know my idea of glamour, it was marrying Julian,' Jacqueline confesses – were photographed in their East 20th Street duplex apartment with the Forties Knoll table in the dining room, the rolled-steel sleigh bed, designed by Julian, in the bedroom and the Max Beckmann self-portrait in the living room. This is in addition to the 'custom-designed home' they have had built on Long Island. 'Young, attractive, active', the captions purred. 'The time, easily, is theirs.'

They have also recently accommodated American *House and Garden* and *Vanity Fair*. *Vanity Fair* tricked them, Schnabel says, into using some pictures taken privately by Helmut Newton whom they had met only once, the night before, at Mr Chow's in Los Angeles. 'This guy wrote that there's a brooding emotionality in Helmut's pictures of me that is never quite achieved in my paintings. It was just a lot of very nasty, bitchy things, and a big mistake as far as I was concerned.'

It was exactly the sort of mistake, however, and exactly the sort of exposure that has led Robert Hughes, the art critic of *Time*, to denounce 'the gross and transparent promotional mechanisms' behind Schnabel's career. 'The larger the art public gets, the more show biz it wants [and] in Schnabel collectors nourished on the legend of abstract expressionism, have found a temporary surrogate for the [Jackson] Pollocks they cannot buy,' he wrote.

Schnabel started to denounce Hughes, claiming that there

is nothing so overestimated as the pleasures of fame, when he was interrupted by a knock at the door. It was a five-by-three-foot floral display, and the two women carrying it could hardly manoeuvre into the room. 'That's why I went with the Pace Gallery,' Julian said, joking-not-joking. 'They send me bouquets.'

1985

JEFF KOONS

'So much of the world is advertising, and because of that, individuals feel that they have to present themselves as a package.' It is one of the most-quoted things Jeff Koons has said. Fresh off the plane from New York (and back on it again in under twelve hours), he had clearly given some thought to his personal self-presentation for an eight-hour stretch that was going to take in a picture session, this interview, a private view of his latest work at the most bijoux of the American dealer Larry Gagosian's several spaces in London, a public grilling at the Serpentine Gallery in Hyde Park, followed by a dinner at which he would be expected to, if not scintillate, then at least give value to the assembled collectors and museum people in an impenetrable, Warholian, Sphinx-like manner. One of the great showman self-promoters of the last twenty years, the bridge between Andy Warhol and Damien Hirst, Koons is aware that, in a world geared to the shock of the new, spooky ordinariness — wife, children, a gee-whizz love of life and the everyday vulgar and unexceptional — can command garrulous attention.

The persona Koons had chosen to come packaged in was, like the work which has earned him a place in the forefront of America's most influential living artists, fugitive and particularly difficult to read. The neat business suit, the clubman's tie and the salt-and-pepper brush-cut hair suggested both the head buyer in the men's apparel department at Bloomingdale's and a retired astronaut still out of joint with life on earth.

'I believe in advertisement and media completely,' Koons has said. 'My art and personal life are based on it.' In an interview many years ago he described his idea of pleasure. Dining with a group of friends, he recalled, he was moved to propose a toast. How lucky he was, he announced, to be in a beautiful place, surrounded by people he liked . . . As he stood there, he remembered, in a state of bliss, it was like being in an advertisement.

Koons had already brought ad campaigns — for alcohol and Nike trainers — into his work, and, with his factory-fresh vacuum cleaners suspended in their neon-lit perspex cases and luxury objects switched straight from showroom to gallery, he seemed to equate art works with commodities directly. Some critics interpreted Koons's work as being a critique of consumer capitalism: he had returned the Duchamp-inspired ready-made to its status as a product. For others though, such as the critic Benjamin Buccloh, Koons was 'only pretending to engage in a critical annihilation of mass-cultural fetishisation'. In reality he was effectively acting out what Walter Benjamin had predicted long ago for capitalist society: the cultural need to compensate for the lost aura of art and artist with 'the phony spell' of the commodity and the star. By 1992, and his very public marriage to the Hungarian-born Italian ex-porn-star Ilona Staller (known as La Cicciolina), he had achieved the kind of crossover celebrity only previously experienced by the artist with whom he clearly has most in common, Andy Warhol.

Show Koons a camera and an audience and, as my few hours in his company were to prove, he effortlessly snaps into 'Jeff Koons' mode. He is disarming, eloquent, charming, intrigu-

ingly wacko — preternaturally knowing and alarmingly innocent; the whole package. Produce a notebook, however, and
proceed to ask him about his work in a conventional interview
situation (in this case, the back seat of a chauffeur-driven car
between engagements) and something within him freezes, a
light clicks off. Like Warhol, whose second-most-famous saying was 'the surface of me is all you get', he feels 'comfortable'
speaking on the phone.

In the gallery, alone apart from a swirling coterie of fashionably dressed, ferociously efficient young women from
Gagosian London and New York, he said he didn't want to
answer any questions because he might get asked the same
ones at the Serpentine later, and the idea of somebody hearing
him say the same thing twice made him feel uneasy: 'It feels
like I don't mean it.'

'What else gets shown here?' Koons asked the woman in
charge of the Gagosian Gallery in Mayfair. 'Oh,' she said,
'Larry calls it his "treasure chest".' It is a tiny space, no deeper
than a department-store window. From the street, Koons's
newest piece, *Cracked Egg (Blue)*, looked like the beginning of
an upmarket window display which would be completed with
bewigged mannequin models later. (The slightly sinister synthetic wigs and disembodied swatches of hair that showroom
dummies wear have been a feature of Koons's recent Easyfun-
Ethereal paintings, overlaid on backgrounds of melted cheese
and syrup-sodden pancakes and other technicolour junk
food.)

Cracked Egg is a sculpture made of high-chromium stainless
steel that has been engineered to standards no less precise, and
to a finish even more reflectively immaculate, than those on
the cars in the Porsche showroom a few doors away. The new
work is in two parts — a six-foot-tall, mirror-laminated egg and

its jagged 'lid' — and is a continuation of the Celebration series which Koons started in the mid-nineties. Previous paintings and sculptures in the series include kitschy inflated Valentine hearts and fake satin ribbons and bows, as well as Koons's signature sculpture, the balloon dog — 'like a balloon that a clown would maybe twist for you at a birthday party'.

It has been claimed that the works in the Celebration series 'conjure up a positive fundamental view not unlike the boundless trust with which a child looks at the world'. As a boy in the provincial backwater of York, Pennsylvania, where his father was an interior decorator, Koons earned pocket money by selling gift wrappings and chocolates door to door. 'I'd present the product, and people would buy it, and it was nice,' he once told David Sylvester. 'I felt it was a way of meeting people's needs. So I was always good in sales.'

Cracked Egg, as the title implies, is the only work in the Celebration series in which fracture or assault of the shiny, happy surface has taken place. Koons is on record as saying that he never consciously sits down to try to create a work that is optimistic and which at the same time has a dark side. He wants his work to be 'a support system for people to feel good about themselves, to have their life be as enriching as possible, to make them feel secure — I don't tend to be pulled towards the idea of making a menacing work.' But *Cracked Egg*, in its shatteredness and sharp edges, seems to cry out for a reading which invokes the spirit of post-9/11 America, and specifically the sense of violation which is evident even now in New York, the city where Koons lives and works.

'It's interesting,' he says. 'They're all about holidays — the hanging-heart Valentines, Thanksgiving, maybe even Christmas. The egg is about Easter, birth and rebirth, in art-historical terms the Botticelli *Venus*. But with the egg there's a sense of loss. There was an abduction. My son was abducted. By my wife.'

Did he ever get him back? 'No.'

Has he remained in touch with him? 'I'm supposed to be able to see him, but I'm not able to. It's complicated. We're supposed to be able to talk, but we can't. I started the Celebration works right before Ludwig was abducted. I continued with them because I wanted to let my son know I was thinking about him. He's fourteen now. When he turns eighteen I hope the first thing he'd want to do is get on a plane.'

Ludwig was born in 1992, the year after Koons began his association with Ilona Staller. In addition to a son, Made in Heaven is the legacy of their collaboration. It is a collection of sexually explicit photographs and kitschy, craftsman-made sculptures of Koons and Staller which marries the pornographic (*Dirty – Jeff on Top*, *Blow Job*) to the teeth-rottingly banal (*Cherubs*, *Three Puppies*).

The photographs haven't lost their power to shock. There was a definite frisson even among the predominantly young, laid-back Serpentine audience when the painting *Ilona's Asshole* flashed up on the multiple video monitors. This was followed by some disbelieving glances when Koons confided that 'what I love about the picture are the pimples on Ilona's ass. That openness, generosity, the sense of self-acceptance.' Back in the car, he explains that the works in Made in Heaven were inspired by Masaccio's *The Expulsion* – 'the guilt and shame on Adam and Eve's faces in the painting. I wanted to make work that showed what it was like to be tranquil and not feel shame about the body. Whatever anybody's history is, it's perfect. It can't be any different. I would tie this to nature.'

Koons's interlocutors in Rem Koolhaas's semi-inflated pavilion on the lawn in front of the Serpentine Gallery were

Koolhaas himself, a Dutchman, and the gallery's energetic young German co-curator, Hans Ulrich Obrist. Koons was bookended by the two European intellectuals who took it in turn to try to penetrate beyond his very American resolve to be 'really friendly, and really positive and optimistic'.

The American Pop artists were not much interested in ideas. Pop art was about 'liking things', as Warhol once said. Koons, who says his art is 'about aspects of entertainment' and believes that 'salespeople are on the front line of culture', is the true inheritor of that tradition. 'You know, Hans Ulrich . . .' he would begin, smiling sweetly, gently refusing a question on the Baudrillardian reading of the commodity-as-sign. Or, again in response to an abstract question, 'Well, Rem, the answer to that is quite simple: the money didn't come.' I was repeatedly reminded of something he once told Sylvester: 'My painting is really, for me, about my background. I was trying to show that I come from a provincial background. Eventually, over a period of time, the provincial always wins.'

When Koons was growing up in Pennsylvania, his father had a furniture showroom which one day would be a living room and a week later a kitchen. 'The fact that Jeff grew up around commercialism and marketing, and the fact that a kitchen wasn't really a kitchen – wasn't really anything – resonates with the hollowness we have today,' his friend Tom Ford, a former creative director of Gucci, has said.

Koons has remarried. He spends time with his wife and their three children on the farm that used to belong to his grandfather in the countryside close to where he grew up. John Updike's family farm, the setting for many of his novels, is also in Pennsylvania. Is Shillington anywhere near York? This draws a blank. 'I don't read books,' Koons says. 'I only see magazines and newspapers. Images. The flood of images. I enjoy narrative through the visual. The great thing about art is that it brings all the disciplines of the world together – literature, philosophy, psychology, science. But, you know, I only really like to be in the studio with the people I regard as my extended family, my assistants. You try very much to be in the moment, looking at everything in the world all the time, putting it into play.'

Dennis Potter was a writer, but he wrote for television, the great indiscriminate disseminator of the visual, so I try a Potter quote on him: 'Capitalism now is about selling all of you to all of you. But they don't know what it is they're selling. The only object is to keep in the game. Which is to keep selling something. And one day we're going to find out what it is.'

'I'm not interested in capitalism at all,' Koons, who used to be a Wall Street broker, says. 'I'm not interested in objects. I don't care about money. I'm interested in people – human desire and aspiration and having daily interconnection with the people I value. I believe in experience, and having transcendence in your life.'

2006

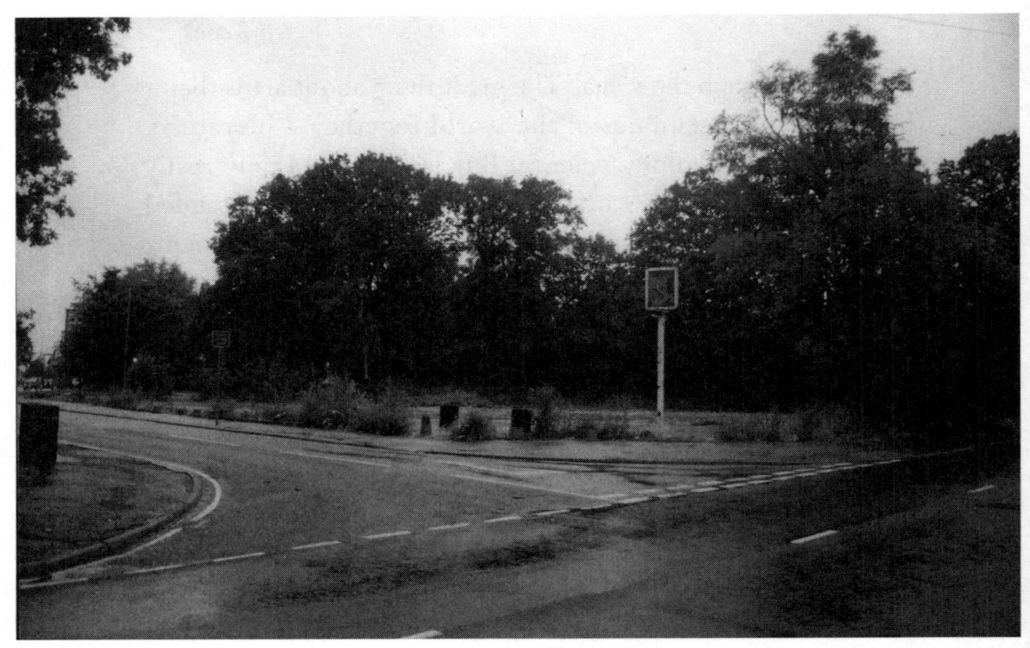

GORDON.
.. AND THEN THERE WAS
NOTHING . . .
GEORGE

MATTHEW BARNEY

Unlike many of his neighbours in the meat-packing district of Manhattan, on the western fringes of Greenwich Village, Matthew Barney chooses not to parade the fact that he spends most of his waking hours locked in a world of weird personal fantasy peopled by his childhood idol, Harry Houdini; a turbaned, swimsuited Gloria Swanson; and a rutting, hoofed and horned satyr, half Bambi, half Schwarzenegger, among others. Polite, quietly spoken and unassuming, he presents himself in the standard downtown artist's kit of washed-out black T-shirt over black Levi's over ruggedly scuffed black workman's boots.

Barney is of only medium height, but he's solidly constructed, with the bunched shoulders of the college quarterback he once was and slabby forearms with the basilic veins standing out on them like dock ropes. There's a kind of bashful Ivy League hardness about him — not the hardness of the gutter fighter, although you get the impression he'd be capable of taking care of himself in a scrap, and he in fact opens by explaining that, if he seems slightly jittery this morning, it's because a few hours earlier he had done what no native New Yorker would ever do: intervene in a violent altercation between two strangers. He had come out of a bar in the early hours to see a man roughing up a woman a block away — he was beating her and dragging her by her hair to where his car was parked. Without thinking, Barney had hot-footed it after them, and ended up having a gun pulled on him.

He was born in San Francisco, grew up in Boise, Idaho, and this was the latest stage in his blooding as a Manhattanite. Stage one had happened soon after his move to the city, three years ago, when the studio he was renting turned out to be part of a drug-dealing operation. The materials the police discovered when they raided him, stockpiled for use in his work, hadn't helped his case: glucose syrup, sucrose, silicon gel, tapioca, sternal retractors, body harnesses, mouth guards, industrial quantities of petroleum jelly and Vaseline. To prove he was an artist, and to get his property released by the court, he had had to make a presentation to the US Attorney General of his tapes and video stills: Barney astride a vinyl-covered contraption, having his midsection pummelled with a hydraulic jack; Barney in a woman's swimsuit and wrap, pantomiming American football moves; Barney scaling a gallery's walls naked, with a titanium ice-screw inserted in his rectum.

The point was to convince the authorities that he was not a felon, or even a run-of-the-mill late-century headbanger, but, at the age of twenty-four, *the* coming new young art star in America, and he obviously succeeded. He has since appeared at the three most prestigious art blowouts of the past year – the 1992 Documenta in Kassel, Germany, and this summer's Whitney Biennial and Venice Biennale – and no gathering of the international avant-garde is now complete without him.

Last summer I found myself in the sub-basement of an underground car park in the middle of Kassel – a subterranean bunker with stained ribbed concrete and diesel puddles, trapped air and signs saying *Ausfahrt* and *Bei Warnsignal* and *Wilkommen in Kassel*. All was chaos above ground: the nearly two hundred artists from thirty-nine countries scattered over nine locations; the art army with its advance guard and big guns and standard mufti and route maps; the scads of museum directors and curators, critics, collectors, artists, dealers, risk analysts, investment consultants, corporate buyers, label lackeys and fashion freaks that the late Peter Fuller took to calling, collectively, 'International Art World Inc.'. A mobocracy sloshing frenziedly about. Zoo time.

Down there, though, away from all that, deep in the belly of the car park under the Theatervorplatz, there was just the steady drip, drip of leaking water ducts and the monotonous herringbone pattern of the parking spaces stretching almost to infinity. But then, uh-oh, here came some people whose stride announced a sense of purpose, and whose logoed tote bags singled them out as fully paid up Documenta-goers. The Documenta-goers disappeared into what I had assumed was a storeroom under the ramps, and so I followed them there. Instead of parking cones and stacking barriers, this room, and the one next to it, housed fetishistic rubber items in dirty fleshy pink – gummy carpets, ribbed rubber dildo-like appliances, lubricated plastics, lozenges of moulded tapioca, soft sinks. They were a kind of fallout from the video 'actions', mounted just above head height and on each side of the door, which showed Matthew Barney being pursued across the level where we were standing by Scottish bagpipers in kilts and climbing naked up the car park's lift shaft.

The atmosphere Barney had created was somewhere between a porno emporium and a public urinal, and the glances exchanged by the smattering of people who had managed to find their way down there, their necks craned to follow the action on the screens, were in keeping with the furtiveness of those places. What was going on here? One clue, both here and, more obviously, in the more recent *Drawing Restraint 7* (in which two muscular young men got up as satyrs cavort and wrestle in a limousine as it silently cruises the bridges and tunnels of night-time Manhattan), is in the apparent references to *Crash*, J. G. Ballard's 1972 novel about violence and sexuality, some of whose wildest sex scenes are set either in a multi-storey car park or in cars. But, while Barney accepts Ballard as an influence, the truth is that he is disliterate in the way of much of his generation: that is to say, he is capable of book-reading when he chooses, but most of the time he doesn't choose. No literary influence can be more than peripheral for him. Instead, at the heart of his work and life are two commanding obsessions, two 'alpha points' of reference. The first is the great magician and escape artist Harry Houdini. The second, more obscure but also more fundamental in drawing together all his work, is Jim Otto.

Jim Otto, a centre for the Oakland Raiders from 1960 to 1975, played most of his football career with a partly plastic right knee. He was Barney's boyhood hero and has now become for him what the Tartar tribesmen who saved his life in wartime were to Joseph Beuys. After Beuys ('all men are artists') and Marcel Duchamp ('anything can be art'), the American Bruce Nauman is probably the person who has played the greatest part in shaping the work currently being made by young artists in Europe and America. 'What Nauman really offers young artists,' Adam Gopnik wrote recently in the *New Yorker*, '. . . is a newly refitted kind of surrealism . . . No one looking at their work would have any trouble seeing that a movement must have once swept through this century's art which put a premium on gruesome fragments, strangled expression, displaced objects, the celebration of the strange and the upturning of the sexually taboo.' It is from this movement that British artists such as Damien Hirst, Rachel

Whiteread and Marc Quinn have drawn permission to use frozen blood, maggots, rotted meat and flowers, ice, household dust and sump oil in their work in recent years. Similarly, Matthew Barney has gone ahead and made dumb-bells and benches out of Vaseline, a blocking sled out of prosthetic plastic, filled a hydraulic jack with glucose syrup and used a wrestling mat with a hole in it stretched open by a sternal retractor. All of these things spring out of the idea, if not the fact, of Jim Otto.

Barney is articulate to the point of garrulousness on the graphic implications of Otto's name, the anatomical significance of the autographic double 'O's he wore on his jersey ('I propose it as a dual rectum or a sort of roving orifice'), and the formal parallels between the two middle 'T's and the goalposts and rams' horns in his videos. 'In the end,' Barney says, 'Jim Otto isn't Jim Otto. He's just a form.' It is remarkable, given the abstruseness, not to say the outwardly berserk nature of Barney's art activity, that it found such easy acceptance. It casts the viewer in the role of crick-necked voyeur, and yet you remain uncertain about the exact nature of what you are being voyeur to.

The night before his New York debut in 1991, Barney locked himself inside the Barbara Gladstone Gallery and climbed the walls. Then he climbed across the ceiling, strapped naked in a harness, and inched himself along by means of titanium ice screws that he planted in the plaster; then he made his way down into the lower gallery, where he hoisted himself into a refrigeration unit, penetrated himself with a pair of the screws, and eased himself on to an accomplice in an 'oo' football jersey lying on his back next to one of the weightlifting benches cast in petroleum jelly. The next day's visitors found the gallery marked with footprints and holes and full of

Barney's gymnasium paraphernalia; downstairs, a videotape of the previous night's climb played.

He had only one solo show in Los Angeles behind him at that point, but a certain buzz had preceded him to New York, the result of art-world gossip and articles in the art magazines. 'He'd really stirred interest among a lot of us who had not seen the work,' according to Elisabeth Sussman, curator of this year's Whitney Biennial. 'So then it came here and the publicity machine went to work on it. A lot of hype around it. Word of mouth in SoHo. But,' she stresses, 'it came at a very low point in the art market bust here, when nobody thought it was possible for anybody to have a major debut. Because nobody had the money. Everybody was selling things like crazy. There weren't waiting lists for artists' work the way there had been in the eighties. So Matthew was like a singular event. There was no other show that year that *electrified* people.' 'By the time the show closed,' Jim Lewis wrote in *Harper's Bazaar*, 'something quite extraordinary had happened: Barney turned out to be the real thing, an artist with a strikingly original and fully realised way of rendering a world.'

Naturally, there were dissenters, mostly among those who had tracked the careers of other young art stars in the previous decade; people like Jean-Michel Basquiat: on the cover of the *New York Times Magazine* at the age of twenty-four, dead of a heroin overdose at twenty-seven and subsequently disparaged by the critic Robert Hughes as an artist whose career 'appealed to a cluster of toxic vulgarities' (including 'a fetish about the infallible freshness of youth'; 'an obsession with novelty'; 'the slide of art criticism into promotion, and art into fashion'; 'art investment mania, which abolished the time for reflection on a hot artist's actual merits'; and 'the audience's goggling appetite for self-destructive talent'). 'Trends can be condensed at will,'

Hughes wrote elsewhere. 'The moral economy of the American art world has been so distorted by the hype and premature careerism of the eighties that a serious artist in New York must face the same unreality and weightlessness as a serious actor in Los Angeles.' This was never a problem in Britain — until the start of the nineties, when what is probably the most exceptional group to emerge from a British art school since the British Pop artists came out of the Royal College of Art in 1962 started to make their presence felt. Damien Hirst and his Goldsmiths contemporaries were unembarrassed about either putting on the hustle or seeing their work in an international context. Hirst, Ian Davenport, Fiona Rae and several others had been shortlisted for the Turner Prize by the time they reached their mid-twenties. Peter Blake is among those who believe it was too much, too soon. 'It's so easy to have one great idea,' he says. 'But it's not enough to base your life on. You're immediately successful and you make your statement and you're left with nowhere to go. You can't go back and, because you haven't learned anatomy, Roman lettering, perspective, architecture, all the things which are the language of art, there's nowhere much to move forward to either. They haven't had a route to where they've got to. They're just there. They're successful with no history and, in a way, no future. It's rather a trap.'

Installation art of the kind that is currently in vogue — 'room settings by numbers, do-it-yourself sculpture, karaoke for curators, art demeaning itself', according to Howard Jacobson; art of 'the quick fix, involving catchy props' in the words of William Feaver — has prompted an almost unprecedentedly violent response from the critics. 'The apotheosis of rubbish on a baroque scale with baroque pretensions,' was Brian Sewell's verdict on this year's Gravity and Grace show at the Hayward. This stuff was nothing, though, compared with the vituperation that engulfed the organisers of this summer's Whitney Biennial in New York, which set out to show work 'that confronts social and political issues'. The *LA Times* called the show, in which Barney's *Drawing Restraint 7* was a major talking point, 'gruesome'; *Newsweek* 'dyspeptically sad'; *Time* 'a fiesta of whining celebrating sodden cant and cliché'; *The Nation* 'mawkish, frivolous, whining, foolish, feckless, awful and thin'. 'There is no point in "reviewing" the carloads of junk that David Ross's apparatchiks have accumulated for the current exhibition as if it had anything to do with art,' Hilton Kramer began in the *New York Observer*. 'Even the people who approve of trashing the museum with this garbage don't pretend to find any aesthetic interest in it.'

'Everybody told me that this was the show everybody loved to hate,' Elisabeth Sussman, the Biennial's curator, says. 'That was the stock phrase. There's always an uproar, and there always has been since this museum opened its doors to contemporary art. So this is a place that comes with an uproar. But I think the reaction was more violent than I was expecting. I think it was more violent than anybody was expecting. Oh, it was *violent*. The first few reviews were by women, and they were quite complimentary. And then the white men started weighing in. They came down the road marching! *Oh yes!* You really felt like you were in the centre of . . . We pushed a lot of buttons. Racism, sexism, all the gender-related issues.' Sussman was instrumental in acquiring *Drawing Restraint 7* — the horny satyrs — for the Whitney's permanent collection. It has qualities that have convinced her it is a 'museum-quality' piece, but, like many of Barney's admirers, she has difficulty in saying exactly what those qualities are. 'He's an incredibly difficult artist to actually say what he's trying to achieve,' she says. 'He seems in a way to be coming from nowhere. And because he came *on us* so fast, none of us have seen a lot of his work. That first show at Barbara Gladstone, that had him climbing up the walls and appearing in drag, was really very impressive. Lots of men responded to that piece because it was very much about homoeroticism. Not in a gay sense necessarily, but the kind of mass-media homoeroticism of Saturday football. Boxing.'

Barney is at least as much athlete as he is artist. He played quarterback and wrestled in high school. In 1985 he was recruited by Yale for its football team; he entered intending to pursue a pre-med programme. But neither the football nor the medicine panned out, so he began focusing on making art — what he calls restraint pieces, environments in which he made drawing as difficult as possible; for example, by attaching himself to rubber cords and straining up an incline to make a mark on the ceiling. They were, in his own words, 'facilities designed to defeat the facility of drawing', and they drew on the knowledge that he acquired as an athlete. 'Football is abstract,' he has said. 'It's all about strategy, about finding a hole in your opponent's defence. And in wrestling, you're taught to internalise manoeuvres until you can respond to information about your opponent completely intuitively.'

'A lot of what he does is physically dangerous,' Richard Flood of the Gladstone Gallery says. 'It's wildly dangerous. At Kassel he had to climb all five elevator shafts, edit the tapes and do the show within a week. The limits he imposes are very tight. But because he sets the rules, he knows the game very well.' Barney has come under attack for trespassing on territory some felt belonged only to the gay community. Flood dismisses this, along with any attempt to link Barney's work to the world of body- and gender-politics. 'So much of the work is performed naked, but the sexuality is never dwelt on. My belief is that it is onanistic or autoerotic rather than specifically hetero- or homosexual. The attempt to politicise the pieces is pure cant.'

Barney has internalised his obsessions so completely that hearing him talk about them is like hearing him thinking aloud in a private language. His thinking is abstract and stylised, like the elaborate 'actions' played out in the pieces. E. L. Doctorow (in whose 1975 novel *Ragtime* Harry Houdini is a pivotal character) once said that what novelists do is bring things together – connect things that have had no previous connection. It is a facility shared by Barney, and it is what makes his work so strange and so compelling, and talking to him such a vertiginous experience. Like Harry Houdini, whose activities were also characterised by simplicity, repetition, solitude, starkness and discipline, Barney works within an entirely enclosed, self-servicing system, and he is unwilling to step out of it to shed any anecdotal light on his life.

During his years at Yale he earned money as a catalogue model, work that he says was 'an interesting way to learn about how flexible an image can be – how the subject must have the ability to evacuate his or her body in order for the transformation to take place'. But it also taught him another valuable lesson. 'I was watching this thing on that famous model,' he says. 'Linda Evangelista, the one with the short hair? And she's talking. She's from somewhere in Canada. I couldn't believe it, hearing her speak. And I thought at that moment she lost all of her . . . resonance, all her flexibility of character. That, I think, dissipates as soon as they open their mouths.' He is similarly impressed by Houdini's lifelong refusal 'to deal with the mystical aspect of his own practice. His practice was physical; it was about a heightened state of body awareness or body intelligence – everything was absorbed through the body. He spent a lot of energy trying to uncover *hoax* mystics.'

After years of mouthing off by the likes of Julian Schnabel and Jeff Koons, such reticence seems admirable; almost a throwback to the days when advanced art was solitary and allowed to develop outside the full glare of public inspection. There are those who see Barney's work as just more 'alien goo' gumming up the system; another example of 'short-impact conceptualism trying to be spectacle'. And it must have occurred to Barney, as the poet John Ashbery once wrote of Jackson Pollock, that he isn't an artist at all. 'But this very real possibility,' Ashbery continued, 'is paradoxically just what makes the tremendous excitement in his work. It's a gamble against terrific odds. Most reckless things are beautiful in some way, and recklessness is what makes experimental art beautiful, just as religions are beautiful because of the strong possibility that they are founded on nothing.'

1993

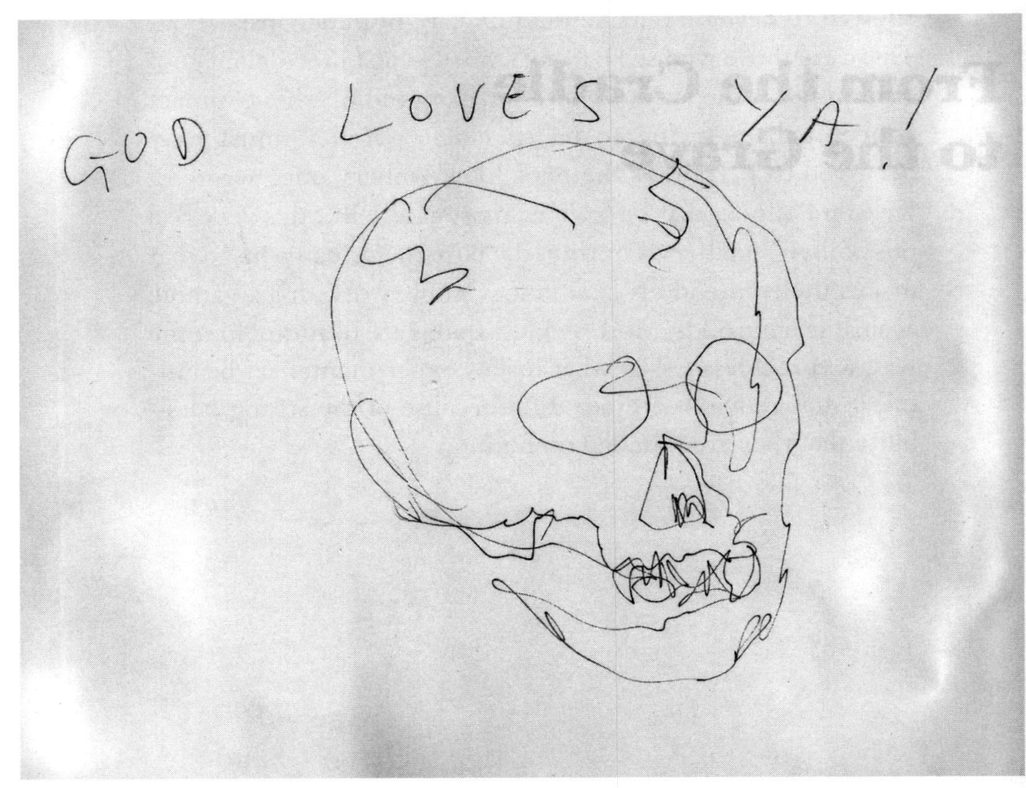

Damien Hirst

USA TODAY

'Tomorrow's world – today!' The motto of the 1939 New York World's Fair is one that sustained Gotham as the cultural capital of the world throughout the whole of the second half of the last, American, century.

USA Today, the title of Charles Saatchi's show of his latest, mint-fresh acquisitions from America at the Royal Academy is, appropriately perhaps, not so ringing, less ebullient. It is the name of a mainstream newspaper. 'It follows that the exhibition title', one of the contributors, the Los Angeles-based sculptor Matthew Monahan has said, 'makes me think of the war in Iraq.' The war and the political environment it has created is a kind of viral link between the work of artists as different as Rodney McMillian, Dan Colen, Matthew Day Jackson and Josephine Meckseper.

'New York, the city that is always its own photograph, the living memento of my childish dream of escape, called to me,' John Updike writes in *Of the Farm*, an early, little-read novel, 'urged me away, into the car, down the road, along the highway, up the Turnpike.'

New York called, and Updike heard it on the family farm in Shillington, Pennsylvania, much as contemporaries and near-contemporaries such as Jasper Johns (b. Augusta, Georgia) and Robert Rauschenberg (Port Arthur, Texas) and Ellsworth Kelly and James Rosenquist, along with Warhol, Lichtenstein, Frank

Stella and Donald Judd heard it in their small towns and provincial cities and came running.

Ignorant of or ignoring Marcel Duchamp's observation that 'artists throughout history are like gamblers in Monte Carlo and in the blind lottery some are picked out while others are ruined', they huddled together in slum neighbourhoods in Lower Manhattan in the way that has since become traditional, with the rats and the cockroaches and the cracks in the wall. Willett Street under the Williamsburg Bridge was one such area, and it was there that Rauschenberg and Johns bided their time and encouraged each other as they planned to take on the abstract expressionists and all their works. Willett Street was 'the grimmest neighbourhood' he ever lived in, Rauschenberg once said. 'It seemed frightening to be inside, and even more frightening to be outside.'

This was all at a time — the mid-fifties to early sixties — when Pollock and Rothko and de Kooning had established New York's hegemony as the art capital of the world, and America, partly as a result of the newness and vitality these artists represented, seemed young and powerful and capable of producing anything at will. 'America embraced the new', Robert Hughes once noted, 'because its enshrined social and technological myth was one of progress. With a little prodding, it was willing to embrace almost any "radical" cultural change as therapeutic. Its cultural industry was announcing fresh, temporarily unnerving changes and telescoping the future into the present . . . Manhattan was the capital of change — the Rome of instability.'

In the twenty-five years up to 1970, the invention of artists in America — their ability to 'make it new' — seemed inexhaustible: abstract expressionism begat colour-field painting which begat the proto-Pop of Johns which begat Pop art proper and an age in which commercial objects for the first time became works of art. This was in response to the market conditions that would ultimately create the post-industrial world. As Warhol was forever telling us, the strange thing about the sixties was not that Western art was becoming commercialised but that Western commerce was becoming so much more artistic.

So America was on a roll; it was the endless wave. And everybody — art impresarios and art stars, dealers, curators, critics, collectors — was delighted to ride it. But then, as the gaudy spree of the sixties abated, something happened: young American artists started to prepare themselves for entry into the booming art industry by studying for degrees in fine art at university. Increasing numbers of them seemed to look on the practice of art as a perfectly viable profession, in which it was not unreasonable to expect a decent financial return. The rapid expansion of the art market — more and more galleries, more collectors, escalating prices, and the social rewards that went with being a recognised artist — attracted bright young men and women who might never have thought of becoming artists if they had been born ten years earlier.

'A dry, academic smog pressed down on the art scene,' the *New Yorker* writer Calvin Tomkins gloomily reported. 'A great many of the college-trained young artists had been spoon-fed large doses of Minimal and Conceptual art in school, and they tended afterward to think in terms of an art reduced to its basic essentials of shape, line, and colour, or else an art in which ideas took precedence over physical artifacts.'

'Floor and drawer art', as the sculptor Richard Serra referred to the fashion for conceptual, documentary and installation work, failed to produce a major American artist in the seventies. 'If we had thought about it from the perspective of old car freaks,' the American curator and critic Dave Hickey has written, 'we would have known and surely would have predicted that the General Motors of the art world – the museums and universities – would ultimately seek to alleviate their post-market status and control the means of production . . . Within ten years, the art world was on its way to becoming a transnational bureaucracy. Everybody had a job description and a résumé . . . I was face to face with a generation of well-educated and expensively trained young artists whose extended tenure in art schools appended to the art world had totally divorced them from any social reality beyond it.'

If Julian Schnabel hadn't come along when he did in the early eighties, the market, ever ready to buy into the cult of the driven and angst-ridden artist, of the heroically suffering self, would have had to invent him. Wall Street was in full flood, the bull market had started its five-year run which lasted from 1982 to 1987, and art, in addition to the varieties of glamorous lifestyle feedback it offered, had become the smart place for futures traders and hedge-fund managers to put their money. Schnabel's paintings on horse hide and broken plates, which were priced at $2,000 apiece in his first show, had jumped to $40,000 apiece by his third. And at the head of the queue was the bright new young collector from England, the newly rich advertising executive Charles Saatchi.

Saatchi bought Schnabel in bulk, along with other big, deliberately crude, neo-expressionist canvases by Schnabel's American contemporaries David Salle and Eric Fischl, and their counterparts in Italy and Germany. The emergence of European painters such as Georg Baselitz, Sandro Chia and Francesco Clemente gave rise to a rash of speculative articles about the end of US chauvinism around this time. 'Contemporary art is no longer a New York exclusive,' Tomkins

announced at the end of 1981. 'Ever since abstract expressionist painting became the dominant international style, a great
many people both here and abroad have seen this city as the
primary source of advanced art . . . The notion that nothing of
interest could be happening anywhere else in the world has
caused much irritation among European artists and dealers . . .
Now the wall of chauvinism, real or imagined, appears to be
crumbling.'

Nevertheless, when Saatchi opened his first private gallery
in Boundary Road in North London in the mid-eighties, the
emphasis was squarely – and, with the single exception of the
German Anselm Keifer, exclusively – on new work from
America. Warhol, Judd, Cy Twombly and Carl Andre were
among senior artists featured in the first shows from Saatchi's
collection. New York Art Now, in the autumn and winter of
1987/8, brought together a group of young artists whose
work had never been seen outside America up to that time.
Peter Halley's cool Day-Glo paintings, Philip Taaffe's 'appro-
priations' of the works of Barnett Newman and Bridget Riley,
Robert Gober's creepy wax castings, Ashley Bickerton's logo-
littered constructions, and – pre-eminently – the former commodity broker Jeff Koons's pristine stacked vacuum-cleaner
and basketballs-floating-in-fishtank sculptures – all of these
had both an instant and a profound effect on the thinking of
Sarah Lucas, Damien Hirst and their fellow students at
Goldsmiths College who made repeated trips across London
to see them. Saatchi's shows by Koons and the so-called 'Neo-
Geo' school were instrumental in firing up a generation of
young British artists who, for the first time since the war, were
able to crowd their New York contemporaries off the international stage.

'You dropped the ball,' I remember a European dealer

telling the young American painter Sean Landers around 1994. Landers stared into his drink. He didn't deny it. So what happened? And what, besides the art world's notorious impatience for innovation and appetite for the briefly new, has happened since George Bush's re-election in 2004 to cause the (mainly European) art journals to start talking about a 'renaissance' in American art and major London galleries like the Serpentine (whose Uncertain States of America is still running) and the RA to mount surveys shows of artists who are still, outside the collecting elites, largely unheard of in their own country?

Several artists in USA Today also had work in this year's Whitney Biennial, a show which was taking place, as its British-born co-curator Chrissie Iles admitted in the catalogue, 'at a moment when world opinion of the United States is at its lowest ebb'. The tendency towards 'obfuscation, darkness, secrecy, and the irrational', Iles added, 'could also be said to reflect the mood in the larger world'. Matthew Monahan, a participant in both shows and hotly collected by the Rubell family in Miami as well as by Saatchi in this country, agreed that the Biennial had 'a nightmarish feeling', but added that it also had 'a pop/punk sensibility typical of US art'.

This contradiction – if that's what it was – was addressed by the Whitney's director, Adam Weinberg: 'For many Americans such events [as the Iraq war and Hurricane Katrina] exist more as the crackle of background static than as a palpable presence . . . This schizophrenic situation gives rise to at least two realities that discomfortingly coexist: one of anxiety, exasperation and despair; and another of exuberance, energy and wishful thinking.'

There are two writers who every one of the forty artists in USA Today are nearly sure to have read. One is Hickey, whose book *Air Guitar*, an exuberant and wide-ranging collection of his art-theoretical and autobiographical essays (he used to be a rock writer, an art dealer, was in a band, was deeply embedded in sixties underground culture, is a long-time resident of and persuasive proselytiser for Las Vegas), has attracted a cult following since its publication in 1997.

The other is David Foster Wallace whose 1,079-page novel *Infinite Jest* became an instant campus classic when it was published a decade ago. Around the time the book came out, Wallace was asked to describe how it felt to live in America, and this was his reply: 'There's something particularly sad about it, something that doesn't have very much to do with physical circumstances, or the economy, or any of the stuff that gets talked about in the news. It's more like a stomach-level sadness. I see it in myself and my friends in different ways. It manifests itself as a kind of lostness. Whether it's unique to our generation, I really don't know.'

Wallace made this observation some years in advance of the events of September 2001 and the subsequent War on Terror. Writing about *Infinite Jest* in the introduction to the story collection *The Burned Children of America* — a kind of literary equivalent of the USA Today exhibition — Zadie Smith also recognised that, post-9/11, 'Underneath the professional smiles there is a sadness in [America] that is sunk so deep in the culture you can taste it in your morning Cheerios . . . You can be unsatisfied in America, or unfulfilled, you can be unrecognised, unappreciated, you can be unbalanced, unemotional, unnutritionally satisfied and unnumerically rewarded, you can be unrepresented and unspoken — but you cannot be unhappy . . . And yet there remains this sadness . . . Wallace identified it: many, many people followed him.'

According to the catalogue, the works in USA Today make 'a firm case for the claim that the US has regained the right to be considered at the heart of all that is exciting, innovative, subversive and questioning in art today'. No doubt Josephine Meckseper, Lara Schnitger, Kelley Walker and the other emergent artists in the show will have had any sadness mitigated, no matter how briefly, by being brought into the Saatchi collection and seeing their work displayed grandly at Burlington House. But they have read their Hickey and so they know the advice he offers vis-à-vis collectors and other art-world 'spectators' in *Air Guitar*: 'They just love the winning side – the side with the chic building, the gaudy doctorates, and the star-studded cast. They seek out spectacles whose value is confirmed by the normative blessing of institutions and corporations. In these venues, they derive sanctioned pleasure or virtue from an accredited source, and this makes them feel secure, more a part of things.'

They will know too that Saatchi's great trophies of the Britart years, paraded at the Royal Academy in Sensation in 1997, had been offloaded at Tesco-like profit within only a year or two of the show moving on.

2006

RONI HORN

'I go north,' the American artist Roni Horn once wrote. 'It's in my nature . . . The desire to go north is an attraction to solitude, open space, subtle expressions of light and time . . . Sometimes going north is about whiteness. Sometimes it's about darkness. I'm attracted to the darkness, it relieves me of the incessant call to visual attention – it opens interior spaces that offer untold possibilities of discovery. This darkness is another form of light.'

Horn has been a 'permanent tourist' in Iceland from her home in New York for more than thirty years. Next week, *Library of Water*, her permanent installation in the small coastal town of Stykkisholmur, three hours from Reykjavik, will open to the public for the first time. Water has been 'archived' from glacial sources in all parts of Iceland, and decanted into a copse-like stand of transparent glass columns which have replaced the shelves where books were once stacked. Some of the columns are clear, others are opaque, with traces of ancient debris drifting in them. The debris is a reminder that the glaciers were formed many millennia ago and are now rapidly receding. Horn describes *Library of Water* as 'in some sense an endgame, since many of these sources will no longer exist in a matter of years'. But *Vatnasafn*, to give it its Icelandic name, isn't primarily an ecological/political work; it isn't agitprop.

Horn imagined *Vatnasafn/Library of Water* as a place for quiet observation and reflection, 'a lighthouse in which the viewer becomes the light. A lighthouse in which the view becomes the light'. This connects it to her work of the past thirty years, which has ranged across drawing and sculpture to photography and essays and whose guiding principle has been anonymity on the part of the artist and minimum intervention in the work's execution. She has spoken many times of her 'desire to be present and be a part of a place without changing it'. Detachment, humility and surrender, that is the ambition. She's there, and then she isn't there, like the weather.

In 'Pictures of Nothing', the series of Mellon lectures on abstract art since Jackson Pollock that he delivered shortly before his death in 2003, the American art historian Kirk Varnedoe made the sometimes overlooked point that not all abstraction has been about 'its noisy, declarative protagonists'; that, in fact, pushing 'a quarter of contemporary abstraction . . . is about whispers, innuendo, confidences exchanged intimately rather than publicly declared'.

'We don't want our personality in the art,' Ellsworth Kelly once said. 'We all had to get over Picasso, because his was "great personality" art. We were trying to get away from the "I", as in "Look how well I do it".'

There is a noticeable strand of solitariness in recent American art — of city-born artists leaving the cities in pursuit of what might be thought of as anti-experience; attempts to quiet the mind.

Kelly's great friend and contemporary Agnes Martin (an artist whom Roni Horn acknowledges she has always had 'the deepest respect for, both the work itself and the lifestyle she chose') fled the Manhattan of the fifties for the flat, open spaces of New Mexico where, for the next forty years, she devoted herself to making paintings which, as she put it, 'have neither object nor space nor time nor anything – no forms'.

The numinous quality of Martin's paintings – the way light seems to be stored up inside them – has inevitably evoked a spiritual experience. Such responses have been encouraged by Martin's writings, which extol the virtues of the solitary life. 'I suggest to artists that you take every opportunity of being alone, that you give up having pets and unnecessary companions,' she once famously wrote. 'I suggest that people who like to be alone, who walk alone, will be serious workers in the art field.'

In the late seventies, shortly after completing her Masters in Fine Art at Yale, Roni Horn took off for Iceland on her own. She had travelled to Iceland for the first time in 1975, hitch-hiking and walking. Now she had a motorbike, and a tent and, for the whole of the wettest summer on record at that point, she immersed herself in all the nothingness and nowhereness Iceland had to offer, a solo traveller across the ice-and-ash desert interior of the island: 'Big enough to get lost on; small enough to find myself.'

'There was a point early on in my visits that I was so taken with this landscape I wanted to experience everything here,' Horn has said. 'Every road, river, mountain, and rock. When I was twenty-two I fantasised about retiring and doing a complete inventory of all the rocks. But short of that, I just went out.'

Often she found herself heading for the hot springs. They became a kind of shelter. 'I found myself pool-hopping to these exquisite faraway places and spending a lot of time in the middle of nowhere, outside, in hot water. In the thick of it, so to speak, alone but protected.' In retrospect, she says she reminds herself in those days of Burt Lancaster in the film of John Cheever's best-known story, *The Swimmer*, about a middle-aged man on his own, swimming home, pool-to-pool, through the backyards of suburban America. 'He was in a swimsuit throughout the whole film and you felt his sensitivity to everything, and his vulnerability.'

In 1982 Horn lived alone in a lighthouse in southern Iceland for two months. Her ambition, she says, was 'to see if I could just let the sea lie before me. I was haunted by this desire — of seeing a landscape as it is when I am not there. I know this sounds absurd, and the effort was full of absurdity, but for me it was a completely new experience, a true adventure. Just being there. Not wanting to change there. This remains an elusive desire. In some sense too simple to achieve. I come to Iceland to discover this possibility still.'

Starting in 1990, Horn began publishing a series of books of photographs, drawings and writings made in Iceland. They include *Lava*, *Folds* (pictures of earthworks, sheep-folds), and *Pooling Waters*, a sequence of photographs of hot pots and swimming pools, all of them part of an ongoing work called To Place. The books struck James Lingwood, co-director of Artangel, the London-based organisation responsible for Rachel Whiteread's *House*, Mike Figgis's film *The Battle of Orgreave* and many other recent pioneering and otherwise unfundable art projects, as having 'something of the quality of a secular devotional'.

Lingwood eventually met Horn in 1998 when she was in London working on a series of large-scale, roiling, uncharacteristically ominous photographs of the surface of the River Thames. There was brief talk about a project in England. But in time the talk turned from England to Iceland and the possibility of Horn making a public project in her 'open-air studio of unlimited scale and newness' there.

Horn was born in 1955. There are now monuments to the

achievement of the artists just a generation older than her all over the United States. Following the model of the Rothko Chapel in Houston, the minimalist shrines range from James Turrell's Quaker meeting house in Houston to Donald Judd's museumification of the entire town of Marfa, Texas, to Walter de Maria's mile-wide *Lightning Field* in Quemada, New Mexico.

These are projects on a grand scale. Roni Horn's *Vatnasafn/ Library of Water* in Stykkisholmur (population 1,100) on the north-west coast of Iceland, on the other hand, is modest, unassertive, and intended to serve the community rather than coerce it into an appreciation (or even a viewing) of the work of one of the more recondite practitioners of conceptual art. In addition to the two installations of Horn's work – a rubber floor scattered with childishly rendered words in Icelandic and English, and the glacial water housed in top-lit, floor-to-ceiling columns – the space will be used by the local community for activities ranging from yoga classes and AA meetings to gatherings of the local (women-only) chess association and reading groups.

Library of Water was the Stykkisholmur lending library until two or three years ago. It stands on a bluff with a commanding view over the corrugated-aluminium-clad buildings of the town and the boats in the harbour in one direction, and deep enveloping views of sea and sky in all the others.

Horn first spotted it when she was driving through Stykkisholmur in the early nineties. 'It wasn't just the look of the building with its gas-station-Deco styling, or the fact that it reminded me of a lighthouse,' she writes in the introduction to *Weather Reports You*, an 'active archive' collecting Icelanders' stories of their weather, published to coincide with the opening of *Library of Water*. 'What really caught my eye was the location at the high point of town.'

Freshly rendered and painted now with the windows cut to the floor, *Library of Water* pokes up into the weather. It sets its face at everything the weather can throw, which in Iceland invariably means extremes of light and wind and cold; visibility often varies from minute to minute. *You Are the Weather* is the title of the dense latex floor installation, which is randomly embedded with words such as 'stormy', 'temperate', 'sunny' and 'chilly', a kind of meteorological map of the mind.

'The weather is constant in its indifference to us and unpredictable in every other way,' Horn told students of the Iceland Academy of the Arts at their graduating ceremony last summer. 'It keeps circumstance complex and beyond our final control. I think it is essential to have something that tells us who we are. And weather has a way of doing this. I have always taken the weather personally.'

Horn is passionate about wet weather in particular, and in fact about water in every state, from ice to condensation. She has a compulsive attraction to water. She luxuriates in it, rhapsodises about it, photographs it, collects it. At a celebration to mark the completion of *Library of Water* in Stykkisholmur two weeks ago, she was coaxed by Lingwood into performing a sort of Allen Ginsberg-like incantation on the theme of water, taken mainly from the Thames piece she had done in London but circumnavigating the grimmer themes ('The river is full of dead bodies and all kinds of darkness'), which she felt were inappropriate to the occasion and the location.

'When you see your reflection in water, do you recognise the water in you? . . . The deserts of our future will be deserts of water.' It was 7 p.m. and still light. The night wouldn't start to set in until around 11 o'clock. The lava-heated and glacier-cooled water, stilled in its columns, did funny things with peoples faces. It folded in the horizon and bottled the sky.

Urine-coloured, sulphurous, sedimented, clear and cloudy, it made Miro-like shapes, a too-rich effect which complicated the room like swirly carpet.

'Water is transparence derived from the presence of everything . . . How does water remain so unfamiliar?' Like all of those present, some of whom had arrived by private plane from America and elsewhere, Horn was in stockinged feet, her shoes deposited in a cloakroom just inside the library door. After a few minutes of reading she requested a glass of water. She kept her gaze locked on what Auden, fellow-Icelandophile, once described as 'the most magical light of anywhere on earth', until the water was brought.

The following morning, despite everybody's best efforts, the floor at *Vatnasafn* was soiled and sticky and imprinted with feet. Although there had been no drink at the opening, it looked like the aftermath of a teenage party.

For years she had kept the art world at bay from her island, carefully guarding what James Lingwood calls 'the delicate ecology' of her relationship to the place. *Vatnasafn* on the morning after offered evidence of what Horn had told the art students in Reykjavik in the summer of 2006: that Iceland is no longer an island, economically, chemically, climatically, or even psychologically speaking. Lingwood spent much of the journey back to Reykjavik arranging to have a cleaner go at the *Library of Water* with bucket and mop.

2007

3 A LITTLE LIFESTYLE FEEDBACK

High Art and the High Life

NAUGHTY

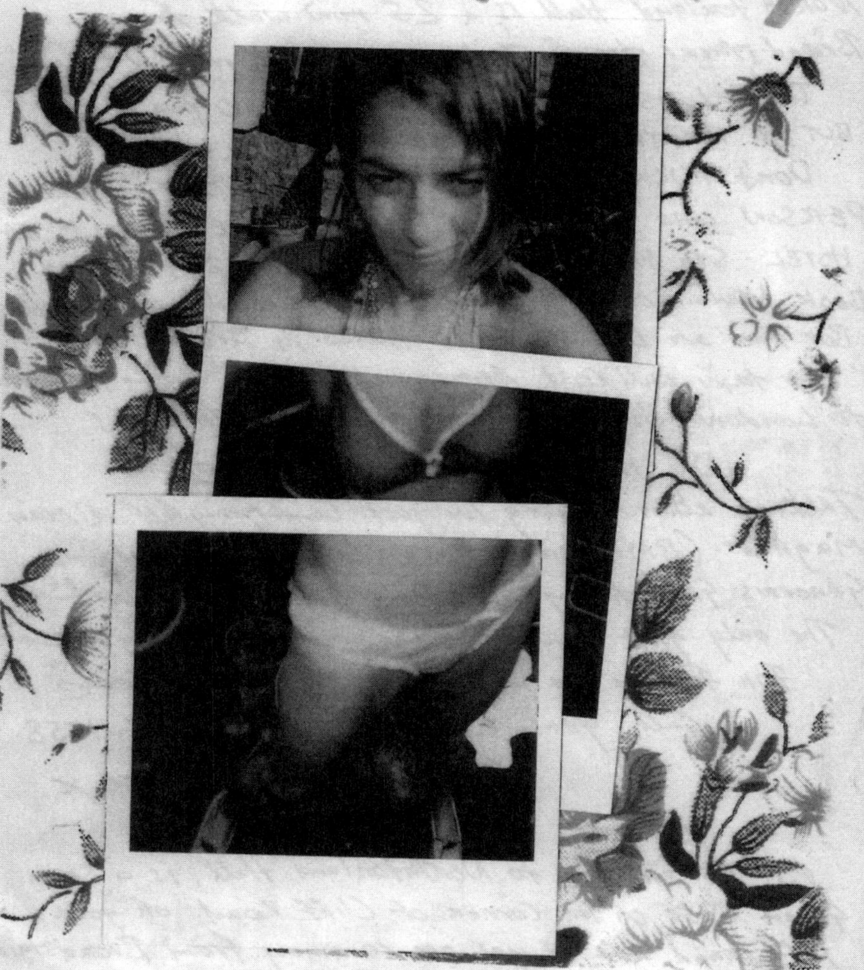

AT FORTY

1990 VENICE BIENNALE

Waiting to board Flight 259 at Heathrow, Norman Rosenthal, exhibitions secretary at the Royal Academy, has the following, Tom Wolfeish suggestion to make: any article about the Venice Biennale, he says, should consist of a single word, repeated beyond tedium to the point of delirium, and the word should be 'hello'.

For Rosenthal, a prominent player in the international art game, the hellos (and an equal number of black looks) have started at check-in, carry on through security, buzz around him like flies on the conveyor belt wafting him to Gate 8, and continue unabated now that he has parked himself in the departure lounge, a deceptively shambling-looking figure in a cream suit.

The Venice Biennale, founded in 1895, is the oldest as well as the most prestigious of all the international art extravaganzas. Others – those in Chicago and Basle, for instance – mainly confine themselves to the business of art, which these days, it barely needs stating, is very big business indeed.

Contemporary art has become currency. But, unlike other areas of risk investment, art is socially smart. 'The public has willed the glamour of big money on to art,' in the words of Robert Hughes, art critic of *Time*, in a way that is historically unique.

At Venice, however, the civilising influence of the city is supposed to mean that the art of the deal for once takes a back seat to the art on display in the fifty-odd national pavilions in the Giardini di Castello and at a bewildering variety of other locations, ranging from an old rope factory to a deconsecrated basilica.

Museum directors and curators, critics, collectors, artists, dealers and what one journal called 'know-nothing gold diggers and fashion freaks' flock to Venice from all over the world every two years.

And it is a representative selection of the British contingent who are assembled ('Hello! . . . Hi! . . . Hel-*lo* . . . How are *you*?' schmooze-schmooze, kiss-kiss), waiting to board Flight 259. The atmosphere is loaded with the latest power perfumes and a palpable social neurosis: am I carrying a full suit of invitations to the *important* parties? Am I going to be able to sleep the sleep of the included?

The art world — the International Art World Inc., as it was ironically dubbed by the critic Peter Fuller — is in reality a hamlet. Not as small a hamlet as it was forty years ago perhaps, when Marcel Duchamp, when asked how many people *really* liked avant-garde art, was able to reply: 'Oh, maybe ten in New York and one or two in New Jersey.' But a hamlet nevertheless.

The art world is a network of competing cliques, cartels, knitting circles and mafias. It thrives on intrigue, gossip, slights, snobberies and petty vendettas. Occasions like Venice are crucial for helping to keep the pot on the boil.

Two figures stand apart from the familiar repertory of travelling players at Gate 8. One — tall, tanned, wearing sunglasses and a mac — is the architect David Connor, a friend of the official British representative in Venice, Anish Kapoor. The other —

small, bearded, sporting a waterproof, shockproof bullshit detector — is the writer Howard Jacobson, who is clearly on a job. You can tell this by the way he looks with his ears and frisks the crowd in a way that suggests that he's got their number: one false move and they're dead.

Rosenthal, the object of Jacobson's severest scrutiny, appears unperturbed.

'You rich collectors,' he calls out to a middle-aged man with a stack of designer luggage on designer wheels, who turns out to be Edgar Astaire, brother of the boxing promoter, Jarvis.

'One bag for each day of the week,' Mr Astaire merrily shouts back, a smile lighting up his tan. 'That's all.'

WEDNESDAY

'This would look wonderful the colour of my kitchen,' Howard Hodgkin said, the first time he saw the British pavilion, a converted tea room overlooking the Giardini, when he showed at the Biennale in 1984. The whole of the inside had to be gone over five times before the correct shade of eau-de-nil was achieved.

This time the floor has had to be reinforced to bear *Void Field*, the largest of Anish Kapoor's sculptures, which consists of twenty blocks of sandstone with mysterious black apertures punched into them.

Kapoor's work travelled to Venice in a convoy of pantechnicons. How Kapoor himself comes to be here is less easy to establish. According to the rumour mill, he was the personal nominee of the director of the Tate Gallery, Nicholas Serota. But Henry Meyric Hughes, the British Commissioner, is unwilling to confirm that Serota even sat on the selection panel.

However it was achieved, Kapoor's presence represents

something of a coup for his gallery, the Lisson, which also supplied Britain's last representative in Venice, Tony Cragg — another sculptor — in 1988.

Strolling edgily around the Biennale grounds in the hour or so before the gates are opened to the first visitors (who are already milling at the entrance), Nicholas Logsdail, owner of the Lisson, is characteristically gnomic about this and his artists' other achievements in recent years, which include two Turner Prizes.

One thing he wants to state categorically — and of course nobody believes him — is that Anish Kapoor's selection for the Biennale came as much as a surprise to him as to the rest of the art world. He dismisses the suggestion that it had anything to do with clever behind-the-scenes manoeuvring or discreet lobbying on his part.

'People come up to me and say you must feel very proud, etcetera. I feel embarrassed, to be truthful . . . I was shocked. But perhaps there's a new establishment. Or [a thought that might be occurring to him for the first time] perhaps Lisson artists have *become* the establishment.'

Prize-giving, which traditionally gave rise to intense political infighting among the nations and some prize dust-ups between artists, was abolished in 1970. Then, because the Biennale was starting to flag without the speculation and the bitching that is its lifeblood, prizes made a comeback in 1988. At present, the sculpture prize is the most sought after. Logsdail, of course, affects a deep indifference. 'The prize is irrelevant,' he claims, 'because it's rigged. Last time, eight out of twelve of the jury voted for Tony Cragg and the prize went to Jasper Johns and the Americans.' He lights his eighteenth cigarette since breakfast. 'I'll say one thing. There will be quite a lot of resentment if Anish wins.'

Within minutes of the British pavilion opening at ten, it's obvious that, in one area at least, it's going to be no contest. Putting its fashion foot forward, Britain has come up with *the* accessory of the Biennale – a stylish carrier bag, 'liveried' in wrapping-paper brown with the words 'Anish Kapoor' and generous easi-sling handles for peerless piazza posing.

Because Kapoor has been profiled in at least nine magazines in the previous five days, and the work has similarly been verballed virtually out of existence, it is the packaging of both the show and Kapoor himself (What's he wearing? Katharine Hamnett? Christopher New?) that draws most immediate comment. And besides, the bars have opened – forty free bars in an area not much bigger than Julian Schnabel's living room.

The Scots, launching their first independent outing, have a piper at their outdoor (i.e. pavilionless) pavilion, plus a variety of canapés featuring baby gherkins, so tempting that people are standing on each other's shoulders to get at one.

The Australians have the James Morrison Quintet with special guest Don Burrows; the Germans boast the longest bar ('hosting facility'), and the Americans are serving champagne cocktails in plastic 'deco' glasses outside a Mussolini-goes-Hip-Hop exhibit which reputedly cost $2 million to set up. There is a dazzling display of costume jewellery here and deep, carcinogenic tans.

National pride is at stake and these things count. The Americans, for instance, have bagged the Palazzo Pisani, where the British are having their party on Friday, for a formal dinner this evening for their representative, Jenny Holzer.

But it's the Australians who draw first blood, with a spectacular reception (catering by Harry's Bar, decor by Tintoretto) at the Scuola Grande di San Rocco.

The Bellinis (champagne and peach juice) are chased by

killer Martinis; the Martinis are accompanied by cool white jazz, and the jazz drifts up the grand staircase to the *albergo* where the wraparound Tintorettos have a brain-burning, hallucinatory effect.

An elderly gentleman casually gropes two female members of his party in a corner; several people have gone into a swoon. And then a messenger from the real world, in the person of the London dealer Bernard Jacobson, blows in. 'Where's the Giorgione? Which one's the Giorgione? I've got a group of people downstairs waiting to go to dinner.'

This includes Howard Jacobson (no relation – 'We're just good friends'). Howard is here as a supporter of all things okker. He loves the Aussies and the Aussies have a transforming power over him. He's stopped looking as if he suspects somebody is about to pick his pocket and become a *mensch*. But it's back to what he himself once called 'the indignity of anonymity' when the orchestra at Florian, the restaurant, pluck their last pizzicato and the bells boing twice.

THURSDAY

Where are you staying? Where did you eat last night? Where are the parties you're planning to get blasted at today?

Social anxiety is the hallmark of jamborees like Venice – a fear of being where it's not when everybody else is where it is. Has Nicholas Serota turned up yet? Yoko Ono? Jeff Koons? If they haven't, where are they? And how do I get in without blowing another £30 on a *motoscafi*?

Arriving by water taxi at the Peggy Guggenheim Museum, for the American party, is a smart move. It avoids the pandemonium going on at the street entrance ('Torture, honey,' Bernard Jacobson's wife, a Biennale veteran, has cautioned) and provides an open run to the bar.

'I love being a groupie. I'm in heaven. This is *heaven*. I'm going to come every time.' This is David Connor. 'I did *World's End* for Vivienne Westwood. I did *Seditionaries* before that for Malcolm (McLaren). I was a punk in seventy-six. I wasn't always the yuppie I am now. I . . .'

Like many conversations started in Venice, it is a conversation that is going to have to be continued later, at another party – the party at the Palazzo Barbero for the Italian sculptor Paolini, perhaps. Or at the *Journal of Art* party at the Palazzo Grassi. Failing these, at the Casino, where the New Museum of Brooklyn is having a thing which doesn't get going until midnight . . .

The comedian Steve Martin, the singer Paul Simon and Aaron Spelling, producer of *Dallas*, are all on Nicholas Logsdail's list. None of them seem to have shown up so far. But the French architect-designer Philippe Starck emerges from the throng in the Guggenheim garden, refills held above his head, to say that the 'Art' concept 'is very convenient for business, for marketing. When it's Art, it's a different price. That's all.'

The French pavilion houses models for a new French pavilion to be built before 1992. One of them is by Starck: 'I prefer to show 'ere a toilet seat, because I think it is more interesting than to show a building. For me to design a building for France or an ashtray or a toilet seat, it is the same thing.'

It is easy, given the relentlessness of the jolly-up, to neglect the fact that not only is serious business constantly being done away from the *mêlée*, in quiet, expensively upholstered corners, but that, for many artists, and especially those just getting a foot on the ladder, the Biennale is a way of bringing their work to the attention of foreign dealers, curators, writers.

One of the British participants in the Aperto, the young section, is Anthony Wilson from Blackpool. His entry is an electronic slide-show conducted at subliminal speed to a soundtrack of 'When You Wish Upon A Star' from Walt Disney's *Fantasia*. The soundtrack is important and so, he points out, is the title of the piece: *Achievers — Strivers — Strugglers — Survivors*.

'It's about all this,' he said this morning, looking down the half-mile of the Arsenale at the 102 other exhibitors from twenty-six other countries — a Kids-R-Us or Do-It-All of the latest tendencies in international 'post-structuralist' thinking.

Wilson found himself in category three of his title when the director of the Tate, who he was meeting for the first time, arrived to view his work. One of his projectors had gone down and he was waiting for a replacement part which the Italians hadn't been able to produce yet.

FRIDAY

The Biennale jury sits this afternoon. Henry Meyric Hughes: 'Rumours start flying around by lunchtime, by Saturday everybody usually knows, but it isn't announced until Sunday.'

By 9.30 a.m. Jenny Holzer is completing her third television interview of the day. TV crews dog her footsteps but, like an atrocity victim or soap queen, she seems to accept this as part of her 'project'.

Anish Kapoor, on the other hand, is starting to show the strain of being what the painter Ad Reinhardt, one of his influences, once called 'the holy-roller-explainer-entertainer-in-residence'.

'He thinks he's going to win the prize,' is the explanation offered by the talented young Scottish sculptor David Mach, still probably best known for his submarine made of tyres on the South Bank.

'She'll get it,' Mach says, as Holzer passes on another tour of the site with a camera crew in tow. 'The Italians are really into that sort of "star" business. We're shoved in here almost as a kind of sideshow. It's a very snobbish affair, this. It fills me full of despondency.'

The experience of 1988, when the venue chosen for the British party was so small that many of the artists' friends couldn't get in, results in a lavish reception – champagne, Tiepolos, ancient Murano glass, candlelight – for 900 this time.

But Bernard Jacobson is still up on his hind legs. 'Have you seen anything that isn't rubbish since you've been here? I don't know what I'm doing here. It's all crap. I'm getting too old for this game. It's for the under twenty-fives.' Bernie is a close friend of Charles Saatchi, and the hot rumour all day has been that Saatchi is about to turn up with the next Mrs S.

SATURDAY

Ten a.m. Anish Kapoor is still sleeping off the night before. Nicholas Logsdail, however, is up and prowling restlessly, waiting for news on the tribal tom-tom.

A call yesterday enquiring about Kapoor's date of birth had suggested the jury were considering him for the under-thirty-five prize, a possibility Logsdail says he finds 'f—ing insulting – it's a prize meant for the Aperto artists and the Aperto is full of shit'.

Breakfast with Kapoor overlooking the Grand Canal. Kapoor's girlfriend and brothers sit at another table. Lady Helen Windsor and a companion occupy a third. It is neither the time nor place to talk about 'post-minimal poetic objecthood', 'metaphysical iconicity' or the Pythagorian and Hegelian references others have detected in his work, so we talk about money, ambition, self-exploitation.

'Were you prepared for the onslaught of the last three days?'

'I was. I have a very good adviser in Nicholas. And I have been to many other art-world gatherings – the reopening of the Museum of Modern Art in New York, and similar equally frantic affairs.'

'Is it necessary to be socially active?'

'I think once the work is properly out in the international world, then it doesn't matter. But somewhere along the way, it seems to matter. Somewhere it seems important to be somewhat public.

'There's so much money in the business now. There's money in the art world like there's never been before. So to see the artist as a pop star is a huge temptation. I think it's really rather terrible.'

'Anish is not being like a prima donna artist if he wants this prize. He's just being like everybody else,' David Mach had said. Where does Kapoor stand?

'The most difficult thing about it is the politics. The rather dirty politics. Maybe it's better not to win a prize, is how I'm thinking now. It's a pain in the arse. The constant frenzy of attention. More talking. More cameras. I don't want to deal with it again. But in a way, of course, you do want it. I mean, who doesn't want to be liked?'

SUNDAY

Kapoor has agreed it would be 'a mega-insult' to be awarded the under-thirty-five prize. Today, at a ceremony attended by the President of Italy, Kapoor (who is nearly thirty-seven) is

246

awarded the Premio Duemila for the best artist under thirty-five. As the American critic Harold Rosenberg once told a friend, 'The art world is a comedy!'

1990

Gilbert and George
and LE MAIRE DE PARIS
VOUS PRIE DE BIEN VOULOIR ASSISTER AU VERNISSAGE DE L'EXPOSITION

GILBERT & GEORGE

LE VENDREDI 3 OCTOBRE DE 18 HEURES À 21 HEURES
MUSÉE D'ART MODERNE DE LA VILLE DE PARIS - 11, AVENUE DU PRÉSIDENT-WILSON 75116 PARIS - TÉL. : 01 53 67 40 00
EXPOSITION OUVERTE DU 4 OCTOBRE 1997 AU 4 JANVIER 1998

Hope to see you there
lots of love
X G + G X

EXPOSITION PRODUITE PAR
PARIS musées
LES MUSÉES DE LA VILLE DE PARIS

INVITATION VALABLE POUR DEUX PERSONNES

site Web : www.gilbertandgeorge.co.uk

ELTON JOHN, COLLECTOR

Liberace called them his 'Happy-Happies' — the mink-wrapped pianos, ermine-lined Rolls-Royces and emerald and ruby-encrusted tennis socks and candelabra that Christie's disposed of at auction in Los Angeles earlier this year for a little over $2 million.

Now Elton John, long regarded as rock and roll's answer to the great sequinned one, has decided to put his own Happy-Happies on the market. In its most ambitious international production since the $25 million Andy Warhol auction in April ('A man destined to remain famous not for fifteen minutes, but for centuries to come'), Sotheby's is selling off Elton's effects in a four-day, 2,000-lot sale that kicks off the autumn saleroom season.

Consistent with a marketing strategy which proved effect-ive with Liberace, Andy Warhol and the Windsor jewels, the plums of the Elton John collection have been touring the world since the early summer like Chaucerian relics. They have trav-elled from Tokyo to New York to Los Angeles to Sydney, and have been the occasion for champagne popping and pocket cal-culating at every stop. The confident expectation at Sotheby's is that all lines into its London saleroom will be jammed for the entire four days as a result.

At the beginning of June, however, the army of bronze and ivory figures, the forests of Tiffany and Gallé lamps, the piles of

Cartier brooches and necklaces and the other contents of the former Reg Dwight's house in Old Windsor were still being evaluated and sorted in Sotheby's storerooms in Bond Street.

A few days earlier Elton had been in to be photographed for the deluxe covers of the four-volume commemorative catalogue. He had left for dinner at Mr Chow wearing one of the lots — an elaborate collar of stuffed satin bananas — over his evening jacket and had then staggered out of the restaurant without it ('They were horrified, the people here. Panic-struck').

Safely retrieved, the bananas were now draped across a piece of sturdy Victorian furniture in the guava-silk-lined office-cum-sitting-room of Lord Gowrie, Sotheby's chairman. The office had been commandeered for the afternoon by Elton and his entourage, which explained the clink of glasses and frequent peals of laughter leaking out into the hallowed corridors around it.

The large room was also filled to overflowing with prize examples of Elton's collecting mania. A square of black velvet contained £90,000-worth of high-octane sparklers, not all of them in the best possible taste ('Van Cleef & Arpels, Los Angeles, that came from. Rodeo Drive. It's very Elizabeth Taylor, isn't it? Ultra-Elizabeth Taylor. It's hideous. Absolutely hideous,' Elton said of an ivory, emerald and diamond elephant-head bracelet, estimated value £2–3,000. 'I looked at it the other day and I thought, How could you have *bought* that? It's an absolute nightmare').

There was a life-size cardboard cut-out of Elton; elaborate stage costumes dripping in bugle beads and marabou, and the Tiffany standard lamp that had stood in his dining room. There was a guitar case full of the 'novelty' glasses for which he is famous, a camisole belonging to Judy Garland in *Meet Me in St Louis*, a crowd of Lalique lamps, and paintings by Magritte,

Allen Jones and L. S. Lowry, all recently removed from the squash court that his wife had turned into a repository for the overspill of his collection.

But, looking around at it all, Elton said the bananas were the only things he was having second thoughts about handing over. 'They look like something they'd give the Queen on a tour of Equatorial South Guinea or somewhere. "Your Majesty, here is something to go with your dreary Hardy Amies outfit,"' he said in a convincing Caribbean accent, and another gale of laughter rocked the building.

The bananas were part of a 'pirate' outfit from the early eighties. Did he come up with the ideas for his stage outfits himself? he was asked. 'I would come up with a couple of ideas, but most of the time I just gave people their head on everything. That's why I ended up looking like a demented drag queen. Because half the people who were designing for me were demented drag queens.' Hilarity in the ranks.

Fixing on a pair of 'outrageous' platforms, lot 144 in the catalogue – 'a pair of monogrammed high-platform boots, the silver-leather zippered boots lettered E and J in scarlet with leather stacked heels and silver and scarlet platform soles (£400–£600)' – one of the secretaries in the chairman's office, too young to remember glam rock, asked had he *really* been able to wear them on stage without breaking an ankle?

'They were daywear, darling,' Elton said. 'I used to run for taxis in those. That's why when the punk thing happened I loved it. There was such a great sense of humour with the punks. I remember seeing a girl run for a bus in the King's Road with her legs tied together and a cannon ball on the side, like a convict. And I thought, Oh brilliant. Only in this country. How fabulous.

'I cornered the market in platform shoes. That has to be the worst era of fashion ever, I would've thought, and I have some of the prime worst examples. The higher they went, the higher I used to get them. When I first joined the football club I was six-foot two.'

It is well known that, over the years, Elton John has put together one of the largest collections of recorded music in private hands. Tower Records would regularly give him the run of its biggest store, in Los Angeles, and he would have to container-ship his purchases back to England. His collecting in other areas, however, was less systematic.

'I can find something to buy anywhere in the world,' he said in one of the quieter moments, 'and I suffered from shipping disease. Only *I* could buy a tram in Melbourne and have it shipped home. Then a lot of stuff was bought at auctions, which I never went to, because otherwise my hand would be permanently up. I've always instinctively bought stuff. Whether it's been a bad investment or a good investment, I've never really bought like that.

'For instance, occasionally somebody might say, "There's an important sale of Picassos — you should go and buy one of them." But I've never done it like that. I don't think there's much fun in that. I mean, when I first started, the best investment was stamps, because there was no duty on stamps. But I can't think of anything more *boring* than going in and out of the country with stamps in my pocket.

'I never know what I'm going to buy. That was the whole great thing about it. I never knew what I wanted. I didn't go out for a certain set thing; I'd just suddenly find things I really liked. That was the whole joy about shopping for me. It was like an adventure. I bought on impulse. I live my life on impulse, really. Always have. When I'm happy, I've always been happy doing that.'

Elton John is a sentimentalist. When Watford contested the FA Cup Final a few years ago at Wembley, his face was awash with tears from 'Abide With Me' to the final whistle. He once admitted that trying to decide whether to get rid of a 1970 T-shirt plunged him into a crisis of conscience. But now he is clearing out everything, from his spectacularly weird collection of Bugatti furniture to his personally inscribed picture of Elvis. Why?

'Because it's time to make our house into a home to live in rather than a place for people to come and say, "Well, that's nice, but where can I put my drink?" It was starting to look like Harrods' warehouse. There was stuff sitting unopened in crates, which was preposterous. Literally everything was covered. Every wall, every surface. It was suffocating me.'

Following hard on the heels of the proposed sale of Watford FC for £2 million to Robert Maxwell (a sale since blocked by the Football League), Elton's big sell-off has naturally given rise to speculation that he is somehow, inconceivably, strapped for cash.

'It was all a bit vague at first and rather intriguing,' Sotheby's British chairman, Lord Gowrie, says. 'Was it some sort of public relations management intended as a corrective to things which appeared in the British press last year? Or did he simply want to raise some money quickly, which, after all, is a perfectly respectable thing to do?

'Then you went to the house and all became clear. He had had a considerable success in his own business that week – a hit record in the United States or something, and there was clearly no shortage of cash. What there was a shortage of was somewhere to sit. He had literally to hack his way up to bed.'

Elton John and Lord Gowrie met for the first time ten years ago when Gowrie was a private dealer in contemporary art. He sold Elton an important Francis Bacon portrait ('a great masterpiece' as he describes it) and this was one of the things he advised him to hold back from the sale.

'Such attics cleared of me! Such absences.' The former arts minister under Mrs Thatcher quotes Philip Larkin in attempting to explain the motives behind Elton John's clear-out (and Sotheby's keenness to assist). 'Collections, you know, are incredibly determining. They determine what curtains or carpets you have or how you decorate your pool room or den. And I think Elton was looking for a different ambience, a different environment in which to live, a different . . . I hate the word "lifestyle". To you or me or lesser mortals than Elton, it's the equivalent of clearing out the attic.'

Put like that, of course, it all sounds very homely. It also sounds as if Sotheby's was unchallenged in its bid to sell off Elton John's combined collections, which is not the case. 'I wish it was,' Charles Allsop, UK chairman of Sotheby's ancient rival, Christie's, says. 'The truth, however, is that we also made a presentation to Elton John which sadly didn't succeed.'

Sotheby's (founded 1744) and Christie's (founded 1766) – 'the two old girls' as Lord Gowrie sometimes refers to them – together control between a third and a half of the international art market. Their combined pre-tax profits for 1987 were in excess of £70 million.

'Everyone agrees that a whole new class of collectors has jumped into the auction market – Reagan-era tycoons who have made a lot of money very quickly in fields such as arbitrage, corporate takeovers, and real-estate development,' Calvin Tomkins wrote recently in the *New Yorker*. 'There are over a million millionaires in the United States today, and more and more of them seem to be buying art.'

The expected downturn in the art market following last October's stock-market crash never happened. If anything, the reverse occurred. The auction houses are now attracting the floating cash of investors wary of Wall Street and the City. In the last year record prices have been the rule at almost every major sale, in every collecting area.

'There are so many more collectors now,' a Sotheby's New York specialist in contemporary art has said. 'And there's a whole new level of disposable income. Some of the new people buy only at auction. They seem to like the auction-room atmosphere, which is sometimes like a roomful of Roman gladiators.'

Contemporary art is particularly 'hot' at the moment. But the supply of masterpieces is limited, and the kind of growth the major auction houses have seen in the last three or four years can only be maintained if they can convince collectors of the investment potential of new categories of auction goods, such as fine wines, antique cars, *haute couture* and pairs of Elton John's boots and glasses.

With its first sale of rock-and-roll memorabilia in December 1981, Sotheby's tapped into an unsuspected but potentially huge and lucrative market. It now holds two sales a year of such items, and has to compete for material – original Beatles lyrics, Keith Moon drum kits, pairs of Jimi Hendrix's trousers – with the rival houses.

'There is practically nothing that we wouldn't have a market for,' the former Christie's chairman, John Floyd, was quoted saying earlier this year. 'There is nothing which is faintly artistic which we wouldn't sell.'

In June, however, Charles Allsop withdrew a batch of 'ancestor skulls' (including 'a rare deformed skull') and 'voodoo heads' from a Christie's sale of tribal art in London.

Allsop, who, in addition to being chairman is his firm's most distinguished auctioneer, also admits to feeling some unease when it came to knocking down the personal effects of the late Sir Cecil Beaton: 'Memorabilia, fine. We all live with hand-me-downs. But I did intensely dislike selling Cecil Beaton's clothes. A dead man's clothes. It just *wasn't* particularly agreeable.'

But both Allsop and Gowrie insist there is nothing new about the current drive to target new categories of buyer and exploit new or under-exploited markets.

Allsop: 'There is nothing new *at all* about any of this. Absolutely not. Look what we did for Beaton. We had a band in the garden playing selections from *My Fair Lady*. That was good marketing, not hype, although I would agree that it's a very fine line.'

Gowrie: 'People – and by people I mean journalists – don't have a very well-developed historical sense. If you do, you know that new money has always bought works of art. Our so-called material age is still a very long way behind the eighteenth century when it comes to self-promotion, showing off, and doing so with knowledge, taste and daring.'

'They came in. They raped my house.' Elton was still doing knockabout, still rolling them in the aisles. 'What more can I say? They took the soap dish out of my bathroom.' (Lot 1615 – 'an amusing soap dish, modern, modelled with a contented bather luxuriating in his bath, his large feet perched on the wide "enamelled" rim, wearing green spotted tie'.) 'It could turn into *It's A Knockout*,' Elton said, 'if they're not careful. I got in just in time.'

He was in the Sotheby's storerooms now, surrounded by the detritus of his life, posing for a picture. 'At one point,' he said, 'they suggested having the sale at my house. At my *house*. Can you imagine? I went crazy. It was impossible to walk through the drawing room for a while without getting a sticker on your forehead.'

Had he given any thought, some spoilsport asked, as to what all this stuff lumped together might reveal about him as a person? None at all, he said. 'Since I've been successful I've always laid myself fairly open. I mean, once you go to football matches and people chant really vile things about you, you can take anything. I couldn't be like Prince or somebody like that. Michael [Jackson]. That's where they get their mystique from. But you can't run away from it. All this is kinda like watching your own funeral, in a sense. It's kinda nice. I like it. It appeals to me.'

On the way out, his eye was drawn to lot 1853, 'A Cutey Doll Radio, wearing a see-through negligee, with dual controls, her body containing the battery.' ('I'm sure this'll fetch a lot of money, darling!') On the shelf next to it was a Tiffany dressing-table set which he said had been a present from John Lennon.

'But you could just lie about these things, couldn't you? "This is from Haile Selassie on his deathbed . . . Lech Walesa gave me this fabulous dining table . . ." And people would believe it. That's the incredible thing.'

Robert, Elton's roadie without portfolio and live-in lodger, meanwhile, was impatient for the collecting bug to bite again. 'All I got left in my bedroom is a plastic Tiffany lamp, a Formica table and a mattress. Cleaned me out, they have. Charming innit?' Robert said, smiling through the tears. 'Knoworramean?'

1988

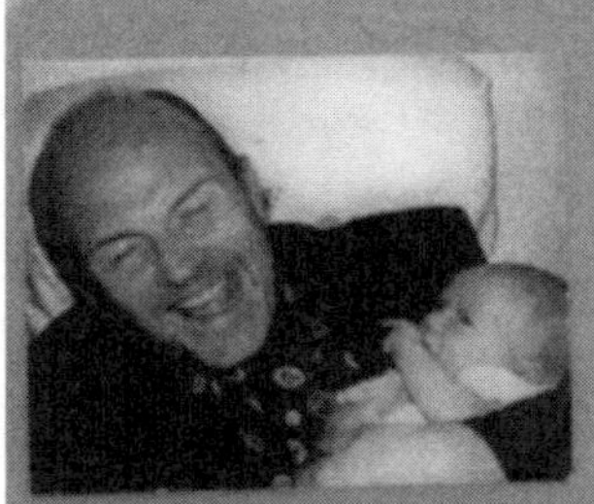

GODFATHER
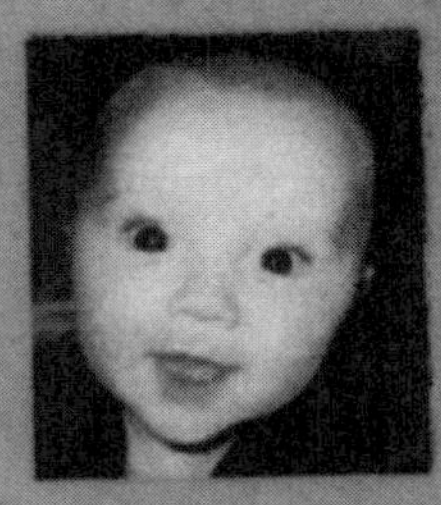
Gordon Burn
to Connor Ojala Brennan Hirst
born April 27th 1995

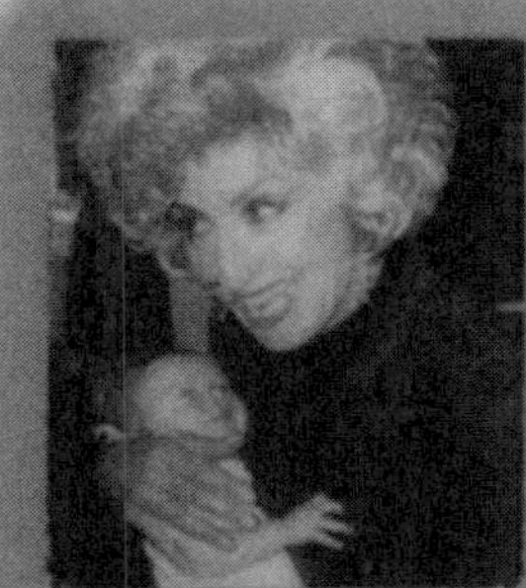
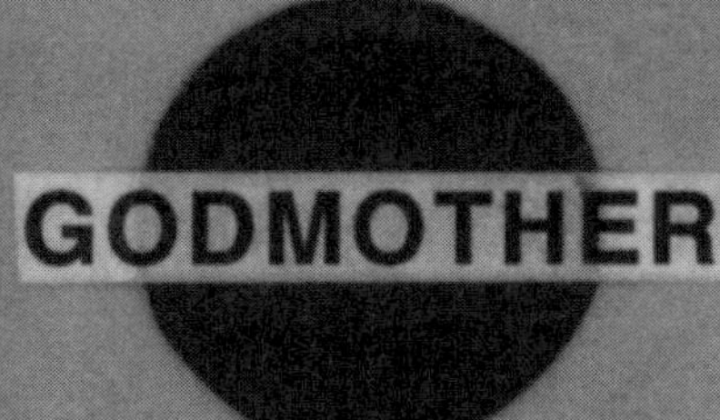
GODMOTHER
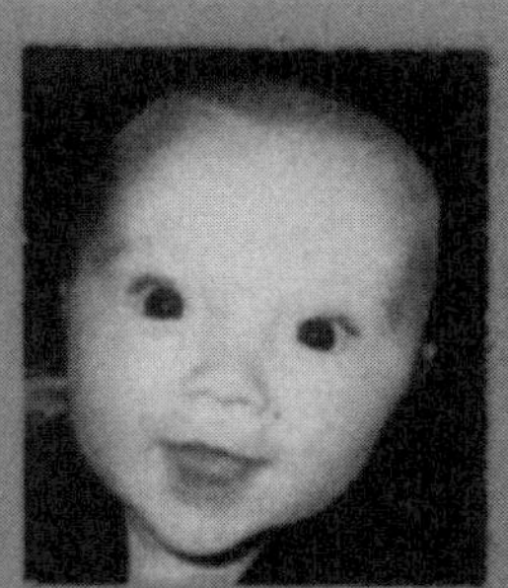
Carol Gorner
to Connor Ojala Brennan Hirst
born April 27th 1995

MODIGLIANI

The apparatus of publicity and promotion that now attaches to the big blockbuster exhibition – the facility visit, the corporate amenity, the preview opportunity, the courtesy blowout – is as far removed from the life led by Modigliani and other *peintres maudits* in Paris in the early part of the twentieth century as can be imagined. This is approximately how far:

In the month of his death in 1920, at the age of thirty-five, Modigliani bailed his friend Maurice Utrillo out of the lunatic asylum where he was incarcerated for the dementia resulting from his chronic alcoholism, encouraged him to knock out two street scenes of Montmartre, rushed them over to his dealer, Leopold 'Zbo' Zborowski, and then the two of them dedicated themselves to getting wrecked on the strength of his small advance.

The next morning, while Modigliani was still unconscious, Utrillo vanished with his friend's only suit and pawned it. A while later he returned in triumph with the rotgut that the few francs he'd been able to raise had bought him. Modigliani's regular boozing partner, Chaim Soutine, dropped in at the studio and 'Modi' told Utrillo to take off his clothes so that Soutine could take them round and hock them and buy more wine.

Food was never a priority, but what food there was tended to come from cadging or handouts or even, on occasion, from foraging in garbage pails. Modigliani and his lover, Jeanne

Héburterne, spent the last eight days of their lives lying on a filthy mattress in a freezing, rat-infested hovel, existing on sardines out of tins; Jeanne was nine months pregnant at the time and committed suicide by throwing herself out of a window on the evening of his death.

These were the conditions in which Modigliani, an Italian, had been living since his arrival in Paris thirteen years earlier, when he set up his first studio in a banged-together shack in what was then the shanty-town district of Montmartre.

During the First World War, in common with many other foreign artists living in Paris, Modigliani had had to depend for his food on the soup kitchens set up by a wealthy American woman. He was still well into his thirties, sometimes getting by peeling potatoes and washing dishes in a local restaurant.

It was hard not to be impressed by the disparity between the starving bohemian striver and the Club Class journalist on the receiving end of the largesse doled out by Fiat, the sponsor of the first leg of The Unknown Modigliani tour, at the Palazzo Grassi, Fiat's 'cultural seat' in Venice. Or was this just being naive as well as ungrateful? It could be argued, after all, that it is simply the inexorable resolution of a process that started even as Modigliani lay gasping his last.

During his final hours in hospital, a Paris dealer, Louis Libaude, scuttled round Paris scarfing up all the Modiglianis he could find, for nothing or next to nothing. Two other dealers approached Modigliani's friend Francis Carco at the funeral on 27 January 1920, to barter with him. 'They talked about it quite naturally as we followed the coffin,' Carco later wrote, 'as if it were none of the deceased's business.' The American patent-medicine millionaire Dr Albert Barnes was on the trail as early as 1922, when he acquired his first Modiglianis: they are among the Masterpieces from the Barnes Foundation which are currently bringing crowds flocking to the Musée d'Orsay in Paris.

'The movement in favour of modern art is intense,' the dealer René Gimpel wrote in a diary entry for December 1928. 'Derain, Modigliani and Utrillo are very much sought after. There is a positive furore for modern decorative art . . .' 'As the boom in his paintings grew after his death,' June Rose writes in her biography, *The Pure Bohemian*, 'landlords advertised free lodgings for artists who would 'finish' Modiglianis and painters were employed to forge his signature and complete his work, with the result that an alarming number of false Modiglianis, from blatant fakes to borderline cases, appeared on the market.'

'Yesterday Hessel bought a fake Modigliani for 55,000 francs,' Gimpel wrote, 'and having swallowed it, he is obliged to shut his trap . . . He is furious.'

Picasso, Modigliani and others, realising that Montmartre was turning into a tourist trap, moved on to Montparnasse, on the other side of Paris, around 1912. After Modigliani's death, Montparnasse turned into a kind of bohemian theme park, full of would-be bohos driving fast cars and drinking champagne in the new nightclubs.

'At a time when it was the fashion to represent painters as over-sexed, alcoholic, brilliant, immoral and full of a dangerous fascination, writers and restaurateurs of the Quarter sensed the need to preserve the myth and the glamour of Modigliani,' Rose writes. 'They grew rich on his false reputation and Montparnasse developed into a leading European tourist attraction, with nightspots offering sophisticated vice, far beyond the means of the poverty-stricken artists of the First World War.'

'I want a short life but an intense one,' Modigliani is

reputed to have said. And when drugged or drunk he was cantankerous, a menace, lurching into traffic, cursing, kicking, scratching friends who tried to help him. At work on a painting, according to one first-hand account, 'his shoulders heaved. He panted. He made grimaces and cried out. You couldn't come near him.'

In the twenties his friend, the poet André Salmon, wrote the book that created the legend of Modigliani, the suicidally self-destructive painter whose genius was liberated by drugs. Several similarly romanticising novels, as well as a play and a film pandering to the legend of 'the drunk of Montparnasse', have appeared since. Accompanying his coffin to Père Lachaise cemetery, Picasso spotted the policeman who had so often arrested Modigliani, standing at attention as the procession passed: 'Do you see?' he muttered to the person walking with him. 'Now Modi has his revenge.'

Like the pre-publicity for a new Rolling Stones tour or Madonna record, or a notorious killer's first day in court, the press preview of The Unknown Modigliani in Venice was a full-dress, international media event. Camera crews from the ten countries which would be receiving the exhibition during its three-year touring life fought for set-ups in front of the 400 or so drawings of nudes, portraits, Pierrots and caryatids, a few of which were still perceptibly creased from where they had been retrieved from waste-paper baskets and straightened out.

Modigliani drew rapidly and incessantly, everywhere and all the time. Friends and others who sat for him have described him in his corduroy jacket sitting on the terrace of the Rotonde or the Dome, a glass of absinthe in front of him, drawing likenesses in acute, rapid strokes. These he would mostly barter for hashish or more drinks. Occasionally when he had a sheaf of drawings, he would try to sell them to a dealer.

There is a story that, on one occasion, rather than part with drawings for less than he thought they were worth, he hung them on a nail in the toilet, having run them through with a piece of string. When his work appeared in London as part of a group show organised by Osbert and Sacheverell Sitwell, an enormous wicker basket full of Modigliani drawings stood by the table occupied by the Sitwells in the centre of the gallery: visitors could choose a specimen for a shilling, threepence less than the price of admission to the exhibition, but very few drawings were sold.

Their conversion into a precious commodity was confirmed by the press conference called at the Palazzo Grassi, which boasted a full panoply of the art world's leading curatoriat. Representatives of the Metropolitan Museum, New York; the Reina Sofia Museum, Madrid; the Ueno Royal Museum, Tokyo; the Royal Academy of Arts and the six other venues taking this gig were arranged at a long table, like impresarios at the talk-up to a big fight.

The ceremony of passing the mike was even observed, with each man (they were all men) being given the chance to enthuse, in his curatorial way, about what boffo business he expected the show to do in his territory.

'Modigliani has long been established as a great artist, but perhaps not the greatest artist,' our man, Norman Rosenthal of the Royal Academy, announced. 'This shows us how he drew on Eastern art, African art, the Renaissance, in his extraordinary explorations of the ear, his explorations of the neck, his explorations of the nose, his explorations of the bodily orifices, of the breasts. Extraordinary, mmm? Modigliani is a greater artist for having seen these drawings, so beautifully installed.' And then he passed the microphone on with an amplified sigh and a hollow ker-thunk.

In the museum's lobby, meanwhile, the licensed Modigliani merchandise was going on display – Modi ties, bow-ties, beach towels, backpacks, playing cards, T-shirts, document cases, drinks trays, sketch books, pens, key rings, necklaces and earrings in precious and semi-precious metals, all in the shape of or bearing the imprint of Modigliani Woman, trademarked for her cylindrical neck, her conical breasts, her oval face, her rhomboidal black slitted eyes. The motif logoised; the modern master given market focus. A bum-bag in Neoprene and a unique elastomeric material! Proof absolute that he has risen above the ruck.

The gulf between Amedeo Modigliani (b. 1884), the booksniff and mother's boy from Livorno, and 'Modigliani', bohemian and transglobal blockbuster, however, only became apparent the next day. Better than the private view, the accidental glimpse.

Saturday in Venice brought what the programme called the 'Official Inauguration', from which the press was barred. But I was travelling along the Grand Canal around midday, when the guests were being delivered to the Palazzo Grassi by liveried launch and *motoscafi* – *ufficiali municipali* and *ufficiali del governo* being glad-handed on to the pontoon, exchanging air kisses; Fiat executives and their partners working their Ferre and Missoni, their Versace and Armani. Again the hint of weirdness, of incongruity, intensified now by witnessing it from the outside.

But there was something else. It took a few minutes, and the physical distancing that resulted from the motor-bus pulling away from the museum, to trace it to the banner advertising The Unknown Modigliani, which spanned the canal. In addition to, and almost as big as, Modigliani's name was another name, so prominent that it seemed to claim equal billing: 'Drawings from the Collection of Paul Alexandre'. This was a slogan that was going to be unavoidable all over Venice in the next three months, as it will be unavoidable in London this year, and every city the show visits up to 1996.

It could be argued that Paul Alexandre deserves this generous acknowledgement, this public twinning. Alexandre was a young medical student, and then a young surgeon, in Paris in the eight years from 1906 to 1914, when Modigliani was a young, starving artist. History has established that without Paul Alexandre, Modigliani would probably have been no artist at all; he probably wouldn't have stayed alive. 'How chic,' he used to say, with the irony of somebody irremediably out of it, 'to be in the swim.'

Modigliani's first years in Paris were the years of early cubism and revolutionary modernist experimentation. But, although Paul Alexandre was one of the first people in Montmartre to buy a major painting by Picasso, and Modigliani one of the first painters of note to fall under Picasso's influence, 'Modi' kept himself resolutely apart from the established social groupings (in particular the *bande à Picasso*). He was an outsider by the force of both circumstance and inclination, and he relied on the regular commissions that Paul Alexandre put his way — portraits of Alexandre's father, his brother, other members of the family — for his meagre subsistence.

'From the day of our first meeting,' Paul Alexandre wrote in May 1954, when he was seventy-three, 'I was struck by [Modigliani's] remarkable artistic gifts, and I begged him not to destroy a single sketchbook or a single study. I put the meagre sources I could spare at his disposal, and I possess almost all his paintings and drawings from this period.'

In the weighty tome accompanying The Unknown Modigliani, though, Dr Alexandre's son Noel falls into the perhaps understandable trap of allowing himself to overestimate his father's role as the nurturer of genius. The title of the book's opening section – 'Paul Alexandre, Modigliani's Chosen Witness' – carries the clear implication that Alexandre was the person chosen by Modigliani as his chronicler and amanuensis. Whereas an examination of the full quote from which the chapter heading is extracted reveals a subtly but revealingly different dynamic: 'I feel that I am chosen to tell the story of your brother's life in Paris, as we were bound by an intimate friendship,' Dr Alexandre wrote to Emanuele Modigliani shortly after 'Modi's' death.

By 1920 Alexandre and Modigliani hadn't seen each other for six years, not since the call-up of 1914: years which produced most of the work – the lengthened and 'distorted' portraits of Soutine, Cocteau, Jeanne Héburterne, the nudes – on which Modigliani's reputation now hangs. More significant, though, is Noel Alexandre's admission that he has set himself the task of writing a revisionist history whose intention is 'to contribute towards re-establishing a truth that is far more noble than the legend'. This, he says, is the fulfilment of his father's ambition, stated as early as 1924, to write a book that would 'put paid to certain persistent rumours' about Modigliani.

Most of these concern his dipsomania and drug addiction and restless promiscuity, words which you can feel sending the blood rushing to Noel Alexandre's ears. The novelist Malcolm Lowry wrote, 'You cannot trust the ones that are too careful. As writers or drinkers. Old Goethe cannot have been so good a man as Keats or Chatterton. Or Rimbaud. The ones that burn.'

Similarly, Modigliani proposed, 'Alcohol is for the middle class evil. It is a vice. It is the Devil's beckon. But for us artists it is necessary.' Once, as he was destroying nearly all of his early work, he explained to his neighbours, who thought that he had gone mad: 'Childish baubles, done when I was a dirty bourgeois.'

When Modigliani arrived in Paris in 1906, he was something of an exquisite, scoffing at Picasso's soiled workmen's clothes. 'For a time he was the perfect student away from home,' wrote Lawrence Werner, 'writing regularly to his mother, and weeping with excitement upon reading her letters . . . [But] within a year, this strait-laced young bourgeois became a Bohemian vagabond par excellence . . . the uncrowned king of vagabonds.'

When a novelist in the twenties decided to update Henri Murger's *Scènes de la Vie de Bohème*, the source of Puccini's opera, it is easy to see why he chose Modigliani as the model for his central character. When he was living with an Englishwoman, Beatrice Hastings, he was legendary for his violent, unpredictable behaviour. 'When she wouldn't open the door to him, he broke the window panes . . . When he finally got in, there were scenes with revolvers and bottles of rum,' reported the writer Max Jacob.

At one party in his studio, incensed by something Beatrice had said, he started tearing down a wall: 'First he scratched away the plaster, then he tried to pull out the bricks. His fingers were bloody and in his eyes there was such despair that I could not stand it . . .' At the same party, Modigliani and Beatrice started fighting until he grabbed her and threw her through a window. On another occasion they set about each other with chairs.

At least since Rimbaud's announced determination to become a visionary through the 'disordering of all the senses', self-destructive excess has been a licensed force in the lives of innumerable writers and artists. Modigliani consumed vast quantities of hashish, morphine, opium and ether all through his adult life, as boosters to the staples of red wine and absinthe.

It is part of Noel Alexandre's task, though, to reclaim Modigliani for respectability. He seems to believe that because Modigliani was 'a remarkably cultivated and educated man . . . a born aristocrat [with] the style and all the tastes', he couldn't also be the man who 'devoted as much frantic distraught energy to self-destruction as to the construction of his talent' whom Claude Roy describes in an early biography. Noel Alexandre reports that, while Modigliani 'had a taste for danger' and thought that 'one should not be afraid to risk one's life in order to expand it', his father never saw Modigliani work 'when he was drugged'.

But in the first volume of his life of Picasso, John Richardson writes the following: 'There was . . . an opium den that Modigliani, already a hashish addict when he settled in Montmartre in 1906, used to attend. It was organised by his patron, Dr Paul Alexandre. A firm believer in the power of opium and hashish to stimulate the imagination, Dr Alexandre had set up an artists' commune in a tumbledown pavilion in the rue du Delta.' Unlike Picasso, 'who regarded his work as sacrosanct and always kept his physical and mental energies tuned to the highest pitch', Richardson sees Modigliani as one of those artists 'who could not function without powerful stimulants'.

I asked Norman Rosenthal, the person responsible for bringing The Unknown Modigliani to London, whether he'd got any sense of a sanitising impulse at work in his dealings with the inheritor of Paul Alexandre's collection. He hesitated for some time. 'Well,' he said, 'probably because they're . . .' 'A nice upper-middle-class family?' There was another long pause. 'They're people who have . . . I'm just trying to think of a nice way of putting it . . . That there was something serious in Modigliani, that there was serious culture in Modigliani, is absolutely without doubt. Whether he got drunk or drugged up to the nines is beside the point. The dignity of the work is important, and whether it makes a serious contribution to the culture, to one's idea of the development of art in the twentieth century. I think we have become far, far too obsessed by biography, in all walks of life. I think it's utterly irrelevant.'

I asked him to tell me what kind of picture he had built up of the man who'd put this collection together. 'Paul Alexandre was a collector of a handful of artists, particularly Modigliani. He believed in him and he was one of those kind of people, it's quite common, who once they hit on to somebody, they buy everything. Everybody makes their own discoveries. And hooray for those doctors, or people who are not within the art world as such, who can commit themselves to an artist whether they succeed or not. There's also a certain degree of accident in these things. It's the constellation of life, which art is very much about.'

'Things are tougher than people,' Bruce Chatwin wrote in *Utz*, his essay on the psychopathology of the compulsive collector. 'Things are the changeless mirror in which we watch ourselves disintegrate. Nothing is more ageing than a collection of works of art.'

Paul Alexandre was born three years before Amedeo Modigliani and lived forty-eight years longer than him, finally dying in 1968 at the age of eighty-seven. By hitching his star to Modigliani's wagon, no matter how honourable his motives, he guaranteed himself a kind of low-grade, second-order immortality.

It is the deal Charles Saatchi is currently making with a

future less likely to be impressed by the man behind 'You Know Labour Isn't Working' and soft Silk Cut S&M than by his premium holdings in Damien Hirst, Richard Deacon, Patrick Caulfield and others whose names, he is smart enough to recognise, are destined to outlive his own.

1994

HELMUT NEWTON

Lunch over, Helmut Newton and his wife June (also a photographer, working under the name Alice Springs) are bowling along the Lower Corniche in the direction of their home in one of the *bon ton*iest of Monte Carlo's many *bon ton* tower blocks. There are banyans and palm trees poking out of the Astroturf and Niarchos's yacht rearing like a great white Waldorf in the harbour, as their little black runabout splashes round the bends of what looks and feels like a life-size Scalextric.

Twenty-four hours earlier, June had been in Milan photographing her husband photographing the kind of image with which his thirty-year-old portfolio bulges: a female 'victim' model bound head to foot in cotton yarn, with her arms strapped to her sides and only her bare breasts exposed.

The picture was for an advertisement scheduled to appear in the same international magazines in which Helmut Newton made his name as a fashion photographer in the sixties, which is evidence of the extent to which he has been able to invest formerly unacceptable sadomasochistic and fetishistic imagery with a significant commodity value.

He has achieved this by bringing it out from under the counter and giving it a titillating, easily assimilable, swank veneer. He has achieved it, in other words, by taking all the heat out and replacing heat with 'irony'. This is not Newton's own word, of course. It is the nature of visual artists (a description that he modestly declines) not to want to discuss what they are trying to 'say' in their pictures. And Newton is no exception.

He has only one weary word, for instance, for those who claim that his work degrades women by presenting them as mute fantasy objects, accessorised with leather and vinyl: 'Bullshit'.

And yet the poster for one of his recent exhibitions, pinned to the wall in his study, could stand as Exhibit A in any feminist case brought against him. It draws its inspiration more from the news pictures that he clips and files compulsively than from any conventional idea of 'glamour' photography. The crumpled blonde looks more like a rape or murder victim than Mimi van Doren.

Newton affects surprise at this. 'It was hot and she's lying on a very rich couch, as a matter of fact.' But, in a languidly inflammatory way, he talks about his models as 'meat' and about models being different from 'real people'. 'A model is not a real person because we pay her *x* amount of money to be allowed to make her into whatever we want.'

His last show in London was ink-bombed by a radical feminist group. But now he feels that 'those women's-libbers are much better. I think they're not as one-eyed as they were. I think they have evolved a lot. And, in any case, my answer to them is what it has always been: I've spent my life photographing women and I think my pictures are a total, 100 per cent glorification of women.'

In the last few years Newton has concentrated exclusively on portraits and female nudes. The demands of the apparently ad hoc, but in fact fastidiously organised, fashion *mises en scène* with which he established his reputation became too much for him and led to a near-fatal heart attack while working on a session for *Vogue* in 1971.

He had received a sharp reminder of this the day before I met the Newtons, when the mask he was wearing as protection against the asbestos dust swirling round the location in Milan had caused him to have palpitations. He had made an appointment to see a specialist the minute he arrived home. Which is news to June.

'Oh, Helmie! To see about your heart?' June asks as Helmut negotiates a typically dinky piece of Monégasque seafront. 'You know what happened to the Shah of Iran, don't you? He had eight *teams* of doctors all over the world. A little old GP is better than all that stuff. Well, I may as well go along and he can check my heart at the same time.'

'No, Junie, stop it. Your heart's perfectly all right. There isn't anything wrong with your heart. You're as strong as an ox.'

'How do you *know*? I'm having palpitations all the time.'

'No, no, no, no, darling . . . She swims three-quarters of an hour a day and I get *so* bored. I used to be a champion swimmer. A really big, big champion swimmer. But hey, listen, don't listen to her. She just wants to be chic.'

The Newtons have been together for more than forty years. They met in Australia, where she was an actress and he, a German Jew, was a refugee from Hitler. It is a relationship that is documented in some of his most memorable pictures.

In 1972, for instance, he photographed June bare-breasted during a dinner they were having together in Paris. 'I looked at her. And I thought the light was nice,' he has said. 'So I said to her, "Open your dress."' Ten years later, he photographed her naked, just after she had undergone major surgery. A deep incision runs from her groin to her navel.

'I was so sick,' she says. 'What could I possibly do? Anyway it was a marvellous way of seeing Helmut, because if he hadn't been able to see me through the camera, he would never have come in. That I know for sure. Because Helmut faints. He's very squeamish. But the moment he came in with a camera and ordered, "Down with the bed covers," I knew that everything was all right.'

'June,' Newton is at pains to point out, 'is not kinky at all. Her upbringing's also very different from mine. I might be kinky, a little bit. But she's as square as you can get 'em.'

It is June, though, who has constantly urged him to keep going when his own, more deliberately commercial, instincts have told him to pull back.

In the period after his heart attack she encouraged him to start taking pictures 'from inside himself', based on memories of his youth in the Berlin of the thirties. In the mid-seventies she talked him out of his initial reservation that getting models to pose in orthopaedic corsets was 'sick'.

Five years ago, he accepted the invitation of two professional couples he met at a cocktail party in California to photograph them having sex. 'I've never published them, and I'm not going to because it would close too many doors for me,' he said as recently as last year. In his New Nudes show at Hamiltons Gallery, however, which runs concurrently with their joint show at the National Portrait Gallery, June has encouraged Newton to exhibit some of his pornographic pictures.

'A lot of people that I know were very much against it. They said I'd gone too far,' he says. 'But I think, at my age, now I can afford to show certain things. I haven't shown the *really* hard stuff. Maybe one day I'm going to do it. I don't know. It's a very difficult thing to do, you see. It's not easy to do pornography and do it well. And I think they're good pornography. June says they're good.'

Kinkiness – or at least an intimation of kinkiness – has become Newton's stock-in-trade. 'I always want more skin,' used to be his complaint. These days, he claims, he doesn't have to press people to perform for his camera: they turn themselves into 'Newtons' without his having to ask. When he photographed his friends, the restaurateurs Michael and Tina Chow, in Los Angeles, she went out and bought the rope with which Newton lashed her to the bar of Mr Chow's restaurant.

'I liked the idea of the elegant woman being tied up. She's a very chic lady. One of the ten best-dressed women in the world. And I said, "You've got such good taste, go and buy me a really good-looking piece of rope." And she did it. And isn't it nice? Oh, it's beautiful rope.'

When Newton was scouting for locations for a travel story around Prague in September, his guide suddenly threw her clothes off in the street and (at least as he tells it) started spontaneously posing for the camera. 'It wasn't my fault. I like photographing at night, and this girl whipped her clothes off, which you can't do anywhere I know of without getting run in. In France people would be *outraged*. But a lady comes walking her dog past the naked girl and she says: "Ah but I was young once. I understand." I almost fainted.'

The notion that Newton belongs to the world of drugs and orgies, bondage and depravity alluded to in his pictures is a common one. But June Newton says she has never met this person. 'Mr Hyde is in his pictures. *Only* in his photographs. He has never scared me. I always think of Helmut as my Othello. He brings all the spoils from the wars home in the form of Polaroids. He throws them down and I know exactly what's been going on; I know exactly where he's been. I see it *all*.'

'A lot of people think that I must be a very twisted person,' Newton says. 'A lot of people also think that I am a jet-setter, that I live a rich life. Well, I don't. I'm a pretty sober person. I haven't often even been drunk in my life. And no drugs ever. I think it's pretty well known all over the place that I never take drugs. I *despise* drugs.'

The Newtons spend every winter in Los Angeles. Do they socialise very much when they are there? I asked them.

'We socialise so much that in three months we only stayed in twice,' June said.

'For that,' added Newton, 'she cooks *every* night when we get home . . . She's a good cook, June. She's a good cook, you know.'

'You sound as if only *I* like going out,' June said.

'Of course you like it. You're a party girl.'

When they moved from Australia to Paris in the late fifties, June gave up her career as an actress because of the language problem. She collaborated closely with Newton on all his fashion work up to the time of his heart attack in 1971. After that, when his work became more personal, she found herself adrift.

'It's very difficult to be the wife of someone like Helmut in a place like Paris. Women are just overlooked completely in France if they don't do something. And I was so desperate to do something. Really desperate.'

She tried painting for a few years but that didn't amount to anything. Photography came straight out of the blue. 'It wasn't even an urge. I started when Helmut was in bed with a cold one Sunday morning and he couldn't make it to the Place Vendôme to let the model boy know. So I went along and took a few pictures, sent them off to the client and was paid a Helmut Newton fee.'

She made portraits her speciality at Helmut's suggestion ('Everybody that's been photographed by her likes her. So she told me'). She got the name 'Alice Springs' by sticking a pin in a map of Australia.

Do they ever find themselves in competition for subjects? 'I am always happy,' Newton said, 'to step into the shadows.'

'Oh!' she screamed. Nervous and rather self-effacing at first, she had started increasingly to pull her weight. 'Oh! Oh!'

But then, when her husband absented himself for a couple of minutes, she quickly said this: 'What everybody forgets is that I could never afford the luxury of being a photographer if it hadn't been, and if it wasn't for, Helmut. The sort of pictures that I do I would never ever make a living at. Maybe if I had two marvellous assistants, then perhaps. But I wouldn't have the same getting-away-with-it feeling, the feeling of complete luxury, that I have.'

The last time they had a joint show in London, in 1983, *The British Journal of Photography* declared June the winner by a knockout.

'Oh that was Mr Thingummy,' said Helmut, 'The little crit who loves you. You should have married him. He was mad about you.'

'He wasn't mad about me.' June drew herself up to her full five feet. 'He just liked my pictures, Helmut. Let's face it. Call a spade a spade.'

1988

4 THE BRITART MOMENT

London as the Art Capital of the World

I think punk and Thatcher are very similar in a way. They're both: Go for it. 'That house is empty. We ain't got fuck all. So we'll be pirates, take it, squat it . . .' I always think Thatcher equals ram-raiding: You wannit, you take it. [The YBAs] all graduated into that moment.

Richard Wentworth

THE CLASH

The 'new wave' had made the charts – the Jam, the Damned, the Clash and the Stranglers all had albums in the Top 30 – but it was clear the reality of it still hadn't penetrated as far as Newcastle. It was a haphazard mob who crashed through the wall of undergraduate stewards at the Students' Union. Inside, they fell in a scrum before a platform dominated by a blow-up of last year's Notting Hill riots.

Their accessories were modish enough – paper clips, safety pins, of course, ripped shirts, plastic sandals – but they were thrown together in a way that confirmed they had yet to be exposed to the real thing. Their idea of what was 'punk' was based on features in the music papers and banner-headline reports in the *Sun*. The rest of the audience was made up of the mildly curious, the openly sceptical, and some who obviously thought they had taken their lives into their hands and had come only out of a sense of daring.

'Punk rock' – 'this grotesque, insulting, anti-life festival of moral and spiritual anarchy', one commentator called it; 'puke rock' to the *News of the World* – had been labouring under an almost total ban for six months, a direct result of the Sex Pistols' conscientious campaign of outrage.

The reasons for the punk explosion – bored and out-of-work teenagers kicking against 'super-groups' too old to iden-tify with, concerts too expensive to attend, songs that were no reflection of their lives — had been widely put about. Still though, very few at the Students' Union in Newcastle had any real idea what to expect of a package optimistically, rather than provocatively, called 'White Riot – 77'. They soon found out.

The Slits are an all-girl group fronted by a fifteen-year-old who, when she isn't holding a dirty mac wide to reveal black latex tights and bikini knickers, is tatting her hair up into tumbleweed with a pink plastic comb. The other girls, sweating inside their own sausage-skin bondage-chic, remain impassive in the face of Ariana's tantrums, which are almost as spirited onstage as they are off, and her nicely obscene line in audience abuse.

The Subway Sect, on the other hand, in their dole-queue rags, determinedly anti-fashion, look like nice boys. When the mood takes them, however, they can be unpredictable. It's not unheard of for the singer to be two songs ahead of the rest of the group, though nobody can claim with any confidence to know when this is happening. And far from being bucked at the sight of an audience dancing, they have been known to stop abruptly and walk off.

''Course, it's not just the music, it's the total attitude. It's the clothes and the way we do things,' Mick Jones, the Clash's lead guitarist, said later. 'I feel a bit like a reason for a ritual.' The abbreviated titles, committed at the last minute to a scrap of paper and taped into the curve of Jones's guitar – 'London-Pressure-Bored-1977-Hate and War-Cheat-Remote-Police-Career-Capital-Deny-Janie Jones-Riot' – effectively capture the spirit of the Clash's music. But it wasn't their articulation of the fears and frustrations of the so-called 'blank generation' that worked on the audience at Newcastle like a shorted circuit: it was the music. It is no accident that, of the words, only the title lines emerge like football chants from an onslaught that has been criticised for being 'screaming, venomous and unrelenting', the very qualities that are, however, its strengths.

In the same way that the skinheads and football thugs were a reaction against the love-and-peace movement of the sixties, so the primitiveness of the 'new wave' can be seen as a reaction against the artiness in rock music that the hippies came to represent. ('Hippy' and 'ageing hippy' are the punk vocabulary's standard alternatives to 'oldfart' and 'boringoldfart'.)

To call the music crude, though – and a lot of it certainly is – is, in a way, to miss the point. 'Dole-queue rock' has taken off the way it has because, for the first time in a generation, the performers are the same in every essential as the people who pay to come and listen. It was the 'rawness' and 'directness' of the Sex Pistols that prompted the nineteen-year-olds who have since become the Subway Sect to turn their backs on A-levels in Barnet a year ago; and Paul Simonon of the Clash only recently removed the dots that guided his fingers along the neck of his bass guitar. 'It only takes an hour to write a song,' is Joe Strummer's line. 'You can play everything inside three weeks. Everybody knows it's dead easy.'

Strummer is the singer with the Clash and co-author with Mick Jones of all their songs, and it is his habit to talk to an audience. 'Aren't you lucky?' he'd scoffed the night before in Middlesbrough, having read of ICI's plans to create more employment in the area. Next day, he would taunt the audience of St Albans with: '*Rock Follies* is on TV. You don't 'ave to come here an' look at us, you know.'

Talking would have served no purpose in Newcastle, though, because it was bedlam from the word go. The 'pogoing' – a dance style that consists of going up to head invisible footballs – progressed naturally into punch-ups, and the wounded had to be hauled up laughing out of the crush. 'I don't give a toss, they can kick hell out of each other,' Mick Jones said when it was all over. 'Most of them kids, they have a good time. They don't feel good unless they go home via the 'ospital . . . If I wasn't like this, I'd just want to be oblivious an' all. Down the terraces Saturday, Clash gig Friday night . . . Go an' bang yer 'ead against the wall.'

It was all good news for the promoter, Dave Cork, an indomitable young entrepreneur from Wolverhampton who had also stepped in as tour manager. 'Look at that, eh? All them pound notes walking in,' he'd said to Joe Strummer, but Strummer had refused to see the joke. ('Tour managers,' Jones said; 'they stink. They ain't talking my language. Same as record company people. If any of 'em show up round 'ere I ain't got nothing to say, 'cause they ain't talking the same language as me. I'm not interested in them at all.') Cork was organising the tour for nothing on the basis that the Clash, very soon, were going to be very big. Not that money, he wanted to make quite clear, was his only concern. 'I'm just pleased there's something new,' he said. 'I'm twenty-five now, been in the business since I was eighteen, and I'd seen it all before. It was dead. But now, all of a sudden, the excitement is there, the way I remember it in the days of Hendrix and the Cream.'

Cork says he lost a lot of friends through his association with the Pistols' Anarchy In the UK tour. And there had been some fears that White Riot might face the same sort of bans when the audience at one of the first shows, at the Rainbow in London, resurrected the old ritual of seat slashing. But once on the road, the tour had progressed without major incident. A basic wage of £25 a week for each of the four members of the Clash, and a bare subsistence allowance for the other groups, plus a blanket ban on room service and the disconnection of all

284

bedroom telephones – precautions insisted on by Cork – had more or less seen to that.

The porter, though, who patrolled them at the hotel after the concert was convinced that the youths littering the lounge were the Sex Pistols, the only group he would claim to have heard of since the Rolling Stones and the Beatles. But, significantly, it wasn't a member of any group who most conformed to the punk stereotype but a wasted boy with Vaselined-up hair, the Clash's chief roadie. 'Rodent' (a nickname derived as much from his real name, Rodney, as from any resemblance he might have had to a ferret) had been moved to rip his arms open one night with the ragged edge of a Coke can to demonstrate his boredom with a roomful of students. To relieve the tedium of the road, he occasionally added to these bloody scars with the serrated edge of a table knife. His background, as far as he'd admit to one, seemed to be public school and prison.

(A punk-in-the-making, to be seen backstage at Clash concerts in the London area picking up points of style, is a spindly boy called Conran, son of the Habitat millionaire and Shirley 'Super-woman'. An extempore equipment humper with a single earring and the beginnings of a proletarian drawl, Sebastian was 'blooded' by being thrown into a swimming pool fully dressed one morning at five. But Strummer likes him: 'He's got a very high-class voice, but he means well.')

For themselves, the Clash's clothes, onstage and off, betray a familiarity with the work of Jasper Johns and Robert Rauschenberg, the American Pop painters, that they don't feel inclined to discuss. Although their recent histories all include squatting and the dole, three of them went to art school, as did their manager and even their sound engineer; but, in keeping with their anti-intellectual stand, they proclaim a profound disinterest in 'art'. Joe Strummer hates the recent translation of 'punk rock' into the more respectable-sounding 'new wave', almost as much as he hates the persistent gossip in the music press about him being a public school boy. ('It wasn't a public school,' he has explained succinctly. 'It was a school where thick rich people sent their thick rich kids.')

'I hate those two words,' Strummer said, '"new wave". I much prefer to call it punk rock. It sounds tougher. Don't know why they use the other words. S'pose they think it sounds artistic.'

Not given much to socialising, Strummer had whiled away the afternoon in his hotel room, stencilling letters that would finally read 'High Tension' across a lime-green shirt to which he had added some black patches and an armband. It was in a feckless attempt to emulate the Clash, the most innovative and probably the most 'committed' of all the groups to be thrown up by the new wave, that Chelsea had just put out 'Right to Work' and the Cortinas were making their bid for the charts with the very catchy 'Fascist Dictator'. But Strummer, who claims to read only the *Sun*, says he knows nothing at all about politics.

'I don't know *any*thing about it,' he said. 'I don't know anything about Marx. I mean, to me, it's just a big snore, because who wants to know about all that back-stabbing? People say our songs are political now because we deal in things that affect daily life, but I ain't got no major plan to save the world. "Just think about who's doing what to you and what you're going to do about it," is all we're saying. "Think for yourself."'

As an illustration of their 'personal politics', the Clash were carrying all the other groups on the tour, thanks to their two-year contract with CBS, reputedly worth £100,000. And Strummer, for one, was feeding people out of his own £25-a-week allowance. Inevitably, though, they were being heckled at their concerts for selling out to 'the system'. 'Geezer down 'ere says we sold out,' Strummer would announce at St Albans. 'Well, if we hadn't signed with CBS none of you lot would 'ave heard of us. So stuff that down your gizzard.'

'The world's full of people who think you've got to adopt the hippy ideal, make everything "alternative", and ignore all the existing structures. Which is a ridiculous idea . . .' He was rummaging in one of the plastic carrier bags that made up his luggage. 'Look, it's *all* business, *I* know that. They only do it for business. Take you down there, sign you up, buy you a drink . . . If they didn't think they were going to make money out of it, they wouldn't give you the time of day.'

Groups are forming and realigning and being snapped up by the major labels faster in 1977 than anyone can remember since the beat boom of the early sixties. The Damned have already appeared on children's television; the Jam and the Stranglers have graced *Top of the Pops*, and Paul Weller, aged nineteen, singer with the Jam, has said he intends to vote Conservative at the next election. Next stop Weybridge, summers on Mustique, partying with Mick and Bianca? What was going to make them any different?

'I don't know.' Mick Jones was lounging on a single bed and his eyes never left the ceiling. 'I don't know the answers. You see, the whole thing we're involved in is full of contradictions. And now compromise is rearing its ugly head. So we contradict and we compromise. So I'm just, like, trying to keep my wits about me, and hopefully . . . you *can* learn from other people's mistakes. I can't quit yet, just because it's getting big,' he said. 'Can I?'

1977

Deer D, Very enjoyable going through this lot - have made suggestions on the FOLLOWING PAGES -

'92/10   '92/16   '92/17
'96/12   '96/19
DEVON 1/7
DEVON 2/5   2/17
LUNDY 1/6   1/11   1/12   1/13
LUNDY 2/1   2/2
LUNDY 3/2   3/4   3/5   3/7
LUNDY 4/6   4/7   4/8-4/9 - 4/10 - 4/11
LUNDY 5/2   5/4   5/10   5/11-5/12
LUNDY 6/2   6/3   6/5   6/6   6/7

Could you get Hugh to check it out as well?
Anyways see you soon
Love

P.S. MY VOTE FOR TITLE IS LOW DOWN ON PAGE NUMBER ⟶ DEVON 2/PAGE 17

Joe Strummer, edits to *On the Way to Work*

CHARLES SAATCHI

When John Greenwood, a painter of odd, amoebic, honey-I-spilled-the-kids figures, turned up at the Royal College on the morning of his degree show in 1990, it was to receive the message which had already set the college buzzing. 'Call C. Saatchi,' it said simply. It was a message that signalled what in fact has turned out to be the case: that the course of his life, and possibly his work, was about to be altered by the intervention of the man whose purchasing decisions are enough to start 'feeding frenzy' among collectors of the fashionable avant-garde all over Europe and America.

Saatchi wanted everything he could have from John Greenwood's degree show, and in addition commissioned a further six pictures. It is this work, along with Saatchi's holdings in the work of five other young British artists, that has just gone on show in the fastness of his private gallery in St John's Wood in North London.

Greenwood, Rachel Whiteread, Alex Landrum, Damien Hirst and Langlands & Bell have only two things in common: a body of work whose bite and intelligence has confirmed London as the number one stopover on the international art safari, and the fact that none of them has clapped eyes on the man whose patronage is largely what has allowed them to go on making their art in the past couple of years.

Charles Saatchi's spectral, mucho-mysterioso, everywhere-

and-nowhere reputation by now is legendary. He moves with stealth, by darkness, swoops while the rest of the city sleeps. 'He's probably at an exhibition now,' a woman who knows Saatchi told me one lunchtime. 'People don't recognise him. He doesn't register. He's almost certainly been to more shows in the last two weeks than you or I would see in a year. He sees everything. He goes to *everything*.'

I dealt with Saatchi through an intermediary — those were the rules of engagement.

First question: would he describe his collecting as: (a) a hobby; (b) an obsession; (c) a dalliance; (d) an investment opportunity; (e) a bid for immortality?

And the message came back: all of the above apart from (e). 'I fear I'll lose interest once I die,' he added enigmatically.

I then tried him with a quote from *Utz*, Bruce Chatwin's essay on the psychology — or psychopathology — of the compulsive collector: 'Things, I reflected, are tougher than people,' Chatwin wrote. 'Things are the changeless mirror in which we watch ourselves disintegrate. Nothing is more ageing than a collection of works of art.'

But this fell on stony ground. Bruce Chatwin, I was told baldly, was one of Charles Saatchi's favourite writers. The non-response was as pure and reverberative as the lofted white space, 'the most beautiful of tombs', in which the Saatchi collection hangs — ten times bigger than the Serpentine Gallery, nearly four times larger than the Whitechapel, 'the nearest thing to a Xanadu of the arts that we have seen in London since the building of Dulwich Picture Gallery', according to the *Guardian* when the Boundary Road museum was unveiled in 1985.

If Robert Hughes is right and the creation of confidence in art as an investment medium is *the* cultural artefact of the last half of the twentieth century, then it could also be argued that the single most important art-world figure of the past decade has not been an artist but a collector.

Being taken up by Saatchi has become one of the conditions of success for an artist in recent years. Being dropped by him, it is now becoming clear, can have equally devastating repercussions.

Geraldine Norman recently reported in the *Independent* that Saatchi sold around seventy works from the seventies and eighties at Sotheby's, New York, last year for upwards of £10 million. The administrators of the Saatchi collection will neither confirm nor deny that this is the case. But Julian Schnabel, an artist whose star ascended in direct relation to the number of paintings Saatchi took from him (he took several dozen), is now on record saying he feels he was tricked and betrayed.

'I thought Saatchi had good intentions. Now it turns out that he's only a superdealer,' the New York-based Irish painter Sean Scully complained after Saatchi unloaded a block of nine of his canvases. All of which was powerful ammunition for the naysayers who see Saatchi, adman refulgent, as being addicted to the constant conquest of new markets, to dynamic obsolescence. A trend junkie, a fashion freak, a connoisseur of the briefly new.

For In & Out of Love, his first solo show last year, held on the upper and lower floors of an unoccupied shop near Bond Street, Damien Hirst took the pupae of a number of exotic butterflies, attached them to canvases, and waited. The emergent butterflies fed themselves from flowers and bowls of sugar water, flew around the gallery space and, at the end of their brief natural life, died. Downstairs, dead butterflies were displayed, wings outstretched, mired in lurid, monochrome canvases.

Without mentioning Saatchi specifically, the critic Charles Hall, in a particularly intelligent reading of In & Out of Love, pointed up the disparity between 'living, beautiful things crawling from the canvas' and 'the imposition of order, the emphasis on display, and the total indifference to function' which are the characteristics of the collector: 'The image of a group of art lovers waiting in vain for their grubs to turn into butterflies,' he wrote, 'is simultaneously chilling and hilarious.'

Charles Saatchi has always got to artists when they were young and, often, unrepresented. He started stockpiling Schnabels while Schnabel's hands were still damp from washing dishes in a restaurant kitchen. He was an enthusiastic supporter of the New British Sculpture when the leading practitioners – Tony Cragg, Bill Woodrow, Richard Deacon – were still in their twenties. Saatchi showed Jeff Koons, Ashley Bickerton, Meyer Vaisman and others of the so-called New York Smart Art or Neo-Geo tendency before anybody had heard of them in Britain.

Since 1989 he has been simultaneously buying into and boosting the reputations of what is probably the most exceptional group to emerge from a British art school since the British Pop artists came out of the Royal College in 1962.

The new generation centres, in part, on Goldsmiths College in South London. The leading figures are protégés of the most influential teacher there, Michael Craig-Martin. Two of his students, Ian Davenport (b. 1966) and Fiona Rae (b. 1963) have already had solo shows with Leslie Waddington and, together with Rachel Whiteread (b. 1963), were shortlisted for the 1991 Turner Prize. Their work was first seen in 1988 in what is already regarded as a landmark exhibition masterminded and curated by Damien Hirst (b. 1965) while he was still a Goldsmiths student.

Even in the depths of a recession, all these artists have waiting lists for their work and Hirst is currently being fought over by New York dealers who see him, in the words of Charles Saatchi, as 'a world star'.

Inevitably, however, as the controversy generated by the Turner Prize last autumn suggested, there are many who feel they have had too much, too soon. More: that in their talents for entrepreneurship and self-promotion they are too obviously products of the me-first, getting-and-spending Thatcher era.

'We taught our students to feel a part of the outside world,' Michael Craig-Martin has said. 'They were not to be intimidated by the market, by critics or by galleries. This particular group were very aggressive in that sense. They wanted to get out there and do it for themselves.'

It is statements like this that make Rachel Whiteread, who went to the Slade, want to distance herself from the Goldsmiths set-up. 'People make art for very different reasons and I think some of the reasons why *some* of the people at Goldsmiths have made art are rather strange and to do with a "career". It's a very American idea.'

Underpinning the antipathy which has built up towards the Goldsmiths artists, and towards British neo-conceptualism in general, is this suspicion that most of its adherents are working, not out of internal necessity, but out of a desire to be successful, even if that means tailoring their styles to the demands of the market.

'Slickness', runs the subtext to this argument, 'is the curse of those born in the marketplace.'

It was another quote, though, from the American critic Barbara Rose, that I passed on to Charles Saatchi for his comments: 'The enemy of the artist today is not public indifference, as it once was, but premature professionalism.'

He came back with a question. Who was Barbara Rose's first husband? Answer: Frank Stella. And how old was Stella when his black-stripe paintings made him a star in New York? Answer: twenty-two.

'There are no rules,' Saatchi said. 'There's no guide to when an artist does his or her best work. I don't know any among the young artists I've come across who are more interested in money than in the integrity of what they are producing. They use surplus income to make grander and grander work.'

Ghost, which Saatchi bought in 1990, is a catafalque-like plaster cast of a room Rachel Whiteread used to live in. She applied plaster to the walls, window, door, fireplace etc., and came away with a faithful copy of the 'negative space' inside the room.

The Physical Impossibility of Death in the Mind of Someone Living, the piece Saatchi commissioned from Damien Hirst for the current show, features an eighteen-foot-long tiger-shark suspended in formaldehyde. *A Thousand Years*, the first Hirst piece taken into the collection, consisted of twin glass cabinets, one containing maggots, the other a rotting cow's head and a neon Insect-O-Cutor. As the flies hatched, they flew next door to feast themselves before being zizzed.

Surrounding Time by Langlands & Bell is one of several beautiful, minimal but difficult to store architectural pieces stockpiled by Saatchi.

'What I can't stand is the British establishment always handing out favours to the artists that they think are carrying on a British middlebrow, middle-class tradition of good value and good taste,' Alex Landrum says. 'Saatchi broke the mould in the sense that he takes anything he trusts. He's completely and utterly ruthless in that respect. If he likes it, he'll show it. He votes with his chequebook.'

'I find the money aspect of my work part of its life,' Damien Hirst states plainly. 'I don't have a problem with it. I enjoy it completely. For somebody to come along and buy something, for it to become a commodity and yet for it to manage to still stay art, I find that really exciting.

'In England people are anti-success, really. If you're struggling and you cut your ear off, they like that kind of an artist.'

Bridget Riley has talked about how she was stunned, on her first visit to New York in the sixties, to see shop windows up and down Madison Avenue stuffed with patterns lifted from her Op art paintings. On this model, Damien Hirst will settle for nothing less than dead cows' heads in the windows of Tiffany, maggot-farms in Macy's.

He's not thinking Riley or Hockney. Not even Koons or Warhol. Damien's thinking the toppermost of the poppermost, Johnny. Damien's thinking Beatles. The clever money isn't saying it couldn't happen.

1992

I must have got him on a good day, because he came back and the answer was yes. After years of asking and years of nononono, it was suddenly yes. Yes, he would agree to . . . well, let's not call it an interview, but anyway an . . . informal chat. On the record. Maybe over coffee. But (this was being relayed by the curator of the Saatchi Gallery, Jenny Blyth) he wanted to keep it fun and, you know, light. Fun. But yes!

In fact I know I got him on a good day because it was a day Charles had gone to look at a new toy. With the New York dealer Larry Gagosian, whom Saatchi has long used to 'disperse' works from the collection that he has blown cool on, or judged are right for the market at that moment, he had been

Rollered down to the West Country to cast a hungry eye over Damien Hirst's first new work for many years, at his studio near Stroud. A day out shopping. So he was up.

But he had been down, a friend had told me – dragged low by the reaction to the Sensation show – 'Young British Artists from the Saatchi Collection' – towards the end of last year in New York. Instead of being a celebration of his collecting acumen and confirmation of his 'modern Medici' status, it had all been elephant dung and city politics and the showboating of Mayor Giuliani instead. 'He was very high in New York,' the friend said. 'He went in to install the show every day. And he was very pleased. But then it didn't go the way he expected at all.'

Plus, in London the 'new neurotic realism' debacle had reportedly got him into a bit of a grump. Neurotic realism. The last big art movement. Remember it? No? That's OK. Nobody else does either. It was a synthetic attempt at having lightning strike twice. To hurry things on. Didn't work. Saatchi himself was rumoured to have found the NNR book he put out, with its tawdry cover and vapid boostering of a new 'tinsel-camp aesthetic', a misjudgement and an embarrassment; evidence that perhaps it isn't so easy to engineer change – to invent the history of British art before it has happened.

So he had been down. But the day I called there was a song in his heart and a spring in his step and he was up. Almost every major talent attracts at least one or two important collectors at an early stage in his or her career. And, to his credit, Saatchi has supported Damien Hirst and a handful of that generation of artists almost from day one. He bought *A Thousand Years* in 1990 from a Hirst-curated show called Gambler. With its maggots and flies and rotting cow's head, and the attendant, almost impossible, problems of storage and installation, it was a work that almost every other collector in the world would have shied away from.

A year later, he paid for the trapping, transportation and preservation of the now-notorious tiger shark and then used his 'top adman' abilities to turn it into a weirdly potent symbol of the age. Pictures of the shark were reproduced with a frequency which invested it with considerable power as an image and deepened its mystery: silent, immobile, latently lethal, suspended for eternity in its secure vitrine, it became a kind of logo of the times; a blank and yet peculiarly charged emblem.

Saatchi says that he believes a thumbnail history of the art of the last half-century would go: Jackson Pollock – Andy Warhol – Damien Hirst. His belief in Hirst's talent – Saatchi has been known to call it his 'genius' – has never been in question. He has always been prepared to get his chequebook out for Damien. And on the day I phoned him he had apparently been in a quandary over which of nearly two dozen pieces to stump up for first. He left Stroud at around four in the afternoon and was apparently still enthusing over the new work with Larry Gagosian at one o'clock the following morning.

So he was up. He had had the pick of some important new work by his favourite living artist and he had come good. *Hymn*, the twenty-foot, ten-ton bronze cast of an anatomical children's toy that he had bought for £1 million, was already on its way to the Saatchi Gallery in North London, trailed by a TV documentary team. The interview was on. But then he seemed to be down.

Supercollector, a book which billed itself as 'a hostile critique written from a socialist standpoint', authored by two British academics, was published in mid-March. 'A new book came out yesterday,' the Bond Street dealer Bernard Jacobson told me. 'Charles must be feeling very hurt.' Jacobson and Saatchi went to school together; they have remained lifelong friends. 'They've tried to make him look ugly on the cover, and he's not ugly. A horrible picture. Charles is a good-looking guy. They've tried to make him look Jewish.'

The next day Jenny Blyth called from the Saatchi Gallery. Our 'informal chat' had been set up for 24 March, a Friday. I could tell from her voice that there was a problem. 'This is embarrassing. I'm not backtracking. But I seem to have misunderstood. Charles doesn't want to do the chat walking around the show. Um, or over coffee. Oh this is all my fault. I said it would be just coffee, but he said it would be like an interview. Charles doesn't do interviews. What he wonders is, could you let him have your questions by fax, and he'll fax you back his replies? It's not very satisfactory, I know. But if you could do that to start with, I'll try and warm it up a bit later.'

A few days later Jenny Blyth called again. She was pitching the idea of writing about some 'post-YBAs' who had been taken into the collection – some neurotic realist artists, in fact. I said I was planning to write about some post-YBAs who weren't in the collection. One of these was Richard Woods, whose new show I'd seen the night before. 'Oh, we like Richard Woods,' Jenny said. 'We've been watching him for a long time. I'll tell Charles to get down there.'

Tuesday, 21 March: I call Jenny with a suggestion. What if I delivered the Q and As by hand? Just handed them over to Charles, with no attempt to speak to him or accost him? Jenny: 'I don't think that's a good idea. I think that would really irritate him. I think it really would. No, Q and A is the way to go. And then if he likes them, the chances are he would just chill.'

It is well known that Saatchi never attends his own openings. Some employees worked for his ad agency for years without meeting him. An often-repeated anecdote describes

Saatchi pretending to be an office cleaner rather than meet clients touring the building. Everything he does that isn't directly centred on his collection (and a lot of what is) revolves around concealment, seclusion, ways of evasion. He seems to be convinced that serious trackers are moving in with their mobile phones and zoom lenses. It's an irrational way of life that has a powerful inner logic. This involves investment in himself as an enigmatic Svengali figure and creating value in the works of art in his collection.

He was able to bring himself to the teetering edge of the interview ordeal, it seems, only as a way of promoting Ant Noises (it's an anagram of Sensation), the show of post-Sensation work by YBA artists which opens at the Saatchi Gallery next week.

His brother Maurice once joked that Saatchi was an acronym for 'Simple and Arresting Truths Create High Impact'. If there is a recurring factor in Charles Saatchi's collecting, then it is surely an attraction to art with high visual impact and shock value – what Bernard Jacobson once described as 'soundbite art'. And the bite about the million-pound bronze that was Saatchi's latest acquisition – that it was copied from a £14.99 Humbrol plastic toy – was soon planted safely in the papers. A full-page story appeared in the *Sunday Times* almost within hours of Hirst's 'big guy' arriving by transporter at the Saatchi Gallery. More importantly, the story was accompanied by a large colour picture of the sculpture which, with the wind in the right direction and the full apparatus of publicity and promotion behind it, was about to begin the crossover to icon status. 'Every photograph,' as Don DeLillo writes in one of his novels, nodding towards Walter Benjamin, 'reinforces the aura . . . An accumulation of nameless energies.'

Much of *Hymn*'s aura at this point resides in the (much reported) price. One million pounds. The magic six noughts. Hirst himself seems to have realised this when Saatchi at one point seemed to be sticking at £950,000 and he insisted on holding out for what he believed was the right amount. 'I said to my accountant, Frank, "Don't forget you can buy a three-bedroom house where I grew up in Leeds for £53,500. It's almost an insult to go fifty thousand short of it."'

Unlike many artists, Hirst is unembarrassed about the money element in his work. In the past he has talked about liking the fact that the work becomes a commodity when it leaves the studio; that it is part of its life in the world. In one of the new sculptures, *From the Cradle to the Grave*, a Coutts gold card signed 'Damien Hirst' balances on its edge on the surface of a desk. 'Whereas art and science and religion you can just about get your mind round,' he says, 'money you can't. People can tell you what things are worth, but it's not what they're worth. Money seems to skitter through everything and be ungraspable.'

Recently, he says, he felt peculiarly wounded when he thought Charles Saatchi had volunteered to deposit half a million pounds ('Pounds, Charles – pounds') in the bank to secure the big bronze man, a sculpture that, as far as Hirst was concerned, Saatchi had never seen. 'I couldn't believe you would do that. I hated the idea that he would buy something sight unseen. Because you make visual art. And for him to do that would mean that it was nothing to do with that. It was all to do with gambling. I thought it was all market concerns. I was quite relieved to find out that he'd seen a Polaroid of it. Basically, he was behaving like a man who'd seen it, and he had seen it. Somebody had slipped him a picture.'

Richard Wentworth taught Hirst and a number of his contemporaries at Goldsmiths College. He is an acutely perceptive commentator on, as well as a wised-up consumer of, popular culture. And Wentworth believes it is significant that Charles Saatchi's latest fetish object started life as a child's plastic toy. 'The joke is that the piece has got aura because Charles cherished the desire to own. If you could ask a five-year-old they could tell you. I guess the message we take away from this is: Charles must have his toys.'

2005

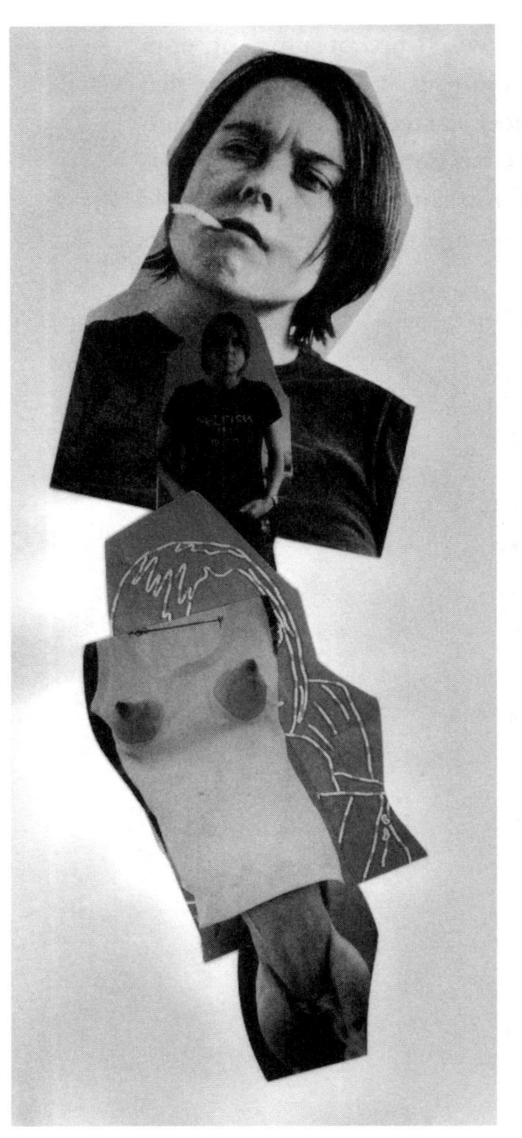
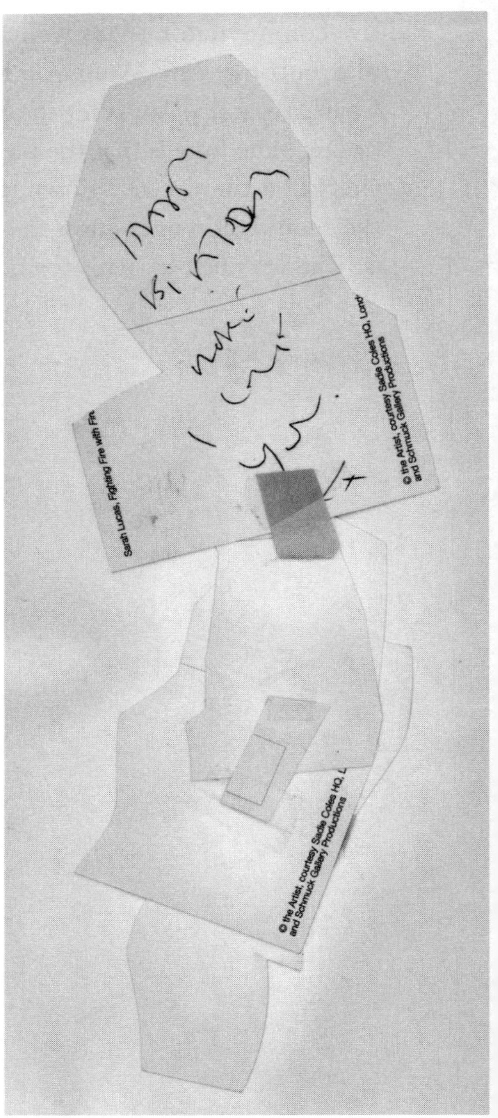
Sarah Lucas, Fighting Fire with Fir
© the Artist, courtesy Sadie Coles HQ, Lond
and Schmuck Gallery Productions
© the Artist, courtesy Sadie Coles HQ, L
and Schmuck Gallery Productions

TURNER PRIZE 1993

Two words – 'Wot for?' – splashed in fresh blue paint on the invitingly white side of *House*, Rachel Whiteread's hard-won cast of the living quarters of a Victorian terrace house in Grove Road, London E3. The raggedness of the letters and the gouts of hard gloss spreading out from them suggest the urgency and vehemence with which they have been applied. A woman with a wallpaper scraper has been given the thankless task of removing the daubings of the day before, which you can nevertheless still make out ('Council houses for all – black and white').

This is art that fulfils the American Claes Oldenburg's prescription of doing something other than sitting on its arse in a museum. It stands on a main artery in Bow, insolently pristine, accusingly beautiful, provocatively blank, and makes people angry. Here they go, turning it on for the print media and for the television cameras; and then they are angry for each other in the dark, when they vandalise the house and graffiti it and kick in the floodlights that have been installed amid the builders' rubble at considerable expense (which, of course, is a lot of the point).

When they're asked, they cite the cost (around £50,000), although *House* has been privately funded. They cite its dumbness and intrusion; its *thereness*, this new blot on their landscape. Nobody, as far as I'm aware, has cited Marcel Duchamp, but they could if they wanted to: he's a copper-bottomed giver of permission in this area; an unimpeachable source.

The guru and presiding genius of postmodern, 'post-object' art, Duchamp didn't say a lot. But one of the things he did say was that the artist was a 'mediumistic being' who performed only one part of the creative act; it was the spectator who completed the process, by interpreting what the artist had done and either accepting or rejecting it. Carl Andre, the maker of *Equivalent VIII* (the Tate's 'bricks', which still have the power to set people's blood boiling), put it this way: 'Experiencing a work of art is as hard a job as to make a work of art.'

The bricks are unemphatic. In the Rachel Whiteread piece there are at least the signs of hard labour, some kind of human intervention. Andre's bricks just lie there, neat, low down on the scale of moral effort. Elegantly lit, they currently flank the entrance to the galleries at the Tate where the work of the four artists shortlisted for this year's Turner Prize is showing – a signal that, after the dainty Degas sculptures and haunchy Rodin bronzes, the visitor should steel himself for a shift in temperature.

The Turner Prize 1993 Exhibition opened to the public last Wednesday morning. Just over an hour later, it closed again temporarily. Galvanised perhaps by the familiar 'call-this-art?', debunking tone of one of the morning's front-page stories ('This seven-ton pile of rice could make a meal for 100,000 people. But is it art?'), or the reservations of Brian Sewell in the London *Evening Standard* the night before ('I thought the prize, according to the rules, was for a British artist'), 'somebody' had thrown 'something' (the gallery was being non-committal) on to the combed, white acreage of *Neon Rice Field*, the installation by Vong Phaophanit.

Vong's background – born in Laos in 1961, but sent to

school in France and separated from his family for twenty years – together with his choice of materials – he has used bamboo, family snapshots and Laotian script, as well as rice – invite a narrative reading of the work, which he nevertheless resists. 'Let me say that what I am doing is not primarily to be understood,' he has said. 'Silence is the only word I have found to describe it . . . silence is to do with the eyes, the look; the look can stop words.' He has withheld the meaning of the Laotian words that are elements in his recent installations – a move bound to be interpreted as a provocation by those who prefer the polite and the undemanding ('the hard work of tradition with armature, plaster and bronze cast') to the difficult and the new ('old boilers, outworn tyres . . . what Walter Pater might have described as "a quaint conceit of Tupperware"' – Sewell again).

The Tate's definition of installation art in the catalogue accompanying the exhibition is compendious: 'Art works which may occupy all or any parts of a space, in or out of doors, and be made of any materials, natural or manufactured, that fit the artist's purpose.' A consequence of the vogue for installation art has been an increased blurring of the divisions between art and non-art inaugurated by Duchamp. Human blood, maggots, rotted meat, fried eggs, sump oil, animal intestines, colostomy bags and kebabs are just a few of the heterodox, 'transgressive' materials that British artists have used in their work in the last two or three years. You would have thought that rice, even seven tons of it, sculpted into deep furrows and laid with twenty-yard strips of orange neon, might have seemed uncontentious in comparison; the result is a space that is meditative, aromatic, Zen-still (and would, if it was awarded on the basis of this show rather than 'an outstanding exhibition' in the previous twelve months, surely win Vong

Phaophanit the prize). But you would have been wrong.

This is work that makes many more than the *Evening Standard*'s critic feel wrong-footed, embattled. Why? It was a question I put to Richard Wentworth, one of the most influential of the middle-generation of British sculptors who, throughout his career, has worked with 'poor' materials (tin cans, Formica furniture, zinc buckets and baths), and who, with his latest London show at the Serpentine Gallery, has probably just booked his place on the shortlist for next year's Turner Prize.

Wentworth said he thought the hostility was partly a symptom of what makes being modern in Britain so hopelessly difficult. '*Everything* in England is a matter of adjustment. We don't *make* a road, we widen one, or we straighten it; or we add on to the house, or we change the telephone boxes. But we're not in the start-from-scratch business.' He also believes there is suspicion of any individual action in what is an increasingly passive, collaborative culture. People will watch *hours* of television, really unquestioningly. The same with films and newspapers. Any collaborative mediation tends to be seen as OK. Then somebody does something which can be identified as being the act of an individual, and it's absolutely horrifying. It's actually seen as a gross impertinence.

'I think people are threatened when commonplace things are used in art because they are very bad at acknowledging the spiritual value they invest in commonplace things, and their own funny little fetishes and behaviours. They talk about their *favourite* garden trowel but, you know, a trowel is a trowel is a trowel. It's as if people can't bear to acknowledge that they're irrational. I think a lot of artists, all they do is manifest, or slightly enhance, the experience of investing everyday objects with those fetishistic qualities.' Hence the loathing for the kind of work that is currently flooding the galleries, and which has dominated the Turner Prize shortlist in recent years.

Wentworth quotes Oldenburg: 'I am for an art that is smoked, like a cigarette, smells, like a pair of shoes. I am for an art that flaps like a flag, or helps blow noses, like a handkerchief. I am for an art that is put on and taken off, like pants, which develops holes, like socks, which is eaten, like a piece of pie, or abandoned with great contempt, like a piece of shit.'

'People are very bad at accommodating the fact that meaning is migrating in everything all the time,' Wentworth says. 'Nothing means what we think it means for longer than a couple of minutes. It's the milk bottle that becomes the Molotov cocktail. It's all on the move. And although everybody's party to that, there's a strange intellectual closure where you hear people saying: "Well it's just a sardine tin. It's only a heap of rice."'

1993

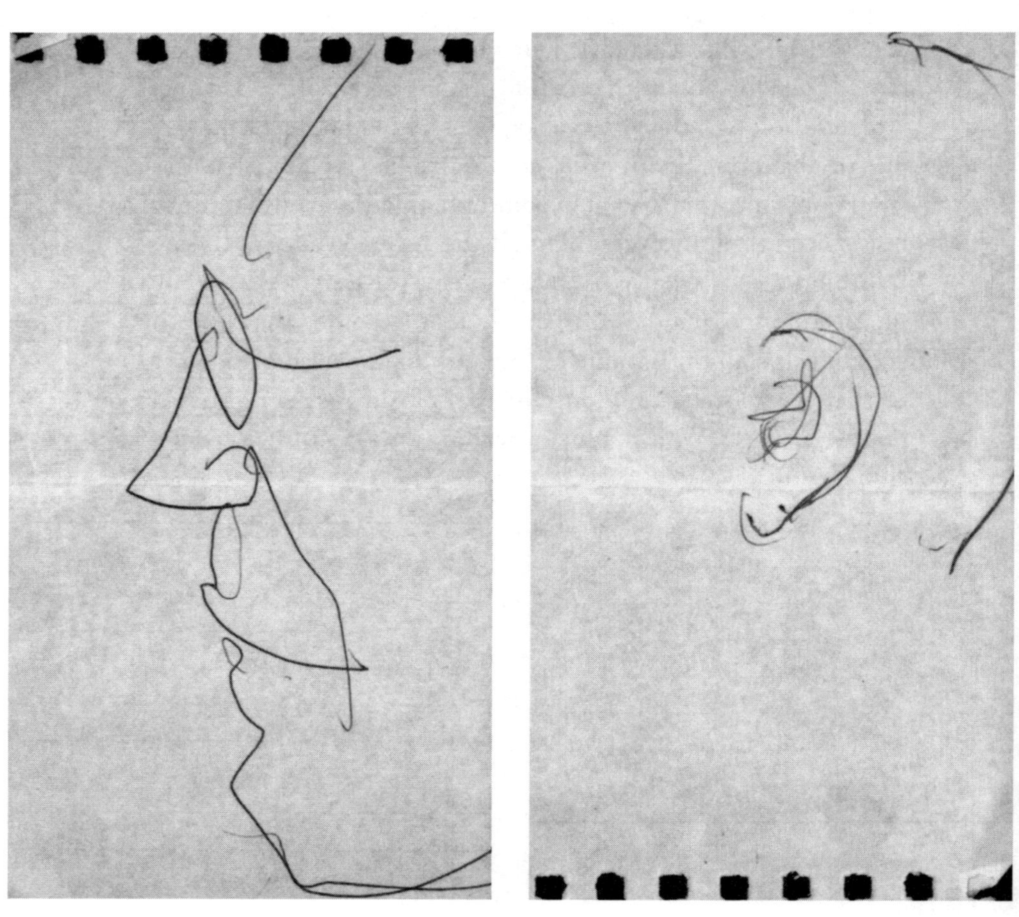

Damien Hirst, sketch of GB

DAMIEN HIRST

The air was charged and crackling and shorting out with opinions, and we pretended we had some. Everyone had opinions. Opinions were demanded in return. The absence of opinion was construed as opinion . . . I began to see opinions arcing in the air, intersecting flight patterns . . .

I was reminded of this Joan Didion quote more than once during April and May, when it seemed it wasn't safe to go anywhere in London (certain parts of London, certain *circles*) without being handed, without being hit upon for, without being fitted up with, vouchsafed, *slipped* opinions about . . . about Damien and the shark. And if not Damien and the shark, then Damien and death, Damien and the demiurge, Damien and the curious case of (the curious case imprisoning) the putrid cow's head.

Was it real? Had breath moved and blood pumped through that piece of offal with the vitreous, opalescent eye, now lolling in the chamber – the 'frame-space' – whose glass panels were turning opaque with maggoty efflorescence, were violently spattered with fly juice? The rotting carcass that even now was sending noxious fatty smells, lardy olfactory discharges, seeping out through the two tiny porthole Vent-Axias, stinking up the shiny acres of the Saatchi Gallery. The key prop in Damien's 'aesthetics of revulsion', as David Cronenberg has referred to his own death-fixated works of venereal and

gynaecological horror, detonated heads, genetic transmutation
— was it real? Well, *was* it?

The North American painter I found myself next to, propping up the bar in a pub off Cork Street one night, said he had
it on the best authority that it was not. The head had been commissioned from Special Effects at Pinewood, he'd heard,
because of Department of Health (Was it? Some Department's) objections to the real thing. Every few weeks Damien
surreptitiously slipped in to lather on another layer of honey,
Pedigree Chum, ketchup, whatever gets flies good and fat and
ready for the Insect-O-Cutor, in whose tin trays they accrete
into twin raisiny hillocks, imperceptibly ascending to the twin
tubes of lethal Alpine blue . . .

Another night, another stranger, happened across in a
restaurant in Gerrard Street, almost Gatlinged the piece of
wind-dried duck he was chewing when he heard Damien's
name uttered by one of the people at whose table he had been
involuntarily parked. Damien Hirst, he volunteered, was overly
prescriptive, too linear, too queasily romantic and ingenuous in
his handling of death and putrefaction. He invoked both
Mallarmé and Wittgenstein in support of this view ('Wittgenstein lived by the idea that whatever happened "externally",
nothing could happen to *him*, to his innermost being. What happened to his body was, correctly, a matter of total indifference')
before paying up and disappearing into the night.

The following day the managing editor of *Modern Painters*
called with the news (it seemed to me gleefully delivered) that
the shark, fridge-freighted from Australia, thawed, preserved,
scrubbed down, stabilised, and suspended in an opaline
formaldehyde solution at a cost to Charles Saatchi of a
rumoured £50,000, had gone belly-up in its tank, and the
Natural History Museum had had to be called in. Then there

was Damien on *The Late Show*, Damien in the colour supplements, Damien photographed by Snowdon for *Vogue* squatting in an aquarium looking like Theda Bara, with crustaceans in his hair and a fat flounder nudging his knee. Suddenly, overnight, a new full-fledged, spud-faced iconic presence!

'Most truly original new art is the result of group activity,' Alan Bowness writes in his pamphlet 'The Conditions of Success', subtitled: 'How the Modern Artist Rises to Fame'.

> The history of new developments in painting and sculpture is largely a chain formed of pairs and trios and larger groupings . . . Artists who emerge from such a situation do not have a consistency of style — indeed, they tend to move to extremes — but there is a consistency of purpose. They want to get to the top.

Comparisons between the Goldsmiths group, of which Damien was emerging as the clear leader, and the Pop artists who graduated from the Royal College in 1962 had become routine by the middle of last year. Now parallels between the Fish Man, 'the Puck of Goldsmiths College', and David Hockney, the golden boy propelled into the public consciousness exactly thirty years earlier when he was photographed by Snowdon in his Elvisine gold lamé jacket, started to become explicit.

The quality that Hirst and Hockney have in common, apart from an inborn genius for generating anecdotal mileage, was articulated by the *New Yorker*'s consistently brilliant young art critic, Adam Gopnik, in a recent piece on Jeff Koons:

> Twenty-five years ago — when ironic displacement became the vernacular not just of art but of pop culture, too, what no-one could have foreseen was that eventually the ironic consciousness was going to pass so thoroughly into the audience that the only way you could tell the artists apart from the public was that the artists were going to be the ones who *didn't* share it.

Gopnik went on:

If a postmodern culture is one in which everything is held ironically —
contingently, at one remove; conditionally, without certainty — then
perhaps nothing in such a culture can ever really be ironic at all. The
people who flourish in such a culture are not the 'pluralistic' ironists —
they retreat into the universities — but those who are able to summon
up enough conviction to be passionate about something, or a series of
somethings.

The titles Hirst gives to his pieces — *I Want to Spend the Rest
of My Life Everywhere, With Everyone, One to One, Always, Forever,
Now*; *The Physical Impossibility of Death in the Mind of Someone
Living* (the shark) — and his public utterances, for example, 'I
sometimes feel I have nothing to say. I often want to communicate this' and 'When we are no longer children, we are already
dead' (the latter from Brancusi) — have no ironic subtext.

The common reviewers' reaction to the Tate's show of
work by those of Hirst's contemporaries shortlisted for last
year's Turner Prize, summarisable as 'There was nothing to
take in except the theory of it', doesn't apply in Hirst's case.
For instance, although it is tempting to yoke the commercial
saw that 'Negotiations, like sharks, have to keep moving forward or they die' to *The Physical Impossibility of Death . . .*, especially in the light of its owner and the circumstances in which
it is being shown, the temptation is to be resisted.

That piece, like all the other pieces Hirst is showing at the
Saatchi Gallery, is a unique product of his own 'chapel of personal weirdness'. A penetrating but plainly stated observation
such as Rebecca West's that 'Natural death seems far less natural than unnatural death — it is much more difficult to understand than somebody dying because they have been stabbed or
shot or poisoned by somebody that hates them' is the kind of
thing that is much more likely to get Hirst's creative blood up.

Similarly, although *A Thousand Years* (the flies and the putre-fying cow's head) invites interpretations of the 'microcosm of the life-cycle', 'microdrama of survival' kind, Hirst has explained that the starting point was, as always, aesthetic rather than sociological or intellectual:

Formally, I wanted an empty space with moving points within it, moving like stars, a solution to the problem of how to suspend things without strings or wires and have them constantly change pattern in space.

(In the Saatchi lamasery, the flies work as a kind of distracting static, flickering on the periphery of the field of vision, 'as of some form of swarming life just outside the range of human apprehension . . . an accumulation of nameless energies', the visual equivalent of the 'white noise' in Don DeLillo's novel.) Hirst's formal preoccupations correspond to Francis Bacon's enduring, and much-quoted, fascination with the 'glitter' of the inside of the human mouth and 'this great beauty of the colour of meat'. If this and Bacon's 'Of course, we are meat, we are potential carcasses' seems to pre-echo Hirst's 'You face the mirror and you look good but you're dying' and his obsession with bringing dead things into the gallery, it is not coincidence.

With Dead Head (1991), which forms the frontispiece to the catalogue of the show that Hirst had last year at the ICA, is a photograph of him posing with the severed head of a Hitchcockian elderly man. *When Logics Die* (1991), the last piece illustrated, also features photographs: one is the gaping, mouth-like wound of a man who has slit his own throat; the other is the bloodied hand of the victim of a road accident. Both pieces date back ten years, he told me, to an adolescence marked by a more-than-usually morbid fascination with dying and death.

I *really* like Francis Bacon, and I'd read the David Sylvester interviews about Bacon's interest in radiography and diseases of the mouth. So I'd gone out and got loads of books. I had a massive collection of pathology books, books of burns and this kind of horrible thing that I'd collected. I used to steal them in Leeds. I was painting all these people with burns and mutilations. I always had a morbid fascination with it. Eventually I couldn't bear them any longer and gave them away. But I went out and bought about six a couple of weeks ago, new copies of the books I'd had when I was young.

Something that really intrigued me about them was the fact that, on the one hand, they were these really horrific visual things, but on the other they were very beautiful, well-taken photographs. I think that's what the interest is in — not in actual corpses, but in the fact that they're *completely* delicious, desirable images of completely undesirable and unacceptable things.

The photograph in *With Dead Head* was taken in a mortuary when he was sixteen.

I was at the point of trying to come to terms with it all. 'This is life. This is death.' And the smile seemed to sum up the problems between life and death in some ridiculous way. When I was really young, I wanted to know about death and so I went to the morgue and I got these bodies and I felt sick, I felt I was going to die an' it was all awful. But I went back and I went back and I drew them and drew them and tried to get the point where death starts and life stops straight in my head. I don't think death really exists in life. It's that kind of looking for it and you can't find it.

Adam Gopnik has written:

What makes Koons a man of his time is that he demonstrates once again that it is possible to be entombed entirely within a bizarre fantasy life and still have a shrewd and calculating sense of self-advancement — that such a state is practically a precondition for real success in contemporary America.

Inevitably for Damien (market forces decree it), contemporary America beckons. He is trying to be as unflinching in his attitude towards the machinery of promotion for which he is the current harvest as he is towards the issues he addresses daily in his work.

I love the fact that you've got art and then you've got all this other stuff that goes with it. I see it as the way the world is. I just hope that I can be kind of like the Beatles. I really like that as a kind of model. I like the way that, without losing integrity, they could change through fashion and not look back at the sixties and vomit when they saw what they'd done.

1993

There is a dream that is apparently widespread among forensic pathologists — the death dissectors, the gore explorers, the rummagers in the tossed-away envelope of the soul, up to their elbows in it. The autopter is performing an autopsy on a member of his family. He has taken out the organs, can't get them back in again, but must finish sewing up the body — which is alive, though dead — by dawn. The harder he labours with the viscera, the more panicked he becomes, the more insistently they slop out again . . . Hearing about the dream I of course immediately thought of Damien, who at this point is up to his neck in it.

'Let's go in.' It's interesting that surgeons and safe-blowers, in their popular portrayals at least, use the same expression to inaugurate their precise, premeditated, violently invasive procedures: the alarm hardware decommissioned and mute; the human wetware morphinised and sundered (inverted, divided).

It was Orson Welles, I think, who described Los Angeles as 'a bright, guilty place'. And that is as good a description as any of the steel-and-glass double chamber that Damien Hirst first showed at the ICA in London in the winter of 1991–2. The bigger component of *The Acquired Inability to Escape* contained a plain table, an office chair, a packet of cigarettes, a cigarette lighter, and an ashtray half-filled with the remains of what are sometimes known as coffin nails and cancer sticks; the occupant had been 'let go'; decruited. The adjacent smaller cell was empty, and the overall effect was, as it was meant to be, atopian — that is, literally, no-place; a sterilised site that was simultaneously fortress and cage and redolent of the walled compounds and 'protected' communities — the 'dumb boxes' with their silent aura — that Frank Gehry had designed in California in the previous decade.

'The work clarifies the underlying relations of repression, surveillance, and exclusion,' the cultural critic Mike Davis has written of Gehry's fortified cells. 'As a prestige symbol, "security" has less to do with personal safety than with the degree of personal insulation in residential, work, consumption and travel environments, from "unsavoury" groups and individuals, even crowds in general.' In other words, the attempt to protect life from external threat often results in a living death.

The Acquired Inability to Escape is the antithesis of the messy animal death represented in some of Hirst's other pieces as *A Thousand Years*, *In & Out of Love* and *Stimulants (and the Way they Affect the Mind and Body)*: it suggests modern death in tiled hospital rooms, and silent technologised removal.

Such hermeticism, asceticism, enclaving and phoney discretion is alien to everything in Damien Hirst's nature. His cannibalising of *The Acquired Inability to Escape* to make two further works — *The Acquired Inability to Escape, Divided* and *The Acquired Inability to Escape, Inverted and Divided* — was a symbolic gesture whose purpose was to (I am guessing) register his sense of becoming trapped within a visual syntax that has made the transition assimilated and repackaged, from novelty to contemporary emblem in a shockingly short space of time.

But more importantly, I like to think, the forensic slicing

up, the going in — 'Let's go in' — was a ventilating device; a tactic designed to demonstrate the futility of the torpid, retreating, life-in-death position that the original work symbolised. You've got to find some way to let ideas come in from the outside, as Hirst once told an interviewer, 'Like holes in the head for eyes or like the holes bored in the skulls of living people in the Middle Ages to let the evil out.'

It is one of Hirst's great strengths, both in the cool medium of his work and the hot medium of his person, that he is always pushing towards full disclosure. It is perhaps significant in this context that the most autobiographical of all his sculptures is one of the few completely liberated from its vitrine. *I Want to Spend the Rest of My Life Everywhere, With Everyone, One to One, Always, Forever, Now* was the 'single' precursor of the 'paired' piece, *Alone Yet Together and in Love*, shown at Jablonka Galerie in Cologne.

At one end a ping-pong ball bobbed insouciantly on its fragile column of air, mimicking the artist's knockabout spirit, vaudeville charm and formidable ability to keep his balls simultaneously aloft and on the line. But the playfulness was counterweighted by the elongated clear-glass plinth to which the air supply was anchored: This presented a couple of uprights with lethal lacerating edges, raw from the industrial cutting, with the potential to inflict horrible damage on anybody unlucky enough to trip and fall. A wall-mounted colour plate of the gaping throat-wound of a suicide, leering like a second lurid slack-lipped mouth and part of a kind of companion piece to *I Want to Spend the Rest of My Life . . .* when it was shown at the ICA, seemed to give notice of the perils of being so beguiled by the charm that you risk tumbling bloodily towards oblivion.

The fact that generosity of intention and devious dark

energies can coexist in the same nature; the fact that individuals can — are fated to — live lonely, even desperate lives, within otherwise mutually sustaining partnerships. These are the great imponderables — the fundamental splits, dualities and twinnings — that, as the world turns, so it has come Hirst's turn to investigate. That he brings to his inquiry such a brilliant, sordid, uncompromising and twisted imagination is our good fortune.

1994

SOME NOTES TOWARD A DEFINITION OF DAMIEN HIRST

By slighting death, by acting, we pretended it was not the terrible thing it was. By our language, which was both hard and wistful, we transformed the bodies into piles of waste . . . Words make a difference. It's easier to deal with a kicked bucket than a corpse; if it isn't human, it doesn't matter much if it's dead. And so a VC nurse, fried by napalm, was a crispy critter. A Vietnamese baby, which lay nearby, was a roasted peanut. 'Just a crunchy munchie,' Rat Kiley said as he stepped over the body.

Tim O'Brien, *The Things They Carried*

— Your new girlfriend's six?
— Yeah, but she's got the body of a four-year-old.

Punchline of a paedophile joke that Hirst memoed
to himself on the corner of a tablecloth in a restaurant.

But you were supposed to put it down the front of your trunks.

Punchline to a favourite Damien Hirst joke.

A wall is a very big weapon. You ram somebody's head into a wall. That's a pretty heavy thing to hit them with.

Overheard.

It is interesting to note a return to the bodily analogy by architects as diverse as Coop Himmelblau, Bernard Tschumi and Daniel Libeskind, all concerned to propose a reinscription of the body in their work, as referent and figurative inspiration. But this renewed appeal to corporeal metaphors is evidently based on a 'body' radically different from that at the centre of the humanist tradition. As described in architectural form, it seems to be a body in pieces, fragmented, if not deliberately torn apart and mutilated almost beyond recognition.

Anthony Vidler, *The Architectural Uncanny*

Every doctor, from time to time, comes across a patient who makes his flesh creep, despite the patient's unthreatening manner and hitherto blameless life. For example, a recent patient of mine exhibited a morbid fascination with the babies bottled in formalin in the pathological museum of the local medical school . . . he thought he might one day bottle a few for his own collection. But in the absence of any concrete evidence of his being dangerous, I am unable to do anything about him.

Theodore Dalrymple, *The Times* (London)

Freud says of the maternal body that 'there is no other place of which one can say with so much certainty that one has already been there'.

The mouth kisses, the mouth spits; no one mistakes the saliva of the first for the second. Similarly, there is nothing impure about dirt. What must be determined are the conditions under which a surface marking is experienced as a stain.

Mostafavi/Leatherbarrow, *On Weathering*

. . . cruel with a cruelty that is linked with an infinite degree of sensibility.

Marcel Proust, *A propos de Baudelaire*

The fact that alloxan, destined to embellish ladies' lips, would come from the excrement of chickens or pythons was a thought which didn't trouble me for a moment. The trade of chemist (fortified, in my case, by the experience of Auschwitz) teaches you to overcome, indeed ignore, certain revulsions that are neither necessary nor congenital: matter is matter, neither noble nor vile, infinitely transformable, and its proximate origin is of no importance whatsoever . . . I would get on my bike and make a tour of the farms on the outskirts of town in search of chicken shit.

Primo Levi, 'Nitrogen', The Periodic Table

The loneliness of voices stored on tape. By the time you listen to this, I'll no longer remember what I said. I'll be an old message by then, buried under many new messages. The machine makes everything a message, which narrows the range of discourse and destroys the poetry of nobody home. Home is a failed idea. People are no longer home or not home. They're either picking up or not picking up.

Don DeLillo, Mao II

It was his idea of beauty that upset me, I suppose. That idea of beauty had taken him to the job in the funeral parlour . . . He frightened me because I thought his feeling for beauty was like an illness; as though some unfamiliar, deforming virus had passed through his simple mother to him, and was even then something neither of them had begun to understand.

V. S. Naipaul, A Way in the World

There is something in these people's lives that is causing them to need to smoke, to expect to smoke, and not to give up . . . Even if they are in work, they are likely to be trapped in one of five jobs that all begin with 'c': cooks, cleaners, cashiers, child-minders, and clerks . . . for the smoker, the familiar packet, the sight and feel of the cigarette, the act of lighting it, the first rush, the whole predictable experience is comforting and enjoyable.

Report of the British Policy Studies Institute, February, 1994

That look – the crazoid look on Damien Hirst's face in *With Dead Head*, the picture of him as a sixteen-year-old, posing with the severed head of an old man in a mortuary – and two occasions I've recognised it since:

(1) Hirst has a copy of *Whoever Fights Monsters* by Robert K. Ressler, picked up at an airport book stand. He opens it at the

black-and-white plates in the middle and indicates a picture whose caption reads: 'One of the two blenders used by Richard Trenton Chase, the Sacramento "Vampire Killer", to prepare human blood and organs for ingesting to "stop his blood from turning to powder".'

(2) Hirst draws me aside during a party at his place and opens a medical textbook at colour photographic plates illustrating female venereal diseases. 'They're like cookery books.'

1994

The London art scene in the nineties has been pretty much a group one. And the group by and large has been the one that came out of Goldsmiths College around 1988 or '89 and showed at the two ground-breaking warehouse exhibitions that Damien Hirst curated: Freeze (1988), and Modern Medicine (1990).

There was an attempt to re-create the spirit of these shows in the winter of 1995, when the Walker Art Center in Minneapolis put on Brilliant! New Art From London. Nineteen of the artists represented went over to America for the opening, and the party was still continuing several weeks later at various locations in London. One night, in the falling-down season just before Christmas, it surfaced in an industrial building close to Smithfield market, where it was the usual happy boil-up of heads, throats, sweat-pasted hair. But with this crucial difference: the palpable sense, shared by everybody present, of living in an unrepeatable moment, of being there *when*.

'The kind of group synergy that can lead to great art — the synergy that once pulled great pictures out of second-rate abstract expressionists — is nowhere in sight,' Calvin Tomkins wrote in his review of Brilliant! in the *New Yorker.* But my intuition is that he is wrong.

The crummy building with the lurching lift and echoey stairs and sodden landings and poorhouse institutional walls . . . the battered sofa and dumpster fridge and skittled bottles of Löwenbräu and Smirnoff and Jim Beam . . . a great silver cycloptic Mitsubishi television and a drum kit on a carpet and the tape of a gymnast looping over against a wall . . . It was generic. Angus Fairhurst had put together a band which, in addition to himself, included Mat Collishaw and Gary Hume – his (and Damien Hirst's) contemporaries at Goldsmiths. Artists in the band, with artists out front – Sarah Lucas, Abigail Lane, Michael Landy, Tracey Emin, Angela Bulloch – supporting them.

Low Expectations' first public performance was the excuse for the party in the studio in Clerkenwell Road. And even those who hadn't been there before, had been there before, had been there before. This was Warhol's Exploding Plastic Inevitable at the Electric Circus in 1965; it was Rauschenberg and Oldenburg and Rosenquist and Poons playing at Bob and Ethel Scull's party, described by Tom Wolfe in 'Bob and Spike', in the mid-sixties, around the time most of these people were being born.

It would be naive to suppose that there weren't the usual undercurrents of competitiveness and petty jealousy and frustration circulating. But as a group and for the time being they present a conspicuous and almost unprecedentedly united front. In Minneapolis, for example, Damien Hirst agreed not to show any of his dead-animal pieces. In the interest (it was said) of group solidarity: it was feared that the controversy they aroused would inevitably overshadow everything else in the show.

It may also be because he felt that his appearance in Minneapolis would shift the balance of attention unfairly in his favour that Damien Hirst did not accompany the others to the opening of Brilliant! Since his first shortlisting for the Turner Prize in 1992, he has achieved the level of promiscuous Warholian celebrity that long ago transcended the coterie journals of the art press: he can turn up as a gossip-column item, a game-show question or an op-ed cartoon. The original title for the film which is his contribution to Spellbound was *Flying* ('Everybody in it was going to have their zips down') — a (possibly unconscious) reference to a career trajectory that has so far defied gravity. The film's central image is of a wartime Spitfire pilot flying mesmerically upwards into the blue beyond: 'You have no sense of time or distance or even gravity and there's a deadly silence. The engine cuts out and there is a sense of nothingness and then a sense of falling backwards . . . back down to earth.' The Icarus plunge is the prevailing counter-image: a doctor is defenestrated; a butterfly burns its beautiful wings on an Insect-O-Cutor. In an early version of the script, a woman falls off a ladder and is impaled on a minimalist steel sculpture by Sol LeWitt: up like a rocket, down like a stick.

In the film there is constant heavy traffic in a skywards direction of the souls of the deceased — of everybody, in fact, unlucky enough to drift into the force field of the dreamy duffle-coated figure known as Marcus Hellman, a kind of unwitting but increasingly witting terminator — a serial killer, or serial *assister* in death. His victims are turned into road rash, wrapped around lamp posts, pitched out of windows; they slit their wrists, stick their heads in the oven, go up in flames.

Any connection between Marcus Hellman and Andy Warhol may be wholly accidental, but the visual referencing of

Warhol images — a car crash, a mid-air suicide, other nods to Warhol's 'death-and-disaster' series — certainly is not.

Warhol (like Marcus Hellman) represents the obverse of Schrödinger's metaphor about the essence of life being the suction of negative entropy from the environment. 'I wonder if Edie will commit suicide?' it is claimed Warhol once said of his former 'superstar' Edie Sedgwick. 'I hopes she lets me know, so I can film it.' Warhol's film *Suicide*, his first experiment with colour, was based on a man who had tried to slash his wrists twenty-three times. (The person involved took out lawsuits and the film was never shown.)

Hirst's preoccupation with death is well enough established by now. But his involvement with film provides a new slant on the old relationship between death and photography (which Roland Barthes defined as the place where death went when religion let it go). There is an obvious correspondence between the rectangle of the film frame which entombs the human image, and the clean geometry of the steel-and-glass vitrines which 'frame' the artificially preserved carcasses of Damien Hirst's farmyard animals. The human context lends a slightly sinister undertow to something Hirst once said about his work: 'I like the idea of trying to understand the world by isolating something from it. You kill things to look at them.'

Marcel Duchamp had 'Rrose Sélavy'. Warhol had Ondine, Ultra Violet, Joe Dallesandro and his roster of spaced-out 'superstars'. During his first burst of fame he hired Alan Midgette, an actor, to impersonate him on a lecture tour, explaining that Midgette was 'more like what people expect than I could ever be'. Hirst's current alter ego is his friend, the actor and Soho prankster Keith Allen, who was in the Blur video he directed, plays Marcus in *Hanging Around*, and is involved in a projected feature film. Marcus represents the parallel existences, the shared selves that the film seems in some way to be about. His is a fugitive identity. He has the name of one Damien Hirst friend, the physical form of another; all his 'wives' are the same woman. 'I just wanted two identities, that's all,' Duchamp said, explaining why he had his friend Man Ray photograph him as a woman. 'It was a sort of ready-made-ish action.' (A Man Ray iron sits on the desk in the psychiatrist's office in *Hanging Around*, alongside Meret Oppenheim's fur cup and saucer.)

Duchamp did not allow his hand to interfere with his mind: an artist was 'just someone who signs things'. Many of Andy Warhol's best-known films were produced and directed by Paul Morrissey; probably half the paintings were created completely by assistants. It's an aesthetic Hirst shares: 'art without angst'.

As you would expect, his approach to film making is similarly lacking in angst. *Hanging Around* inevitably incorporates many of the motifs he has made familiar through his art – butterflies, ping-pong balls, dying cigarettes, dead meat, bug zappers – but it doesn't set out to be an art film.

Unlike some of his contemporaries, who equate roughness of execution with rebelliousness, and sometimes confuse the untrained look with sincerity, poverty, even purity of intention, Hirst has always eschewed the gimcrack and the home-made. This was true even of the shows he curated as a student: they were designed and catalogued to a professional standard. He has always gone in for technical perfection and finish, a kind of surface glamour. Even when working with dead matter (entrails, preserved flesh) – he has always rated high production values over experimentalism.

Just as Hirst's Blur video harked back unexpectedly to Benny Hill and Dick Emery and Saturday-morning television,

Hanging Around is a challenge in some ways to the normal notions and practices of the art film.

There are no scratches or stains or multiple superimpositions. No arbitrary zooms, focuses, changes of angle and depth of field and light intensity. There is a narrative: actors and a story. It is realistic. Naturalistic, even. Reading it on the page, you would expect the pivotal monologue of Philip, the old airman, to be delivered in a flat, uninflected, deadpan (arthouse) manner. In fact it is done in character, straight, with an accent, almost soap-operatically, like a scene from *Z Cars*.

In one scene in the film a woman tells her husband, 'You have to come down. People are expecting you.' He replies, 'I'm not in a fit state, Camilla . . . Just go down and be a good hostess, will you?' The man happens to be a junkie; the woman is wearing a Rifat Ozbek outfit based on a Damien Hirst spot painting. But it is an exchange that suggests *Emmerdale*, not Terence Rattigan.

As the film critic David Thomson has pointed out, all but a few movie fanatics have seen more moving imagery on a television screen than at the movies; television is on 'like the light'. Like most of his generation, Damien Hirst is not a film buff but a channel surfer. 'I'm more interested in Roald Dahl's *Tales of the Unexpected*,' he says, 'than . . . I don't know . . . Richard Lester.' His film could be seen as being in the long tradition of 'found' objects, which achieve their power as art by being removed from their normal context and placed in a gallery setting. By this logic, *Hanging Around* could be slotted into a normal evening's viewing without causing undue alarm.

The working title of the film, *Is Mr Death In*, is an anagram of Damien Hirst. (Others, he points out, are 'A denim shirt', 'Near mid-shit', and 'Ten mad Irish'.) So it is effectively 'Damien Hirst by Damien Hirst'.

Lines of dialogue echo titles of pieces: 'All day long telephone numbers come into my head and I get this strange urge to dial them.' The party in the film takes place in the Notting Hill house where Damien hosted a lavish party last year. An actress wears an outfit virtually identical to the one that his girlfriend Maia Norman wore to the Turner Prize dinner in November; Marcus Hellman's son is his own son; friends play the wives. So how autobiographical is it? 'It's only autobiographical,' he says, 'in the way that wiping your bottom is a self-portrait.'

The plot of *Hanging Around* is reminiscent of David Cronenberg's *The Dead Zone*. Significantly, though, Hirst says the effect he was aiming for owes more to the closing sequence of John Huston's *The Dead*, with its ecstatic melancholy and ghostly light and the incantatory repetition of a single word: 'falling . . . falling . . . falling . . .'

1996

This is what it's like. It's like: I'll do a magic trick, and I want it to be amazing. But if anybody asks me how to do it, I'll show them exactly how to do it. I want you to be amazed twice. Once you're amazed because it seems impossible, and then you're amazed because it's fucking easy. That's what I like.

Damien Hirst, 1997

To amuse His Royal Majesty he will change water into wine. Frogs into footmen. Beetles into bailiffs. And make a minister out of a rat. He bows, and daisies grow from his finger-tips. And a talking bird sits on his shoulder.

There.

Think up something else, demands His Royal Majesty.

Think up a black star. So he thinks up a black star. Think up

dry water. So he thinks up dry water. Think up a river bound
with straw-bands. So he does.

There.

Then along comes a student and asks: Think up sine alpha
greater than one.

And Žito grows pale and sad: Terribly sorry. Sine is between
plus one and minus one. Nothing you can do about that.

And he leaves the great royal empire, quietly weaves his way
through the throng of courtiers, to his home in a nutshell.

Miroslav Holub – *Žito the Magician*

When he opened a London office some years ago to deal with
his proliferating outside involvements – restaurants, videos, a
record label, album covers, books, films, TV commercials,
interviews, litigation: everything that wasn't art, in other
words – Damien Hirst called it 'Science'. It says it on a brass
plaque fixed to the wall, next to the plaques of the other
strictly white-bread businesses in Bloomsbury that share the
building: 'Science'. It's what you hear a voice announce every
time you phone: 'Hello, Science.' The 'Science' logo is two
spots – a detail of the parent 'Damien Hirst' logo made familiar through the series of spot paintings that take their names
from psychotropic drugs, and the most successful example of
the brass-necked branding of an artist in the dour ('provincial,
marginal, literary, cute' – Robert Hughes) history of art in
Britain.

To anybody who has followed his career, the bright blameless twinned spots of Hirst's office logo ineluctably suggest
nostrils or eyes or other human holes. This is because in the last
few years the Hirst iconography has entered the common consciousness so completely in Britain that even people with only
a passing interest in art are likely to be familiar with his – *whey-*

hey! – orificial fixation ('Come to my big opening!'), and with statements like the following: 'I remember once getting terrified that I could only see out of my eyes. Two little fucking holes. I got really terrified by it. I'm kind of trapped inside with these two little things to see out of.'

The other reason that we might associate pretty, abstract signs on a sheet of headed business paper or compliments slip with baser human referents in an almost Pavlovian way is because Hirst has been relentless in placing medical science – forensics, pathology, gynaecology, pharmacology – at the core of what he does. Almost uniquely among artists of his generation, he has committed himself to working in the space between science and art in much the same way that artists of the older generations have been trying to act in the gap between art and life that Robert Rauschenberg first laid claim to in the late fifties.

Like writers such as Don DeLillo, Richard Powers and others, who have acknowledged the poetic lure of modern jargon from science, sports and Madison Avenue in their fiction, Hirst located an unlikely poetics in the boilerplate prose of the scientific paper and pharmaceuticals catalogue, and in the disease- and death-tainted artefacts of the mortuary, the pharmacy and the lab.

Isolated Elements Swimming in the Same Direction for the Purpose of Understanding. The Physical Impossibility of Death in the Mind of Someone Living. Anaesthetics (and the Way they Affect the Mind and Body). Looking Forward to a Complete Suppression of Pain. When Logics Die. As titles, these were not only unusually resonant and intelligent in themselves; they announced the arrival of an artist different and brave enough to use contemporary science to clarify, celebrate and enhance the range and depth of his work.

In this Hirst stood apart from the normal run of 'Artistic Minds' (as Miroslav Holub described them) whose 'primal and direct communication with the nature of man and things is still seen as an alternative and more genuine path of human creativity, opposing the analytical, cold and cynical scientific approach. Frequently', Holub went on, 'we find that artists believe, at least in private, that they are fundamentally opposed to this science, to mimical science which is designed to endanger their minds, their aims and their ways of life.'

Holub was a scientist – a distinguished immunologist – as well as a poet. Like the poet and doctor William Carlos Williams (who famously stated that 'The poem is a machine made of words'), Holub felt no sense of contradiction between his two callings. In fact, he believed that a scientific idea – 'reduced to its components, verified and sieved, criticised and revised by scientific observation' – had a great deal in common with the more self-consciously 'creative' utterances belonging to 'the so-called creative professions': 'Both the scientific and poetic communications are a function of condensation of meanings, of the net weight of meaning per word, of inner and immanent intensity. Opposed to other written communications, they are – at their best – concentrates, time-saving devices.' Throughout his life, Holub wrote against the (perceived) breach – 'the romantic disjunction' – between the poetic impulse to imagine and the scientific gift for accurate observation; 'between free invention and strictly rational reflection'. Put another way (to quote Holub quoting the Polish writer Stanislaw Jerzy Lec): the hay smells different to the lovers than to the horses.

Francis Bacon said repeatedly that he was committed to 'the brutality of fact'. Echoing this, Damien Hirst has said he likes 'the violence of inanimate objects'. Typically this has meant everyday objects – Formicaed tables, office chairs, ashtrays – being bifurcated and mutilated in predetermined, precise ways in a symbolic enactment of the 'hurtability' of human beings. At other times, the violence has resided in Hirst's choice of object – most characteristically, medical apparatus and equipment with the power to lift pain and its attributes out of the body and make them visible. Duchampian ready-mades have been transposed from the morgue and the operating theatre to the gallery on the basis of the cold cargo of dread and terror that they carry.

Sometimes I Avoid People (1991) consists of two coffinated glass cases, one vertical, one horizontal. Each case, which contains compartments for the storage of bodily waste, is supplied with medically useful gases – oxygen, nitrogen, an oxygen and helium mix – from a range of colour-coded cylinders. *Naked* (1994) is a glass-fronted steel cabinet containing scalpels and bone saws and other cold instruments of the surgeon's violently invasive trade. In *He Tried to Internalize Everything* (1992–4), an anaesthetist's black rubber mask and Halothane dispenser and a swivel chair whose back has been grievously broken – cut through the spine – are encased in one of Hirst's signature twin-celled, glass-and-steel vitrines.

These things are the furniture of our bad dreams, and of the death rooms. The direction of Hirst's work has always, notoriously, been towards death and dwindlings. He has said, 'I like creating emotions scientifically.' His 'inanimate objects', characterised by their hypothermic, sterilised, hospital 'wipe' aesthetic, are among the last things seen by many people in their earthly lives. His disinhabited dumb boxes speak of modern death in tiled hospital rooms, and silent technologised removal. They speak, that is to say, of how death has become increasingly mediated; of how the technological media, which enormously reinforce and heighten the illusion that death happens only to others, have put a distance between us and our own dying.

Wittingly or not, this is another area of interest that Hirst shares with a postmodern writer like DeLillo. Discussing DeLillo's novel *White Noise* (1984), the American academic Michael Valdez Moses has noted that one of its themes is how 'the technology of the hospital functions as an extension of the public media, of television'. He quotes the following passage:

You are said to be dying and yet are separate from the dying, can ponder it at your leisure, literally see on the X-ray photograph or computer screen the horrible alien logic of it all. It is when death is rendered graphically, is televised, so to speak, that you sense an eerie separation between your condition and yourself. A network of symbols has been introduced, an entire awesome technology wrested from the gods. It makes you feel like a stranger in your own dying.

The latest pieces of medical equipment to be brought by Hirst from the hospital into the gallery are the gynaecological examination couches, incorporated into the two new (living) fish installations in Theories, Models, Methods, Approaches . . . *Lost Love* and *Love Lost* are two gynaecologists' offices entirely submerged in water. In one, hundreds of jewel-like African river fish swim around the forceps and past the coatstand and through the stirrups of the couch. The fish in the other are big black carp that, even before the piece was ready for shipping, had started to impose themselves on their surroundings. In time, everything – the adjustable stool, the white examination coat, the advanced technology – will be coated with green algae.

As with all of Hirst's most powerful work, these are sculptures that provoke a multiplicity of interpretations. They could be alluding, for example, to the nineteenth-century eagerness to open up the female body and see deeply into the secrets of creation, which was central to the process and method of science itself. This passion for observation and analysis among the Victorians was manifested first in the development of scientific, medical and gynaecological instruments. Alternatively, there are a number of broad-brush references to low-budget horror films and to cult slasher pictures in the new work. Hirst has admitted that the various messages in lipstick and blood (in *An Unreasonable Fear of Death and Dying* and *Figures in a Landscape*, for example) were prompted by similar messages in *The Exorcist* and *The Shining*. And so it wouldn't necessarily be a mile wide of the mark to hazard that the dreamy, gynae-centred narratives of *Lost Love* and *Love Lost* allude to David Cronenberg's creepy 1988 film *Dead Ringers*, in which twins Beverley and Elliot Mantle invent a large instrument for gynaecological surgery, the Mantle Retractor. 'Gynaecology is such a beautiful metaphor for the mind/body split,' Cronenberg once said. 'Here it is: the mind of men – or women – trying to understand sexual organs.' The duality of mind and body has been one of Hirst's most persistent themes. And a second quote from Cronenberg chimes suspiciously well with Hirst's avowed motives for making these unnerving, hypno-trippy twin chambers.

Cronenberg: 'The . . . reason gynaecology weirds men out is that they are jealous. They've never gone into why. Men who put their fingers up their girlfriends can turn around and say the concept of gynaecology is disgusting. What are they talking about? . . . What makes gynaecology icky for people is the formality of it. The clinical sterility, the fact that it's a stranger . . . Everyone agrees to suppress any element of eroticism, emotion, passion, intimacy.'

The performative, gross-out, slyly provocative part of

Hirst's personality is the other side of him that is given rein across much of the new work. It accounts for the sense of a layered existence inside the most complicated and debris-littered (and probably autobiographical) of the sculptures. *Lost Love* and *Love Lost* in particular, it seems to me, can be read as a paradigm of the artist's personality (and, in many ways, of the practice of science itself).

Science (like art) is traditionally regarded as a combination of intention and surprise. 'In working,' Francis Bacon once said, 'you are really following this kind of cloud sensation in yourself, but you don't know what it really is. And it's called instinct.' Sol LeWitt goes further. 'Irrational thought', he advises in *Sentences on Conceptual Art*, 'should be followed absolutely and logically.'

In this exhibition, *A Way of Seeing* and *The Way We Were* tell how the rigour, the relentless objectivity, the heroic caution of science constantly come under threat of being undermined by human thought-habits: by superstition ('magical thinking'), say, or emotive distortion. Hirst has commented in the past that the spot paintings could be what art looks like viewed through an imaginary microscope: 'A scientific approach to painting like the drug companies' scientific approach to life.' And the scientist in *A Way of Seeing*, cocooned in his clean, well-lighted box, breathing in, breathing out, is intent on looking at this abstract, atomised version of the world – a world supported by the most minute entities, such as the messages of DNA, the impulses of neurons, and quarks, and neutrinos wandering through space since the beginning of time.

A fully technologised being himself, and therefore a realisation of the dream of modern technological science – the conquest of the final natural limit, death – Hirst's animatronic man is a modern exemplar of rigid, consistent and unchanging intellectual control. Only the sand and the seaside paraphernalia in the outer corridors of the vitrine suggest that he is missing the breezy and blowy, non-objective world; the seas and beaches.

In stark contrast, the Hammer horror nocturnal experimenter that we are meant to deduce from the ancient laboratory equipment and the other props stored in the melancholy cell of *The Way We Were* is the embodiment of what happens when dispassionate scientific method inadvertently admits mystical elements and human wishful thinking – what the science writer Stephen Jay Gould calls 'hope'. (In *Something Solid Beneath the Surface of Several Things Wise and Wonderful* we witness the incursion happening mid-title.) It is as if, Hirst seems to suggest, we keep our Dark Ages permanently with us, both in our societies and in our individual psyches, ready at any moment to undermine the painstaking evolution of the mentality and methods implied by science.

In *A Way of Seeing* we are presented with a cool room dedicated to the proposition that the world is comprehensible, controllable, everything correctable. (The cigarette ash in the ashtray – always a locus of horror for Hirst: the horror underlying everything; the horror that can overwhelm everything at any moment – offers the only clue that this might not be the case.) *The Way We Were*, on the other hand, is a hot environment – literally, thanks to the old single-bar electric fires leaking their warmth; and metaphorically, thanks to the scientist's overheated, almost Guignol-like imagination, rooted in the unruliness and dishevelment of life.

I think we are to infer that *A Way of Seeing* and *The Way We Were* are interior landscapes. They have this in common with two of the other paired pieces, *Lost Love* and *Love Lost*, in which the dreamscapes of the fishes – the pretty darting fish and the glooming phallic fish – envelop and transform the actuality of the world.

In *White Noise*, DeLillo's narrator, a college professor, has the following small-hours conversation with his wife:

'You have a vague foreboding,' I said.

'I feel they're working on the superstitious part of my nature. Every advance is worse than the one before because it makes me more scared.'

'Scared of what?'

'The earth, the sky, I don't know.'

'The greater the scientific advance, the more primitive the fear.'

Postmodern society is supposed to have become fully demystified and secularised. But like DeLillo, Hirst illustrates for us what Horkheimer and Adorno termed the dialectic of enlightenment, the paradoxical way in which scientific enlightenment reverts to new forms of mythology.

As Valdez Moses has pointed out, the concluding passage of *White Noise* reveals the quintessential postmodern environment, the supermarket, to be completely saturated with the aura of the sacred:

The terminals are equipped with holographic scanners, which decode the binary secret of every item, infallibly. This is the language of waves and radiation, or how the dead speak to the living . . . Everything we need that is not food or love is here in the tabloid racks. The tales of the supernatural and the extraterrestrial. The miracle vitamins, the cures for cancer, the remedies for obesity. The cults of the famous and the dead.

The patina of accumulation is something that has interested Hirst from the beginning. He has spoken often in the past about the profound impact that Mr Barnes had on his life and his working practice. Mr Barnes was Hirst's neighbour when he was a young student, newly arrived in London. Mr Barnes was a magpie collector, an obsessive hoarder of all the ephemera and detritus of his life. Then one day Mr Barnes disappeared, and Hirst let himself into the house to find out what had happened to the old man.

'It was like going through layers of time,' he has said of what he discovered. 'From the top to the bottom it was piles and piles of collected shit, like every toothpaste tube he'd ever used rolled up and stored in bags. Everything was collected and had a place, alarm clocks, and God knows what, heads from statues he'd found in graveyards, everything you could imagine, even money in parcels. I couldn't get to the things underneath immediately, but as you ploughed through it and got to the bottom I found a more and more organised man. It was like going back through his life, sixty years of time in one room.'

The action of the world on things became one of Hirst's driving obsessions. Time passed, and he started to use the worthless bits of flotsam that he'd retrieved from Mr Barnes's house to make small, Schwitters-like sculptures. For somebody who had always found trying to paint an ordeal — 'I could never paint. I was always terrified by a white void. I just couldn't choose what to paint there' — the collaging offered a lifeline back to art. 'With the collages,' Hirst has said, 'I found I could work with already-organised elements. And in Freeze [the group show of his contemporaries at Goldsmiths College that he organised in a disused warehouse in South-East London in summer 1988] the artists were kind of already-organised elements in themselves. I arranged them.'

A group show by young New York-based artists at the Saatchi Gallery in London at the end of 1987 — New York Art Now, which included work by Ashley Bickerton, Jeff Koons, Robert Gober, Peter Halley and Haim Steinbach — had a galvanising effect on Hirst and many of the other British artists of his generation who have since come to prominence. The commodity sculptures of Koons in particular (he was still in his vacuum-cleaner and floating-basketball phase), but also the slicked-up, deadpan work shown by Bickerton and Steinbach, helped Hirst towards the possibilities that he's still excavating. Except that, instead of Hoovers and lava lamps, the found objects that he chose to 'recontextualise' included surgical instruments and pharmaceuticals cabinets; also the internal organs of cows, bulls' heads, fish, a fourteen-foot tiger shark and a number of farmyard animals — cows, a calf, a lamb, a pig — suspended, either bisected or whole, in formaldehyde (the Natural History series).

As early as 1992, though, Hirst was adding to 'minimalist' work, that prided itself on an almost antiseptic clarity, other works that were more opaque and even, on a couple of occasions, dared a narrative element. In place of the poetic-associative, largely abstract combining of collage, he brought objects together so that they conspired to suggest a linear reading — a 'story'. *The Asthmatic Escaped* (1992), for example, depicts just what you would expect from the title: one half of a large vitrine contains a tripod camera; the other half contains a pair of jeans and dirty trainers discarded on the floor alongside an asthma inhaler.

In the same year he showed a large vitrine installation which was clearly meant to depict the suicide of a young woman. The glass walls of *She Wanted to Find the Most Perfect Form of Flying* are semi-obscured with blood, and blood stains a chair, a table and various scattered items of clothing. Only a white coat on a hanger, reminiscent of the white lab coat in *Lost Love*, has escaped the carnage. (Interestingly, a goldfish swimming in a bowl and the personal effects of a woman, giving a clue to her personality, are further links between the bloodbath of *The Most Perfect Form of Flying* and the site of conception that is the ostensible subject of *Lost Love* and *Love Lost*. 'I can make art about love but I don't know how I'd deal with sexuality,' Hirst once said. 'It always turns into murder for some reason.')

'He started off putting things on his desk for functional reasons, like everybody does in their life,' Hirst has said of Mr Barnes. 'And then he put so much on the desk that it became an object in its own right, and then the room itself became an object. At some point it stopped being functional and became art. Art without a viewer.' A number of pieces in Theories, Models, Methods, Approaches . . . have obviously been allowed to accumulate in this way; to grow cumulatively like fungal matter.

The result is that, shorn of their minimalist lack of affect, the vitrines of *Concentrating on a Self-Portrait as a Pharmacist*, *The Way We Were* and *From the Cradle to the Grave* have started to look less like the transparent cages of Bacon and more like transparent huts or sheds — vernacular structures found in back gardens and yards, where the cast-off stuff of life tends to multiply and moulder.

In *The Way We Were*, the surface of a vitrine has been broken for the first time, and articulated with the handles of swords. The swords themselves have a nostalgic charge that is in keeping with a work assembled from knocked-about remnants of the past. They are redolent of the magicians' boxes of vaudeville and childhood television, into which the magician's assistant disappeared, to be spun and apparently pierced and penetrated with sabres, only to emerge unscathed. The actual figure in *The Way We Were* — a crippled-child collecting box of the kind that used to stand outside post offices and chemists' shops — recalls the 'column' that used to stand at the centre of

Kurt Schwitters's *Merzbau*; it was surmounted by the cast of a child's head, taken from Schwitters's own son after he died in infancy.

'The past is hidden somewhere outside its own domain in some material object which we never suspected,' Proust wrote. 'And it depends on chance whether or not we come upon it before we die.' There are reminders of Proust here, and also of collage-period cubism, in the way Hirst makes a kind of expressive lyricism and hermetic poetry out of tatters and *tchotchkes* and less-than-skip-quality junk.

It took fifty years and Robert Rosenblum to 'contaminate a bit the pristine air' that cubism had earlier been breathing by indicating the abundance of witty, topical, and, at times, even smutty double and triple entendres in the work of Picasso and Braque. The incorporation of (often sensationalist) newspaper fragments and other 'visual offences culled from urban life and popular culture' into their still-lives, and Picasso's well-documented delight in true crime and cheap detective stories, find their equivalents in the lurid 'red-top' newspapers that crop up as compositional elements in several of Hirst's new works and – especially – the stroke books and pulp paperbacks that are semi-submerged in the theatrical gore of *An Unreasonable Fear of Death and Dying*. The can of Charm air-freshener ('Nature's Way') standing on the blood-spattered cistern and the cable news spooling out on the television – it's a matter of time before the room meets itself in its first mention or possible appearance in a bulletin – are just further plebeian facts of modern life.

In an earlier version, the television shows a looped sample of what has become known as 'wild programming': a shark doing its shark thing in the open sea. This is of course a reference to what is probably Hirst's most notorious work, *The*

Physical Impossibility of Death in the Mind of Someone Living. But it is also yet another emblem of how contemporary 'reality' has become completely mediated and artificial: cable nature, available twenty-four hours a day to the National Geographic and Discovery Channel subscriber. Heidegger's general term for this technological approach to the world – nature as the consumable product of consumer culture – is *Ge-stell* or 'enframing'. By means of enframing, which is the essence of technology, nature is 'revealed' to be at man's disposal, and in so doing is transformed into a *thing* which man chooses to consume at his convenience.

When he decided to make *The Physical Impossibility of Death . . .*, Hirst lifted the phone and placed an order for an adult shark with a shark hunter who was unknown to him and who lived in a town he had never visited, ten thousand miles away in southern Australia. It is something he has since said he regrets doing and would never do again. So the target of the word 'Die', finger-painted in blood on the bathroom door in version one of *An Unreasonable Fear of Death and Dying*, could conceivably be seen to be the killer (the shark) rather than the implied (human) murderee. Hirst's contrition for what he now apparently regards as the pointless death of a living creature seems to be reflected in the filtration units over the *Lost Love* and *Love Lost* vitrine tanks which – sculptural qualities aside – are immensely more elaborate than anything that could be needed to simply deliver warmth, air and light. Unlike the Insect-O-Cutor in *A Thousand Years* that zapped flies at random, fried and obliterated them, the plant of the fish pieces is there to keep the kinetic elements in shape and alive, and available for eternal scrutiny and inspection.

*

More than once, after breaking a table full of glasses and china, he would sit conspicuously in a corner booth and play with the sharp fragments, casually making designs as his fingers dripped blood onto the table-top . . . [It was] a display so exaggerated, so singular, that people began coming on Tuesday nights just to see it; a display so memorable, so widely witnessed and reported, that for decades afterward, [his] reputation rested almost entirely on [it].

He [then] stuffs his penis into a hot-dog bun and tapes it on, then smears his ass with mustard . . . He approaches the table and sits nearby, drinking ketchup and stuffing his mouth with hot dogs . . . Binding his head with gauze and adding more hot dogs, he finally tapes his bulging mouth closed so that the protruding mouth looks like a snout . . . He stands alone, struggling with himself, trying to prevent his own retching . . .

These two descriptions – the first by two of Jackson Pollock's biographers, Steven Naifeh and Gregory White Smith; the second by a spectator at one of Paul McCarthy's messy, sacramental performances in the early seventies – come perilously close to describing the Damien Hirst of contemporary London legend.

'I find myself becoming more and more yobbish,' Hirst once said, 'when I expected to become more intellectual.' The new work *Death Is Irrelevant* shows how the strategy he has applied in life has carried over to the art. It is what many people would see as a deliberate desecration of the wistfulness and quiet elegance of its precursor, *I Want to Spend the Rest of My Life Everywhere, With Everyone, One to One, Always, Forever, Now* (1991). It is up to others to make links between *Death Is Irrelevant* and Grünewald's or Bacon's crucifixions, or the bone-figure style of Picasso if they want. Hirst's task – apparently the latest stage in a developing aesthetic – is (he appears to be saying) to disappoint expectations of what his art should be by floating a turd in the proverbial punchbowl and subverting the pleasant appearance of things.

342

He has always candidly used drugs and drink as a way of isolating himself from banal experience and to bring him to something original or extraordinary in the moment that nobody else can see. He is a showman artist in the tradition of the Victorian decadents like John and Sargent. 'It's about expectation,' he has said. 'It's theatre. It's about raising expectations and lowering expectations. It's very theatrical . . . I like to imagine that art is more theatrical than real.'

Hirst has developed a performance persona that is intended to both shore up and disconcert the hooligan genius reputation he has been cultivating now for the best part of a decade. And the role he has been touring for the last few years – the period of the gestation and completion of the work in Theories, Models, Methods, Approaches . . . – is that of the famous fuck-up, chaotic and wilful, and permanently, maddeningly out of his tree. To the point where it is often impossible to know (perhaps even for the artist himself) where 'theatre' ends and reality begins.

The eerie carnival that Hirst's life sometimes seems to have become (he has long been a staple of the gossip columns and a favourite of the voracious English tabloid press) is punctuated by performance-like acts that combine parody with self- and other-directed aggression and bathetic self-abasement. 'He wanted total fulfilment and satisfaction. But he didn't call it art. And that's why it gets to me,' Hirst has said of the most important artistic influence in his life, the semi-derelict Mr Barnes. 'To ignore everything and get involved in this creative process, and it just merges into your life and your life merges into it, and that's it. It's a complete fusion of art and life . . . I want art to be life, which it never will be.'

'The aesthetic of aftermath' is an expression that has been used by the critic and curator Ralph Rugoff in connection with the work of performance-based artists such as Chris Burden, Cady Noland and Paul McCarthy, whose gallery practice involves the display of 'performance relics'. 'The aesthetic of aftermath' is a term that can be applied to certain sculptures in this show — *Figures in a Landscape* and *From the Cradle to the Grave*, for example — which reek of violence and which continue a tradition inaugurated by Pollock's action painting where, as Harold Rosenberg declared, 'the canvas was no longer home to a picture but to an event'. In an insightful essay on the work of McCarthy, Rugoff continues:

This notion of the picture plane as an arena of evidence marks a conceptual shift in Modernism, a movement away from the autonomous art object to a growing focus on works or environments that bear the imprint of prior activities . . . an art of forensic traces and evidentiary values . . . Faced with an art object that is positioned as relic, clue, left-over or aftermath, the viewer is required . . . to connect the past to the present.

Concentrating on a Self-Portrait as a Pharmacist is an inventory of relics connected with Hirst's struggle with painting. Having cleared the studio of his assistants, he entered the shower-sized inner vitrine and performed the painting — or, more accurately, the sculpture of a painting. 'They're about the urge or the need to be a painter above and beyond the object of a painting,' as he once said of the spot paintings. 'I've often said that they are like sculptures of paintings.'

Many writers have pointed out the similarity between Hirst's framing vitrines and what David Sylvester has called the 'spaceframes' — most commonly, the simple introduction of a rectangular linear frame around the human image — in Francis Bacon's paintings. Hirst has come to be seen as the natural inheritor of Bacon, and it can be no accident that the most legendary of his actings-out have happened at the Colony Room, a place indelibly associated with Bacon and the mythology of haute-bohemian London. (When she opened the club in 1949 – it's really only a narrow, single upstairs room – the owner, Muriel Belcher, had paid Bacon £10 a week for a while to bring in his rich friends and generally tout for her.)

Damien clenched naked into a foetal position behind the bar in the Colony Room; Damien trouserless at the piano; Damien daubing a big black swastika on his chest . . . Why are these theatrical presentations of himself so insistently familiar? Answer: because they are (probably conscious) re-enactments of Bacon's 'inner scream'; of the convulsed and isolated 'rough beast' that Bacon returned to again and again in his painting, just as he was habituated to the perpetual twilight in the cramped 'interrogation green' Soho room with its dull gilding and its vicious gossip, which he internalised and reproduced obsessively as a hellish psychic landscape over the four decades of his career.

To this point, human absence has been as crucial to Hirst's endeavour as human presence was to Bacon's. 'Before,' Hirst said recently, 'it was the lack of the human figure; an implication of absence. And – this is what makes it most poignant – of human absence from a man-made environment . . . Only objects are left – man-made signs which, in the absence of men, have become objects.'

Although, as Richard Flood and others have pointed out, Hirst has studiously avoided the human body in his work, he has been aggressive in his referencing of it, through inanimate objects, animal carcasses: surrogate humans.

Theories, Models, Methods, Approaches, Assumptions, Results and Findings marks a departure. Now the human presence – skeletal, mechanical, bin-bagged, prosthetic, painted – is real. This show is dominated by a human figure: the twenty-foot, six-ton bronze cast of a child's anatomical learning toy called *Hymn*. The fragility of existence has been Hirst's big theme from the beginning. It's why he puts things behind glass, and in formaldehyde in big steel-and-glass cases: to hold off the inevitable decay and corruption; as part of a futile effort to preserve them.

Casting human organs in bronze would seem to be a parallel process: a way of rendering them invulnerable; immune. 'Solidity – and people always look for solidity – I think is a great strength,' Hirst has said. 'I love the idea of solidity. But to actually find solidity in my body means that I will be a skeleton.'

Time works its relentless erosion. 'Death subtends life, or underlies life,' the pathologist F. Gonzales-Crussi writes, 'and the action of time consists in peeling away successive layers so as to render death ever more visible.' The bright nursery-coloured paint over the surface of *Hymn* is like skin; like skin, it will decay. All that is solid, as Marx wrote in *Capital*, volume one, melts into air.

2000

Four years ago, for his last major show, at the Gagosian Gallery in New York, Damien Hirst made a piece featuring a giant beach ball bobbling on a column of air. The ball was multi-coloured and the box around the air supply was also brightly painted and carnivalesque. It was a sculpture that suggested playfulness and buoyancy and barmy insouciance and all the things that people already associated with Damien Hirst. He was the recognised ringleader and alpha talent of the most startling artistic development in Britain in what we must now call the last century.

Loving in a World of Desire was a refinement of *A Celebration*. At least, one of Hirst's most innocent and affecting apprentice pieces, in which party balloons, some of them partly deflated, float in front of a bright striped party backdrop. It is a sculpture out of a time and about a time when all of it was easy and like a party. You had an idea and you grabbed it and — hey! — next day you were in the papers.

Now he has produced an uncomfortable new piece which relates to these earlier works the way the fresh-faced young friend from your youth relates to the stranger with the frail, wintering, chemotherapy look, passed unexpectedly in the street. All the colour has been leached out, and the easy optimism of the 1995 work has been replaced by what seems to be an overt acknowledgement of ominousness and even dread.

The beach ball in *The History of Pain* is white — ectoplasmically white and precarious; the top of the box above which the ball is suspended is pierced by several dozen rasped and hungry Sabatier knives. The briefest choking of the air supply and the ball will be punctured and instantly shredded. The fragile balance destroyed.

A friend (it was Joe Strummer) misheard 'The History of Pain' as 'The History of Fame' and went on referring to it by this title. Which gave Hirst the idea of tweaking the original sculpture into a second version. The cloned work will be identical in every detail: same bubble-like inflated ball, same fierce long knives. The only difference is that *The History of Fame* will have an audience track — rumbles of anticipation when the ball drops close to the knives and appears to be in danger of bursting; groans of disappointment when it floats clear of the daggers and the carvers.

The period of neglect for an avant-garde artist has shrunk for each successive generation of artists in the past hundred years. It is no longer possible – or it seems no longer possible – for an important avant-garde artist to go unrecognised. And artists are no fun once they have been discovered.

Having soared so high, so fast, and having struggled with what he calls 'a difficulty with art' for the past four years, Hirst knows he has arrived at a crucial point in his life and his career. He says that if his adventures in the catering trade and his other excursions have taught him anything, it is that if he's not an artist, he's nothing. But he believes he has been hearing the grinding of knives for some time now. 'The art world's very shallow,' he says. 'The art world lets you down. It's very shallow and very small and it's very easy to get to the top of it. And then you burst through the top of it and you've got no idea where the fuck to go. You know, they've all been waiting for me to die. Now they're all phoning up. I've got so many people on my back trying to get me to make things, pushing in the wrong direction. It's a constant effort telling people to just go away. I mean, everyone's your friend.'

It can be deduced from the Sabatier sculptures, and from a number of the other sculptures that he has made for a major show in New York in the autumn, that Hirst's first work of the new millennium has taken a turn towards the nakedly autobiographical. Care will be taken wherever *The History of Pain* and *The History of Fame* go on show to make sure than nobody can put a foot on the pipe delivering the air supply.

He was drinking a Steelworks. This was a new one. Just soda plus a dash of Angostura bitters and a twist of lime. Non-alcoholic. But fashionable, because Damien Hirst was drinking it. Soon a woman at the next table was ordering a Steelworks, and then a woman at Princess Diana's old table behind the column, away from the window.

It was Steelworks all through lunch. Then a hot-towel shave and a haircut. And then Coca-Colas all the way through dinner. Even at the after-hours club round the corner, he stayed stubbornly on the wagon.

The next morning he was bright and early and in boisterous high spirits, which an unscheduled taxi ride between Reading and his new studio in Gloucester could do nothing to dent. For two hours we got the story of the Ebola virus, complete with detailed descriptions of the *vomito negro* ('Black vomit,' Damien explained helpfully; 'it contains the lining of your lungs as well as blood') and typical Hirst-like actings-out and grotesque embellishments. He'd read *The Hot Zone* through all of one night, pacing the bedroom of his house in Devon, heart pounding, his eyes on stalks, horrified and yet electrified by the horror.

He's always working on sculptures. Even at his drunkest you can sense him thinking; always looking, looking, looking. It troubles him; he sometimes wishes he could stop looking. He's on the lookout constantly for something that can be used.

In addition to a change of clothes, his luggage consisted of a copy of the *Fortean Times*, a copy of *Viz* and a heavy leather-bound academic volume on blood. The single word 'Blood' filled the whole of the spine. Blood is the symbol linking most of the new work he has been making. Blood and smoking. Blood and smoking and violent death. Sometimes, such as in a piece called *An Unreasonable Fear of Death and Dying*, the blood is graphic, splattered all over the rugs and furniture and glass of the vitrines. In *An Unreasonable Fear*, a chainsaw saws an armchair in half and a shark plays on a tape loop on the television; a can of Charm air-freshener ('Nature's Way') stands on the blood-spattered cistern, behind the door with the word 'Die' finger-painted in blood.

In other instances, the blood is merely implied. *Adam and Eve (Banished from the Garden)* features two corpses on mortuary trolleys, buckets, bones; an unfinished cheese sandwich rests on one of the corpses. *Figures In a Landscape* is a vitrine divided into nine cells. Each cell contains bulging black bin bags deodorised with sachets of Haze concentrated fragrance gel and 'Superfresh Neutradol'. 'Stop me B4 I kill again', reads the message written in lipstick on an old wardrobe mirror.

We arrived at his studio at a time when Damien is often just falling into bed. And immediately, as if to announce his arrival, the peace of the countryside was shattered by the sound of security alarms going. The alarms started going and then phones started ringing to say the alarms had been triggered. He couldn't find the phones. He couldn't find the switches for the lights. The codes for the digital pads to stop the alarms bleating were written on another piece of paper.

There is a new piece called *Looking Forward to the Total and Absolute Suppression of Pain*, in which four TV monitors simultaneously and at ear-splitting volume play four different commercials for Neurofen, Solpadeine and other headache tablets. The first ten minutes at Stroud was like being in an opened-out version of it.

There was an element of theatre involved, of course. Hirst is a showman artist in the tradition of the Victorian decadents like Johns and Sargent. The 20,000 square feet of studio in a Cotswold village is his recently acquired Xanadu; a bolt-hole to withdraw to and 'sit the fuck down and concentrate on working'. 'I love the fact that there's no windows,' he said. 'It's completely separated and isolated from anywhere else. It's a personal space. It's out of London.'

It's a vast hangar-like building. In addition to his own work, it houses work by Warhol and Peter Halley, and by Goldsmiths contemporaries like Angus Fairhurst, Rachel Howard and Sarah Lucas. There's a conference room and a dining room, a gallery and a kitchen with a walk-in freezer. 'I blame Charles Saatchi,' Hirst said. ''Cause when I was an art student, I went down to look at his space and I just wanted one. Immediately. I mean, art looks great in there. Art looks great in here. So you make art for it.'

Inside, when the lights did finally come on, the immediate impression was of menace. It felt a dangerous place. In addition to the Sabatier knives jutting skywards, the whole studio had been turned into a labyrinth of steely, reflecting surfaces and lacerating, industrially cut edges. There were (real) skeletons and blood; (prosthetic) human body parts arranged on shelves and bagged in bin liners; surgical instruments and corpses. And towering above it all, the sculpture that Hirst refers to as 'the big guy' — a twenty-foot, ten-ton bronze cast of an anatomical child's toy that Charles Saatchi was four days away from buying for £1 million to add to his collection. The whole of it the fruits of two years' labour and a million-plus dollars.

Over the past fifty years the vocabulary of art has expanded towards the inclusion of everything. Everything seen in a certain way becomes art; is art. Children's plastic toys and cheap domestic detritus are scattered through Hirst's new work. It was seeing his son Connor, who's five, playing with the figure from Humbrol's Young Scientist series that made him decide to cast it in bronze. 'I might even get sued for it. I expect it. Because I copied it so directly. It's fantastic. I just thought it was so brilliant, and it was so accurate, it was like a chemistry set, and I loved it that it was a toy. I wouldn't have done it with a teaching hospital one. This is much happier, friendlier, and more colourful and bright. Like plastic! The paint on it's like skin. It'll decay. I liked it for that reason. Eventually what you'll be left with is the paint hanging off and this big, fucking grand iconic sculpture.'

At home in Devon he has a fish tank with fish in it swimming around in rubbish. One fish is from the village pet shop, the other's from the fair, and they share their tank with a pair of false teeth, a model shark, and an old beer bottle. 'It's like the bottom of a beck [a stream]. All trash in it.'

In his studio near Stroud he had two fish tanks, each room-sized and each with a gynaecologist's examination couch in it. *Love Lost* and *Lost Love* are two gynaecologist's offices underwater. One contains hundreds of jewel-like African river fish. The fish in the other are big, black carp that have already started to impose themselves on their surroundings. These are clearly works that cry out for prolonged critical analysis and deep psychoanalytical investigation. They are haunting (consciously so) and beautiful. Their creator, of course, refuses these kinds of 'higher' interpretation. 'They're pretty direct,' he says. 'There's something really simple. If you've got a gynaecologist's office underwater with fish swimming about, then there's something fishy going on. An' fishy fannies comes straight after that. I think. In the logic of it. I quite like the idea that the doctor's had to take his watch and his rings off [they are part of the furniture of *Love Lost*], so that you get the doctor's personality into the hand that's going to finger about with you down there. The woman's got her shoes on the floor, and there's the coat and the handbag. So there's a hugely sexual element to it. An' women smell of kippers.'

'I find myself becoming more and more yobbish,' Damien Hirst once said, 'when I expected to become more intellectual.' This has partly been a defence mechanism. His lack of house-training, a talent relatively recently acquired, has kept him out of polite society and therefore away from contaminating conventional ways of viewing the world. He has always used drugs and drink as a way of isolating himself from banal experience and to bring him to something original or extraordinary in the moment that nobody else can see.

He has always drank and drugged. But he has also always been a ham. 'It's about expectation,' he says. 'It's theatre. It's about raising expectations and lowering expectations. I've always done that. Regularly, when I used to go to openings, I used to go in looking like a tramp. Then I'd go in a suit, then I'd go in like a tramp . . . So people would just be going, "Damien's losing it, oh wow, he's really on top of it, omigod, he's losing it, no he's on top of it . . ." And they never know where the fuck they are.

'The way I got involved with the art world . . . You get people to think one thing, and then you come round from another direction. I mean, you do it in an art work. I think that's what all artists do. They draw you into some sort of belief system and then – bang! – they hit you with something else. The one-two. Bacon does it. With a kind of bareness of paint, or a sensuality . . . Michelangelo does it. Everybody does it.'

Damien has always been able to charm his way out of things that would get other men done over or put away. The hooligan genius of recent Soho legend seemed, through his innate taste and acute intelligence, to be incapable of putting a foot wrong. Sometime during the making of this current work, though, a subtle shift occurred. He was banned from the Groucho Club after complaints from members. He dropped his trousers in the bar of his Dublin hotel last month, where he was directing a Beckett play for television, and a female guest is persisting with her threat to sue after he inserted a chicken bone in the end of his penis. More recently, Norman Rosenthal, the exhibitions secretary of the Royal Academy, arrived at the Academy Room in Soho and found Damien trouserless at the piano.

'So what's new! Will you tell me when I haven't done that?' he says. And then: 'I think I've spread myself so thin. I was just drinking too much to be concentrating hard. So something's got to give. Blackouts. I used to never get blackouts. I get blackouts now. I got involved in drink and drugs, didn't I? Mixed. So it's a completely different thing. I mean, I always mix my drinks. I don't stick to one drink. And then I started taking cocaine and drink. And I think there's some point when you do that where it becomes a different drug in its own right. When you add two chemicals together, you get a different chemical. There's a balance I was after between a certain amount of this and a certain amount of that. Like a fucking alchemist.

'But then overnight I turned into a babbling wreck. It was completely overnight. I've spoken to Maia [his partner] about it. It happened like that . . . I started to blow gaskets and pop rivets. I mean, it's been incredibly hard work not doing anything for four years, in terms of the art world. And I haven't done anything for four years because until now I've not felt it was any good. There's a kind of hunger. Well, you just have to starve people. You have to convince yourself that the art world's not going to go away if you go away.'

Since his last major gallery show, he has concentrated his energies in the commercial arena. He went into partnership with Marco Pierre White at Quo Vadis in 1996; then he opened Pharmacy, a restaurant, with Matthew Freud and others at the beginning of 1998. He believes now that maybe the restaurants were more effort than he admitted. 'It just wasn't art at the end of the day. You end up getting involved in fucking aprons, knives and forks, pots and pans, all the shit of life that you don't really want to get involved in. Stocks and shares, ties, boots, Blu-Tack, glue, string . . .

'Doing Pharmacy made me realise why you're not allowed to touch art – why it says, "Do not touch" in art galleries. You go in after a week and it's fucked, you know what I mean? It's like all the things that can go wrong in your house if you get shit builders in, combined with letting a herd of elephants rampage through the art gallery.'

Damien Hirst joke:

Q: 'What's the biggest thing you've ever killed?'

A: 'My career.'

He says this is the clue to the lipsticked inscription 'Stop me B4 I kill again' in the brilliant bin-bag sculpture. 'I thought it was quite funny to have that, as a kind of cry to the public . . . It comes from *The Shining*, where he writes "Redrum" on the mirror. And in *The Exorcist* when she's possessed and it's inside her, she writes on her chest "Help me" from the inside. Like trying to get out of your predicament. I said the other day to Maia that I feel a bit like I don't want to be Damien Hirst, and it's too late to do anything about it. I don't like being "Damien Hirst", I've decided. But you can't avoid it. So I think on the next mirror I'll write, "Help me".' Pause. Switch to camp delivery. '"I'm just trying to make the best of a bad job, really".' Prolonged laughter.

2000

GALLERY BRUNO BISCHOFBERGER
THE BEAUTIFUL AFTERLIFE
for Gordon + Carol
all my love
Damien Hirst
'AV A FAG FOR FUCKS SAKE

RICHARD BILLINGHAM

These photographs are about my close family. My father Raymond is a chronic alcoholic. He doesn't like going outside and mostly drinks home brew.

My mother Elizabeth hardly drinks but she does smoke a lot. She likes pets and things that are decorative. They married in 1970 and I was born soon after.

My youngest brother Jason was taken into care when he was eleven but is now back with Ray and Liz. Recently he became a father. Ray says Jason is unruly. Jason say Ray's a laugh but he doesn't want to be like him.

Richard Billingham, 11 March 1996

Obviously Richard has asked himself what he must have done to deserve Ray and Elizabeth. But, equally obviously, Ray and Elizabeth must at some stage have wondered what they did to end up with Richard, a royal pain and a regular viper in the nest, constantly mooching, always lurking with his Nikon loaded, relentlessly in their face. ('Out the way, fookin' David Bailey.')

Liz clocks Ray one and Richard is on hand to get it (carefully composing the picture so that the kitchen knife, which may or may not have had a part to play in the action, in the ritual — this is the implication — bloodletting, juts up into the bottom of the frame). The Billinghams settle down to enjoy a quiet TV dinner, and Richard materialises behind the set to squeeze off frames that show more flesh than Elizabeth probably intended, and both parents dribbling gravy down their fronts. (There are two added compositional bonuses here: the correspondence between the tattoos up Elizabeth's arms and the pattern on the Ming dynasty-style wallpaper behind her; also the fact that one of the dogs, parked in between its owners, is making a meal of its hot pink privates.)

The intrusiveness appears to be unremitting and total and to have gone on for at least a couple of years (it was actually six). Richard's brother, Jason, retires to his room to roll a joint and Richard moves in to snatch a shot that makes him look like a bloated, smear-head Francis Bacon. Somebody (probably Jason) ices a cock-and-balls on a birthday cake (which is also conventionally decorated with two hearts, and the names 'Ray' and 'Liz'), and Richard turns it into a still-life. In a few instances, the images are so raw that it feels indecent to scrutinise them too closely; just as in real life you would increase your pace, look away, pretend not to have seen (you didn't ask to have your face forced into this stuff), here the impulse, when you come to, say, Richard's picture of his father sprawled in the toilet, door open, flies gaping, is to turn the page quickly. You don't, of course. Or, if you do, you soon leaf back pruriently, sneaking up on it, to check the precise nature of the crud caked around the outside of the toilet bowl (shit or puke?) and to register the irony of the mop and bucket (itself splattered) by Ray's elbow and the clasp/anchor of the deodoriser outlined against the smashed-up plastic seat.

The phrase 'a tourist in other people's reality' is one that is engraved on the hearts of all photojournalists and of all those reporters who have heard it. It was coined by Susan Sontag in her well-known assault on Diane Arbus, whose pictures of drag queens, freaks, the deformed and the retarded (and, it shouldn't be forgotten, of Sontag herself, posing with her son) she accused of 'lowering the threshold of what is terrible'. 'To the painful nightmarish reality out there,' Sontag wrote, 'Arbus applied such adjectives as "terrific", "interesting", "incredible", "fantastic", "sensational" . . . To photograph people, according to Arbus, is necessarily "cruel", "mean". The important thing is not to blink.' Arbus herself once said she thought that 'all families are creepy in a way' and tried to bring that out in her work.

Martin Parr has been the best-known inheritor of the Arbus tradition in Britain in recent years. *The Last Resort*, published in 1986, was a series of pictures of working-class families up to their necks in fast-food and garbage in the run-down northern seaside resort of New Brighton. The pictures were luridly coloured and grabbed, carpetbagger-fashion, without the permission, and often without the knowledge, of the people in them. 'They are the objects I am using,' Parr has said of the ice-cream guzzlers and ketchup squirters and naked, dirty children. 'I knew where people would gather. I knew that at the end of a bank holiday there would be litter, and I knew I wanted litter to feature.'

Like Roger Graef and the makers of the BBC's 'fly-on-the-wall' documentary *The Family*, Nick Waplington moved in on the tenants of a Nottingham council house to get the pictures that were eventually collected in his book *Living Room*. This was an exercise in 'humanistic photojournalism', in the tradition of Dorothea Lange and Walker Evans: Waplington said he saw himself as being intimately linked with Janet, her partner and her children; that in a way, their story had become his story; they knew what was happening in their pictures and how their lives were going to be represented.

But in the cases of both Parr and Waplington all we are talking about in the end are degrees of distance. The impulse, no
matter how well-intentioned, was journalistic: both went out
looking for a subject – for material; both went visiting the
natives to bring back news of their exotic doings and strange
gear.

Part of the voyeuristic appeal of photography is the licence
it gives us to look at people who can't look back. 'We can look
at people's faces in photographs with an intensity and intimacy,' as the American critic Adam Gopnik has written, 'that
in life we normally reserve for extreme emotional states – for
a first look at someone we may sleep with, or a last look at
someone we love.' And not just people's faces, either: their
pot-plants, their carpets, that odd stain to the right of the fireplace, just above the Eiffel Tower ashtray and below the wall-
mounted rifle, also make themselves available for forensic
examination. In Martin Parr's and Nick Waplington's – and
now Richard Billingham's – photographs, ordinary objects
tend to assume a previously unlooked-for, occasionally sinister
significance, the way they do, after the fact, in police scene-of-
crime pictures.

In the most heat-filled situations – Liz drawing her arm
back, about to lay one on Ray; Ray lurching floorwards, about
to crack his head; Liz weeping in the kitchen after what has
probably been a run-in with Jason – Billingham is able to maintain a steady hand and a cool, appraising eye. Note, for example, the way Ray is toppling towards the square of canvas on
the floor, as if he is about to frame himself, rather than brain
himself (he is, in fact, doing both). Or how the china orna-
ments, the dollies and doggies, Liz's treasured possessions,
echo the fragility of Ray. Or the way Jason is always hovering
just at the edge of the picture whenever there's a bust-up

brewing. Or the slice of bread lying behind Ray's head as he lies in bed in one picture and the pile of bread standing next to a heaped ashtray in another, as unlikely as the box of Yorkshire puddings on the bedroom table in the lovely double-portrait of Ray and his dog . . . Take all this as evidence of Richard Billingham having the splinter of ice in his heart that Graham Greene said all true artists need.

Many Victorians were afraid of photography. Like Balzac, they believed that 'every body in its natural state was made up of a series of ghostly images superimposed in layers to infinity, wrapped in infinitesimal films'; being photographed caused people to slough off images like dead skin.

On the evidence of *Ray's A Laugh*, Ray and Elizabeth Billingham are people who bleed unselfconsciously and often, either as a result of casual, sometimes self-inflicted violence or simple accident. Metaphorically, though, this is a set of pictures which shows two people skinned alive.

Unlike most actuality photographers, who invest much of their energy insinuating themselves into the kind of situations where, if they hang around long enough, they might hope to catch reality off guard, Richard Billingham found himself in a situation where everybody was off guard all the time; where all guards were down by virtue of his relationship with the participants and his father's addiction to the brackish brown stuff which is visible in reality or by implication in all of the pictures.

The appropriateness of exposing what, in some quarters, will be seen as the squalid details of feckless, even useless, lives is inevitably open to question. Billingham will be criticised for exploiting the openness of his brother and his parents. And there can be no doubt that implicit in the pictures is the boast that what we are being asked to admire is a consciousness of a different order from those surrounding it. Richard Billingham has made it over the fence; he has escaped into a different reality. Some of the pictures have already been shown in a Bond Street gallery, which must have made for an even more awkward viewing experience than coming face to face with them in a book.

Ray's A Laugh is a remarkable document for a number of reasons, almost none of which have to do with the broader, boilerplate social and political implications of a family struggling at or below subsistence level. (For the record: Ray Billingham has been unemployed since he was made redundant from his job as a machinist in a Birmingham factory in 1980. His drinking predates the redundancy by many years. Elizabeth Billingham has never worked.) It is a brilliant essay on the psychopathology of family life which is also brave enough to suggest that destitution — more: squalor and degradation — can produce images that are not only *not* ugly, but actually galvanising and beautiful.

Billingham's pictures reminded me of something Francis Bacon once said to his friend, the wildlife photographer Peter Beard, after Beard had shown him photographs of the carcasses of thousands of elephants. 'Dead elephants are more beautiful,' Bacon said, 'because they trigger off more ideas to me than living ones. Alive they just remain beautiful elephants, whereas the other ones are suggestive of all types of beauty . . . All kinds of images crowd into you from seeing this particular image.'

On a different occasion, Bacon spoke to Beard about his fascination with street accidents: 'If you see someone lying on the pavement in the sunlight, with the blood streaming from him, that is in itself — the colour of the blood against the pavement — very invigorating . . . exhilarating . . . In all the motor accidents I've seen, people strewn across the road, the first thing you think of is the strange beauty — the vision of it, before you think of trying to do anything.'

It seems pretty obvious that Richard Billingham's concerns are aesthetic rather than purely documentary. A picture of his mother doing a jigsaw puzzle, for example, is all about the formal concerns of composition and texture and pattern: the 'sky' cigarette box and the sky of the worked puzzle provide the only areas of flat colour; the only solace for the eye. The chaos of pattern and colour that is evident in many of the pictures seems an accurate reflection of the chaotic nature of the life that is lived inside the Billinghams' flat. But, whereas his wife sleeps under a lace canopy, next to a doll in a lace dress, there aren't even sheets on Ray Billingham's bed, only heavy brown blankets like blotting paper, blotting him up.

A confirmation of its value as a functioning unit, perhaps, is the fact that the family has hatched within itself somebody with a sensibility as refined, and potentially unique, and an eye as acute as Richard Billingham's. Billingham himself appears only once in his family portrait — a spectral figure reflected in a dressing-table mirror, camera masking his face, in a picture of Ray on one of his good days: clean, almost smiling, and dewhiskered.

I had just started typing that last sentence when the phone rang and the operator asked if I would accept a call from a 'Richard Bellingham' who was in a phone box in Birmingham. He was on his lunch break, it transpired, from the KwikSave supermarket where he currently works. He provided some biographical and technical particulars (age twenty-five, uses a Zenith or ordinary automatic camera, gets the films processed at the local chemist). Then he hurried to point out that he didn't consider himself a photographer and that *Ray's A Laugh* was likely to be his first and last effort in the photographic field.

He trained as a painter and started taking pictures of his father as back-up for some paintings he planned: every night he came in from college and Ray would be lying passed-out on the bed; checking his breathing was always the first thing he did. 'So taking pictures was also a way of preserving him a bit at the start.' Seeing him on his back in the toilet was – is – an accepted part of family life. A familiarity with Francis Bacon's paintings and his liberatingly unorthodox view of the world also helped. Billingham seems to have more or less committed Bacon's interviews with David Sylvester to memory.

For some reason I asked him to tell me the names of the pets, the cats and dogs, who climb all over the pictures. 'Pebbles and Peppy are the dogs,' he said. 'The cats' names are Shadow, Tiddles, Snookums and Sheba . . . Have I said Shadow?' There was the vague hum of shopping malls and out-of-town hypermarkets and rural factories. 'It feels strange standing here saying this.'

There was something about all this – something about his pictures – that was strongly reminiscent of the stories of Raymond Carver, in which a recurring image is of a man at home alone during the daylight hours, lying drunk on a sofa. Billingham's, like Carver's, is an indoor world, with grime and net curtains obscuring a reality that would otherwise go unsuspected and unreported; the strangeness of the everyday.

Raymond Carver once amended Tolstoy's definition of talent as being 'the gift of seeing what others have not seen' to suggest that talent, even genius, is also 'the gift of seeing what everyone else has seen, but seeing it more clearly, from all sides'.

Among Elizabeth's tattoos you can make out 'Raymond'

inked onto one arm, and 'Jason' on the other. You can't read Richard's name, but he had assured me it was there along with his father's and his brother's. 'They like me,' he said. 'They like what I do. I want them to see everything.'

1996

Somatheeram Beach
Somatheeram
AYURVEDIC BEACH RESORT
Chowara P.O., South of Kovalam, Trivandrum - 695 501
Phone : 0471-481600-603 (4 lines)   Fax : 0471-480600
Photo : Salim Pushpanath
Produced by Dee Bee Venture, Pushpanath Ave, Kottayam 686 041
INDIA   1.00
INDIA   5.00
SANCHI STUPA
Gordon Burn
3 Beaufort Mansions
Beaufort Street
Chelsea London SW.
ENGLAND

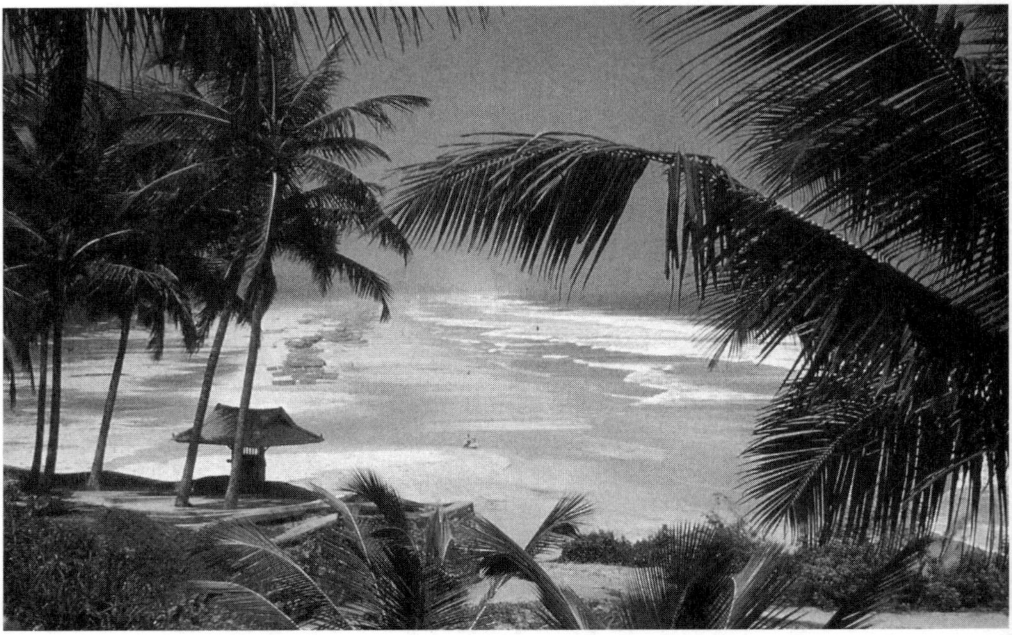

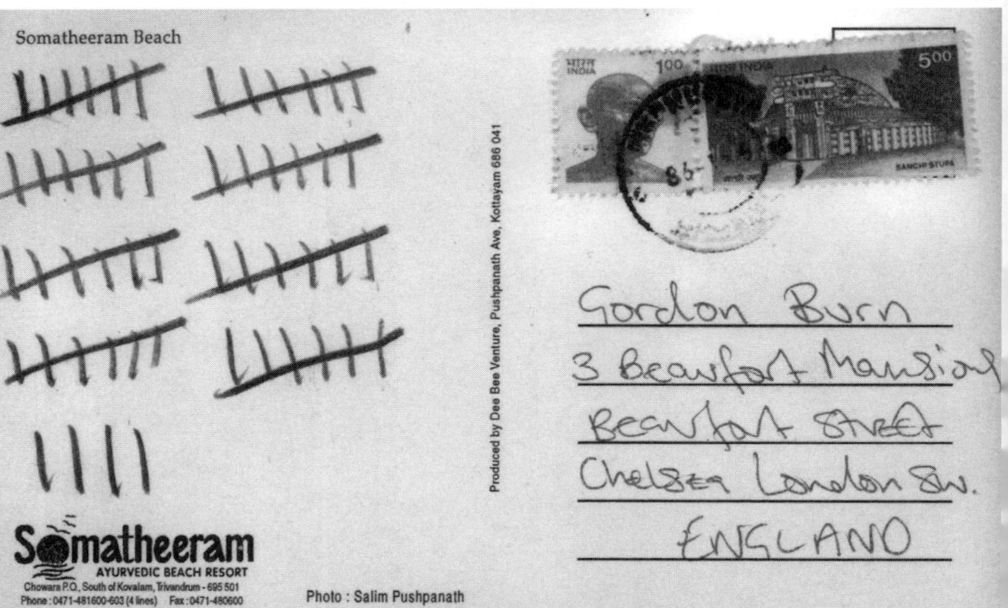

Sarah Lucas

SARAH LUCAS

Our first conversation was about a jacket that I didn't realise was her equivalent of Warhol's platinum-white wig or Gilbert and George's tweedy old Civil Service flasher suits; a jacket that was part of her armour – part of the personal mythology she was in the process of constructing for herself at the time.

It was in a pub after a private view. I had never met Sarah before, knew nothing about her. I didn't know she was an artist. What I remember thinking (and eventually – almost immediately – saying) was that she was the most concentratedly, even obsessively, down-dressed person there. Not unfashion or non-fashion or junior bohemian or just fashionably grungy, like many of the others surging around us, but aggressively anti any notion that clothes might do more than provide a cover in which to walk out in public.

Her hair was parted in the middle, thin and long and hanging in rats' tails as if she had just eaten a bag of chips with her fingers and run her fingers through it. She was wearing road-diggers' jeans with a broad brown belt that puckered the inches of excess denim where it dragged them in around the waist. Big pants. They ended at some kind of scuffed and nondescript platform boots with about six inches of material turned back over on itself at the ankles. This was three or four years ago, so it's difficult to be absolutely specific, but there was probably some thick-washed, charity shop woollen, possibly a starveling muffler, almost certainly a non-designer (YHA rather than YSL) backpack with an emergency bottle and her cycling stuff in it.

The main exhibit, though, eclipsing everything else she was wearing in the clapped-out stakes, was the jacket: a short, Wrangler-style leather jacket that had apparently once been brown but was now as white and cracked and dry as the Bonneville Salt Flats in Utah. It looked like a shitty jacket that had been repeatedly allowed to get soaked and then hung up in front of a fire to get even shittier.

There used to be an old poet who went around Soho stinking of his own excrement. This wasn't an accident. It was a statement. He used to enjoy seeing how long it took people to edge away, and Sarah reminded me of him. Her address – the fag in the hand, the feet set wide apart, her head cocked back – was spoiling-for-a-knuckle confrontational. Her face was pale, innocent of any hint of make-up, with two angry cross-hatchings of colour burning high on her cheeks.

She reminded me then, as she does now, of Joan Littlewood, the firebrand of E15, always photographed in her dustman's jacket, embroidered with the red lettering 'Borough of Hackney', her man's shirt and her jaunty slouch cap. Sarah claims never to have heard of either Joan Littlewood or Brendan Behan, whose plays *The Quare Fellow* and *The Hostage* Littlewood put on at the Theatre Royal, Stratford East, in the fifties. But she recently had herself photographed in a big topcoat lurking outside a men's toilet in an inner-city park, looking exactly like Behan in a picture taken forty years ago. The only difference is that, whereas Behan has nothing more unconventional than a rolled-up newspaper about his person, Sarah is carrying a heavy ugly grey fish, its tail on her shoulder, its slack mouth suckling her finger.

As usual, it is difficult to extract from her the thinking behind this weird picture. 'I just think it's funny to loiter around outside a men's toilet,' is all she is initially prepared to offer. 'I got really stinky. It was hilarious, walking around with it.'

Nietzsche wrote that he wanted to say in a page what anyone else would take a book to express – and what even then they wouldn't have succeeded in expressing. Michael Tanner has written of the philosopher E. M. Cioran, a follower of Nietzsche, that he 'writes with a kind of fastidious weariness, as if what he has to say is nothing very surprising, but he knows that people are, by and large, too stupid or too wilfully self-deluded to agree with it; so he needs to descend to explanation and even a little argument'. Sarah Lucas's approach to her work is similarly withholding, equally aphoristic: she supplies a sentence and leaves it to the serious viewer to turn it into a paragraph. 'There's always that bit missing in Sarah's work,' is how Damien Hirst puts it. 'There's no way out, no way in, but you're in. It's like a bogie on your finger. That's what makes her so brilliant.'

'Fish,' Sarah is finally pushed into saying. 'They recur in my life quite a lot. I can eat a crab in a really efficient way. I've always liked fish. I think it's the smell – the sexual connotation.' The most notorious use of fish in her work occurs in one of her simplest and most successful pieces, *Bitch*, already established as one of the signature British sculptures of recent years. *Bitch* consists of a simple enamel-topped table on castors. A white T-shirt has been pulled over the legs and part of the table-top at one end, and two melons dropped into it to simulate heavy pendant breasts. At the other end hangs a vacuum-packed kipper. The result: the stereotypical stroke-book image of a woman bending forward, offering herself; a pastiche male fantasy that, as reclaimed by Sarah Lucas, is simultaneously crude, repellent, engaging and funny.

The picture of her loitering outside the Gents with a garoupa is the latest in a series of photographic self-portraits that she has been making in the last few years. 'The idea of taking the liberty of doing a self-portrait', as she puts it, came to her in 1990, when she photographed herself as a piece of jail-bait eating a banana. This was later incorporated into a much larger panel featuring paste-ups of leggy lovelies and buxotics from the *Sunday Sport*, the paper she plundered for a lot of her early work.

In all the pieces featuring images of herself — Sarah sitting on the tailboard of a lorry drinking a can of Tennants; Sarah lounging, legs apart, in an armchair, big boots pushing up into the foreground; Sarah under a line of washing in a forest clearing, staring down the viewer on the other side of the camera — she comes over as the hard case; the boy slag; the bit of rough. ('My life, if I live to be five million years old I will never be able to work out how birds' minds tick over.') In all of them she is wearing serious bovver-wear and a scowl and trousers. In all of them she is wearing the crappy Wrangler jacket. We know the pose. It is one of the staples of late-twentieth-century culture. It is Gavin Turk as Sid Vicious as Elvis Presley as John Wayne. (*Get Off Your Horse and Drink Your Milk*, a Lucas piece consisting of six pictures of a naked man doing things with two digestive biscuits and a bottle of milk, takes its title from a line in a John Wayne western.) She has made a wax mould of her middle finger giving the finger (*Receptacle of Lurid Things*, 1991). She has exhibited the steel-toecap Dr Martens boots that she wore for years, with razor blades inserted between the soles and the uppers: the title — *1-123-123-12-12* — alludes to the world of sound-checks and roadies, another

370

world from which women, unless they're groupies, are effectively excluded.

'Anyway,' she said on that first occasion, after the argy-bargy over her jacket had gone on for far longer than was sensible, full of her standstill swagger, 'who asked you to stick your fucking oar in?' It was then she let go the laugh that distinguishes her from the well-hard, transgendered 'Sarah Lucas' of the pictures. Her face was transformed by paroxysms of happiness, and her laughing grew progressively louder, drunk on the sense of its own audacity.

Earlier this year, during a panel discussion at the Royal Academy, Sarah Lucas was asked to talk about the jostling for position that the art student putting the question said he assumed must go on among the current generation of so-called 'Britpack' artists. 'It's the survival of the fittest,' she said. 'In many ways it is that. But there's lots of ways to be fit. It's not like the dole. You can't get in the queue and get your whack.' More recently, she had this to say on the same subject: 'I'm not into being "top sculptress". It's just not up my street. Having said that, I have made some fucking excellent sculptures. I feel I have to say it because there are some people who don't realise it for some reason.'

Sarah Lucas isn't exactly unknown. She has had solo shows at White Cube and Anthony d'Offay in London, at the Barbara Gladstone Gallery in New York, and in a number of European museums and galleries. Charles Saatchi collects her work, and she has been included in all the big showcase exhibitions for the new English art.

She has been a powerful presence at a time when presence has counted for a lot in the London art world. The bars at the Groucho Club, the Soho House and the Atlantic, and at St John near Smithfield Market, have felt like Max's Kansas City in New York in the sixties, as described by the art historian Thomas Crow: 'It was in this competitive fish bowl that artists had to establish and maintain a dominating personal aura, that is, if dealers were to be successfully cultivated, critics cajoled or intimidated, and fascinated collectors convinced that supporting this art offered an entrée to flattering recognition and a share of the glamour for themselves.'

At thirty-four, Sarah Lucas is a few years older than the artists who came out of Goldsmiths with, or at around the same time as, Damien Hirst. Anya Gallaccio, Abigail Lane, Georgina Starr and Sam Taylor-Wood are a few of the younger female artists who would admit to being encouraged by Sarah Lucas's example. Her personal style has also been influential. 'She's managed to find a completely genuine way of being,' a woman who knows her told me, 'and her femininity shines through it. There's no artifice involved, which is very liberating for women. No tricks or games with hair and breasts and high heels, and yet she's totally like a woman in every way.' It was noticeable that Siobhan Feahy started to look like Sarah earlier this year, around the time she commissioned her to design the cover for the new Shakespears Sister album.

And yet the fact remains that she is still probably the best little-known artist of an unusually talented generation. Hers was the name that most people were surprised to see left off this year's all-male shortlist for the Turner Prize. 'I think my work is both what I like and what I'm like,' she once said. 'I make things how I am.' How she is is pretty intractable, which probably explains why she hasn't yet broken through.

While he is fighting off young artists who want him to do for them what he has done for Damien Hirst, for example, Sarah has consistently refused to sign an exclusive contract with Jay Jopling and White Cube. 'He could represent me very well,' she says, 'but I've always had qualms about how well I want to be represented. I'm not that interested in being part of some establishment or other. I'm interested in what next I'm going to do in the world, not even as an artist. I'm in it for the long haul.'

She has always had a compulsion toward the margins, and it is an instinct that the developments of the late eighties reconfirmed. In 1988, when Damien Hirst curated Freeze, the warehouse show that sparked the current art-buying boom, all the work in the show sold except hers (a brick wall that she hung on a brick wall). 'I wasn't interested enough in it,' she says now. 'Sitting at home grappling with a piece of aluminium; taking up my space, not going anywhere. The futility and ridiculousness of doing this kind of stuff.'

So she stopped. While the others were jetting around the world, being photographed by Snowdon, powering ahead, she worked in bars. Ever since then, in a way, she has been defined by the success of the people she knows. Grenville Davey, whom she used to live with, won the Turner Prize in 1992. Gary Hume, whom she also lived with, is tipped to win it next week. One of her closest friends, Angela Bulloch, used to live with Damien Hirst; her current boyfriend, Angus Fairhurst, is a friend and occasional collaborator of Damien's. Rachel Whiteread, generally recognised to be one of the most gifted artists to come out of this country since the war, is younger than her by a year.

Although superficially their work and their working methods could hardly seem more different – Whiteread cerebral, considered, concerned with surface and finish; Lucas impulsive, intuitive, happy to muck along with whatever's to hand ('All her work has the appearance of being proper sculpture and mine hasn't,' Sarah says) — there's an interesting overlap of subject matter between them. Both have worked extensively with ordinary household objects: tables, chairs, mattresses, baths. But whereas Whiteread tends to be interested in the 'auratic', in histories of use and the melancholy of absence, Lucas is more likely to be drawn to ugliness or shabbiness; to 'anti-beauty'. She's also capable of making that rare thing: the postmodern work of art whose aim is to raise a smile, even a laugh. In 1992 Whiteread made *Untitled (Amber Mattress)*. Two years later Lucas also worked with a mattress in a piece she called *Au Naturel*. Whiteread's was a poetic evocation of the site of birth, copulation, illness and death, moulded in translucent rubber. Lucas was only interested in the copulation part: to a stained mattress dragged in off the street she added two oranges and a cucumber (the shagger) and two melons and a fire-bucket (the shaggee) in order to put a new spin on the old East End joke: 'You're fucking me, aren't you? I can hear you.' *The Old Couple* consists of two wooden chairs: in the middle of one there's a wax penis, on the other a set of Burroughsian vaginal teeth. 'I like her. She's a laugh.' This would be Sarah's ultimate compliment.

She comes from Islington in North London, where her father worked as a milkman most of the time she was growing up. 'What I'm like is so much to do with how I grew up and where,' she says. 'And, if you like, that is my point of view, and I try and make things according to my own point of view. Maybe it's something that I might find funny, the tone of someone's voice. It stems from that.' It is only relatively recently, though, that it occurred to her to bring who she is to her work.

By 1990 she was 'just moseying along in life; I didn't care so much about art any more'. That summer she went with Gary Hume to Rome, where Barbara Gladstone had offered him a place to work. Like the American Bruce Nauman, the person who has been the single biggest influence on Sarah Lucas and her contemporaries, and who has recalled that his defining moment came in 1966 when he found himself spending most of his time alone in a storefront studio, equipped with a fresh postgraduate degree and no materials to speak of, she decided to work with whatever was cheap and available. In Rome, surrounded by all its art and antiquity, she chose to make lists of obscenities – the colloquial names of sexual parts and sexual practices written out on four-foot strips of paper. 'Arse Eater, Arsehole Bandit . . .' was one. 'Ball Bag, Banger, Bell Ender, Bollocks . . .' was another.

Back in London, she started working with the *Sport*, collaging, overpainting, blowing up spreads into seven-by-ten-foot posters. *Sod You Gits*, featuring a woman as a topless kissogram dwarf, and *We Score Every Night* were shown as part of her first solo show in London in 1992, along with *Penis Nailed to a Board Box Set*, a 'game' derived from a topical tabloid news article about the imprisonment of a group of consenting male sado-masochists. A couple of weeks later she showed *Two Fried Eggs and a Kebab*, another literal translation of a woman-hating obscenity she had been hearing all her life. 'It was good frying the eggs every morning,' she has said. 'I felt a bit like a dirty old man.' The piece was snapped up by Charles Saatchi.

It was around this time that Sarah met another lapsed artist called Tracey Emin (Tracey had seen the kebab piece and thought it looked like her), and the two of them embarked on an intense relationship that lasted for twelve months. Early in 1993 they took over the lease on a former doctors' surgery at 103 Bethnal Green Road, in the East End of London, and opened for business as The Shop, selling T-shirts daubed with slogans like 'Complete Arsehole' and 'Fucking Useless', key rings, mugs, mobiles, decorative penises, and one-offs such as an octopus made from tights stuffed with newspapers and wearing a wig, all of which they made themselves. Sarah greeted customers in a T-shirt that said 'I'm so fucky', while Tracey's asked 'Have you wanked over me yet?'.

There were art-historical antecedents for The Shop: most obviously Claus Oldenburg's Store on the Lower East Side of Manhattan in the early sixties and, more recently, the American artist Mike Kelley's 'dirty' dolls and second-hand knitted, stuffed toys. But Tracey Emin says that none of that was in their minds: doing The Shop was a way of cementing their friendship by making something together. 'The question was: "Are we going to fuck each other, are we going to head-butt each other? What are we going to do with all this welling, this ball of energy?" The Shop was so much more than just a relationship.'

For a while, Emin and Lucas cultivated a joint persona: The Birds. 'We're birds,' they told a television interviewer, before dissolving in giggles. According to Tracey, most people who met them thought they were a couple at the time. They weren't. They believed that what they had together transcended sex.

At the end of six months The Shop closed as planned. There was a party, and the following day Tracey incinerated everything that was left. The boxed ashes formed part of her first show at White Cube. A few months later Sarah showed her 'immaculate bollard' at the gallery – a concrete bollard bearing the inscription 'Fuck me while I'm sleeping'. It was called *Headstone for Tracey*.

'Something you have to remember about Sarah. It's a simple thing,' Tracey says. 'Quite often when you see her art, it's something you've never seen before. That's why people have problems with it.'

Sarah incorporated a toilet into her work for the first time last year. In *One Armed Bandits (Mae West)* the toilet was paired with a man's singlet and underpants draped over a chair and an erect penis made of wax; there was a cigarette end floating in the dingy bowl.

At the minute she is showing another toilet in a gallery in Berlin. This time the bowl is clean, the toilet is plumbed, and the flush-cistern works. It is just an ordinary toilet standing in an empty room surrounded by white walls. Nicole Hackert, who runs Contemporary Fine Arts with her husband Bruno Brunnet, 'launched' the toilet the night before the private view. 'Somebody had to do it,' she said. 'We stayed in drinking wine with Sarah and Angus, had a very nice evening, and after three hours I thought, somebody has to do this job.'

The gallery is in what, until six years ago, was the communist part of Berlin. In an effort to achieve the 'blooming landscapes' promised by Helmut Kohl on reunification, the eastern half of the city is a single building site. To get to Contemporary Fine Arts it was necessary to walk on duckboards across mud, surrounded on all sides by the things that have become the common currency of installation art in recent years: scaffolding, skips, portable cabins, rusting metal plates, slabs of paving, mounds of gravel, sand, cement. It was some of these same workers, from the former GDR, who had installed Sarah Lucas's toilet in the room where they had expected paintings to be. It wasn't possible to explain to them that the aim of *arte povera* sculptors was to remove the 're' from 'represent'; to force the viewer to confront the naked reality of the object, its likeness to nothing but itself. But Bruno Brunnet believed that the men who had carried out the job had got something useful out of it, none the less.

'They don't understand anything about it, but you saw it

from their faces and from their behaviour that they had changed a little. Maybe only for ten minutes or for half an hour . . . It meant they got out their tools, the plumber, the electrician, they did things they had not done before. This was good. There was an energy. They think a little bit that we are crazy, but not stupid-crazy; crazy in a good way.'

Did he think of the toilet as sculpture? 'It's very pure,' he said. 'I wouldn't call it a sculpture. It's not the word which comes to my mind.'

'What would you call it, then?'

'I don't know. I would call it . . . a toilet.'

One afternoon a couple of weeks ago I was having a drink with Sarah in the Chelsea Arts Club when a member of the bar staff asked if she could have a word with me in private. It was just that . . . well . . . this was embarrassing, but an elderly female member was complaining that she had just passed a man coming out of the ladies' toilet, and seeing as I was the only man in the bar . . . That is, there was me, and there was Sarah, in a man's shirt and man's trousers, her hair shorter than it was.

When I got back to the table I asked her: why do you look the way you do? 'What I like to do with my appearance,' she started, then stopped. Then she collected herself — as usual, she had a fag on — and started again. 'I've always had this idea about what people mean by how they dress. I mean, in the detail, men included — like whether they have their shirts done up or not done up, how their collars are, how their tie is in relation to their shirt, and all the nuances about how anybody's dressed, and what they're trying to say about themselves. And what they're trying to say about themselves is always what you know already: they're trying to muscle up to some cliché or other. I'm not trying to put forward something; I'm trying to avoid a lot of things. I try to be fairly neutral, in the same way that I try to find a neutral table for a piece of work.

'The upshot is that I don't look lairy particularly, but I do look a bit odd. But I can live with that. I've found what I am. I define myself against what I don't want to be, really. There's a heck of a lot I'm not saying because I don't want to say it. It's quite like the sculpture: there's a lot of stuff left out.'

Her conviction is contained by a natural sweetness that the people who don't know Sarah never see. They see the acerbic bitch of the art; the you-could-have-knocked-me-down-with-a-starting-handle street tough. They see her as trivial or vulgar, which she knows. She knows she's not as articulate as she could be, probably should be. It's typical of her well-concealed worritable nature that she's already trying to get her articulate bit together for a lecture she's booked to give at the Tate Gallery at the beginning of next year.

'For once in my life,' she said, 'I feel I've got a lot of thoughts. I'm not even sure what they are, and it's not to do with wanting to preach about anything, it's to do with who I want to be . . . The whole glamour dimension that's on the art world, I can enjoy that as much as the next person – having a good time, getting really pissed up, doing lots of drugs all night, being somewhere with a whole bunch of people and it's all on. It's all on. But I find I can be totally bored even when I'm having a really good time. Then I crave solitude, but if I'm solitary for a day, I've had enough of it already.

'I dunno,' she said, lighting up again, flashing a screw-you look at the old woman who had mistaken her for a boy. 'Where's it all going? What are we fucking up to, if anything, that we all think is so important?'

1996

'There has always seemed something grim to me about Mary McCarthy's dogged insistence on remaining angry for forty years,' the literary critic James Wood wrote recently. By the same token, there has always seemed something unfeasibly heroic about Sarah Lucas's determination, still going full-tilt at the age of forty-three, to live life at the pitch of a delirious Jimi Hendrix solo – the lewd, endlessly deferred climax of 'Voodoo Chile', say, when it seems he can never get back from where he's gone.

'I feel so overwhelmingly excited by everything at the minute I can hardly sit still,' Lucas said on the phone when we were arranging to meet. To which the only possible reply was: 'So what's new?' In her best work, thinking and doing seem to be the same thing, detonating in the same moment. It's why she prefers to work at home, between the washing-up and reading the paper and, probably most profitably, in the heavy hangover hours, when she can make connections between a zinc bucket, a raddled pair of tights and a Fray Bentos boil-in-the-tin steak-and-kidney pie that nobody other than maybe Les Dawson would think to make. Leaving the house to toil in a studio she says is 'too much like going out to do a job'.

For Lucas, the rush-of-blood moment, the sudden move-ment and making is the object. She can be equally headlong in her day-to-day life. She recently leapt on Damien Hirst in a crowded bar at the Groucho Club in Soho and wrestled him to the carpet. She said she was going to bite his tongue off and put it in his pocket and afterwards Hirst admitted that there was an instant when he thought she might do it.

She has always been a singular person, and the most unabashedly, all balls out, rock 'n' roll of the YBAs. It was Lucas who came up with In-A-Gadda-Da-Vida as the title for the show that she did with Hirst and Angus Fairhurst at Tate

Britain last year. It came from what Doug Ingle, keyboardist with the psychedelic rockers Iron Butterfly, managed to mumble while wastedly trying to convey to a label executive that the band's 1968 album was going to be called *In The Garden of Eden*.

Led Zeppelin figure in a couple of her titles. *Spam Zeppelin* ('resin, acrylic paint, fibreglass, wanking mechanism') is a spin on 'spam javelin', rude-girl slang for an erection. *1-123-123-12-12*, the roadie-mantra title of one of her still bruisingly original early pieces, consists of a pair of cherry-red Dr Martens with a razor blade inserted lethally in each toecap.

'A bloke for the nineties' is how Hirst once described her, an allusion to the gender ambiguity that she simultaneously played up and interrogated in a series of now very well-known photographic self-portraits which showed her in heavy boots and jeans, fag dangling, legs splayed, looking truculent and hard as fuck for the camera.

Gratifyingly for her, there was a period a few years ago when David Bowie, the great soaker-upper, appeared in magazines and videos looking like a Lucas doppelgänger, and he was emulated by what at the time seemed like legions of models and members of boy bands. Meanwhile, for a show in Berlin in 2002, Lucas revealed that one of her earliest influences on the gender-bender front, or ambisexual 'caper', as she herself would say, was, not entirely predictably, the seventies Arsenal legend Charlie George.

She painted portraits of Charlie (the drug double entendre was purely intentional) on newsprint and on garish pizza flyers that had been pushed through her door, and they could have been portraits of her young self in a red Gunners shirt: same lank, centre-parted hair; same 'standstill swagger'.

A more abstract rendition of Charlie in the same show

came in the form of a porcelain toilet bowl, painted red outside and in, apart from a collar of white, and suspended from the ceiling by a rope. Dangling next to the toilet was another bathroom fitting: a bidet that had been given a coat of matt black and wired up with a tiny, flickering, urine-coloured bulb. This was titled *Susan Farge*, the name of Charlie George's wife. Three walls of an adjoining gallery were lined with Duchamp-style urinals, each painted in team colours and carrying a facsimile autograph of a player of the Charlie George era.

As is nearly always the case with Lucas, she was working on several levels here. One was autobiographical: she grew up in Islington in North London, where she still lives, and Charlie George was a friend of her brother's; they lived on the same estate. 'It's a local thing,' she says. 'Local to me. His wife lived two doors from me and he lived like three blocks away. It was a big moment when he drove up and parked outside his father-in-law's house in a Jaguar. He was the first, I suppose, "famous" person I knew. But also football was local in those days. He went to the Holloway school where a lot of the Arsenal football team then would have come from, selected from the schoolboys. I've always lived within the sound of the Arsenal crowd, more or less all my life. One of the things that interests me about that is just how different all that stuff is now. "Local" is hardly there.'

The Charlie George installation was only the most recent example of Lucas's fascination with the social spaces that men carve out and aggressively make their own. Snooker halls, nicotined sheds, changing rooms, truckers' cabins, public bars and dodgy urinals keep on turning up repeatedly in her work; territories from which women tend to be excluded except as the objects of casual put-downs, dirty jokes, or as pin-ups on the salted-peanut card hanging next to the pork scratchings behind the bar.

Lucas read all the standard feminist texts as a student (Andrea Dworkin later used one of her sculptures, *Bitch*, for the cover of a book) and then, believing they could be narrowing, or at least over-prescriptive for an artist, abandoned them. 'I've decided I don't want to be the individual who is harping on continuously about a particular issue,' she announced more than a decade ago. 'I know someone's got to do that job. I just don't want it to be me.'

Recent titles such as *What a Bloke! (We All Went Out With Him Sometime)* and *Geezer* may be ironic, but then again maybe not. It is on the swampy ground of ambivalence that Lucas has sunk the foundations of her work. 'I quite like insinuating myself into blokiness, definitely,' she says. 'I do love it. I love all the banter. That's why I would say something spurious like I'm a better bloke than most blokes. But it adds so much to the work I do that I'm a woman doing it. And that fascinates me, why it should be so much more powerful because I'm gender-bending, in a way. But it is.'

Of all the unpredictable twists and turns which kept the YBA saga bobbing high on the media agenda for the best part of a decade, one of the least explicable was Lucas's decision at the height of her notoriety, when her pieces were starting to go for six figures at auction, to become a barmaid. Well, not a barmaid exactly, and it was only for a day a week. But around 1998 she decided to work shifts at the Colony Room in Soho, which was going through difficult times making the transition from being the home of Francis Bacon and the old-school bohemian pissheads of the School of London to accommodating Hirst and Lucas and their lairy, loved-up pals.

Why was she doing it? It was a question that many people

kept asking. Was it a grunge enactment of Manet's Bar at the Folies Bergère? Or a literalisation of John Berger's theory of female objectification which, at the time of its publication in 1972 ('Men look at women. Women watch themselves being looked at'), had hinged on women's historical lack of real-world power or independence? Ask her over the drink she was busy serving and she'd give enigmatic answers like, 'I know it's not proper rhyming slang or anything, but I always think of half a lager as a Mick Jagger,' or talk about her work as an artist being in the tradition of British slapstick comedians like Benny Hill or the Carry On crew.

I have a strong image of her around this time, backstage in the tiny musicians' bar at Ronnie Scott's Club in Frith Street. Ian Dury, then dying of cancer, had just performed a set for a TV documentary. Lucas was a fan: in her cups she often gives singalong renditions of 'Billericay Dickie' and 'What a Waste', belting it out like some androgyne Marie Lloyd or Gertie Gitana. She loved Dury; his work clearly echoed her own obsession with punning, tabloidised reality. But until the painter Peter Blake brought them together backstage that day, Lucas and Dury had never been introduced. She was touchingly shy and uncharacteristically abashed. She told him about how she used to serve him tea in the days when she was working at a kiosk in Regent's Park but never let on she knew who he was. After a very few minutes, she said she had to go; she had to 'be back at work'.

Dury no doubt thought she meant back in the studio or at her gallery, rather than round the corner pouring drinks for the halitoxic members of the Colony Club. 'It was one of those times,' she says now, 'and they come round on a kind of loop for me, of not wanting to be pushing what I'm doing; of wanting a bit of breathing space. For years and years I did work in bars, and it didn't make me feel in a lowly position. It gave me quite a strong sense of myself, in fact. I've never believed in those notions that dignity lives in status or in how much money you've got. It's good to remind yourself. And it seemed to work out all right. I also thought I might drink a bit less if I was that side of the bar,' she adds, 'but I didn't.'

Lucas is occasionally snapped at A-list events and gallery openings, but she is not part of the moveable feast of paparazzi targets in the way that contemporaries such as Sam Taylor-Wood and Tracey Emin, for instance, are. She seems to have an antipathy to modern celebrity culture and doesn't appear to be media-needy in the current way. One of the reasons she gives for why she has stopped making the photographic self-portraits in recent years is that she started to suspect they might just be feeding the worldwide lust for celebrity and iconomania, rather than commenting drily on it.

She spends a lot of time at a house near Alburgh in Suffolk these days that she co-owns with her dealer Sadie Coles. It used to be the home of Benjamin Britten, who composed his music in a shed in the garden, and this has been her introduction to Britten, Purcell, Vaughn Williams and the English song tradition.

The counter-tenor Alfred Deller played in the background all the time we were speaking, and provided the soundtrack to the video clips and pictures she brought up onto her computer screen. They were taken at a dance performance she had been involved in a week earlier at the Kunstverein in Hamburg, where the survey show of her work that is about to arrive at Tate Liverpool was on. It featured her partner Olivier Garbay in a chiffon sheath dress and red high-heel shoes dancing to moves that had been choreographed by their close friend Michael Clark, and incorporated the rough building-site gestures that she has hijacked and recast as the language of her work: the finger; two fingers; the sign of one forearm jacked up under the other that means 'up yours'.

God Is Dad, the title piece of her recent show at the Barbara Gladstone gallery in New York, featured a globe-shaped bulb glowing through the crotch of a pair of tights. The review of God Is Dad in the *New York Times* concluded that it was all about incest. This is news to Lucas, but she remains unfazed. 'People are always suspecting me of being abused,' she says. 'Some people. Journalists. Not everyone. But it does come up that people think there's something about me that suggests I have a very dark past. And that's why I'm sexually twisted, or something. That's what they're reading from the work.'

Damien Hirst has never made any secret of the fact that Lucas is the artist among his contemporaries that he most admires. 'Sarah's out there strapped to the mast like Turner in the storm, making excellent pieces over and over again,' he said five years ago. More recently he has put his money where his mouth was by buying back all her outstanding early work from Charles Saatchi.

No Limits!, the title of a piece she made in 1999, always seems to have been the general idea. 'I don't want to be scared of anything,' Lucas once told me. 'I hate excuses. Loathe excuses. I don't want to make them, I don't want to listen to them, I don't want to live one.' And there is the sense that, maybe alone of the generation of artists she came up with, she is the one left still living the life.

'I sometimes wonder how long I've got,' she says. 'I feel all right, but I'm still smoking like a trooper, I still drink like billy-o. Not a great deal has changed in that department. I don't take as many drugs as I used to, but I still do. I haven't got to that point of giving anything up, even though the balance shifts a bit

. . . I'm not complaining, it just makes you wonder, doesn't it? Because it's completely random how much that stuff affects you and how much it doesn't. It's something you can't know in advance. Everybody to a certain extent will be a victim of what their life has been.'

2005

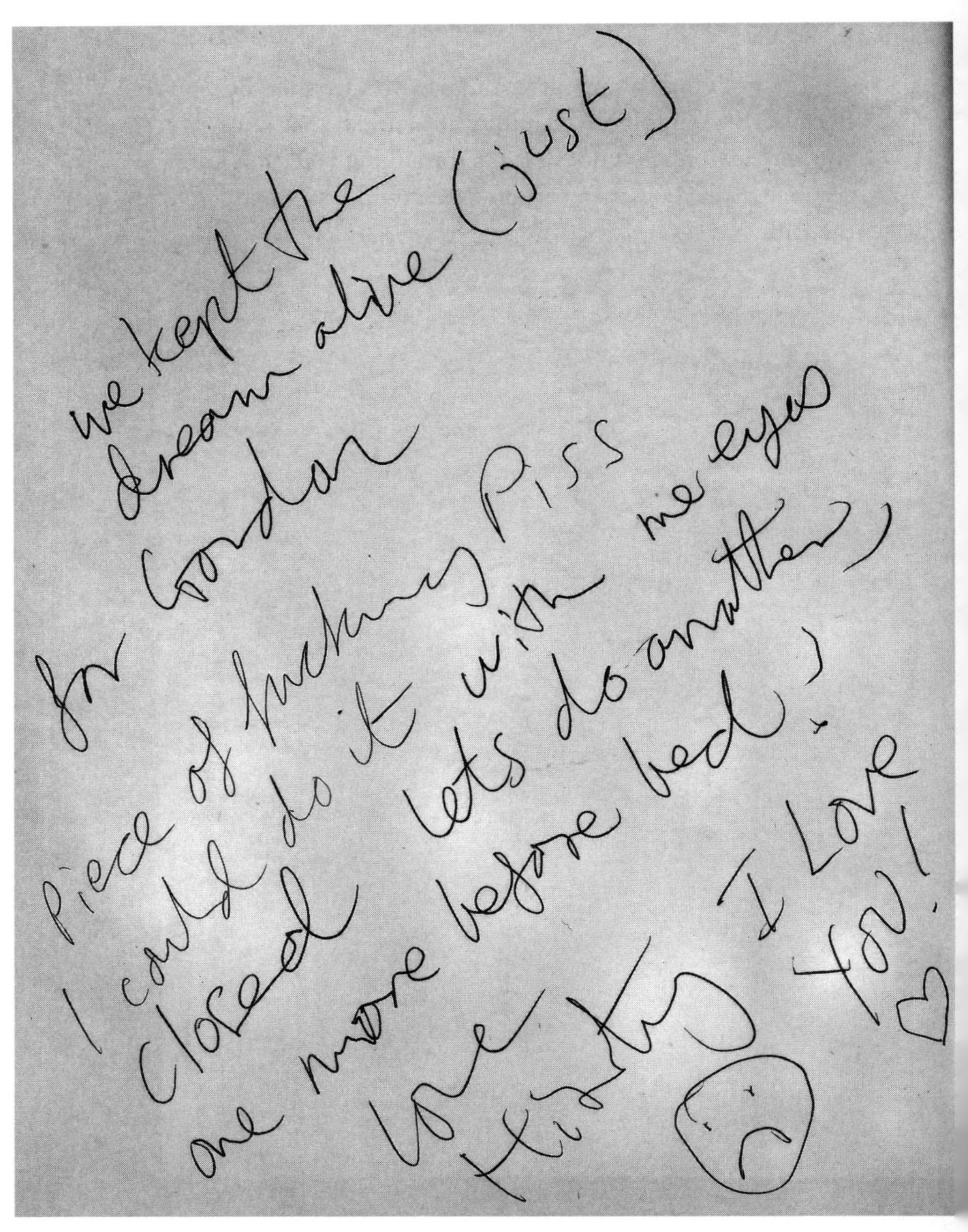

Damien Hirst, dedication to GB's copy of *On the Way to Work*

SENSATION

Banging. Sorted. Mental. Wicked. New words for new ways of living in an old country. Large. Skanky. Blimey! (shading out of the childlike wonder of the pop mentality here, into rote MTV irony). Top tip! Brilliant! Phwoar!

Betcha By Golly Wow. This could have been a good title for the show of work by young British artists from the Saatchi collection, which is just about to open at the Royal Academy. The record was a hit in 1972, so they probably danced to it at junior discos. It's corny/clever, 'selling' in a sly, self-deprecating way, and suggestive of the we're-all-dumbed-down-now *Sun*speak that it predates by a few years.

Instead, the show is to be ho-humly called Sensation (no exclamation mark), a word which will be emblazoned on the belly of Burlington House, the home of the RA in Piccadilly, like a Nike swoosh on the master of the hounds' well-filled twills, or a logotype splashed across the stirrups and snaffles printed on his lady wife's headscarf. Bleeuuuurrrgh! Beg-pardon, guv.

On second thoughts, though, perhaps 'Sensation' isn't such a bad title. It suggests the gulf that exists between all the heat generated in the media kerfuffle surrounding the Damien Hirst generation of artists, and the coolness – that is the affect-lessness; the loss of sensation; the starey cold stoniness – in the work itself.

'Sensational'. This was one of the adjectives applied by Diane Arbus to the nightmare reality she cruised New York photographing every day. 'Terrific', 'interesting', 'fantastic', 'brilliant'. These were others. Arbus made her name in the sixties taking pictures of the subliterate and the disliterate, the pain-crazed and the deranged, transsexuals and circus freaks. To photograph people, according to Arbus, is necessarily 'cruel', 'mean'. The important thing is not to blink. With Andy Warhol, she was an originator of that new kind of ghostly, frozen, remote look at death and suffering and decay.

In a now famous attack on Arbus's work, Susan Sontag accused her of being 'devoted to lowering the threshold of what is terrible', and continued: 'By getting used to what, formerly, we could not bear to see or hear, because it was too shocking, painful or embarrassing, art changes morals — that body of psychic custom and public sanctions that draws a vague boundary between what is emotionally and spontaneously intolerable and what is not. The gradual suppression of queasiness does bring us close to a rather formal truth — that of the arbitrariness of the taboos constructed by art and morals. But our ability to stomach this rising grotesqueness in images (moving and still) and in print has a stiff price. In the long run, it works out not as a liberation of but as a subtraction from the self: a pseudo-familiarity with the horrible reinforces alienation, making one less able to react in real life.'

Some of Sarah Lucas's early pieces, which started finding their way into the Saatchi collection from about 1990, bear a superficial resemblance to Arbus's work. *Sod You Gits*, for example, is a huge seven-by-ten-foot blow-up of a spread from the *Sunday Sport* in which Sharon Lewis, a topless midget, tells how she became the smallest stripper in the world and learned how to drive men wild by showing them her breasts. *Fat, Forty and Flab-ulous* features the twenty-five-stone wife of Reg Morris who grew so large her husband decided to get rid of her by putting her up for sale. She is photographed naked (front and rear) except for a pair of fishnet stockings.

In Diane Arbus pictures, the point would have been to gaze on the women's reality with curiosity and detachment; to confront the horrible or, at the very least, the potentially embarrassing, with equanimity. It is this flat-eyed gaze that Sarah Lucas appropriates and parodies in a recent photographic self-portrait, in which she stares sullenly into the camera, a fag-end clamped sluttishly in the corner of her mouth, its coil of ash ready to drop, direct eyeballing anybody with the Niagara Falls to eyeball her. It is a pose, of course, a semi-fiction, as Martin Maloney points out in the Sensation catalogue: 'She took [Michael] Landy's idea of the object as a tool of class visibility and directed it towards herself . . . Her appropriation of a young, working-class male's interest in violence, sex and alcohol was unapologetic. By adopting it she exposed it.'

It is role playing as we have come to understand it through the work of Gilbert and George and Cindy Sherman. Frontal, insolent, the unintimidated direct address to the camera. This is a look we think of as traditionally 'masculine'; certainly as unfeminine. It is a look that many of us instinctively associate with the murderer Myra Hindley, and, in particular, the picture that Marcus Harvey has used as the basis for the painting that has turned him into a (reluctant) headline-hitter during the slow news weeks of the summer.

It is the belief that it is the terribleness of her 'inner being' that can be plainly seen etched on the thirty-year-old police mugshot of Hindley — the cavernous upturned eyes, the heavy bones, the holed hedge of bleached-blonde fringe, the fondant of deep shadow, like a choke collar, under Hindley's chin — that gives it its power as a symbol of evil.

In the sixteenth century, Protestant iconoclasts believed that evil influences could come into the body through the eyes, and corrupt the viewer. And the events of recent weeks have shown that it is still possible to hold these views, four hundred years later. It was inevitable from the start that *Myra* would mobilise powerful opposition from predictable sources. At the beginning of August the *Sun* printed the telephone number of the Royal Academy and urged its readers to bombard the switchboard with protests about the hanging of a picture which — an essential part of the 'outrage' ritual — only a handful of people at that point had ever actually seen.

Peter Blake happened to be at the Royal Academy that Saturday morning. It was the day of the porters' annual coach trip to the Ascot races, and one man was having to field all the calls. Many were abusive, and a few threatened violence. 'Unless you tell me it's withdrawn, I'm coming round to the Academy and I'm going to stab the first person I see,' Blake heard one caller say.

The alleged charlatanism of contemporary art has always been good copy. It is even better copy now that London is 'swinging' again ('ablaze with a giddy energy', in the words of *Vanity Fair*), and young artists like Damien Hirst and Jake and Dinos Chapman enjoy something approaching pop-star status. In the thirties, as Anthony Everitt has pointed out, the joke was usually about reclining nudes with holes in their stomachs, and well-hung angels. In the more recent past, there has been the noise around Carl Andre's bricks at the Tate, a display of soiled nappies at the Institute of Contemporary Arts and the torching of David Mach's submarine made out of tyres on the South Bank, in which the arsonist ended up killing himself.

In the last few years, their engagement with the real world (the lavatory as art, the racehorse as narrative sculpture, the avalanche of cartoons and one-liners about pickled cows and sharks) has seen British artists turning up in the mainstream media, usually to be cackled at, in unprecedented numbers. This reached some kind of crescendo at the end of 1993, when Rachel Whiteread's *House* went up on Grove Road in the East End and Whiteread was judged to be both the best artist in Britain (by the Turner Prize jury), and the worst (by the group of rock-biz pranksters calling themselves the 'K Foundation'). A book about the project references more than two hundred press and television mentions. 'I only read the tabloids,' Damien Hirst has said, 'when I'm in them.'

The case with the most obvious relevance to the controversy surrounding Marcus Harvey's billboard-size painting of Myra Hindley is probably Andy Warhol's thirty-six-feet-square painting derived from the 'wanted' posters for the thirteen most wanted men in America. It had been commissioned for the New York State pavilion at the 1964 World's Fair, but the sponsors' protests over such a perverse official advertisement meant it was whitewashed over within hours of its installation. (The Royal Academy has given Harvey an assurance that his painting will be withdrawn from the show only if they feel the safety of any RA staff member is threatened.)

Andy Warhol, though, was Andy Warhol; he was a creature of, by and for the media; a lifelong media tart and headline junkie. Marcus Harvey, by contrast, is not a controversialist. With him, it really has been a case of backing into the limelight, and he has found even that can be unnerving.

'"I'm going to stab the first person I see",' he repeated ruminatively, pouring a rubber latex solution into a mould. When it had hardened, the mould would make the head of

Adolf Hitler, its mouth opened in an un-Hitler-like guffaw. The head would go on the body that was already made and waiting in the studio, leaning forward, right hand extended, taking a child by the hand. '"I'm going to stab the first person I see".' I had told him what Peter Blake had overheard at the Royal Academy, and it was a phrase Harvey would keep returning to, saying it under his breath really, rather than speaking it, in the course of the day.

'You decide to make a piece, you've got to fund it, and then you don't know if it's going to work,' he said. 'I was prepared to let the thing just wither and die in my own studio if that had been the case. Or you've sold it, and after two years of thinking [Charles Saatchi] doesn't like it, he's bored with it, he's frightened of it, I'm not going to see it again, suddenly – bang! It just explodes all over you, with "I'm going to stab the first person I see". Now the only time I get to see it and evaluate it for myself is in a hallowed institution. I haven't had time to form my own relationship with it yet.'

The studio is behind a breakers' yard in Brixton, South London. In addition to the Hitler paraphernalia – histories, texts, pictures blown up to poster size and taped to the wall – it is filled with pallets on which hundreds of plaster moulds of squeaky nursery toys, bath-time ducks, tea-time cakes and biscuits are stacked. There are also moulds of a baby's hands and feet, the feet plunging, soles-upward, into the choppy picture plane, as if it was water, the hands emerging from it, like a diver coming up for air. (Seeing a hand 'beckoning' from its shallow grave was how the police, combing Saddleworth Moor in the mid-sixties for Brady and Hindley's child victims, discovered the remains of John Kilbride.) The plaster moulds are the components of a three-dimensional, even more monumental version of the painting of Myra Hindley.

Any portrait of Hindley of course was going to be contro-versial. A portrait measuring eleven feet by nine was bound to be interpreted as an affront to common decency and a chal-lenge. A wall-size portrait of Hindley in which the basic pic-ture element is a baby's hand, simultaneously clawing and constructing, obliterating and making, and repeated hundreds, perhaps thousands, of times across the surface of the picture was seriously – some might say recklessly – raising the stakes. In his on-the-record remarks, it seemed more important to Harvey to be candid than to bring the temperature down.

'It's a terrifying image,' he said, 'and I realised I had been attracted to it lots of times, just pulled in by it. It's quite excit-ing, it's very uncomfortable. I was very aware that the pull of the image was a sexual thing and that that is part of the taboo that increases its appeal.

'The whole point of the painting is the photograph. That photograph. The iconic power that has come to it as a result of years of obsessive media reproduction. And I don't really want to get beyond that. I'm not going to read a lot of trashy books to find out the nuts and bolts of the case. I know enough to know that she probably didn't do any of the murders, that she was just in a relationship where she was probably too attached to the man who was doing it to extricate herself. That her life was probably too dull and boring to throw the relationship away . . . I don't believe that's thirty years' worth of reputation as one of the most vile and notorious murderers in British criminal history.

'This is the crucial issue: she didn't do the murdering, but she was a female who ignored her motherly instincts. That is her great crime. It was compounded by the unmentionable sin of looking like everybody's idea of what somebody who commits that crime should look like. It's more than the embodiment of evil. It's the realisation of a certain kind of Nazi/Marilyn Monroe/Frankenstein fantasy. A kind of dumb insolence. I think there's a lot of sexual appeal to men, and definitely to a lot of women as well. That is what we're not admitting to ourselves. And that is why the first reaction [to the painting] is to condemn. The only way you can talk about the power that image has is by allowing it to operate on people. And that meant making it big. You're in a sea of Myra, lashing over you. It felt very uncomfortable right from the outset. I was troubled by it. But there seemed to be no other way of doing it.'

Unlike most of the other young British artists in the Saatchi collection, Marcus Harvey's background is in 'pure' painting. For the past three or four years, he has plundered top-shelf magazines for pornographic images of women. *Julie From Hull*, *Golden Showers*, *Doggy* and others are dense smearings of paint applied directly to the canvas with his fingers in a process that he describes as 'orgiastic'. It takes him half an hour to get the muck off his hands after finishing a picture. 'I feel like a murderer,' he once said, although he probably now regrets it.

He was at Goldsmiths in the early eighties, when neo-expressionism was the prevailing style and the lack of spirituality in our materialistic world the dominant message. 'I had these very kind of . . . religious ideas about how you proceed in art. You sweated and suffered and, if you were lucky, when you were old and wispy, you might sell a picture. And to do anything other than that was just a frivolous load of bollocks that would come to nothing.'

The two Hindley pieces and the Hitler-and-child tableau are a move in a more conceptual, ideas-based direction. Using the hands to depict Hindley's face, though, instead of the more conventional brushes and paint, was a tactic he said he was driven to by the desire to sidestep the inevitable allegations that, just by painting it at all, he was lending a gloss of glamorous allure.

'I just thought that the handprint was one of the most dignified images that I could find. The most simple image of innocence absorbed in all that pain. And that kicks the thing into reality. There's an absolute realism. It's a real event. I realised you had to break the surface of this image, so it's not just a glamorous posturing. That wouldn't have been enough. It wouldn't have struck the nerve you needed to strike if you were going to get people to recognise that what they loved to hate — what gave it the heat — was the idea that a woman and innocent children were in there, and the children were dying.'

The result is a remarkable, refrigerated piece of work with a chill that seems to stain the air around it. It's a chill to which even the person who made it is not immune. 'I became very aware that I had completed the person, and that they were looking back out at me. I was very aware of having created the thing. Then I did become kind of concerned about the potency of it, of what I'd done.'

Norman Rosenthal, the exhibitions secretary at the Royal Academy, believes it is the single most important painting in the show and the one that informs everything else. 'I mean, I would rather live with something a little more decorative, like a Gary Hume. But I believe the Myra Hindley painting is a very, very cathartic picture. It is an incredibly serious and sober work of art that needs to be seen. It means nothing in reproduction. Its facture, its aura, its immanence. These are things which have to be experienced. To take it out would reduce the temperature of the show radically.'

Rosenthal believes that there is 'a place in the world for lightness and a place in the world for darkness'. But the evidence of his eyes must have told him that it is in the dark places – 'the mind's swampy sewer', to quote one American critic – that most of the best artists of the current generation have been grubbing for inspiration.

'There's something very macabre about what I do . . . twisted and macabre,' Cindy Sherman said recently in an interview in the *Guardian*. And 'macabre' is a word that has been used in connection with their work by everybody from Rachel Whiteread to Alexander McQueen, who paraded dead animal parts on the catwalk in his last Paris show.

As a preoccupation, of course, this is not new. There can't be many people left who don't know about Francis Bacon's habit of haunting medical bookshops or his fascination with the 'glitter' and 'incongruous beauty' of the inside of the human mouth. (Perhaps less well known is his fondness for remembering that Sigmund Freud had in his possession a set of particularly horrendous photographs from the Viennese police archives, and Bacon's own irregular visits to the Black Museum in Scotland Yard.)

With Dead Head (1991) is the picture of Damien Hirst as a sixteen-year-old, posing with the severed head of an old man in a mortuary. *When Logics Die* (1991) features two photographs: one is the gaping, mouth-like wound of a man who has slit his own throat; the other is the bloodied hand of the victim of a road accident. Shortly after these were shown at the ICA, Abigail Lane moved in and decorated the walls of the same gallery with her blood-splattered wallpaper: the pattern came from a scene-of-crime photograph showing the trace of hands, printed in their own blood. Her show also included a dismembered body, cast in red wax, and a looped tape of terrified whimpering sounds coming from behind a closed door.

Lane and Hirst were students at Goldsmiths at the same

time, and she remembers his atrocity books doing the rounds. Mat Collishaw took a forensic pathologist's picture of a bullet hole in the top of a man's head, blew it up from five-by-four inches to twelve-by-eight feet, called it *Bullet Hole* and hung it in Freeze, the hit show put on in a deserted warehouse in docklands that almost nobody saw and that everybody remembers seeing now.

Others – Marc Quinn, the Wilson sisters Jane and Louise, Richard Billingham and (especially) the Chapman brothers Jake and Dinos – have since taken the aesthetics of revulsion to places even David Cronenberg probably didn't know it could go. 'Vomit', Jake, the younger Chapman brother, once said was the response he wanted from the viewer. 'No, laughter. And then vomit. Money. No – I don't know.' Six Feet Under, the Chapman brothers' show opening at the Gagosian Gallery in New York later this month, will apparently feature a mass grave. 'There'll be grass and trees and lots of mutated figures looking down into a pit.'

In 1993 the American critic Adam Gopnik gave what was happening, not only in Britain but internationally, a name: the High Morbid Manner. Picking up where Susan Sontag had left off a generation earlier, he described works in which 'bodies rot, faces are filled with maggots, surgical instruments and examination tables are on display' as representing 'if not the spirit of the age, then at least the mood of the moment': 'A detached, distanced, oddly smiling presentation of violence – a pageantry of violence – is, as every evening's television and every summer's big movie demonstrates, as much the popular fashion as the avant-garde one . . . The shock of the new, which for most of the century could reside as much in a black square as in a slit eyeball, isn't available any longer. It's not possible to shock any more by being new. The only way to shock is by being shocking.'

'I want to give succour,' Gary Hume once told an *Express* reporter, whom he had already floored by saying that, outside of art, nursing was the only other field he was interested in. What was shocking about this was that it was said without any obvious irony. Hume is the orchid in the dung heap; the poppy amidst the current carnage; a painter with a deliberately cloying confectioner's palette and a hallucinatory menagerie of owls and puppy dogs, teddy bears and bunny rabbits, prayerful model girls and low-wattage celebrities which can induce a sort of sugar shock in the viewer.

Hume is unblushingly (although not doctrinairely) pro-life. When he does produce a creepy or crapulous image, such as *Baby*, it is to throw the surrounding ordinary goodness into sharp relief, as the Italian critic Francesco Bonami has pointed out: 'It looks like all the energy of this artist has been concentrated in the effort to reveal a world of nasty images that veil the true beauty of a world inhabited by beautiful people and beautiful things.'

But there was a time, and it wasn't very long ago, when Gary Hume could conceivably have qualified for membership of the High Morbid tendency. When he was still a student at Goldsmiths he started showing life-size paintings of doors, but not just any doors. These were hospital doors, complete with finger and kick plates and porthole windows. Which naturally led (although he says it was never his intention) to speculations about 'cheerless hours of fearful loneliness', and lines of thought whose only direction was towards dwindlings and exits and death. It was possible to link this work with work being done at the same time by, say, Rachel Whiteread, who made her first bed piece two months after her father died in 1989. They are both suffused with what Saul Bellow calls 'street sadness'; the same easily identifiable ache of urban melancholy.

But, where Whiteread went on to cast mortuary slabs and discarded mattresses, Gary Hume turned his face towards a brighter day. Like Mat Collishaw, whose subject matter has shifted from suicide, rape and pornography to pictures of himself in Arcadia catching fairies, Hume has, very successfully in the last few years, produced a body of work embodying his belief in 'colour, form, laughter, innocence, attraction, beauty'. That's what he's for. He is against 'pain, loss, grimness, paranoia'.

'It's much easier to be disgusting, I find. It can have weight. Take any of the subjects that are illegal or disgusting or question the given morality, and you've got weight. And weight is one thing artists are desperate to have,' he says. 'But I didn't want to rely too much on that type of weight. I was more interested in how you can get weight somewhere else.'

He says it would be a distortion to see Goldsmiths, at least during his time there, when his contemporaries included Michael Landy, Angus Fairhurst and Fiona Rae, as a forcing ground for High Morbid Manner artists. 'I think it would be a mistake to call Goldsmiths, instead of the "cool school", the "macabre school". The driving force was wit and formalism. Punning. I think the horror came later when everybody had left college. When you move from the college environment to the non-college environment, a kind of grimness sets in straight away. And then Damien had created his own supreme place. It's like you wake up one morning and realise all your friends have been eight times to the Groucho Club and you haven't been once.'

In fact, Hume was one of the big successes of Freeze. Charles Saatchi bought one of the door paintings and then, when he had a solo show with Karsten Schubert, bought a lot more. 'I want it, I want it all, and I want it now' is the motto that Doris, the first Mrs Saatchi, once said should be engraved on all great collectors' hearts. But 'Buy cheap. Buy early. Pile it high' has been her husband's purchasing policy since Charles and Doris went their separate ways.

Being taken up by Charles Saatchi has become one of the conditions of success for an artist in recent years. The benefit to Saatchi of having a virtual monopoly is early access to some of the best new work at prices he essentially controls. He is dedicated, serious and assiduous, and he gets everywhere, as Richard Wentworth confirms.

'You're being an assessor at the Slade, in what is essentially examination conditions, and he'll just appear. This little figure appears in the background. He's gone shopping, and he's the first in the line. It's like Hitchcock . . . People perceive a proper collecting culture in this country, and it's not there. There's Charles Saatchi and there's no one else.'

1997

GARY HUME

Like his pictures, which resist any easy reading – super-gloss recapturings of fleeting or stolen moments: a human shadow thrown on a wall, rain pattern on a pavement, clouds reflected in a puddle, and other glimpses of sweet city sadness – it can take a while to get your ear in with Gary Hume.

One of the many can-he-be-for-real? moments happened at the end of our second meeting when conversation turned to ballet, which he has become a fan of, and *Swan Lake*. He was on his feet, grinning and doing the little mincing shuffle of the cygnets in the corps de ballet. 'How gorgeous it would be to walk down the street with the cygnets all around me,' he said. 'They'd just be fluttering around me, protecting me, keeping me safe. All totally delicate and fluttering and forming patterns, going into a right old flutter. Beautiful.'

He did the little mincing move again, fingers interlaced in front of him, eyes turned to the ceiling, in the living room of the large house into which he has recently moved with his wife, the artist Georgie Hopton. There was a rip in the armhole of his jumper but only wear-marks on the socks that moved over the rug which is a copy of one of his paintings – brown leaves and branches against a background of pale cerulean blue. 'Like coming out of the saloon bar and falling over,' he said, 'and what you see is sky and trees.' The view from the gutter.

The space under the floorboards of the house is packed with business cards and the swarf and metal shavings of the small industrial firms that occupied the building before Gary took it over. 'Reggie and Co.', an antiquated illuminated sign on a building on the opposite side of the road says. 'Miss Smith. Coats and Suits'. The sign is made of dozens of individual silver bulbs that echo the glitter in the paint on one wall of the kitchen. 'That magic twinkling thing,' as Hume had (typically obliquely) said earlier, using one of his favourite words – magic – in a quote culled from *The Great Gatsby*.

The role Gary Hume has cast for himself is a kind of ragged-trousered visionary – William Blake to Damien Hirst's Les Dawson, say. He has been working on a series of Angel paintings this year and is unembarrassed to say that he likes the idea of 'imagining an angel looking'. It seems entirely fitting that Blake, who conversed with angels and spirits and practised the mirror (or backward) writing that Hume has occasionally used in his paintings, should be one of the dead artists he 'calls down' when he finds himself in trouble in the studio and feels moved to ask for assistance from one of the greats. Picasso, Marcel Duchamp and Andy Warhol are others on the list. 'I called someone new the other day,' Hume said, 'which I don't normally do. I've been shouting at Beuys a bit, but he's pretty reluctant. It's just people who've cut the crap. And when I'm calling on their help it's because I'm in crap. And so they come down and just . . . you know, help me out a bit.'

Six years ago, in the comedown period from his first flush of success and totally blocked, he went into the council estate that backs on to his studio, looking for a four-leaf clover to bring him luck. He couldn't find one, but he found a common three-leaf clover and painted that. It led to one of the great epiphanic moments in recent art. 'I said, "That's Tony

Blackburn!" I saw the invisible thing that just needed covering. The invisible painting that just needed a cover on it.' He paired this with a painting of another low-wattage celebrity, Patsy Kensit, and then painted two three-leaf clovers together and called it *Polar Bear*. His friends were worried, especially as he had spent the months before this nailing potatoes to the wall.

'I was just trying to give Patsy Kensit and Tony Blackburn — not that they asked for it or necessarily needed it — but I wanted to give them some dignity through our common experience with them,' he says now. 'We all have our ups and downs like that. Theirs are in the public domain and most people's are in the private. But using the public domain as my subject matter, I could recognise some dignity there, through these feeble attempts at success and failure.'

And the 'potato sculptures'? 'Your staple diet is art, and it's all fed by this, like, tuberous underground stuff, and the fruit is all underneath, and all the other stuff is the vegetation — the greenery that you don't really want. What's underneath is the potato, and the potato grows underground as well. And with this tuber I was making it very clear that . . . I was a bloody potato.' He has an infectious laugh which he has a tendency to collapse in at odd times. And then when you ask him what he's laughing at, he'll say, 'Nothing.'

When he first started making the pictures for which he is now famous, they were regarded as clashing, hideous colours, totally disgusting; the sort of colours nobody liked. Paintings made by somebody who had no sense of colour — was using horrible colour — and whose form was crude. Gary talked about their 'strange banal gorgeousness': 'I can bear looking at them for days on end, living with them. Beautiful, sensuous and intelligent, hard, deep, soft'; they were about 'romance, beauty, fame, emptiness'. Everybody else just wondered what he was on.

He did use colours from the trippy part of the spectrum: loved-up yellows, slatherings of whizzy greens and pinks. He dreamed up a hallucinatory menagerie of owls and puppy dogs, teddy bears and bunny rabbits. His Girls of the Year (very good, these) had blank expressions and bee-sting lips and zonko party eyes. Sex-doll lips. Kandy-kolored hair.

It occurred to me to ask him whether he ever used drugs to put his head in another place. 'So tell me, Gary, about the part drugs have played in your work.'

'Never taken them in my life.' Big laugh. 'OK. I drink too much and I take a bit of cocaine every now and then. And some speed, and some E, and some Viagra. Just like anybody else. Normal amount.

'I hardly buy any drugs, the truth is. The only time that ever kicks in is when I stay in the studio and look at the pictures for a little while and try and see them from a different point of view. I don't use drugs as a way of making pictures. Never have.'

At Goldsmiths, when he was there in the late eighties, he was in a group that included Mat Collishaw, Damien Hirst, Abigail Lane, Michael Landy, Sarah Lucas (Hume's girlfriend for several years), Simon Patterson and Fiona Rae. Their tutor, Richard Wentworth, hid all the walls, so they had to confront each other. Students were treated as working artists from the moment they arrived at the college and the course prepared them for being professional artists after they had graduated. Wentworth remembers the atmosphere being intensely competitive. 'Everybody had the chance to talk to everybody, and there was a sense that ideas belonged to people. One of the things that is never articulated was that there was an exhibition space right in the centre of the building which was fought over. The desire to expose your work, which was done every week, was truly incredible. And then there would be a sort of Peking-style crit, with people hanging on the walls, which everybody wanted to go to. I'm talking sixty, seventy people. And a real energy.'

A great deal has been said about the 'Thatcherite' ethos which produced Damien Hirst and his contemporaries. But Wentworth believes their formative experience happened a decade earlier, with punk. 'I think punk and Thatcher are very similar in a way. They're both: Go for it. "That house is empty. We ain't got fuck-all. So we'll be pirates, take it, squat it . . ." I always think Thatcher equals ram-raiding: You wannit, you take it. They all graduated into that moment.'

Gary Hume was an early flyer, one of the big successes of Freeze, the landmark show that Damien Hirst organised and curated in Docklands in 1988. Charles Saatchi bought one of Hume's early door paintings and then, when he had a solo show with Karsten Schubert, bought a lot more.

After our first interview a couple of weeks ago, Gary told me that he had staggered home and collapsed into bed; it had been a 'nightmare'. 'What I disliked about it – and it probably isn't true; it just felt like it,' he said when we met up again, 'was that it was about all the stuff I don't care about. Like the amount of success, the amount of money, the amount of feelings about other artists . . . All of that stuff, which is just totally peripheral to me. That stuff is just totally not my bag.

'The strange thing about art and artists is that we support each other. We know that we are the poets out walking in this valley, and that we are surrounded by the beasts and the charlatans, and that we must all be together.'

He says, 'Age is making everybody into themselves. Once

upon a time, the competition was about "I'm interesting: I'm more interesting than you, I'm more talented than you, I've got better insight than you." Whatever. Now the competition is: "What in itself is interesting? I can only be like me; what should I be interested in?"'

When newspapers give a list of the artists represented by Jay Jopling at White Cube – Damien Hirst, Tracey Emin, Antony ('Angel of the North') Gormley, Marcus ('Myra Hindley') Harvey, Marc ('blood head') Quinn – the name of Gary Hume, one of the gallery's biggest money-spinners and currently probably its most fashionable artist, is always missing. To achieve crossover success – to become a celebrity artist, one of those remembered names – history has shown that you have to become known for being known, even among people who have no idea why what you are known for matters. Hume is not a headline grabber; there have been no extramural sensations or scandals to bring him to the attention of the non-art-going public.

All he can offer in the way of narrative interest is the crisis his career was thrown into at the beginning of the nineties when he decided he could no longer go on turning out the door paintings that had made his reputation, and he embarked on his personal long dark night of the soul. Journalists tend to gratefully fasten on to this troubled part of his biography, his suffering moment, which he now actually remembers as 'great fun' and 'totally liberating'. In many ways, he was unlucky to have arrived at the perfect vehicle for his talent and his intentions when he was still so young. He was a student when he started showing life-size paintings of the now near-legendary hospital doors.

'I think that when I was doing the doors I was a bit more . . . bleak,' he says now. 'I didn't have very much faith, making those. I really didn't have any faith in any transformative power of an art object. Art was to help define our hideous place – the hideous place that we're in. And that was something in me while I was making them. When I stopped, I looked around for something equally pure. And all I could find was doubt, fear, masturbation, plants, flowers, holidays, friends . . . That's what it is. That's what I had.'

The door paintings were magisterial and austerely beautiful. But Hume is alive to the danger of regarding them as the ideal object and the pictures he has been making since as merely 'the multifarious bits'. 'I think the doors are more obviously art. How clear and pure and blank it all is. It's more refined. It's more special. And what I'm doing now is more like life itself, which is a lot more confused. The only difference between the doors and everything I've made since is that the doors are perfect.'

Although it is no longer the case, 'decorative' was a dirty word in the world of art professionals in the early nineties. And Hume says that he unnerved himself when he stood back and realised that, after years of striving to achieve the cool and the uninflected and distant, he had made his first decorative painting. 'I looked at it and thought, Fucking hell, what have I done here? This is just too much. Can I accept it? The prejudice thing I've always been interested in: the prejudice to do one thing and not another. And for somebody to not like something for their own prejudicial reasons, was absolutely OK. That, in fact, might well be its point. Its point might well be for you to say, "I can't stand that. That is a big pansy flower." Its point may well be for you to say, "Big pansy flower; don't like it." That's its job in the world. So that finally allowed me to make big pansy flowers. I've chosen to say "yes" to making things, and not be worried about it.'

His loyalty to paint in the age of photography and video and the scatter installation had always set Hume apart from the other YBAs. Now his refusal of the big themes – life, death, hot and heavy existential angst, a kebab way of knowledge – put him right out on a limb.

Hume says he cries easily – 'at the drop of a hat'. It's a heartening admission from somebody so closely identified with a group culture that has sometimes seemed to be characterised by drunkenness and laddish pranks and loud, even occasionally thuggish-seeming, behaviour.

In the crazy days of the Britart boom, Hume was as full-on as the rest of them, partying for England. Two or three years ago, though, he started to pull back to the point where now, making art on an industrial scale with a battalion of assistants, he hardly goes out at all. He exists only in his work, is how he now sees it; he doesn't exist anywhere else. He's nothing apart from his paintings. 'I've been feeling a bit fluey,' he said one day when I phoned up to check on something. 'I've been wandering around flipping through channels on the television, feeling I should go out, but I didn't want to. Then just now I started drawing up a new painting, and suddenly I feel fantastic.' The knowledge that his one-time falling-down friends were still out there somewhere on the razz, caning it, possibly contributed to his powerful sense of well-being.

He says he feels 'fragile'. And, unlike some other boy YBAs, Hume seems entirely at ease with the softer, more feminine, side of his personality.

Some of the first paintings he made in the new style now seem emblematic of the male/female split. In them, muscular male torsos, based on some *fascisti* public statuary he saw in Rome, are set against a ground of kitschy garish flowers. In *Jealousy and Passion*, a woman's lipsticked smile, clipped from a magazine, has been pasted onto the face of the preening Adonis – a reminder, according to Hume, that 'the woman in you is laughing at you'. But when I suggest that it is reminiscent of the endlessly debated difference between (pretty) Matisse and (rugged) Picasso, it is rewarded with one of Hume's typical gnomic utterances: 'I think Picasso is more feminine than Matisse. Matisse is more like a queer, and Picasso's a woman.'

Hume's work doesn't tug at your sleeve; it doesn't beg to be noticed. It doesn't chew up the furniture or piss on the carpet. In a time when shock has become a convention, it is almost freakishly well behaved. Many of the paintings are built on nothing more concrete than a glance or a mood or a gesture: their special aesthetic sex appeal derives from the fact that something that can last for a fraction of a second – a rushing, fugitive thing – can take weeks to fix in paint. The colours are blocked in painstakingly with a fine, tiny brush to give a flat, graphic impersonal style that leaves no trace of the hand.

'It's all been done,' Hume says, 'this romantic idea of brush marks and expressive movement. To me, that clutters the expressiveness of it. Not always, not as a rule. But I don't really want to see this person doing it. Saying that, I would look at a Basquiat or something, and I marvel at his mad activity and I love the fact that he was out there being busy and doing this. I like him. I like him through his paintings. But I also like paintings or things where the artist isn't as involved. It's the viewer and the painting that matters. Well, mainly it's just the painting that matters, and the painting doesn't need me. In that lovely emptiness, that beautiful emptiness, there's anything. So I don't clutter it up with me.'

For the three big shows he has had this year – in Venice, in Edinburgh and now at the Whitechapel in London – he has made three series of line paintings which spoof the spontaneity and gestural freedom — quick images achieved by quick paint-ing — of abstract expressionism. They remain playful rather than bombastic, which is always the danger when you're mak-ing pictures as big as the ones Hume is now making. 'If you're doing the drunk thing,' he says, 'you have lots of great bombas-tic ideas, and they're always really regrettable in the morning. And they're the ones you might get tired of. But if they're not bombastic telefantastic, then I think I can live with them.'

Irony, which he has a clear disposition for, is another thing he is now prepared to go the extra mile to erase from his work. 'There was a really concerted effort to give that up. That was a hundred-per-cent not having it. When I gave irony up, I took on embarrassment. And I preferred embarrassment. I thought I could hide, and I didn't want to hide. When you're making something, all the time there are moments when you're pleased and when you're not pleased. And there were certain things that pleased me, I could see how they were working and why they would work; I could see their success. But the type of success they were having was something I wasn't interested in. They don't stay around.'

Hume gets many of what have been described as his 'bru-tally agreeable' images from newspapers and magazines. 'I like them being pathetic in some way,' he has said, 'or upsetting. If I'm slightly upset then they seem appropriate.'

'The subject shouldn't really matter,' he told me, 'whatever it is. The subject can be anything, supposedly. Because what you're after is the content. And the content is beauty and love and loss and fear and hope, and Hume sometimes just mucking about. And just a bit of quiet, amazing, pleasurable self-reflection when you look at it.

'I have to take it as a given that I have got a certain ability to do something. I can be an artist, which is to take something and transform it into another thing. I can just see something, and I can see my painting. I know that I can make a painting there. It's the fading thing,' he said. 'They're just about to fade, I think. I like things that are just about to go. Everything's leaving. Death is never far away from me. When you make something, death can't help but be in it. Like I said: that fading moment. Time to go. Even as you're looking at it, it's already leaving you. You want to imbue it with that just-about-to-go bit.'

Attempts have been made to link Gary Hume to the Pop artists of the sixties. But Pop art wasn't much interested in ideas. Pop art was about 'liking things', as Warhol once said. Hume is closer to the tradition of minimalism and Duchamp-inspired conceptualism. He is making idea-based art. With the best of his paintings, seeing them becomes thinking.

'The surface of me is all you get' is his most often quoted comment on his work. ('The surface of me is getting bigger and bigger,' is how he currently glosses it.) Because of its lack of conventional 'humanist' content, Hume's painting is often viewed as bland, even blank. In fact his work is anything but dehumanised or lacking in expression. His representation is objective, but it is not unfeeling. In particular, he has a strong and genuine affection for women, who light up many of his best pictures.

'What is a lovely line? A nude woman is just a gorgeous line,' he says. 'Many lines of excellence. In my looking at women, I look at them in many different ways all at once. I'm shifting constantly, readjusting myself. So I wanted to make paintings that could look like that. Could be my pictures of women. How I readjust my gaze all the time and still keep the women like themselves. Make them still be them.'

The time is long gone when he thought you were supposed

to be serious, 'and do something for civilisation'. He believes his work lacks the professional finish of museum-quality art, but ('I don't want to sound like some cross-legged yogi') he has got to a place where he prefers that to the perfectly achieved thing. 'I'm probably not going to develop to a final state as an artist. Like, become better and better, and more and more refined. Become "pure". I don't think that's going to hap-pen to me, because I don't really see that as something I want to explore.' He also has no plans to beef up his 'banal' subject matter.

'What is the point of needlessly being cruel to my paint-ings, just because I can? Just because people like them, I'm supposed to go into some weird kind of psycho fucking anger? I don't see what the point of it is. Why be cruel? The hard thing is not to be cruel with these things. The hard thing is to be gen-tle and accept them and allow them to be made. To help the paintings get to themselves. That's the hard thing to do, to keep that going.'

1999

TRACEY EMIN

'The great British art disaster' was a phrase Tracey Emin was using yesterday in the wake of the destruction of two of her best-known, and therefore most valuable, pieces in the fire that gutted the Momart warehouse in Leyton. Like all her contemporaries, she is consummately media-savvy, and she was using the expression sardonically, quoting the broad-brush media take on the story.

But, typically, she was also using it in a felt way, projecting human qualities onto the chipboard and corrugated-iron beach hut from the seafront at Whitstable which was one of the hundreds of art works from the Saatchi collection which are believed to have been destroyed in the blaze. They were qualities that were always inherent in the title she gave the ramshackle and inherently worthless structure when she decided to wrench it from its moorings and reconfigure it as art in 1999: *The Last Thing I Said to You Is Don't Leave Me Here*.

These are the words, Emin says, that have been repeating in her head as pictures of the beach hut and her famous tent (*Everyone I Have Ever Slept With 1963–1995*) have flashed up in round-the-clock rotation in television coverage of the fire. Like down-at-heel hotel rooms in the novels of Graham Greene, these were powerfully eroticised spaces with associations which spun out far beyond the aesthetic, not least for Emin herself. 'It had stood in Whitstable for twenty-five years before I had it,' she says of the blue-painted shack that she bought with Sarah Lucas and shared with her boyfriend of the time, the gallerist Carl Freedman. 'It travelled to America and back again. It had a life. Like the tent. It had real spirit. I never imagined them not being in the world.'

Early yesterday Emin sent out a text message to the world at large that read like one of her banner blankets: 'I was OK now I'm HURT. BUT NO ONE DIED and IDEAS CON-TINUE. The WAR in ARAQ', she added, in trademark Mad Tracey from Margate spelling, 'is WRONG x.'

Speaking later, she explained that the bit about the war wasn't as much a non sequitur as it appeared to be. 'It's hap-pened – the British art disaster – and it's in the papers between this war, with people being bombed at their wedding, and five hundred people being washed away in flash floods in the Dom-inican Republic. So it's very difficult as an artist to say that I'm very upset – I'm going to cry because my art has been burned.'

At the same time, Emin recognises that, in a society united not so much by common beliefs any more as common images – images like the ones with which we have come to be on first-name terms: the bricks, the bed, the tent, the shark, the blood head, Myra, the cows – the violent destruction of these images is not nothing; the Momart fire is high up the news for a rea-son. 'Oh it's part of the national psyche now,' she said. '"Art collector". Everybody knows what that means. People didn't need it spelling out. When those pictures of the burning build-ing came on the television everybody knew. Everybody knew definitely something has happened.'

It explains, perhaps, why news reports have talked of works of art – insensate objects, after all – having 'perished'. Of members of the art community as they gathered for an Edward Hopper dinner at Tate Modern on Tuesday night being 'profoundly shocked and saddened by the news'. The uncertainty, and the time it has taken to positively identify the works that have been destroyed, have increased the similarity between this event and others, such as plane crashes or mining disasters, where it is human lives that have been lost.

A painting had an active life of about thirty years, according to Marcel Duchamp; after that it died – visually, emotionally and spiritually. Ready-mades, on the other hand – works of art created not by the hand or skill but by the mind and decision of the artist – can be replenished to infinity. If lost or destroyed, a ready-made could be recreated without difficulty by anyone, which gave it a sort of permanence denied the masterpiece. So when his sister, in the course of clearing out his Paris studio, threw out both his bottle rack and his bicycle wheel which she decided were useless junk, Duchamp simply went down onto 14th Street in New York where he was living and bought more of the same.

Since the Momart outpost at Leyton went up, some commentators have made a qualitative distinction between paintings and 'real' sculptures lost in the fire – one-off, handmade pieces which it is impossible to replace – and 'found' objects such as Emin's beach hut and nylon crawl-in tent which they have implied it is simple enough for her to go shopping for at a branch of Millets or an ordinary high-street camping shop. To argue that, though, she maintains is to miss the point.

'[The tent's] a seminal thing. It was that moment and that time in my life. It's me sitting in my flat in Waterloo sewing all the names on. It took me six months to make. It just fitted inside my living room, which was ten foot by twelve, and the TV just fitted inside the tent. I couldn't remake that time in my life again any more than I could remake the piece. And anyway, I haven't slept with anybody for a year.'

In her castings of the insides and undersides of common objects such as wardrobes and baths and beds, it is the space left by an object when it is gone – negative space – that Rachel Whiteread is memorialising. 'A commodity is an ideology made material', Michael Landy took as his slogan when he publicly ground all his worldly goods to dust at an abandoned Littlewoods store in Oxford Street in London a couple of years ago. Item A4 in the inventory of destroyed belongings was *Be Faithful to Your Dreams*, 'embroidered Tracey Emin handkerchief in box from Momart'; item A90 was *Clown*, a gloss painting on wood by Gary Hume, the destruction of which almost caused a rift in their friendship. Hume was uncomfortable with it at first. He said he understood the idea but he didn't like it much. In the end though, like Willem de Kooning, who fifty years earlier had reluctantly donated a drawing to Robert Rauschenberg who wanted to transform it by rubbing it out, Hume liked the result: he has admitted to being nearly moved to tears by what Landy had committed himself to achieving.

'It's funny, because once you rub something out, it's still there, really, isn't it?' Damien Hirst once commented of the de Kooning–Rauschenberg collaboration. 'I mean, it actually physically is there. It's not like a blank piece of paper.'

For now, Emin's tent and her seaside beach hut and other works yet to be identified are ingrained on the common memory. The original Duchamp ready-mades disappeared eventually, but their subversive power did not cease to grow.

2004

KARSTEN SCHUBERT

History is likely to record it as the most momentous encounter between an artist and a dealer since that long-ago day in the mid-fifties when Leo Castelli, on the verge of becoming the most influential dealer of new art in New York, paid a visit to Robert Rauschenberg's cockroach-infested loft in the armpit of Manhattan in order to 'discover' him, and ended up discovering Rauschenberg's lover and downstairs neighbour, Jasper Johns, instead. 'I saw evidence of the most incredible genius,' Castelli would later recall, 'entirely fresh and new and not related to anything else.' He had stumbled, in other words, into the situation that every dealer (and collector) dreams of — a brilliant young artist whom nobody else is on to, who can still be bought cheap.

Damien Hirst and Jay Jopling met each other for the first time on the night of 23 May 1991. The following exchange cemented what has to be the most singular — and rewarding, in all senses of the word — relationship between an artist and a dealer in this country.

Hirst: 'Do you know what I like about life?'

Jopling: 'No. What?'

Hirst: 'Everything!'

The reason it can be dated so precisely is that it was the night of an opening at the Karsten Schubert Gallery in Charlotte Street in London. Schubert at that point had cornered the market in what the world did not yet know as Young British Art. (A book paid for and published by him in 1990 called *Technique Anglaise* would help define the movement which has been instrumental in shaping the profile and debate not only on contemporary British art, but art internationally, for the past decade.)

Schubert had been fast off the mark. It was always said about him that he had a good ear. He had got to the degree shows at the then just emerging Goldsmiths College well ahead of anybody else. Freeze, the now near-mythical Docklands show of work by Damien Hirst and his contemporaries, had happened in 1988. By 1991 the Karsten Schubert Gallery already had Angus Fairhurst, Mat Collishaw, Michael Landy, Gary Hume, Anya Gallaccio and Rachel Whiteread (who didn't go to Goldsmiths but is always lumped in with the YBAs because of being represented by Schubert and collected by Charles Saatchi). It was a killer hand. Only the trump card was missing.

Karsten Schubert, of course, knew Damien Hirst. By the early nineties there were very few people in the London art world who didn't know him. 'He was trying to take over the world even in 1985,' Rachel Whiteread has said, 'and he hadn't made anything!' Schubert had known Hirst – small, furious, bluntly made – for three years. But it was another dealer, a new face, who Damien Hirst went with in 1991.

'Jay [Jopling] was very into making it very, very sexy in that tabloid way,' Schubert says. 'There is a history in England of people being negative about contemporary art. As a result, the press was not interested in it, or only in the most negative, carping manner. And then over the past twelve years it has become this amazing mainstream thing, with artists making the front page. I remember Jay saying that it might be a good thing to encourage this, with very judicious leaks to the tabloid press.

'There was a lot of spin there. All that, of course, was new. And if you talked to oldies in this business they kind of shuddered a little bit. It just was not done before. You wouldn't leak things to the gutter press. And you would not employ PR people. When it started happening, I felt very much in two minds about it. But once a new standard was set, you couldn't not do it. It's like, I don't think politicians should spin-doctor. But then that's a very naive, old-fashioned notion of what should and shouldn't happen. They do. Jay is amazing at it, he is brilliant and his energy level is extraordinary.'

Schubert says this in the spare, wood-panelled flat in Soho where he now lives and works. Norman Rosenthal, who staged Sensation at the Royal Academy in 1997 and who's curating a second bad-mannered exhibition at the Academy this autumn, is his immediate neighbour. Schubert, who moved to England from Germany in 1984, is resolutely unraucous. 'The wrong man at the right time,' as one of his former artists, Angus Fairhurst, calls him, now lives quietly, dealing privately, representing only two artists: the painter Bridget Riley and the sculptor Alison Wilding. (He says he also 'helps Michael Landy a bit'.)

He seems thoughtful and bookish. In the three years since his gallery folded he has written a book on museums. So, yes, he had them all. Eldorado was his for the taking. But he found himself temperamentally unsuited to dealing with the drinking and drugging habits, the mental-as-anything, round-the-clock caning it, no-limits way of living of the brashest and best of the farkin young farkin British farkin artists. He was around it for a while and then decided he didn't want to live the life.

The dean of art writers, David Sylvester, recently had this

to say about dealers: 'They buy and sell portable objects that can easily cost more than a castle or two. They survive by out-witting some of the world's most cunning and ruthless manipulators of wealth, and they also know how to charm the old rich, key sources of supply. When they deal in the work of living artists they shape the careers of some of the most charismatic and paranoid individuals of their time.' They have also, Sylvester might have added, got to be prepared to party hard. To get off their faces and stay off their faces 'from late', as the sign in one of the London artists' favourite after-hours drinking holes has it, 'till unconscious time'.

In the early 'bonding' period of their association, Jay Jopling has said that he was out of it for a year, going to parties, going to bars, staying wrecked with Damien Hirst. It has come to seem like a precondition for anybody with serious ambitions to be a player in the London art game. Even the now unlikely-seeming Anthony d'Offay could occasionally be put in touch with his inner delinquent by Gilbert and George, the British stars of his very starry international stable, who have just jumped ship to Jopling's new White Cube 2.

Eventually his non-participation in the high-jinkery disqualified Karsten Schubert in the eyes of some of his artists from being the kind of dealer they wanted to represent them. 'He wanted to engage with an older age group,' Angus Fairhurst says. 'He didn't want to engage with what was happening now. He had it all in the palm of his hand and he didn't know what to do with it.' Fairhurst is now with Sadie Coles HQ, whose flagship artist is his girlfriend, Sarah Lucas. The three of them can often be seen hard at it in the Groucho Club and the Colony Room, hitting the old falling-down lotion. The fact that Fairhurst is selling better than he ever has, and Lucas has lately hit a purple patch in her career, Sadie Coles believes

is directly connected to what appears to be the seamless marriage of their working and social lives. 'How can you sell art if
you don't know what's the story? The closer you get to somebody, the better the job you're going to do for them. When
they're pissed, that's when they're often talking about ideas.'

Coles is regularly out until four or five. But she's always at
her desk in the gallery by ten. 'She looks pretty ropey at her
desk,' Karsten Schubert says. It's a joke. They're friends. But
it's a joke he's pleased to be able to make from the outside,
looking in. 'It became intensely social,' he says, 'and it still is.
The Americans, for example, are always gobsmacked when
this group arrives. They hadn't seen anything like this. I think
there is something wonderful about it. They are working all the
time. They are always in the studio. Looking, looking, looking.
But there is also a drawback there, which is that one can
become very claustrophobic. And it also becomes incredibly
tiring. I just couldn't do it.'

The residual mainstream, establishment aspect of the
Karsten Schubert Gallery for the span of its life between 1987
and 1997 was embodied in the person of a minor royal, Lady
Helen Windsor, the daughter of the Duke and Duchess of
Kent, who worked at the gallery for five years from 1988.
Karsten Schubert was young and cutting-edge. But it is clear to
him now that he clung for too long to conventional notions of
what a gallery was. 'Having a big space was what a gallery was
about. And then suddenly there Jay was in this little thing
[White Cube]. It gave him great flexibility. It was a completely
new way of dealing with contemporary artists, not having a big
space. Nobody understood that then. I remember thinking at
the time that what he proposed was a very radical departure.
Jay turned it upside down. It was very, very clever.'

Jay Jopling opened for business in 1993, just after the

recession had receded. Other West End dealers like Karsten Schubert were reeling. It now seems that White Cube was tailor-made for that moment, although it wasn't so obvious then. 'Boys don't like other boys seeing them when they've got small things,' I remember Damien Hirst saying just after Jay Jopling opened modestly in St James's. He was only half joking. It was a while before White Cube came to seem pacy and cool and agenda-setting, not least to the artists. Not having a big space. Nobody understood that then.

Around 1989 there had been some talk of Karsten Schubert joining forces with Anthony d'Offay to put on a big show of Hirst, Sarah Lucas, Gary Hume and other artists of the emerging Freeze generation. 'I remember there was a meeting with all the artists and d'Offay,' Schubert says, 'and he turned to me afterwards and said could I tell him which would be the greatest, most important of these people? It ended up in the usual d'Offay mind-fuck way where he said, "If it works, I want to represent them; if it doesn't, you can have them back." So I said no thank you.'

It was another two years before Damien Hirst's and Jay Jopling's paths crossed after an opening at the Schubert Gallery. Hirst and Schubert could have done business with each other during that time, but they didn't. 'I just couldn't see it. He was making very, very big demands. There was already talk about the shark in formaldehyde at that point. There was a recession, and there were already eight artists. And in a way, the beauty of the Damien–Jay situation was that Jay arrived with a clean slate. There was just no more room for anyone else with Damien. This needed full attention. And Jay was in a position to do that, and he did it very, very well. It's very well matched. There's a sense of showmanship and a sense of theatre.'

By the beginning of 1991 Schubert already had his own leading young British artist; he had Rachel Whiteread. They stayed together for six years and in that time Whiteread won the Turner Prize and established a huge international reputation as an artist. One of the peculiarities of the art business is that artists and dealers hardly ever have contracts binding them together. Whichever party wants to walk, can walk. And, for reasons which have never been made public, Rachel Whiteread left the Karsten Schubert Gallery in 1997 to go to Anthony d'Offay. For Schubert, it was the final straw. To the amazement of many people, he closed down the business.

He says, 'I think it's become more difficult for artists. Because as a result of becoming faster, it's also become more volatile. Unfortunately this audience, which is so big now, is so fickle. Many people treat it like the fashion world and change the art on their walls the way they change their wardrobe. They're just looking for the latest thing; they all zoom in.

'An English collector said to me something really funny the other day. We were talking about the whole situation and he said, "Look at it this way: there were four cubists, five abstract expressionists, four Pop people, three minimalists, there were probably four people from the eighties, and then you've got fifty young British geniuses."

'I think part of the anxiety that is starting to become apparent now is that it is starting to dawn on people that it is beginning to shake down. You know, history, it's a fantastic process. It's also one of the cruellest processes going. Which is: you just edit it down to the bones. That is what history does. There isn't room.'

2000

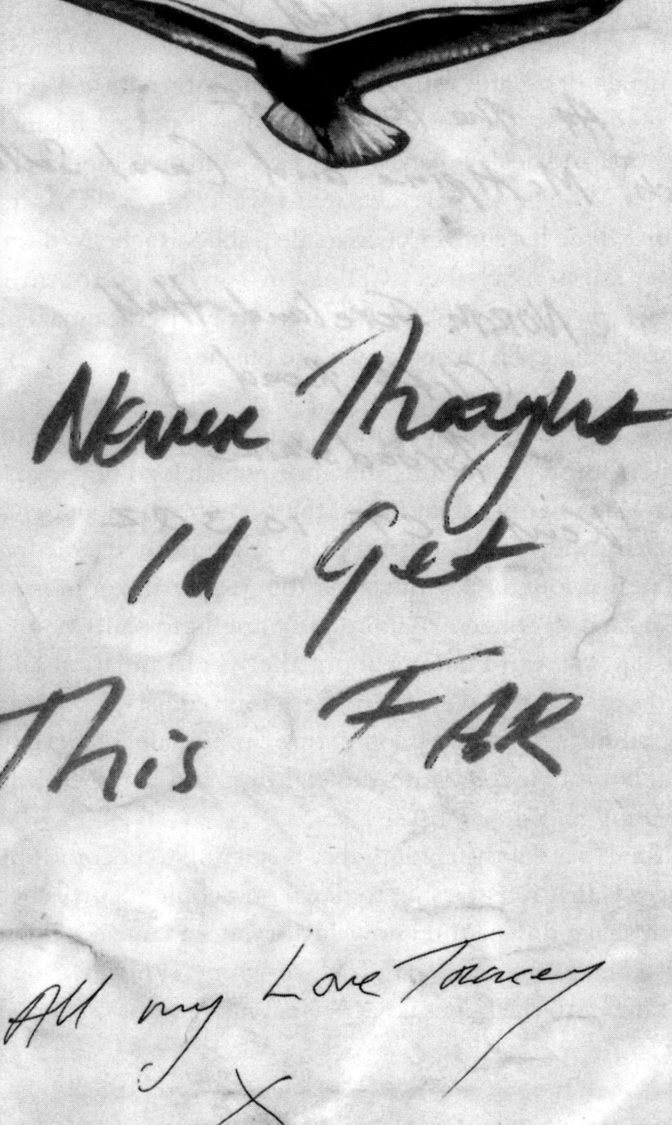

Never Thought
I'd Get
This FAR

All my Love Tracey
X

BRIXTON BREAKERS

There's romantic squalor — the *nostalgie de la boue* kind of squalor: Soutine and Modigliani in their shit-pile in Montmartre in the First World War, pawning their clothes for rotgut wine and ether and opium; Francis Bacon shuffling around among the rag-piles in his mews studio in South Kensington, living like a poor man with lots of money. There's picturesque squalor. Champagne and mousetraps. And then there's squalor that transcends the merely squalid.

Brixton Breakers fitted into the last category. Oh, it was brutal. It was a breakers' yard in London SW9 that did exactly what it said it did on the board by the gate: it broke things; bent and totally totalled them. Mostly these were cars connected to some insurance fiddle, stripped and crushed and cubed. They also did respray jobs on stolen cars — 'hot motors'. And that wasn't the half of it.

They dealt drugs in the Breakers at night, hooded figures in the dark; and some nights had all-night yard-style parties. Booma-booma-booma. Gerry, the guy who ran it, was a biker, and other bikers from his gang or chapter or whatever would zoom over and hang out. Gerry's clothes were black with sump oil; they were slick and ebonised. His nails were black and his eyelids and scalp. The artists speculated on whether the chairs in his house were also like that, and his cups, and his children.

Gerry had a sidekick called Chico. Chico wore a greasy mac and bred puppies and was dubbed by the tabloids 'The Most Evil Man in Britain'. He ran a puppy farm in Brixton Breakers, right in among the totalled Toyotas and hot motors. Feral dogs. Now and again he'd throw them a bootful of raw chicken. Oh, man. Sometimes the feral dogs would escape from their compound and set about people – chase and bare their teeth at the artists. People using the alley down the right side of the yard were particularly susceptible. This was the way to the studios. It was a rat-run, pitted and cratered. The craters were full of oil and ooze. The rats came to feed on the heaps of crap dumped at the top of the alley by the fly-tippers. Heels of bread and stiletto shoes and burst mattresses. Rats the size of cats. It was bleak and cold and weird. With all this going for it, naturally it was going to attract some of the best artists and finest sensibilities of their generation.

Damien Hirst made all his formaldehyde pieces at Minet Road: the cows, the lamb, the cow's heads, the pig. He did the spots there and the giant spin paintings with the mad Minet Road titles: 'Beautiful, cheap, shitty, too easy, anyone can do one, big, motor-driven, roto-heaven, corrupt, trashy, bad art, shite, motivating, captivating, over the sofa, celebrating painting.' Marcus Harvey made one of the most powerful and notorious paintings of the nineties there – his billboard-size portrait of Myra Hindley daubed in children's hands.

And after the artists came the collectors, dragging their Lobb and Gucci through the mire, braving the verbals. 'Oy, where'd you get your driving licence, on a milk carton?' It became a compulsory stopover on the international collectors' circuit. People came with chauffeurs. David Bowie came to fling paint on a spin painting with Damien. You wouldn't leave your car to go round the corner for a coffee. There were muggings. A woman artist was mugged twice, both times in the morning. It was scary.

Daniel Coombs spent six weeks clearing car parts out of a space behind Brixton Breakers with Richard Clegg, another former student from the Painting School at the Royal College in London. Clegg had always been a bit iconoclastic. He'd been the singer with an anarcho-punk band called Monkey Island and had wrecked the floor of the gallery at the college with a degree-show piece made from 2,500 bars of Sunshine soap and cataracts of sump oil. So he fitted right in.

Daniel Coombs, though, had stuck to conventional painting. In 1994, the year before he moved into Minet Road, he'd sold a group of surreal Bauhaus-meets-Butthead canvases to Charles Saatchi. In 1996, Coombs was in Young British Artists 6 at the Saatchi Gallery and then saw his work being shoe-horned into the new art movement Saatchi tried to launch just last year: new neurotic realism.

But the very particular circumstances at Minet Road soon got to him. It was a wart of land and a jumble of old clapped-out buildings in the middle of a modern council estate; the last remaining trace of a life that had once been lived there. He stopped making paintings and started making assemblages from the rubbish heaped outside the studio door instead.

'It felt like a kind of quite alien environment, in a way. I felt alien and isolated and didn't quite know what was happening at first. I found it hard to use a brush and do sensitive paintings. But the strangeness of the place drew us together more. It made us all take quite a hard attitude to our work. It made us want to do something quite brutal. Everybody who produced beautiful work there was influenced by the surroundings. Marcus [Harvey] definitely. He was just starting the *Myra* piece when I moved in, and I remember being impressed by this giant canvas laid out on scaffolding. It was exciting to think of Damien Hirst making his stuff there. If somebody produces something really outstanding, it gives you an impetus to compete with them.'

In his book *The Conditions of Success* the former director of the Tate Sir Alan Bowness puts forward the view that most truly original new work is the result of group activity:

I do not believe that any great art has been produced in a non-competitive situation: on the contrary it is the fiercely competitive environment in which the young artist finds himself that drives him to excel . . . Pollock, Rothko, Newman, Still and de Kooning were all linked together in friendship and rivalry. A post-expressionist generation of distinction – Johns, Lichtenstein, Rauschenberg, Warhol – was to follow them. Artists who emerge from such a situation do not have a consistency of style . . . but there is a consistency of purpose. They want to get to the top.

Daniel Coombs and Richard Clegg and their contemporaries from the Royal College who followed them to Brixton – Ian Dawson, Martin Westwood, Chantal Joffe – were the second tribe to colonise Minet Road. The first settlers came from Goldsmiths College and included Damien Hirst, Marcus Harvey and Hugh Allan. In fact, these three were the core of a tribe within a tribe: the Leeds lot.

Hugh Allan, who now runs Damien Hirst's studio and is his business partner in Science, had grown up next door to Marcus Harvey in Leeds and they remained best friends. Damien, who was a few years younger, had been a friend of Hugh's brother. They all went to the Jacob Kramer College of Art in Leeds, and then, at different times, to Goldsmiths in London.

Marcus was the trailblazer, and once he was settled Damien came to check it out. 'I'd led the way in terms of a career – of going to college and becoming an artist. I showed Damien what to do, in terms of it being possible to do this. I think with-out me being there, he might not have chosen the same path. I really do think that. But he came down, tapped into the actual mechanics of the art world by getting a job in a gallery [dogs-bodying at d'Offay], and then just took off in the inside lane. When I had these very kind of religious ideas about how you proceed in the art world – you sweated and suffered, and if you were lucky when you were old and wispy, you might sell a pic-ture – he just did not do shit like that. He just got on with life, you know; making life comfortable.

'There's no . . . He's the most guilt-free man I ever, ever experienced. That's what the contrast between the two of us is. He just went for it. And he didn't have a plan before, or a model. Damien's his own model. Fearless. He found out that if you are your own person, you've nothing to fear in life. Especially in this [art] world. Being, you know, a genius of a geezer, and such a great personality and sense of humour, sense of adventure in life and death and everything, he just knew: "I can't go wrong. There are so many fucking tossers. Whingeing neurots. I'm like a rock in a stormy sea." And then suddenly he blazed away. He ripped the air out of everyone's lungs.'

By the time he discovered Brixton Breakers and Minet Road in the early nineties, Damien Hirst was already in the thick of the kind of celebrity that hadn't been seen in the British art world since the days of David Hockney. He needed somewhere fairly rough and ready because he was about to extend the Natural History series of sculptures that had started with *The Physical Impossibility of Death in the Mind of Someone Living* – Saatchi's fourteen-foot tiger shark.

To all the other noxious odours at Brixton Breakers was added the stench of formaldehyde. In a scenario that recalled the heyday of *la vie bohème* in Paris, when the stink of a side of beef that Chaim Soutine was painting had his neighbours running for cover, the people in the flats on the Loughborough estate complained that formaldehyde fumes were seeping in their windows. Looking down from the balconies they could see figures in dry-suits and face masks pumping formaldehyde solution into bits of animal carcass using twenty-four-inch syringes.

Over time, the bleakness of the surroundings – the damp and coldness and lack of even basic amenities (black fungus would creep up over the surface of a picture very quickly); the operatic scale of the squalor – seemed to encourage an unorthodox approach to methods and materials. It was as if the toxic nature of the landscape in which they were working gave them permission to do things that a politer set-up would have withheld.

Among the younger group of artists – the second wave – Richard Clegg started working with stainless-steel sink units and then, in *The Unknown Collaboratives*, with a hard-setting polyurethane, while Daniel Coombs went on piling up his detritus. At the RCA, Ian Dawson had worked fairly conventionally with wood and metal. In Brixton, he built everyday household objects into heaps – dog bowls, bins, baby baths, picnic chairs – then took up an oxyacetylene burner to fondue the plastic into free-standing Jackson Pollocks. Saatchi took three. Even Martin Westwood, whose work has a marvellous Jasper Johns stillness to it, a steely cerebral quality, started mutilating his canvases and winding the painted strips into spheres, which were then mounted, fungus-like, on the wall. Only Chantal Joffe kept more or less obdurately to the path she had been travelling before she arrived at Minet Road.

The only change was that, perhaps as a reaction to all the gigantism and physicality going on around her, her already small paintings of children and adult pornography got even smaller. 'They're quite a macho group of people,' she says, 'and those studios were really open. They made each other more ambitious: "Oh I did an all-nighter." They were going for that kind of mythical bonding. Which they could laugh at as well. The music went with that. Loud and hard. You know: "We're here because we're hard." I like to work silently. But even I was aware of making work that would stand up in that space.'

At the beginning, they split into two camps: the Leeds lot and the rest. 'It wasn't easy to move into the Amish,' Hugh Allan says. The division was acted out in the arena of The Hero of Switzerland, the nearest pub: if you were Leeds you turned left into the pool room; Royal College you turned right into the lounge. But then, largely through Richard Clegg and Marcus Harvey, the demarcations disappeared. Damien Hirst had already taken his dangerously anarchic sense of mischief to the West End by then and was cavorting with a new group of friends at the Groucho Club. By chance, Ian Dawson was taken on as a construction worker at Pharmacy, Hirst's restaurant project in Notting Hill. He'd put in an eight-hour shift, and then do a few hours down at Brixton Breakers. It was sheer economics, he says, that drove people there. 'It was the cheapest studio space in town by a mile. But there was a grimness to it. I'm fucking glad that place is over. We were all just waiting to get out of there at the end.'

The end, when it came last summer, came quickly. A big fire spread through the breakers' yard, and a week later Gerry, the gaffer, was found dead in the alley among the rubble. The fork-lift that he had been using to shift the burned-out cars had flipped over and crushed him. As a spectacle in a place that had seen the production of so much (museum-quality) art whose theme was catastrophilia, it must have seemed grotesquely

appropriate. (Catastrophilia: The longing for something terrible, for something that is terribly high, sad, or far, terribly
mean, dangerous or lovely, as long as it's terrible.)

'It was all very odd and very tragic,' Dan Coombs says. 'It
was just like the last . . . It was like the finally horrific thing that
could have happened.'

2000

RACHEL WHITEREAD

'Perhaps a good place to start is if you would tell me the thinking that took you from doing a big, monumental, politically highly charged piece – the Holocaust Memorial in Vienna – to about as far away from that as you can get, which is a cardboard box, basically.'

So there we have it. At last. After months of fevered speculation and stop-at-nothing, daredevil spying missions, the truth is out. The ace Rachel Whiteread has been hiding up her sleeve for a year is a box of the common-or-garden cardboard variety. Fourteen thousand of them, in fact, or at least their ghostly plastic apparitions, stacked up into a vast walk-through installation called *Embankment*. Whiteread's 'warehousing' or B&Q-ing of the Turbine Hall at Tate Modern.

But Whiteread's cardboard boxes are to boxes what Carl Andre's notorious Tate firebricks are to . . . well, bricks. 'I wanted to start with something that was as dumb and inert as I could find, that wasn't a brick,' she says, perhaps pointedly. As the maker of *House* and the Holocaust Memorial she speaks as somebody who has been through the wringer of public controversy. In the weeks leading up to the unveiling of her Turbine Hall installation, she has been desperate to avoid cooked-up tabloid outrage of the kind that led to Andre's bricks being doused with blue vegetable dye and to the conservative commentator Paul Johnson referring to supporters of contemporary art as 'brickies'.

For the time being, she remains 'completely braced'. 'In the early stages, when I was still making collages and just working all this stuff through,' she said, 'I had to try to figure out whether or not it was really dumb, actually; just too stupid to do. "Is that all she could come up with, a cardboard box!" But after about three months mulling it over, it struck me that if I could find a way of making these boxes in totally mass production, then I could make it work. So that you could make the inside of the Turbine Hall almost like landscape, as well as like this massive storage area.

'I don't think it's going to be like a room full of cardboard boxes. It's going to be a room, I would imagine, full of light and space and built elements, and you'll figure out what they are, but it might take a bit of time to do that. It's going to be a spectacle, and theatrical, and it has to be. It's the only way to deal with that space. And I have to make that jump. That's what I've done. And that is how it has to be done.'

Whiteread lives and works in a former synagogue in East London. Parts of Bethnal Green have been 'chi-chified', as she describes it, but it remains raw. 'We still have prostitutes standing on our corner, and people crapping round the back of buildings,' she says. 'So the charms are still there.'

But inside her own space the atmosphere is almost sepulchral. The studios are big and airy and quiet as cancer. She has made it that way. She started out on her own with small objects and pieces of furniture that she had foraged for in local junk shops or dragged in off the street. She cast their insides and undersides in damp-looking, mottled white plaster whose surfaces registered all the signs of wear and tear — dust, snot, wads of gum, dents and makeshift repairs — that the bric-a-brac had accumulated in the course of its life, and which would have remained unrecognised, and certainly unmemorialised, without her intervention.

She associated the casts of wardrobes, tables and sad single beds that were among her earliest pieces with her childhood in Muswell Hill in North London; working alone in her studio, casting objects with which she was familiar, connected her to her family. *Yellow Leaf*, for example, was the cast of a table similar to the Formica-topped extendable one that her grandmother had kept in her kitchen. *Shallow Breath* was the cast of the underside of the bed on which, according to her mother, she was born.

Her eureka moment came in 1990 with *Ghost*, a plaster cast of the 'mummified air' inside a room in a Victorian house in Archway Road, similar to the one she grew up in. *Ghost* looked like a catafalque or a tomb. There were echoes of Reginald Christie and 10 Rillington Place. She once worked in Highgate cemetery fixing lids back onto crumbling coffins, and she would go on to explore an interest in the macabre, with urine-coloured castings of mortuary slabs and hair-clogged sinks. When I was working on a book about the West murders in Gloucester in the mid-nineties, she indicated that she might be interested in visiting the house in Cromwell Street where a number of bodies of girls and young women had been buried under the patio and in the cellar, but then apparently had second thoughts. 'While I was deliberating about whether to go or not, I dreamed that I was a wall in the house, like the image in Polanski's *Repulsion*,' she later said. 'I dreamed I witnessed the horrific events of the past fifteen years. I woke up screaming and decided not to go.'

Charles Saatchi bought *Ghost*. Whiteread was shortlisted for the Turner Prize in 1991, and became the first woman to win it two years later. It was then that the art world – 'a carnival with a casino attached', as somebody once described it — came slowly seeping, and then rushing in. That year, 1993, was also the year of *House*, a project with serious political and social overtones which nevertheless saw her catapulted out of the arts ghetto and into the maw of the tabloids, an arena where Damien Hirst and his more frolicsome contemporaries were already at play.

Rachel Whiteread didn't go to Goldsmiths. This was more or less the first thing she ever said (hissed, really) into my tape recorder. She went to the Slade. Nevertheless, along with Hirst, she was part of Young British Artists 1 at the Saatchi Gallery in March 1992, the show that gave a name to a new, cocky, very un-English approach to making art, and history will always lump her in with the YBAs. And for a while, like everybody else, she was swept up in the mood of boosterism and celebration. 'But I just wasn't from that same mould, you know,' she says now. 'I just had come from a different place.'

Her mother Pat was an artist, a socialist and a great supporter of the feminist cause. Her father was a geography teacher who later worked as a polytechnic administrator, and was a lifelong supporter of the Labour Party.

Their serious approach has rubbed off and has earned Whiteread a reputation in some quarters as an earnest individual. I recently ran into the photographer Johnnie Shand Kydd. He was looking triumphant. 'I've just been to take a picture of Rachel,' he said. 'And I got her to smile!' In 1997 Shand Kydd brought out a collection of pictures taken in the eye of the Britart maelstrom, and although she was around — 'I partied along with everybody else. We all partied hard' — Whiteread doesn't crop up in any of them. (Well, there is one, but it's a straightforward — non-singing, non-dancing, straight-faced — portrait in her studio.)

438

The truth is she is warm, if slightly guarded, and laughs easily. 'I think the difference between me and some of the other YBAs,' she can say now, 'was that I was ambitious for the work, and not ambitious for myself. You know, personally. And I think that's quite a big difference. Of course it was interesting watching people like Damien really playing the media; just working out how to do it, and doing it. And he did it very well, actually. I just wasn't so interested in all of that.'

Interestingly, she makes a link between her own generation and British artists of the prewar years, and nominates an unexpected pacesetter: Henry Moore. 'A few years ago I went to Moore's studio, and it's kind of fascinating going there, because you see there's a few sheds and outbuildings that have fake skies painted on the walls on the inside. And I was asking, "What's that about?" And they said, "Oh that's for the maquettes." They used to make the maquettes, then photograph them very low, like Albert Speer when he wanted to persuade Hitler to build whatever. Then Moore would go over to Canada, America, Australia with the photograph and say, "I've got one of these, one of these, or one of these. Which one d'you like?" So he was the first British artist, I would say, that . . . You know: hustlers. People that really know how to get it all working for them. It's why there's a Henry Moore on every street corner in every city.'

She says that after she had completed the Holocaust Memorial for Judenplatz in Vienna, she felt she was under great pressure to become, in the Moore tradition, a career memorial-maker. 'But I don't do that. I don't work like that. I've made four public sculptures, and people think you're producing products. But I think a lot of the time, making good pieces of work is a completely cathartic process. It's about the whole life; its about all experience; it's about everything that happens. And if you can channel it out somehow . . .'

The Holocaust Memorial was a draining experience. It was a political and bureaucratic minefield, and took five years to achieve. At the same time the thirteen-ton sculpture she had been commissioned to make for the fourth plinth in Trafalgar Square was being dogged by what seemed like insurmountable technical problems, and she was constantly flying round the world repairing pieces and installing shows. When she moved house, she made the decision to step away from her role as hands-off executive 'producer' of large public sculptures and to go back to her original, solitary studio practice. 'I was feeling, not that my touch had necessarily gone, but it was all a bit out of control and I just wanted to go back, into the studio. I think I wanted this studio to be my studio, rather than me and my assistants'. I didn't want all the chaos of the last place. It was mine, and I wanted it to be mine; and to do that, I had to physically make the work in it, and so it was a case of trying to work out what that was.'

Fixed to the wall of the room that fills the upper space of the former synagogue in Bethnal Green are two mementoes of Whiteread's past: one is the battered box her family's Christmas decorations used to be stored in all the time she was growing up. The other is a set of photographs of the interiors of three cardboard boxes, ascending in size, each box containing a broken Pyrex bowl. This is an art work made by Pat Whiteread, who went into hospital for a standard investigative procedure two years ago, but died.

Whiteread was devastated by her mother's death, which happened to coincide with other major upheavals in her life: moving house, moving studio, the arrival of a son. 'My mother's house was still full up of stuff. And my house was still full up of stuff from having moved and still having the builders in. So I was in this place of literally not being able to unpack my life, my mum's life — my parents' lives.

'She'd lived where she was about ten years; not really a long time. But a lot of stuff that she'd never unpacked from before just stayed in the basement. So there was layers of stuff down there that was very peculiar going through. All our toys. All very mouldy. Everything I looked at looked like a still from a film. A film of my life. And I felt I was going mad. Because every single thing had a significance — connections and associations which you couldn't stop. And I really thought, I'm going to go insane here if this carries on. It did subside. But you know in movies when they do a fast flashback of things, like in *Terminator* . . . If that had gone on for a long period I think I would have ended up in therapy. Because I really was thinking, I can't live the rest of my life in having to repeat these memories. I really couldn't do that.'

The realisation that the cardboard boxes where much of her past and present life were stored could be turned into sculpture crept up on her slowly. She started to become more interested in what had once been in the boxes — cans of soup, bolts of material — than what they currently contained. 'I love it when there's been a circular object, whatever it is, inside,' she says, 'and it's been moved around a lot in transit, so you get these beautiful drawings, circular shapes.'

She had been looking for an object that she could build with and use as a standardised unit, much as Carl Andre had used bricks. She went into what she describes as a 'casting frenzy' as soon as she realised cardboard boxes were it. 'I became fixated. Looking for boxes, finding very specific ones, working with them, crunching them up more.'

Surprisingly, perhaps, she collects dolls' houses, old used ones that she buys on eBay. And the boxes they come in — 'like a TV box that may have been totally reconfigured – they'll cut a bit, and then they'll stick a bit down . . . They're people who don't have any idea about three-dimensional things and practicalities, and the way they do it is in such a fantastic, bodgy way' – have provided her with some of her favourite moulds.

The castings in the installation at Tate Modern are light, translucent skins which she believes will illuminate the space. The sculptures she has made for her show that opens at the Gagosian Gallery in London later this month, on the other hand, are heavy plaster casts. 'This is much more my sculpture,' she said, unlocking a ground-floor door. 'This is what I do in the studio.'

It looked like a storeroom at first: dusty white boxes piled on pallets and stacked under cheap tables and chairs. Your eye skidded over it. There was little sense of display. You couldn't tell it was the work. But then its slowness started to resonate – to impose itself, really. And you were reminded of the groupings of plain flasks and bottles painted for decade after decade in the middle of the last century by Giorgio Morandi, who was nicknamed 'Il Monaco' ('The Monk'). Also of the blank windows of *House*.

'I had a few years where I was feeling . . . I suppose a bit mid-career,' Whiteread said. 'It happens with everybody who's been doing anything a certain amount of time: you start scratching your head. And I feel I have refreshed myself.'

2006

GILLIAN WEARING

> If, as with Emerson, Williams seems to 'ask the fact for the form', the form, once it comes, is free of the fact, is a dance above the fact.
>
> Charles Tomlinson, Introduction to
> William Carlos Williams, *Selected Poems*

For some reason every time I applied myself to thinking about Gillian Wearing and her work (the deadline was looming) I found myself thinking about William Carlos Williams – Williams, the poet of inarticulate America; a poet who distrusted articulacy – and Williams's elusive, famous little poem – only sixteen words – 'The Red Wheelbarrow':

> so much depends
> upon
>
> a red wheel
> barrow
>
> glazed with rain
> water
>
> beside the white
> chickens

Like Wearing, Williams, a family doctor for most of his life in small-town New Jersey, believed in embracing the immediate and the local, the what-is-to-hand in the where-we-are. The great attraction of Williams's poetry was its insistence that intelligence is inseparable from the whole range of immediate, physical, bodily perception. He set out to develop a language that was 'an action upon the real' rather than a discourse of abstractions about it.

The blocked verbal facility of the people he encountered daily on his rounds was for Williams a constant rush and excitement ('It's the anarchy of poverty/ delights me . . .'), and the artlessness of ordinary speech came to replace 'high-end' aestheticised language and the conventional poetic formulas in his work. 'Colleges and books only copy the language which the field and work-yard made,' Emerson had said. And 'the speech of Polish mothers' was where Williams insisted he got his English from: 'Anything is good material for poetry. Anything. I've said it time and time again.'

'That words set in Jersey speech rhythms mean less but mean it with more finality,' was Williams's great technical perception, the critic Hugh Kenner once observed. Which reminded me of something Gillian Wearing has said about her own work's investment in the completely defenceless simplicity of personal speech, and its implicit belief in a kind of heroism among damaged people and diminished things: 'I'm more interested in how other people can put things together, how people can say something far more interesting than I can.'

Starting out, I had an idea that the matter for this essay on the awkward and, in important ways, unknowable work of Gillian Wearing was going to consist of 'found' material like the sometimes funny, sometimes vulgar, often banal and uncomfortable thoughts and words of strangers that she incorporates into her gnarly photographic and video art. And one day when I should have been at home working on what you have in front of you now, I stepped out of a London restaurant into driving rain. Diagonally opposite the restaurant was a second-hand bookshop, and I ducked in there for shelter. It was musty-smelling, with a dinging doorbell and flattened cardboard boxes on the floor to take up the wet. The owner was sitting in a low, busted chair in his topcoat with the collar pulled all the way up, playing bridge or patience or another card game on a grey box computer.

My eye was almost immediately drawn to some white writing on a red spine: '*I Wanted to Write a Poem* by William Carlos Williams'. This was the first edition of a 'talked' book, published by Beacon Press in Boston in 1958. Set on their own in the middle of the first page were five lines of the poem from which the book got its title:

> I wanted to write a poem
> that you would understand.
> For what good is it to me
> if you can't understand it?
> But you got to try hard —

This book stood next to a long-forgotten novel by Djuna Barnes. And, slipped between them, a skinny filling in this melancholy modernist sandwich, an issue of the University of Minnesota Pamphlets on American Writers, number 24, dated 1963, subject William Carlos Williams. The pamphlet fell open to page 24, where 'The Red Wheelbarrow' was reproduced. Page 25 carried 'Danse Russe', a Williams poem I hadn't come across before but which, for reasons that to even casual Wearing-watchers will seem obvious, wrote itself straight into this space:

> If when my wife is sleeping
> and the baby and Kathleen
> are sleeping
> and the sun is a flame-white disc

> in silken mists
> above shining trees, –
> if I in my north room
> dance naked, grotesquely
> before my mirror
> waving my shirt round my head
> and singing softly to myself:
> 'I am lonely, lonely.
> I was born to be lonely,
> I am best so!'
> If I admire my arms, my face,
> my shoulders, flanks, buttocks
> against the yellow drawn shades, –
> Who shall say I am not
> the happy genius of my household?

'In the Video Diary and Video Nation TV spots,' Wearing has said, 'you see people acting silly in their own homes – and that's since camcorders have come out. People have wanted to record themselves being wacky; this is the "true" them. But they're doing it in private. I'm sure that many people have done a lot of dancing in their bedrooms, but taking that fantasy and putting it somewhere it's alien – that's where you can start questioning.'

The twenty-five-minute video *Dancing In Peckham* (1994) shows Wearing herself dancing to a soundtrack (Nirvana's 'Smells Like Teen Spirit', Gloria Gaynor's 'I Will Survive') that she is unspooling silently in her head. The 'alien' environment the spectacle unfolds in is the placelessness of a small shopping-mall arcade – a locus of the new form of solitude endemic in what Marc Augé has defined as 'the space of non-place'.

'A person entering the space of non-place [motorways, air-port lounges, cineplexes, destination retail 'experiences'] is

446

relieved of his usual determinants,' Augé writes. 'He obeys the same code as others, receives the same messages, responds to the same entreaties. The space of non-place creates neither singular identity nor relations; only solitude, and similitude.' To give vent to unembarrassed self-expression and self-display in such a non-place then becomes an act of wilful and (this is the implication) punishable transgression.

It has become a commonplace in the environment of the image that images accumulate sensation around themselves the more they are reproduced and repeated; they grow an aura. And, thanks to a number of high-profile murder cases in Britain in recent years, a suggestion of the uncanny – the spectre of death stalking through the centre of life; the notion of demonistic or magic forces – has attached itself to suburban malls like the one where Wearing filmed herself disco dancing in South London. (She had previously used the down-at-heel, no-longer-modern Peckham mall as a background in *Signs ...*, 1992–3.)

In what was to be the last hour of her life, the popular television presenter Jill Dando was caught by CCTV cameras shopping for an ink cartridge for her printer in King's Mall, close to the BBC. The grainy stutter-frames of the three-year-old James Bulger walking through the central precinct of the Strand shopping centre on Merseyside hand-in-hand with his two schoolboy killers became some of the most deeply ingrained images of recent times.

There is an aggression involved in every use of the camera. And inevitably there is an evidentiary quality – a starey cold stoniness – to the Dando and Bulger pictures. Although mechanically captured, they imply the slyness and patience of the snooper, the stalker, the lurking feral paparazzo photographer. They suggest the privileged view vouchsafed her killer, crouching, unseen, in the bushes in the front garden of Jill Dando's house at Gowan Avenue in Fulham.

Perhaps it was these conventions that Gillian Wearing was testing when she put on a bandage mask and had herself spy-cammed as she walked to the local shops for *Homage to the Woman With the Bandaged Face Who I Saw Yesterday Down Walworth Road* (1995). The visual vocabulary that, as regular television grazers, we have all internalised — the extreme graininess, the ethereal steaks and smudges — is in evidence. The snatched quality of such footage has come to be seen as a guarantee of its authenticity. The rawnesss of the pictures (often combined with ticking digits at the top of the frame or the bottom) has become code for the real world happening in real time — for reality caught off guard, in what we might think of as the in-between moments, when crimes and catastrophes happen. Much of their power derives from the fact that they were never meant to be seen. Only the calamitous events to which they have become connected have led to them being retrieved.

The difference in this instance is that Wearing herself is the embodiment of the uncanny, if you accept the psychoanalytical interpretation of the uncanny as being 'something that ought to have remained secret and hidden but which has come to light' — 'a sense of something new, foreign and hostile invading an old, familiar, customary world'. And another difference: the woman in the bandage mask returns the gaze; stares down the starers; she looks back.

What is it with Wearing and masks? 'Celebrity', John Updike has written, 'is a mask that eats into the face.' Unlike a number of her friends and contemporaries among the Young British Artists pack, Gillian Wearing hasn't become a promis-cuously photographed party presence, an instantly recognis-able household face. In *Self Portrait* (2000), though, she wears a mask that reads as a photo-fake, digitally doctored version of her own features. It has no physical texture; none of the complicated tonality of a living face; none of the greasy lustre of living skin. The hard-shadowed eye sockets and deep caves of the nostrils are unnerving. The face appears virtual; incorporeal. Less Lara Croft than Larkin's stone effigy on an Arundel tomb.

In these ways *Self Portrait*, and the more recent self-portraits as various members of her immediate family (*Self Portrait as My Mother Jean Gregory*, and so on), are reminiscent of the computer composites that Nancy Burson has made, using 'wrinkle masks' taken from the family members of long-missing children to digitally 'age' the children's faces in order to give an approximation of how they might look in the unlikely event of them still being alive.

In the work of an earlier generation of English artists – the portrait paintings of Francis Bacon and Lucian Freud, most notably – the body shape is clearly modelled by the life inside it; there is a sense of internal pressure pushing the skin into its uniquely complex shape. But with Wearing, as with a number of other notable artists of her generation, you never know whether there is a (real) face or only a ghastly void behind the crude disguises and prosthetic masks.

In his 1991 novel *Mao II*, Don DeLillo has the following passage: 'He knew the boy was standing by the door and he tried to see his face in words, imagine what he looked like, skin and eyes and features, every aspect of that surface called a face, if we can say he has a face, if we believe there is actually something under the hood.'

'There are signs everywhere [in US fiction] of the end of what I would call the physiognomy tradition,' the novelist Charles Baxter recently wrote. 'In writers like Don DeLillo, there is the . . . suggestion that the individual face simply has no importance any more . . . In DeLillo we enter a world where we cannot really know much of anything, particularly about other people. Other people may have some sort of individual reality, but it is not very likely to appear on their faces or to be visible anywhere else . . . If there are no real individuals left, why bother describing their faces. You will have to find something else to describe.'

We have come to a point where more and more of us, not only the famous, benefit from packaging ourselves in congenial forms. The packaging, like the masking that is such a feature of Wearing's work, is a form of self-protection. Because it can be perilous to go out there as yourself in a time when personality has replaced output as the measure of fame.

Confess all on video. Don't worry, you will be in disguise. Intrigued? Call Oprah, Jerry, Kilroy, Trisha. Come on. You can be real or fake-real so people think they're seeing reality when they're seeing something they invent. We are all creatures of the electronic limbo. Call Gillian.

2004

MICHAEL LANDY

At a formal dinner given for Michael Landy at Tate Britain on Monday night, there was an uneasy moment – four minutes of extended social embarrassment, in fact – when the director of the gallery stood up to speak. As he offered his entirely deserved congratulations to the artist for what has a better-than-even chance of turning out to be a famous piece of work, and continued through a roll call of all those who had helped to make it possible, some joker in the next gallery (a caterer? a sweeper-up?) went on whistling obliviously as he worked.

He whistled 'Danny Boy' then segued into an Irish Saturday-night version of the Jim Reeves weepie 'Welcome to My World (Built With You in Mind)'. The Duveen galleries, where the whistling was coming from, are stone-walled, barrel-vaulted, 300 feet long and perfectly echoic. It is the kind of cathedral-like space dedicated to the exaltation of high art where a low art like whistling would seem to have no place. Known as 'the Duveens' after Sir Joseph Duveen, the antiques dealer who funded them, they were added to the Tate in 1937, the first public galleries in England designed specifically for the display of sculpture. They are a reminder of a time when popular culture was more constrained, because there was another culture which was more dominant.

Very clever of Michael Landy, then, whose last show at Millbank was Scrap Heap Services (1995), a bitter satire on the expendability of working people, to record his father, long unemployed as the result of an industrial accident, whistling slightly wheezily and wistfully to himself, and to use this as the soundtrack to *Semi Detached*, a new installation gathered together from the pieces of John Landy's life. The soundtrack intruded on the dinner in much the same way as the life-sized replica of his parents' Essex house that he has had constructed intrudes into the lofty interior of the Duveens.

Who would have known that such a small house, uprooted from its suburban plot, could look so big? The chimney barely makes it under the skylight; the outer walls leave only narrow brick alleys as a pedestrian way in. Or that such a modest house, planted in a space that has previously been home to Richard Serra's dumb-faced lead bomb shelters and Richard Long's Niger mud circles, could look so imposing?

62 Kingswood Road, Ilford IG3 8UD. It is just a house, in all its pebble-dashed, net-curtained, nylon-windowed, slightly run-down boring ordinariness. Untampered-with. Unamplified. A ready-made. A 'found' object in the Duchampian tradition. Except it is the object Michael Landy found himself living in when his parents decided to move from Hackney in East London to Ilford in Essex for the sake of Michael, and Maureen and Lisa, his sisters. (Hollow laugh from Landy. 'That's why I became a runner. I spent my whole childhood running.')

The Landys' happy, unremarkably ramshackle life was upended in 1977 when John Landy, an Irishman working with other Irishmen digging a tunnel in Northumberland, was buried alive after the roof of the tunnel collapsed on his head and shoulders. He suffered severe injuries: his back was broken and, in the language of industrial tribunals and compen committees, he was considered 'a total wreck case'. In the years since the accident, disabled and increasingly immobile, he has progressively withdrawn from the world. His world has largely become contained within the walls which have been recreated down to the smallest paint stain and rust blemish at Tate Britain — traces of the earlier stages in the history of the building and the human life associated with it. As the brick crumbles and the materials weather, the house becomes its own record of everything that has happened to it.

John Landy is a link with the older world of hard, itinerant manual labour. 'Labour' is the first word to appear in the long, slow panning sequence of the video Michael Landy has made of his father's rough, randomly accumulated bedside possessions. It is twinned with the logofied red rose of New Labour and appears on some kind of promotional literature which has found its way onto a shelf which is weighed down with the dusty evidence of his former life as a DIY fanatic: the camera lingers lovingly over cable clips, welder glue, car indicator lights, chainsaw brushes (neatly bagged and labelled), heel grips, a magnifying glass, a collection of torches. A chainsaw and all-purpose Power Devil are kept to hand (and in good condition, though they're hardly used any more) in the bedroom.

A second large video screen on the reverse of the house's facade shows a sequence of changing images drawn entirely from the collection of instruction leaflets, DIY manuals and home-improvement magazines that John Landy has collected over decades, both before and after his accident. Photographs and line drawings of optimistic young couples and growing young families, hell-bent in pursuit of the modernity, pureness and newness that was all the rage, alternate with illustrations of how to deal with blocked guttering, eroded surfaces, skinned knuckles, clogged drains.

Landy found it too unnerving trying to interrogate his

father directly with the camera. Instead he pays attention to the small things in a house – and in a life – that are often only noticed in their absence: a fridge light; the chest freezer in the dining room switching through its cycle; the ball of fluff spinning on a thread above the radiator; the ticking of a clock.

Taped to a wall through the weeks that 62 Kingswood Road was being replicated at Tate Britain was a plan and elevation of the house pocked with the hundreds of individual peculiarities – every sore, scar and bricky pockmark – which Michael Landy had spotted and was anxious to bring to the attention of Mike Smith and the construction team. The people applying the finishing touches to the kitchen extension last weekend looked more like make-up artists than conventional chippies and painters, stepping back to appraise, and then going in with a fine eyeliner brush to finesse a scab by the door.

When are ordinary houses usually scrutinised in this way? By police forensics teams and in the visual vocabulary of newspapers and television, when something out of the ordinary, often macabre, has taken place there: the school caretaker's house at Soham; Jill Dando's house at Gowan Avenue in Fulham; 25 Cromwell Street. The wadded albums of photographs that the 'factors' worked from showed the skin of the house in eruptive, forensic detail. The elevations which Michael Landy marked up were strongly reminiscent of the body maps that cosmetic surgeons prepare (and Jenny Saville has painted) prior to an operation.

Many of the artists of Landy's generation, while studiously avoiding the human body in their work, have been aggressive in their referencing of it. Damien Hirst's use of animal carcasses has always been insistently anthropomorphic. Sarah Lucas has used dead poultry, fried eggs and assorted fruit and vegetables. Rachel Whiteread has cast the insides of wardrobes and the undersides of beds as well as mortuary slabs and discarded mattresses. But it was with *House*, her 'mutilation', according to hostile critics, of 'the archetypal space of homeliness', that Whiteread inflamed a debate which, a decade later, is still difficult to make sense of.

Two decades before Whiteread, the young American sculptor Gordon Matta-Clark had drawn a line with a chainsaw through a house in suburban New Jersey, and later installed the four roof corners of the building in a gallery. More recently, the German Gregor Schneider has systematically mutilated the house he inherited from his parents to the point where Schneider himself claims he can no longer distinguish between parts that have been added and those that existed before. In all these cases the point has been the transposition of the familiar into its opposite: the uncanny, and stories of boarded-up houses whose secrets might only be imagined.

For *Semi Detached*, Michael Landy's family home has been bisected and a hundred feet of gallery space placed between the two halves. The video presentations are where the lived life of the house would be. But he is insistent that his intervention stops there. He would have uprooted 62 Kingswood Road and moved it across London, if that had been possible. The choice of ready-mades was based on visual indifference, at the same time as a total absence of good or bad taste. Duchamp once talked of 'signing' the Woolworth Building in New York and that's what Landy would have liked to do with the house where he grew up. It is in its implacable, unassuming ordinariness that his interest, and all his interest, resides. Nothing terrible, and possibly nothing even particularly wonderful, has ever happened there. Just a set of unremarkable lives rubbing against each other, moving through time.

This is by a broad margin the most sentimental project to

which Landy has committed himself to date. *Break Down* (2001), where he took all his possessions, including works by other artists, and systematically ground them to dust, was a definition of unsentimentality. The final piece to go, inventory number C714, was the piece that Landy was most attached to – his father's old sheepskin coat, purchased shortly before he had his accident and paid for over a year by Landy's mother even though it was too heavy and uncomfortable by then for John Landy to wear. *Break Down* was a ritual acting out of the disintegration which is the only end of every human life. 'It's like my own funeral,' Landy said at the time, 'but I'm here to watch it. I'm still alive.'

He says he is already dreading the day in December, six months in the future, when the house at the Tate will have to be demolished and taken away in skips. 'In a strange way, although it's only been up less than a week, it feels more real to me than the real thing.'

His father, though, already has first claims: the drainpipes, the guttering, the white PVC door and white plastic windows are all making the trip to Ilford and 62 Kingswood Road.

During the filming for *Semi Detached* a curious thing happened: they had to remove a lot of the stuff in which Michael Landy has invested so much meaning so that the camera could move freely in his father's room. At the completion of filming, his dad didn't want it put back. Now a move to Jaywick or Clacton or somewhere on the south coast is on the cards.

Reminiscing about the interiors of his youth, the Viennese architect Adolf Loos observed that he did not grow up in a 'stylish' home. The house was his family's product, not a work of art. 'It was our table, ours!' The house was never finished; 'it grew along with us and we grew within it'. It possessed neither style, strangeness, nor age.

456

'Art is what we do. Culture is what is done to us,' Carl Andre once said. With their move, it's fair to say the art will have gone out of the Landys' unassuming semi standing on Kingswood Road.

2004

COLONY ROOM NIGHTS

Performance Bar Art

S + T

....

invite you

to join them in an evening of performance bar art

Weds 29th September 1999

....

From 6 - 11.00 p.m.

at

THE COLONY ROOM CLUB. 41 DEAN ST W1V

Invitation only

JANE AND LOUISE WILSON

Place in preference to people. This is the principle that has driven the work of the video artists Jane and Louise Wilson. The Wilsons are twins and originate from Newcastle. The first fact is currently not that obvious: Jane's hair is dark and short, her sister's sun-bleached and longer and she is the slighter of the two. That they are Geordies, though, is indisputable: they tend to address the loftiest art-world panjandrums as 'pet', and still refer to cigarettes, as hardly anybody in Newcastle ever does any more, as 'tabs'. This has the (probably intended) effect of encouraging people to underestimate them.

The Wilsons seem outgoing, gregarious and no less sociable than the rest of the YBA tribe, of which they are fully blooded members. So it is intriguing that in their work, which is typically shown in technically complicated, multi-screen installations, they have concentrated on depopulated industrial dumps and military prisons and other alienating, slightly sinister crannies of the modern built environment. These have included the former Stasi headquarters in Berlin, decommissioned missile bunkers at Greenham Common and a hallucinogenically post-industrial microchip factory in Northumberland.

Their last major show, at the Baltic in Gateshead, was called A Free and Anonymous Monument and took as its focus a modernist folly made of reinforced concrete which the artist Victor Pasmore designed for the new town of Peterlee near

Newcastle in 1958. Pasmore's Apollo Pavilion was built as a symbol of the supposed regeneration of the region in the Macmillan years, much as Owen Luder's brutalist high-rise car park in Gateshead, famous now only for being a key location in the 1971 gangster film *Get Carter*, was meant to stand as proof of the role the region had to play in Harold Wilson's much-speechified new era of 'white-hot' technology. Today both Pasmore's pavilion and Luder's multi-storey car park are in states of mouldy dilapidation. The 'indestructible' cast concrete that both structures are made of has become porous with stress cracks and deep chemical stains. Bushes have taken root; steel supports nudge close to the surface like bones.

Now the Gateshead car park is the centrepiece of a short film the Wilsons were commissioned to make to mark the twenty-fifth anniversary of the Great North Run, which attracts an entry of 50,000 runners every year and takes place in Newcastle tomorrow.

The split and tiled screens of *Broken Time* are often busily pixellated with people — swelling streams and rivers of runners channelled along motorways and bridges and culverted into the dimly lit underpasses at the perimeter of the city. The title is apparently a reference to time off allowed to industrial workers with an interest in sport. But the emphasis is not on the athletes in their gaudy near-nakedness and driven pursuit of personal bests, but on the urban landscapes that the race draws them through.

Crowds in these numbers themselves become a place. The city is surveyed from the upper decks of Luder's modernist ruin and the viewer is invited to note the changes that have taken place. But it is not only the Newcastle skyline that has been invaded by shapes which were unimaginable thirty years ago. Who could have predicted that health and fitness and endurance running would become a mass leisure activity with its own rituals of dressing and behaving and a booming micro-economy? Or that a day would arrive when there would be more visitor destinations for art and culture than shipyards on the Tyne?

In their film the Wilsons show how even spectating has advanced to become its own kind of performance art. They are excited by the way people on the route take possession of places that were never meant to invite human occupation: the cobble-crusted oases, for example, where vast V-shaped concrete buttresses make contact with the earth and are normally unreachable across the lanes of speeding traffic. Or the slip roads of the elevated motorways that the buttresses are supporting, where pedestrian interlopers could normally expect to be mowed down. I took *Broken Time* to be in part a reiteration of Corbusier's belief that architecture 'is appreciated while on the move, with one's feet . . . while walking, moving from one place to another'.

This was in early August. And then, as is often the case when an artist has cottoned on to something which the rest of us haven't yet been able to articulate, something unexpected happens which confirms their vision and slightly alters our perception of the world.

On 28 August Katrina happened. And soon our screens were awash with horrible images which, in their depiction of crowds roaming in places that crowds don't normally go, were uncannily like the scenes of recreational human displacement that the Wilsons had captured at last year's Great North Run. Prisoners from New Orleans jail herded onto a ramp of the collapsed and flooded freeway. The showpiece Superdome flayed by the storm and transformed overnight into an over-crowded and insanitary shanty town. The impoverished and the elderly lined up along the central reservation of a flyover awaiting evacuation eight days after the hurricane hit.

Last week there was a preview screening of *Broken Time* in London, at Soho House, the private members' club. The club's faux country house interior is piquantly familiar from the pictures accompanying numerous colour supplement features on its members, drawn from the media community. There was a disjunction between this louche atmosphere and the exertions of the half-marathon runners on screen whose laboured gasps and wracked breathing are the only soundtrack to the film.

It played on a loop. Loving close-ups of desolate urban spaces and refuse – piles of plastic bottles; foil capes lifted on the breeze like Warholian litter. Many shots are unpeopled. The Wilsons' interest is in absence rather than presence: the traces left when the spectacle has moved on.

I thought of the sludge marks left on the houses of New Orleans as the flood slowly receded, and how the Wilsons could be the ideal chroniclers of the disaster. They are fascinated by the corporeal aspect of buildings: by what happens when the newness and cleanness become stained and defiled. By the fact that ageing is inherent in all construction, and the knowledge that even the solidest structures, and the oldest cities, can disappear.

2005

5 THE 'DEGENERATE SUBLIME'

from Luc Tuymans *to* Neo Rauch

Well at the
end of the day

the only interesting
artists are
the ones that

say:
Fuck off this is
what I think!

and don't
ever loose

your sense of

humour.

W.

Dame

LUC TUYMANS

The most memorable public works of art in Britain in recent years have been spontaneous, temporary and death-related: the third-world shrine-making at the Kop after Hillsborough; the Di-and-Dodi altars and the field of flowers in Kensington Gardens after Diana; the trenches and embankments of flowers that marked the murders of James Bulger and, more recently, Sarah Payne.

It isn't possible yet to say how the new invented tradition of laying cuddly death totems and flowers at the scene of an accident or other bloody event started, although the roots probably lie in the street shrines of South America and India. What is clear is that it was an artist, the American Mike Kelley, who identified the sinister aspect of 'the pathetic's darker side' when he started using stuffed animals in his work in the eighties, a decade or so before shopping-centre and suburban street-corner shrines became a familiar part of the emotional and media landscape — of the media spectacle — in this country.

Kelley rescued chewed and smelly teddy bears and bunny rabbits from jumble sales and thrift stores and arranged them, clumped or individually, on dirty blankets on the polished terrazzo floors of galleries. Although still virtually unknown here, Kelley has been a major influence on two generations of British artists who have used abject and degraded materials as a matter of course in their work. 'There are often unacknowledged but painfully obvious things going on around us,' Liam Gillick, an artist who came through Goldsmiths with Sarah Lucas and Damien Hirst, once said. 'Kelley, and others such as Raymond Pettibon, Jim Shaw and Sue Williams have reinvigorated the debates around where we all stand in relation to shitting, dying, feeling paranoid and not really caring.'

But for many years Kelley had a hard time of it in America. He has made 'dolls' out of faeces. *Nostalgic Depiction of the Innocence of Childhood* shows a naked man and woman squatting on the floor astride soft toys. The man's buttocks are smeared with a dark chocolatey substance and he appears to be rubbing a fluffy rabbit up against himself. 'His body of work is often taken as a demonstration that art not only doesn't have to be appealing,' one critic has written, 'but that anything appealing in it is by definition not art.' Kelley's 'transgressive' representations of American life still tend to be viewed there as just another embodiment of its ugliness.

I thought about Mike Kelley and his failure to return my calls (he is a notoriously reluctant interviewee) on the way to see Luc Tuymans in Belgium. Like Kelley, Tuymans is drawn to the banal and the dejected and to bilious, highly uncomfortable representations of childhood. Unusually (almost uniquely) for a sought-after young artist, Tuymans is a painter. His paintings typically have titles such as *Repulsion, Embitterment, Incest, Resentment, Child Abuse, The Murderer*. On a material level, they are pitiable objects, thin and slapdash, the pictorial equivalent of Kelley's rag-doll installations. 'A lot of my imagery has a sense of cosiness which is turned into something terrifying. Anything banal can be transformed into horror,' Tuymans has said. 'Violence is the only structure underlying my work.'

Kelley and Tuymans are two of the dozen or so artists in Apocalypse, intended to be the big autumn blockbuster show at the Royal Academy, designed to have them chewing the carpets in Great Missenden and Orpington. Subtitled Beauty and Horror in Contemporary Art, Apocalypse is meant to be a kind of son-of-Sensation. In the show's catalogue, the co-curator Norman Rosenthal quotes Nietzsche on the importance of facing up to difficult knowledge, 'although it may be ugly and even deadly': 'Artists . . . are best positioned to affect our knowledge by confronting us with a synthesis of new and often shocking realities . . . The ability to look, make and map where no one has looked before is the aim of every artist and exhibition.'

Already, though, a month before Apocalypse opened, David Lee, reliable no-goer and naysayer, had delivered his verdict to the London *Evening Standard*. 'Disgusting works with profane titles, profane works with disgusting titles, disgusting works with disgusting titles by disgusting artists.' Rosenthal is pissing in the wind.

The day I travelled to Antwerp to meet Luc Tuymans was the day after the funeral of the murdered eight-year-old Sarah Payne and the newspapers all carried front-page stories and pictures. The Eurostar was full of the kind of photographs that had dominated the papers all summer: photographs of Sarah Payne's grieving parents and her brothers and sister; photographs of floral tributes and Beanie Babies and weeping neighbours; photographs of the small white coffin in its Victorian hearse.

The papers had also been full of other, angrier pictures all summer, in the wake of the *News of the World*'s 'name and shame' campaign against paedophiles. Pictures of smashed windows and daubed houses and 'vigilante' marchers with children in prams and banners saying 'People don't want no paedophiles here', 'No paedophile scum on this estate'.

'Memes' is Richard Dawkins's word for those ideas (rituals, rumours) that now and again surge through the culture, that proliferate and, sometimes, develop seemingly without specific ownership or particularity. When I had finished reading about Sarah Payne's funeral, I turned to the book of Luc Tuymans paintings that I had brought with me, and the commentary to the paintings that Tuymans had attached. *Body*, one of his best-known images, shows the headless and legless torso of a school-age girl. It is ghostly with a dull, cracked surface, and bled of all colour. 'It is the torso of a doll, with a zip fastener in the middle so that you can open it up to put in stuffing and give it volume, a meaning,' Tuymans says of this small work. 'You can hardly see that the body looks as though it is injured, suffering the effects of cruelty. The zip fastener acts like a wound, like a cut.'

Body is the painting of a child that is in fact a doll. *Silence* depicts a doll that turns out to be a child. It is equally anaemic; equally mute. 'Beneath its closed eyes two colours appear, green and orange, which, taken together, form a superimposition. They indicate that the face is maimed from within, that it is ill,' Tuymans explains. 'It is as though the child has been infected by a virus which has spread through its whole body. The painting corresponds to complete silence.'

There are others: *Silent Music*, which is an airless nursery room, stuffed with sinister furniture; *Smell*, based on the deodorant blocks you find in toilets; *Incest*, the abstraction of a hand sticking through something. The surface of *Gas Chamber*, on the other hand, which you would expect to be blackly sombre, is suffused with a honeyed orange glow. 'The picture radiates both fear and human warmth. That's actually its meaning. To approach the really terrible thing that cannot be depicted.'

'Phantom figuration' and 'ghost painting' are some of the things Tuymans' style has been called. His pictures are universally bleak, gloomy even; indifferent; petrified. They seem shockingly casual – casually daubed with a scratchy brush while his mind was absent, thinking of something else. Tuymans' paintings are like half-thoughts; they are notoriously elusive (but they stay around – they are haunting; they haunt you): they have been likened to overexposed photographs, or barely legible images on shrouds.

We departed Lille and I flipped to the front of the book, where there was an interview with Tuymans. Q: 'Some of your paintings focus on the representation of childhood. Some details induce the viewer to think about childhood as fraught with horror, with unease, open to torment, abuse, ailment.' A: 'The idea of fear is pretty much embedded in my personality. Constant fear and constant uneasiness . . . Fear of the dark, of physical mutilation, which were instilled very early on in me.' In answer to another question: 'For me, it's impossible to make a joyful painting.'

His studio is in a working-class district of Antwerp, mainly occupied by Moroccans. Now aged forty-two, Tuymans has had the place – 'I regard it as a kind of protective shell' – for more than half his life. He doesn't live there any more, but it's pretty obvious that the cheerless atmosphere and air of near-dereliction sustain something that he needs for his painting, much as Francis Bacon liked to throw on dust, dirt, candle wax. (Norman Rosenthal says he found Tuymans' studio strongly reminiscent of Bacon's reeking, rubbish-strewn London studio in South Kensington. For the record, Tuymans is not an admirer of Bacon's; he finds him an 'utter academic'.)

Tuymans works onto unstretched canvas, nailed to the wall —
paintings of King Leopold and other emblems of the Belgian
imperium in the Congo, when I was there; pictures that were
uncharacteristic of Tuymans in their generosity of scale and use
of colour and even allusions to a narrative element. Also some
smaller works, painted direct onto newspaper, for an upcom-
ing show in Japan.

Most of his pictures depict rooms. Some of the rooms are
evidently, or by implication, the scene of a crime. *Bloodstains*
and *Child Abuse* are self-explanatory. *Apple* is the image of a
decaying apple, taken from a police archive photograph of a
murder scene. Tuymans works in a very small room with a big
mirror. It can feel as if there's something a bit Rillington Place
about it, a bit immanent and loaded — forensic, evidentiary —
when you come to it fresh from the work.

Plus Tuymans isn't exactly overburdened with social skills.
He seemed offhand and quite prepared to be disliked, always a
good sign. He chain smokes. He's arrogant. A mountain of
dog-ends was spilling out of a deep bowl onto the floor. For an
ashtray he used the kind of small round mirror you expect to
find in a budgie's cage; it sat on the arm of an armchair that had
its stuffing poking out looking, with the light swimming in it,
like the kind of indeterminate, shifting image he likes to make
in paint. A scab that turns out to be an embroidered flower. A
skull that turns out to be the X-ray of a diseased tooth. An
obscene gash that turns out to be the shadow thrown by a small
girl's knee.

Tuymans says he likes an image to stale. He picks it and then
lets it hang around long enough to go dead on him before he
tries to resuscitate it in paint. No painting takes longer than a
day, an unbreakable rule. There are preparatory drawings and
watercolour sketches and then — indifferently, eventually — the

small, malignly resonating, creepily beautiful, real thing. Occasionally the thing Tuymans finds on the wall staring back at him has the power to unnerve even him. This happened with the painting called *Child Abuse*. 'The colours are exaggerated, ugly. They glow dimly . . . I painted the picture quite unconsciously, and even I was shocked by the result . . . The idea of subversion, a perversity, becomes apparent in it.'

Tuymans' work, like much of the work on show over the next three months at the Royal Academy, represents a kind of anti-sublime – what the artist Jake Chapman has called, only half-jokingly, a 'degenerate sublime'. It takes art about as far from the pleasure principle as it can be taken. In Tuymans' case, this is conscious. His work, he will patiently explain, sets out to reveal the cruelty and harshness of things. He despises a painter like Kandinsky for whom painting aspired to the condition of music. There's no place in Tuymans' life for music. He never listens to the radio. He told me he has never bought a record. 'Never. Not one. I have no urge to buy – what you call them – CDs. I'm not so much interested in the spiritual aspects of culture – "beauty" or poetic descriptions of beauty don't seem real enough for me. Reality is actually far more important than any form of spirituality. Realism. It's much more interesting to crawl from underneath to the so-called top.'

It is all obviously a long way from Matisse, who famously spoke of his art of 'serenity, balance and repose' as providing restoration 'like a good armchair'. But maybe this is inevitable. Good art sucks in the psyche of its time, and our time isn't about beauty and order and the imitation of nature. Disorder, fear, Bacon's 'smell of death' were the central twentieth-century experiences.

Antwerp, where Tuymans lives, and Mönchengladbach on

the German–Dutch border, where Gregor Schneider, another Apocalypse contributor, has a house, are both about seventy kilometres from Charlerois in southern Belgium. Charlerois is where Marc Dutroux lived. Dutroux, who still hasn't come to trial, is accused of the abduction of six young girls and the murder of four of them. Two of the children, just eight years old, were kept locked in a small cell in Dutroux's basement, where eventually they starved to death while their captor was in prison for four months. After the police arrested Dutroux, they discovered two other abducted girls, aged twelve and fourteen, still alive in the home-made dungeon. 'They were held in a white-painted concrete "cave" measuring 2m by 3m,' *Time* reported. 'The cell was cleverly concealed by sliding doors behind a basement cabinet.'

There is an uncanny correspondence between this description of Dutroux's terrifying 'dungeon' – and the disgusting reality of the Wests' cellar in Cromwell Street in Gloucester – and the dark, dank room that Gregor Schneider has installed at the Royal Academy. It is the cellar of his own plain house in Rheydt, a suburb of Mönchengladbach, hacked out stone by stone and removed bodily to London.

The atmosphere of ominousness and dread that the three spaces have in common may be coincidental, but it isn't accidental. Although he is still only thirty-one, Schneider has an interest in murder and what he calls 'places charged with a strong past event, but from which the event itself is absent' which dates back many years. His work, according to Rosenthal, 'exists in a space between the normal and the pathological'. The 'guest room' of Schneider's house in Rheydt has no windows and is clad with sheets of soundproofing and an insulating lead covering. (Luc Tuymans has coincidentally done a set of paintings called Sealed Rooms. Mike

Kelley has incorporated crawl spaces into several works.) The house is riddled with the crawl spaces and deep shafts that Schneider has been excavating and modifying and concealing since he was sixteen. As a schoolboy, he obsessively photographed a place in the woods where a female art student had been murdered.

The interesting thing is that both Tuymans and Schneider had been set on their paths for many years before the national trauma of Dutroux. For his last show in New York, it was naturally assumed that Tuymans was making allusions to the paedophile scandal that had wracked his country, and to the occasion of the White March in Brussels, when 300,000 took to the streets to protest against the official incompetence and corruption that had made the system rotten. It was natural to assume it. But it wasn't necessarily the case.

'Until that point,' Tuymans says, 'everybody looked at Belgium as being like a small country in which people are a little bit stupid but they like to eat well. They don't think that much. Then with this Dutroux character, the whole perception changed. It has been a very disgusting time for this country because it just depoliticised everything. In that you have these house fathers that come onto the streets with white balloons and some fucked-up consciousness, which is naturally very hypocritical. Because all those men probably would have liked to fuck a Thai girl of fifteen years old, but not the innocence of the nation. It has completely psychologically disturbed the country. And it has created tendencies which are not really worthy to talk about, I think. Like this Dutroux being talked about as "the face of evil". Which is like the Middle Ages, to iconise the evil in a person in such an unsubtle way. Like a witch-hunt . . . We have come to be seen as what we are, of course — a very corrupted society, to a point exceedingly sinister. But the system was dissolute and rotten to the bone far before Dutroux.'

The mass demonstrations in Belgium happened in 1996. A year later they were re-enacted in microcosm in London when relatives of child murder victims and MAMA (Mothers Against Murder and Aggression) descended on Burlington House in Piccadilly to plead with people queuing for the Sensation show not to enter because it featured a billboard-size portrait of the murderer Myra Hindley by Marcus Harvey. Shortly afterwards two men vandalised the picture. The *Mirror* featured the damaged painting in full colour on its front page accompanied by the caption: 'Exhibited by the Royal Academy in the so-called name of art, defaced by the people in the name of common decency'.

Myra, like everything else in Sensation, was owned by Charles Saatchi. Saatchi's position as the most powerful collector of this kind of art in Europe is unassailable. It is precisely his status as a 'power mongrel' which makes Luc Tuymans disinclined to sell to him. 'The grip he holds has molested a lot of possibilities,' Tuymans says. 'In the last ten years Charles Saatchi has stripped the art of its political content.'

Tuymans' work would be drowned out in the Saatchi collection (as it might well be in the bombast of Apocalypse). It doesn't make a lot of noise. Like the guest in Schneider's lead-lined room, the paintings fester inside their own repelling, chilly aura. His aim isn't to beautify something that is already in the world, merely to state its (often unpretty) existence. 'To be unspectacular. To be spectacular in all the unspectacular ways.' They remind me of something Italo Calvino wrote just before he died: 'Knowledge of the world means dissolving the solidity of the world . . . Were I to choose an auspicious image for the new millennium, [it would be] the sudden agile leap of the poet-philosopher who raises himself above the weight of the world, showing that with all his gravity he has the secret of lightness, and that what many consider to be the vitality of the times — noisy, aggressive, revving and roaring — belongs to the realm of death, like a cemetery for rusty old cars.'

2000

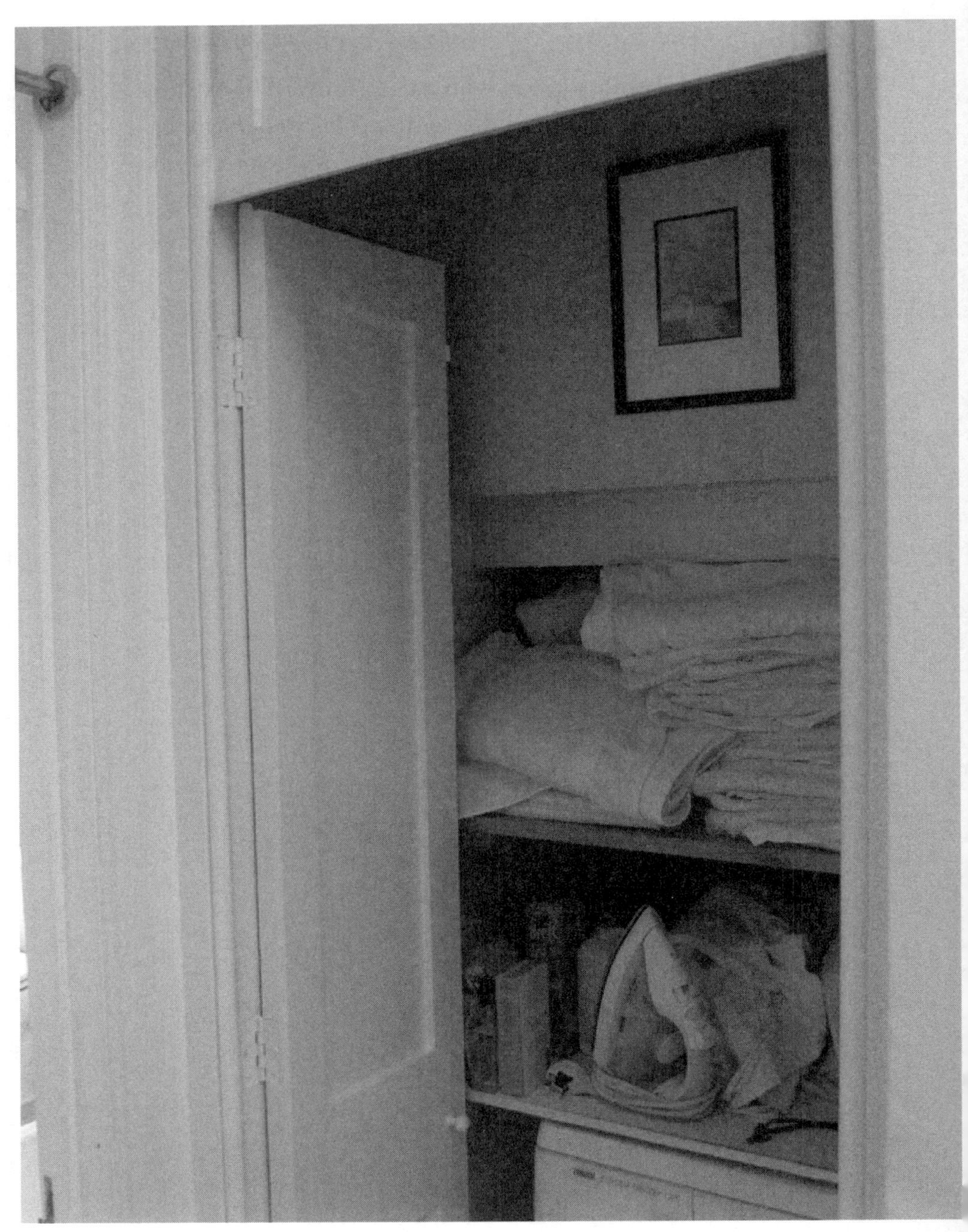

Gregor Schneider, *Liebeshaus*, in GB's airing cupboard

GREGOR SCHNEIDER

Whose house is this?
Whose night keeps out the light
In here?
Say, who owns this house?
It's not mine.
I had another, sweeter, brighter
With a view of lakes crossed in painted boats;
Of fields wide as arms open for me.
This house is strange.
Its shadows lie.
Say, tell me, why does its lock fit my key?

Toni Morrison, 'Whose House Is This?'

It's my home, and I have worked to make it beautiful. Nothing bad ever happened to me here. No grisly murders were committed here and no bodies buried. It is not a house of horrors but a very nice home.

Sonia Sutcliffe, wife of Peter Sutcliffe,
the Yorkshire Ripper, speaking in 1982

The Yorkshire Ripper was the first serial killer I wrote about, in a book published in 1984. I returned to the subject for the second, and final, time in 1998 with *Happy Like Murderers*. This told the story of the West murders — also known as the 'House of Horror' murders — which came to light in the pretty English cathedral town of Gloucester in 1994. Fred West was a self-employed jobbing builder. Together with his much younger wife Rose, West sexually tortured and murdered thirteen young women and girls over a period of about twenty years. The bodies, including that of the Wests' sixteen-year-old daughter Heather, were buried under the patio, in the cellar and under a bathroom floor of the outwardly unremarkable house where the couple lived with their remaining seven children at 25 Cromwell Street.

The Wests worked in tandem, cruising the streets for female hitch-hikers, runaways and girls from broken homes. They trussed them and gagged them with masking tape and kept them hanging from beams in the basement until their lust had burned itself out. The victims were decapitated and dismembered and forced into narrow pits in the ground.

It is well established that Gregor Schneider has a lifelong interest in scenes of crime. As a schoolboy he obsessively photographed a place in the woods where a female art student had been murdered. He has been interested to discover 'whether a scream would stay behind in a room after you had left it'. Under the floors at Unterheydener Strasse 12 in Rheydt there is a birdcage, dead animals, inflatable dolls. 'I'd love to stop someone getting away one time,' Schneider has said, 'but I have never dared to yet. I'm one of those people who live double lives and go out into the park at night and sift through the litter bins and secretly take something home with me . . . I assume that there are others working at it and I will probably never meet the best ones.'

Schneider's work, like the work of many of the artists he showed with in Apocalypse at the Royal Academy in London in 2000, represents what Jake Chapman has called a 'degenerate sublime'. In a way, Schneider is part of a tradition in German art dating back to Otto Dix and George Grosz who, in the period between the wars, produced numerous gruesome images of the *Lustmord* – sexual murder. In some of their paintings and drawings the criminal has the unmistakable, if caricatured, features of the artist himself.

The Wests were arrested in 1994. Fred West hanged himself in prison before he could be brought to trial. In 1995 Rose West was found guilty on all thirteen counts of murder and jailed for the rest of her life. By 1995 Gregor Schneider had been locked into his parallel endeavour at Haus ur in Rheydt for ten years – 'Wall before wall, wall before wall, wall behind wall, passage in room, room in room, passage in room, wall before wall, blue paper area on wall, room in room, room in room, red stone behind room, lead around room, lead in floor . . .'; the litany of burrowing and secrecy and obsessive, tireless shape-shifting and modification that is now so well known.

Writers rarely read their old work: I hadn't opened *Happy Like Murderers* for several years until I returned to it for the purposes of this essay. Fred West, of course, was a creep and a degenerate, an amoral psychopath. Gregor Schneider is incontrovertibly a person of high artistic seriousness – a serious artist who, in order to achieve a special kind of beauty – the dire excitement of fear; the terrible beauty of the cheapened urban experience – is prepared to transgress the established order of things. Two very variously evolved examples of what we think it means to be human.

And yet, re-reading what I had written about the murderer West's devotion to his house and his fetishistic absorption in his materials, I was struck by the disturbing adjacency of transgression in its violent and artistic forms – of the nuzzling closeness of artistic creativity and violence. Impressed, also, by how, implicitly, and even explicitly ('I'd love to stop someone getting away one time'), Gregor Schneider's work challenges our easy assumption that art is something always good and at worst benign.

For example, Schneider: 'I am always making, I always have to be making things. That is my personal problem . . . My work is really about the fact that I am always starting work again.'

Happy Like Murderers, pp. 185–6:

His house would exist in a state of becoming which would last not just for two or three years but for nearly twenty years. All his life in this house. Constant digging, demolition, excavation. The house was a building site. Always Fred did the work. Fred alone or Fred working with somebody else. When he wasn't at work he was working on the house. Re-wiring, re-plumbing, roofing, digging up floors, pouring new footings. New roof. New windows. He painted the outside. Cladding. Skimming. Decorating inside. Always rubble and noise . . . After Rose – perhaps even before Rose – the house was his most precious possession. He invested everything he was and had in it. He had an impoverished, perverted and murkily complex interior life. And whether he intended it or not 25 Cromwell Street would in time grow into the fullest expression of it. He loved the house. He was so proud of what he had achieved that he would strike up conversations with strangers in the street and invite them in for a guided tour of it . . . He would waylay them and give them the tour . . .

Making and constructing. Working and making. Activities that always held more meaning for him than unmaking a person. Buckets of lime. Sacks of cement. Sewer pipes. Shovels. Back axles. Ice-knives. Rakes. The sheath knife that he always carried on his belt. An actual dagger, used for laying felt . . . He loved the house. He was so proud of the house. Every penny they had for many years went into the house. The house that they built with their bare hands together.

Schneider: 'As soon as someone spends any time in a room, you accept it as a normal room.'

Schneider: 'Corpses always lie in the cellar. Perhaps I am the one that can't get out.'

Happy Like Murderers, pp. 198–9:

Fred didn't allow anybody down in the cellar in the beginning, only himself. He'd just lock off the doors and do what he was doing. He'd just bolt them shut and they would hear the sound of work being carried out. For years he would say he was going down to see to the drains in the basement to stop this water coming up. A preoccupation that started in the weeks before and the months immediately after moving into Cromwell Street. From the beginning the many possibilities of the cellar excited him. He was going to have it as a bar with card schools. He talked a lot about making films in it — bringing in prostitutes from Birmingham and elsewhere and making home-made pornographic movies. Or he could make it his torture chamber, he joked . . . A break in the sewer pipe that ran under the house and a rise in the water table were the reasons he gave for the powerful attachment that became evident between Fred and the cellar at Cromwell Street. He could stay down there for hours apparently trying to work out a way to stem the rise of thick murky water that had reached ankle-height and was relentlessly rising. To repel the inrush of the sewage — the thick, consistent water — that all the time now in their new home was threatening to engulf them.

Not difficult to see from this how the cellar represented the unconscious for the psychoanalyst C. G. Jung. Jung compared the rationality of the roof to the irrationality of the cellar. Up near the roof all our thoughts are clear. In the attic it is a pleasure to see the bare rafters of the strong framework. In the cellar darkness prevails both day and night, and even when we are carrying a lighted candle we see shadows dancing on the dark walls. In the attic rats and mice can make considerable noise but they are easily frightened into returning to the silence of their holes. The creatures moving about in the cellar are slower, less scampering, more mysterious.

Scenes from the early life of Gregor Schneider show him to be death-bothered and indicate an incontrovertible disposition, well in advance of the usual childhood fascination with bogeymen and creepy-crawlies, towards the black-hearted macabre.

Schneider grew up in a landscape of dust and fumes and

dirty, heavy industry. Rheydt, his home town on the outskirts of Mönchengladbach, where he still lives, has traditionally been a centre for opencast mining, although many of the mining villages are now shut down and deserted. The house he grew up in was part of the lead-making factory that has been in his family for five generations. The house – now known to gallery-goers internationally as Totes Haus (Dead House) ur – acted as a kind of baffle between the factory and the Schneiders' Unterheydener Strasse neighbours, who have always taken exception to the unsightliness and the noxious gases Bliewerk Schneider emits. Schneider's father used to run the business; two of his brothers have taken over since their father's death.

Little Gregor (he was born in 1969) must have been a worry to his mother. He was not as other children. None of his friends, for example, lay in bed at night working out the practicalities of how to completely isolate themselves – from noise, from evidence of any other living presence – by lining their rooms with four-foot layers of lead, glass fibre, soundproofing materials and other stuff. (*Completely Insulated Death Room* would be finished in 1991.) None of them coated their faces and naked bodies in a doughy mixture of meal and water and cycled through the cold to school; or, if they did, they certainly didn't refer to the end result as 'body art'. Gregor was an avid admirer of a Canadian called John Fare who removed various bits of his body in a slow and bloody process of auto-amputation.

Home alone, Gregor filled a coffin-shaped box with wet cement and lay face down in it, with a chisel at hand in case things went kerflooey. The original idea had been to make a second impression of his back and, unaided, flip the first entombing slab on top of himself, but this proved impractical.

Around this time he was earning pocket money working at the local Catholic cemetery, where he learned many things. One of these was never to take the position at the front left of the coffin because that was where you caught the worst of the death smell. Sometimes his English is not so good: he mimes bending to take the handle of the coffin; he shows you how they slowly lowered the ropes into the grave. Three funerals a day. In between he got a lot of reading done. He smiles broadly.

When he was sixteen, Schneider's parents moved to the suburbs, leaving him in the house overlooking the factory yard in Rheydt on his own. When he paid him a visit his father hurt his leg in one of the several traps Gregor had set in the floor. There's a B&Q megastore conveniently situated on the other side of Unterheydener Strasse, and Schneider started making day-long visits. He bought industrial quantities of plastic sheeting, cement, piping and ventilation grilles. The lead, whose lethal molten condition and psychedelically coloured drying surface had always absorbed him, came free.

Without knowing exactly what he was doing, or where it was leading, he set to work. Walls were built in front of walls, windows in front of windows, ceilings were rigged to rise and fall unseen. His *Coffee Room* rotates 360 degrees imperceptibly on its own axis: leaving by the door they arrived through, visitors risk stepping into a void.

In 1997, as work on the West book neared completion, Gregor Schneider swam into my consciousness for the first time. He had a show just before Christmas of that year at the Sadie Coles Gallery in London. In addition to the glitter ball from the 'brothel' in the cellar, and unplaceable lumps of debris from the house in Rheydt, *Puff* (Knocking Shop) featured a series of small, amateurishly framed, black-and-white photographs of the rooms at Haus ur. *Liebeslaube* (Love Nest) showed a narrow cell with a bed, a bath and a hotplate: the idea was that it contained all that was necessary for human existence and the person inside need never leave. What it didn't show was that the room was entered by a damp crawl space under the sink. I bought the picture and fixed it to the cladding around the cold-water tank in the airing cupboard. It still hangs in the dark in the airing cupboard, along with the clean linen, and the dirty washing, and the washing machine.

A couple of years ago Schneider started working with human 'collaborators'. In *N. Schmidt* (2001–3), Schneider's probably fictitious 'lodger' had to lie on a gallery floor playing dead. In *Old House-Slut* (2000–3), a woman had to lie on a gallery floor looking raped and dead. For *Rubbish Bag in Wanking Corner* (1999) Schneider himself crouched in the bag of the title for seven hours, all-seeing but invisible, and nobody ever knew he was there.

Die Familie Schneider last autumn in London featured living, breathing, wanking people and represented a startling, and hugely risky, change of direction. Adjacent houses in a Victorian terrace in Whitechapel in East London had been acquired. The houses were decorated and 'distressed' to Schneider's exact specifications. Down to the tiniest wallpaper tear and fungoidal ceiling stain, they were identical. For the duration of the show they were be occupied by two 'families' of identical twins whose movements throughout a seven-hour day were co-ordinated precisely. Only one visitor was admitted at a time. Nobody under the age of sixteen was allowed in. The address was available only on application.

Shortly before the opening, I talked to Schneider in one of

the upstairs bedrooms at number 14. It had been given a kind of seedy cheap glamour: cream 'boudoir' carpet, cream vanity units, what Schneider described as 'porno' mirrors. There was no natural light; a wall had been erected in front of the window; we were in a room-within-a-room. From the street, though, it looked as if the window and the room behind it were still as they were; 'normal'. Both houses were, in fact, sealed off from the outside world. They were flocked and dado-railed tombs.

Schneider had just been back to Rheydt to make a decision about a headstone for his father, who had died recently. As the artist of Family Schneider this responsibility fell to him. In his role as altar boy, he attended at the ceremony when the new Catholic cemetery opened. 'It was empty. Now my father's in,' he said. 'Now it spreads and spreads.'

It grew late. It had been raining. We walked in the direction of Whitechapel via the London Hospital. Outside the hospital, a young woman was screaming into a mobile phone; she was sobbing and screaming, her body shaking. An IV patch showed in the space between her top and her trousers. 'I'm fucking cracking up! I can't fucking take it!' We sought help from two paramedics who were having a smoke by their ambulance. They shrugged. 'We don't work here. We just bring them in.' But they went over to the woman, who was spasming now and had slumped to the pavement.

We were headed for the Blind Beggar, scene of one of the Kray brothers' most notorious gangland slayings. The twins' portraits grace the walls. There are posters advertising Kray walks and Jack the Ripper tours, something I thought Schneider would be interested to see. But he stopped suddenly. He felt tired, he said. He thought he should go home.

I suspected that he wanted to see what had happened with

the young woman, not in a voyeuristic way but to reacquaint himself with that kind of abjectness and human misery. To look at it and remember and take it back to the houses where in the morning work would be continuing with the mildewing and bruising and the calling back of things which might or might not have happened inside those walls.

'Anything bad ever happen in this house, Frank?' a house-hunter asks the realtor-narrator of Richard Ford's novel, *Independence Day*.

'Nothing I know about,' Frank Bascombe replies. 'I guess all houses have pasts. The ones I lived in all sure did. Somebody's bound to have died in some room here sometime. I just don't know who.'

2005

COURT ARTISTS

Priscilla Coleman got her first sight of Rosemary West at an early remand hearing in Gloucester. 'Big ole baggy ole T-shirt,' she remembers. 'Big ole hangin' boobs. She didn't look like a prostitute to me, not how you expect a prostitute to look. You expect a prostitute to wear, you know, make-up.'

By the time she came to trial more than a year later, 'the most depraved woman on Earth', as the tabloids dubbed her, had respectablised herself with an ersatz gentility which she displayed in court every day: the matronly dress and little ankle boots that one of her daughters had kitted her out with; the bows of exaggerated deference towards the judge; the wearing of a poppy in the week before Armistice Day. Prevented by an Act of Parliament dating back to 1925 from drawing even a line in court, Coleman jotted notes to herself about all of this, as well as West's habitual notepad and balled tissues and beakers of water. She noted her comparing manicures with the female prison officer sitting in the dock beside her while the court heard details of child rape, sado-masochism, sexual abuse and torture.

Searching for the terribleness of her 'inner being', reporters and court artists scrutinised Mrs West compulsively for six weeks, hoping to catch a glimpse of the intimate and unintended. She showed signs of agitation sometimes: her tongue would flick out, a finger would wipe behind her enormous glasses. She appeared to cry in earnest, although reflexively, whenever her daughter Heather's name was mentioned. Called to the witness stand for her evidence, she proved lumpen, intractable, as uncommunicative as the walls and bricked-up windows of the house at 25 Cromwell Street.

'I found her easy, to be truthful,' Coleman says of the many portraits of Rosemary West that her ITN contract required her to make. 'Oh, easy. I thought so. You could almost put on a disguise of Rose West in a way. Her big glasses. Her little boots. Her slightly kinked hair. It got easier. Just automatic, really.'

The French artist Christian Boltanski once spent a year clipping images of criminals and their victims from *Detective*, a weekly tabloid that focuses on grisly tragedies. What attracted him to these images was the fact that, once a photograph was separated from its caption, it was impossible to distinguish victim from criminal. 'He has the face of a Nobel Peace Prize winner,' Boltanski has said of the Nazi war criminal Klaus Barbie. 'It would be easier if a terrible person had a terrible face.'

'One of the most shocking things', Nicci Gerrard wrote about the trial of Harold Shipman, the family doctor from Cheshire who was found guilty of murdering fifteen of his female patients, 'was how Shipman did not become a figure of horror, the stuff of our nightmares . . . He is a smallish, thinnish man with a respectable paunch. He has a pale grey beard and dark grey, thinning hair and wears grey-brown suits, conservative ties, thick-lensed spectacles. With his dry and narrow face, his scratchy, pedantic voice, his tetchy manner, he is like an old-fashioned schoolteacher or a middle-ranking civil servant.'

'I imagined him to be an ugly hunchback wi' boils all over his face,' Carl Sutcliffe said when his brother Peter was named as the Yorkshire Ripper. 'Pete had everything going for him. Nice house, steady job, enough money, good-looking . . . He were totally different to what I imagined this murderer to be.'

At the centre of the media spectacle surrounding every sensational murder trial in this country are two near-primitive, inextricably linked, instantly recognisable ritual events. The first involves the arrival at court of the accused, head wrapped in a heavy coat or prison blanket, stumbling, blinded; the nightmare image of a hooded, stooped, creeped-out creature. The second, following hard on the heels of the first, is the creature revealed: the artist's impression, in scumbled chalk and scratchy pastels and deadline-chasing approximations, of what the prisoner looked like in the dock. And what he looked like (it is almost always a he) always has a touch of the Madame Tussaud's about it; specifically, the Chamber of Horrors, a fixture of the waxworks dating back to the eighteenth century when it was known as the 'Separate Room'.

In the case of both Tussaud's and the courtroom artists we are offered a representation modelled directly from an actual body in a tenebrous medium which appears somehow to incorporate sloughed skin and cobwebs and dust. The subjects of the drawings have temporarily travelled to another realm, one where we hope never to have to follow them. They are experiencing a different consciousness or state of being, removed from the banal circumstances that circumscribe all our lives.

Although they are increasingly under threat, and are currently being squeezed by transcripted re-enactments (Sky) and 360-degree electronic simulations (ITN, BBC), these archaically hand-crafted depictions have earned a place in the visual language of print and broadcast journalism. They declare their independence from the incessant flow of images made possible by the camera, and cut through the astonishing, wearying density of the advertising environment.

489

Curiously, waxworkers have always been women. And all the main British television outlets have traditionally turned to women artists to bring us the news – darker and darker news, in the words of Don DeLillo, of a world of extreme anger and danger – from the back of the cave.

'History in a hurry' is a well-established definition of journalism. And sometimes court artists like Priscilla Coleman and Julia Quenzler, who works for the BBC, only have fifteen minutes to weigh up a defendant (or defendants – in the recent case of the Afghan hijackers there were thirteen in the dock) before scuttling off to fix as much as they can on paper before the image begins to dull. Because the law only allows them to make written notes in court, they write shorthand remarks about size of head, shape of nose, colour of tie, haircut etc., without taking their eyes off the prisoner, as well as cryptic comments such as 'gt bones . . . v. pretty silver hair . . . a v. glam older man . . . like an eagle' (Priscilla Coleman on Lord Hutton).

Quenzler and Coleman spent half their summer at the Hutton inquiry at the Royal Courts of Justice in the Strand. I came across them one morning hurrying through the courtyard that separated Court 73 from the gloomy, lancet-windowed, Victorian Gothic dungeon where they were doing their drawing. It was the day the Prime Minister was giving evidence. And after a succession of senior civil servants and distinguished balding men with beards – spooks in suits; tedious to draw – anticipation was high and the adrenalin was pumping. They both had to have drawings ready to be filmed by 11.30 in time to go out on the lunchtime news.

'He is so nervous,' Quenzler said of Blair without breaking stride. 'He doesn't know what to do with his hands. He doesn't know what he's doing with his glasses. He's wearing new glasses. They're off. They're on . . .' She flipped open her notebook to a page which seemed to show a flock of seagulls flying in formation. This was a note to herself about the way Blair chopped and sliced, unflaggingly articulated with his hands. 'He seems very unnerved, and I have to say you can hardly blame him. He's the most nervous witness we've had so far.'

It's a point of honour with both women not to make any preparatory drawings before going into court. They see their task as being about reacting and responding in the moment. (They drop dark hints that not all of their colleagues work like this.) The work is not an attempt to recreate something; it's an account of seeing it. 'You have to be prepared for changes, alert not to what you're expecting, but to what you see,' Quenzler says. 'On the day – posture, attitude, body language. There's no point in depending on photographs. Forget photographs. You're in real trouble if you go down that road.' Coleman said Tony Blair was somebody she had found particularly difficult to second-guess. 'Is it going to be the face-lift look, the blond look, statesman grey, tanned, drawn, jowly, new haircut . . . I think he did a Caesar haircut one time.'

Coleman's and Quenzler's drawings seem a fair reflection of their personalities. Quenzler: focused, precise, detailed, forensic. She is English, camera-shy (weirdly – or probably because of the fact of spending her life interrogating other people's faces), lives in a chocolate-box cottage in a village in Sussex, has been a court artist for more than twenty years. Coleman's sketches are animated, quirky, boldly coloured within the restraints of such a muted form, with an abundance of surface energy. She is American, born in Houston, married to an Englishman, retained by ITN for fifteen years.

Julia Quenzler has a tendency to home in on the principal

players in a case: terse two- and three-handers, featuring judge, defendant, counsel for the defence or prosecution, enough to give her producer room to roam around within the frame. Coleman's pictures, by contrast, are teeming, Rowlandson-like, even Hogarthian, occasionally almost verging on the carnivalesque. She has a talent for particularising the large supporting cast in her drawings as well as the main actors and is a popular figure around the Royal Courts of Justice and the Old Bailey for this willingness to look beyond the depersonalising court mufti. (There may be a canny business sense at play here as well, of course: barristers and others are always asking for her work for their chambers, and the greater the number of recognisable figures, the wider the circle of potential buyers.) And it always helps to have contacts. On the occasion when a prisoner managed to vault the dock and punch Judge Ann Goddard in the face, Coleman's eyes, as she puts it, were on another case. But the clerk of the court was not only happy to describe to her what had happened so she could recreate it; he climbed on the bench and posed as Judge Goddard's attacker for her in another part of the Bailey. 'I think there was glass, too. So I had to get shards and water. But Judge Goddard's always easy to do. Motherly like. And always red lipstick. Bright red lips are almost her trademark.'

When her drawing of Tony Blair was finished – it had taken her a little under half an hour; her reputation is largely based on her quickness – Coleman rushed it over to 'the island' to be filmed. 'The island' is how everybody in the media contingent refers to the paved area around the church of St Clement Danes which has squatted in the middle of the main thoroughfare between Fleet Street and the Strand for several centuries. It shares the spit of land with a below-ground gentlemen's toilet and a statue of Samuel Johnson. A Caffè Nero beaker, a balled sandwich wrapper and a plastic mineral water bottle had been wedged in the space between Dr Johnson's feet. The church was hemmed in on one side by equipment trucks and outside-broadcast vehicles and on the other by the paraphernalia of the half-dozen camera crews who were bivouacking there for the duration. White lights came on as the reporters, tied and suited above the belt, bejeaned below, ran through their pieces to camera. Coleman whipped her drawing out of a portfolio and Blu-Tacked it to an engraved tablet set into the church wall commemorating the day in 1958 when the Queen dedicated St Clement Danes to the Royal Air Force. Her fingers were stained from the pastels; she used her thumb to muck around a bit of background colouring, stepped back, and mucked around some more. Her Pradas were deep in pigeon droppings – 'pigeon doo-doo', as she calls it – and, as she waited for her cameraman to come and shoot her drawing, a woman arrived with a bag of breadcrumbs for the birds that descended in a flea-infested grey cloud from the roof of the church.

One of the other court artists, Elizabeth Cook, who is retained by Sky, frequently does her drawing in full public view out on the pavement and she says she has been added to the tourist itinerary, the guides on the sightseeing buses pointing out this piece of street theatre – 'All her own work!' – as they pass along Fleet Street and across Farringdon on the way to the Old Bailey and St Paul's.

'Fleet Street', Peter Ackroyd notes in his 'biography' of London, 'is an example of the city's topographical imperative, whereby the same activity takes place over hundreds of years in the same small area.' George Cruikshank drew the condemned cells behind the 'dreadful walls' of Newgate prison, which was eventually demolished at the beginning of the last century to make way for the Old Bailey. The most notable painter of the day, Sir James Thornhill, visited the legendary robber and prison breaker Jack Sheppard in Newgate in 1724 in order to complete a portrait which was then sold to the public as a mezzotint. Thornhill's son-in-law, William Hogarth, 'himself could not resist the lineaments of the condemned', according to Ackroyd. 'When in 1761 Theodore Gardelle was about to be hanged at the corner of Panton Street and the Haymarket, Hogarth captured his countenance "with a few swift strokes".' The press room deep in the bowels of the Old Bailey where today's court artists do their work is on the site of the dungeon where prisoners in the seventeenth and eighteenth centuries were literally pressed to death: they were stripped 'and put in low dark chambers, with as much weight of iron placed upon them as they could bear, and more, there to lie until they were dead'.

'What does it mean psychologically and socially to be a woman . . . imagining slaughter, trauma, combat and atrocity?' Elaine Showalter asked in the *Guardian* recently, reviewing Pat Barker's latest novel, *Double Vision*. 'In interviews, Barker has described the novelist's role as akin to the therapist's — the invisible witness, protected from contagion . . . She sees the novelist as "totally involved but also totally detached . . . enabling you to take hot coals out of the fire without being burned". This oven-mitt view of authorship, however, seems naive or evasive, especially from a writer so immersed in psychiatric and psychoanalytic theory. Having written profoundly about the counter-transferences in the therapeutic relationship of [the psychologist W. H. R.] Rivers and [First World War poet Siegfried] Sassoon, Barker cannot believe that the artist is immune to horror and trauma.'

'The point is not to be upset, to be able to confront the horrible with equanimity,' Susan Sontag wrote — not with approval — in *On Photography*. 'Gazing on other people's reality with curiosity, with detachment, with professionalism . . . The important thing is not to blink.'

Many of the cases Coleman and Quenzler have to sit through involve men terrorising and torturing or murdering helpless women and children. They have to look at the accused and fix his image on their retina; imprint it on their brain with no guarantee that they can ever erase it. In her early years, working for a television station in Texas in the seventies, Coleman had to do many drawings of prisoners being given lethal injections. These were reconstructions made on the basis of what her cameraman and other eyewitnesses were able to tell her. But she says she would have watched if she could. She joined the queue to witness a lethal injection once but didn't get in. She says she would watch today if somebody asked her.

'I did the Candy Man who killed his own son on Halloween for his insurance. I worked from reference photos of him strapped to the gurney. I did Carla Fay Tucker, the axe murderess . . . Oh, tons of them. But I guess Texas is really so full of this kind of thing that it got so everyday we stopped covering it. Terrible, I know, but it's a fact of life.'

When I asked her whether the evidence of sordidness and corruption she was continually exposed to had changed her view of human nature, she said, 'You want to know have I become a horrible old cynic? Well, the way I see it is it's like dealing with things in the emergency room. There might be blood and guts everywhere, but you still have to get on with it.'

Coleman is not listed under that name in the telephone directory. Quenzler asked to be described as living in 'just say Sussex'. 'I won't answer any questions about my personal life,' was the first thing Elizabeth Cook said when I approached her for this article. She is the only court artist with a website. ('She stares at criminals', it informs us.) I had emailed her about an interview but she had been too nervous to open it. 'I do get inundated with, how shall I say, unnecessary messages,' she said. 'I don't want to encourage anyone.'

In the United States, artists are allowed to draw in court, and even at executions. One of them — Howard Brodie — has achieved talk-show status. An American writer has recorded how, throughout one case, the judge repeatedly told Brodie how honoured he was to have him in his courtroom. Brodie was a role model for Priscilla Coleman when she was a student just out of art school. And Julia Quenzler, who is self-taught, also encountered him many years ago when she was living in America, drawing the patrons in Beverly Hills nightclubs for twenty dollars a throw.

Howard Brodie's commitment to objectivity is something they have tried to emulate. Sympathetic without being overwhelmed; engaged but at a distance. Both agree that this is the ideal. But Quenzler acknowledges that she has been known to weep in court — 'It's the look on the faces of families of children who have been murdered when the verdict comes in and they finally have to acknowledge that this is the man who killed their child. The combination of relief and the grief is so horrific.' Priscilla Coleman says that among the things her years in court have taught her is that 'you have to keep your eyes open and be safe all the time. But women have to do that all the time anyway.'

But is it art? It isn't portraiture in any accepted sense. Portraiture belongs to the drawing room. Portrait painting tends to be consensual, a transaction voluntarily entered into by artist and sitter. It used to be congratulatory, although there are numerous examples of subjects who ended up feeling defamed or deformed by the way they had been fixed for ever in paint – Churchill, for example, who had Graham Sutherland's painting of him destroyed; and more recently Prince Philip, after he had agreed to sit for the young portrait painter Stuart Pearson Wright. Francis Bacon believed that a portrait is a form of assault, and one which may endanger the psyche. 'You have turned me into a devious-looking mountebank, full of violence, awkwardness, atrocity and stupidity, without recognisable likeness,' Thomas Carlyle roared at one of his immortalisers.

Earlier this year the three Real IRA terrorists who were eventually found guilty of being involved in the BBC and Ealing bombs were allowed to decide whether the drawings made of them in court suggested 'negative impact' or not. They decided that those made by Siân Frances, a freelance, did – they made them look 'sinister' – and her drawings were banned.

Art can be news. But news is different from art. Coleman and Quenzler describe themselves as 'artist/journalists'. Their presence in court adds a 'human element' to the coverage, and the human dimension is what can make the difference between art and news. The bold-stroke style of their drawings, their gropings and approximations, the technical flaws, speak of 'authenticity' and 'candour'. In the same way that blurred or smudged or hard-pushed telescopic images have become conventions of the tabloids' style, visually stating the technical compromises the newspaper will make in its commitment to presenting the 'real' story, the court drawings embody the immediacy of events; the sensationalism of the spectacle. Like the hacks, the court artists come to work with an empty bucket, and somebody fills it up every day.

On the opening day of the Hutton inquiry, Geoffrey

Robertson QC, representing ITN and Sky News, put the case for allowing the evidence of the inquiry's more public witnesses to be broadcast. He raised a wry smile from Priscilla Coleman when, as part of his argument, he described her drawings, and the drawings of the other court artists, as 'cartoons'. (James Dingemans, counsel to the inquiry, would later complain to the *Times* that the sketches being made of him were 'terribly inaccurate'.) 'I knocked Geoffrey Robertson out of shape because I did him too heavy,' Coleman says. 'I'd seen him in *Neighbours* — oh, it was *Home and Away* — and I remembered him being kinda, y'know, doughy'. Robertson called and wanted assurances that the picture would never be used again. She told him he knew she couldn't do that. '"You should know that, Geoffrey," I told him. "You're a barrister."' He bought the drawing.

2003

GEORGE SHAW

How does it go, 'an exile at life's feast'? George was waiting at the station, slightly agitated on account of the abuse he had just had hurled at him from some yobs in a passing car. George is an artist and therefore has no discernible shape to his day: he walks backwards and forwards to the studio where he paints, he clutters up the pub when he might be expected to have his shoulder to the wheel, he mooches about. The Erewash valley – 'the awful Erewash valley' as D. H. Lawrence referred to the place where he was born and grew up – is a place you either stay in or leave; hardly anybody is perverse enough to move there to live. As an incomer, George stands out. 'In London,' he said, 'I was regarded as a great hulking working-class piece of shit. Here, I'm seen as an Oscar Wilde figure, skipping through the daisies.'

A hungry reader, he feels slightly ashamed to be seen reading a book, or to be thought to have any interest in reading. 'Because I could be identified as being . . . well, a cunt, really.' He used to be a vegetarian and a teetotaller. Now he eats meat and sometimes has solo drinking sessions in the pubs of Langley Mill and Eastwood that go on so long that when he stands up to go home, he falls over. All the time he's sitting in pubs thinking, he's writing notes to himself about what it's like sitting in pubs having thoughts about . . . nothing much, and time hanging heavy. He reproduces these in a spooky, poison-pen upper case and has them printed as loose-leaf pamphlets with titles like 'Sort Of' and 'Nothing Much' and 'Nothing Really Happened'. 'What you writin', yooth?' is something he gets on a regular basis from the former colliers with an angry if indistinct blood memory of the superior little booksniff, Lawrence. The only reason George can think why the baboons heckled him was for being posey enough to wear sunglasses on a sunny, late-summer day. And this after his strenuous efforts to drink and meat-pie himself 'into normality'.

What a grim place Langley Mill is, just the godforsaken railway station with its urine-soaked stairs and a frayed straggle of shops gloated over by Angelo's Vegas-style chippery ('Cheapest chips in the area'). The Railway Tavern is a square lavatorial pile. Pictures of the Aldercar and Langley Mill ABC hang in the back saloon. It is noticeable that everybody in them – clean-up men, trainers, whippety boy boxers – is white; the milky, transparent white that is given a cold blue undercolour by the skeins of surface veins and seems to actually glow in the gloom of the cracked dark leather and the dark wood of the back bar. A mugshot of Hitler with the slogan 'En Memoriam' has been fly-posted on the building opposite, at the derelict corner of Elmor Street and Station Road, and is probably not unconnected to the low-placed 'I love Pakistan' sticker in the window of Khan's convenience store just a few yards away. A bunch of scrawny youths, close cousins of the boys in the boxing pictures, hang around the entrance to Heanor Haulage with a couple of pit bulls on makeshift rope leads. They saunter over to the barred side window of Khan's and bunch together in the furtive-conspicuous attitude of children pretending to carry out – or actually completing – a heavy drugs deal.

Langley Mill is in the valley; Eastwood, Lawrence's birthplace, is on the hilltop a mile away, with Derbyshire off in one direction and Nottingham in the other. The last pit in the area closed in the eighties. Two generations ago there were ten coal mines in just a few square miles and the landscape all around was filled in in shades of black. In an often-quoted essay written in 1929, the last year of his life, Lawrence railed against 'ugliness, ugliness, ugliness: meanness and formless and ugly surroundings, ugly ideals, ugly religion, ugly hopes, ugly love, ugly clothes, ugly furniture, ugly houses . . . Pull down my native village to its last brick,' he concluded, 'and make an absolute clean start.'

Today the countryside around Eastwood is blistered with man-made hills that have cattle grazing on the lower slopes. The scars of the mining past have been landscaped and reclaimed; rustically concealed. The waste tip from Brinsley colliery, where Lawrence's father worked and where his grandfather had the contract to supply thick flannel vests and moleskin trousers to the miners, has been swarded over; the railway line along which the coal wagons trundled is a nature trail; the headstocks are a picnic area. In place of the old industry, a new industry has sprung up which advertises itself in heritage signs and the names of a dozen pubs and eating places around the town: the Lawrence Snackery, the White Peacock Tea Room, Chatterley's Restaurant. There is a tourist trail, in the form of a blue line painted along the pavements and footpaths, that brings you to every Lawrence-connected building still standing. Passages from Lawrence's writing are embedded in bronze like presidential crests in certain pavements; his personal symbol, the phoenix, in polished steel in others. The terraced house where he was born, in Victoria Street, has become a Birthplace Museum. Even the rainbow — symbol in the eponymous novel of 'the earth's new architecture, the old, brittle corruption of houses and factories swept away, the world built up in a living fabric of truth, fitting to the over-arching heavens' — has been adopted as a trading name and a logo by the local bus company.

'It really makes you wonder what they would do, doesn't it?' George said. 'What they would call everything. It seems so weighted, it's almost perverse. It's almost like an unhealthy perversion of the area. It's been bent. I've always suspected that there's a degree of hostility about it all.'

You have to cross a footbridge over the motorway, coming from Langley Mill, before you reach the 'Welcome to Eastwood' sign. Somebody recently added the words 'brown town', which George guessed might be to do with drugs, 'brown' being a street name for heroin and the combined West Indian and Asian populations of Eastwood being nil. On the main shopping street in Eastwood, close to the Birthplace Museum, there are other signs: 'Say no to asylum seekers' stickers on the lamp posts; 'Where have all the boot boys gone' spray-painted on a wall. What is George doing here, in this place with its unwelcoming attitude to outsiders and its threatening atmosphere, where just standing on the wrong piece of blue line at the wrong time could easily lead, as he puts it, to you being kicked in?

The easy answer is that George met Kathryn, a teacher, and fell in love, and Kathryn comes from round here; she has family in the area and doesn't want to move away. But George is an artist, as we have already established, and art is rarely that simple or straight-ahead. Art notoriously likes to stray to those places where it most risks having its world view contradicted and its windows put in. Before moving to the Midlands, George was living in London where he had a nice life: the Royal College, parties, openings, an ambitious young gallery, buyers for his pictures, a fast-growing fashionable reputation on the art scene. When all he really wanted, it turns out, was the bum's rush, the cold shoulder, to reclaim his birthright as a neurotic boy outsider; which, of course, is something you can only do when you're on the outside.

That's why hard-drinking, horny-handed, philistine East-wood was the perfect place for sensitive, bookish, mother-fixated 'Bert' Lawrence and his fictional alter ego, Paul Morel of *Sons and Lovers*, to grow up. 'A bit poetic or a bit staying-in and a bit . . . wimpy, probably. A bit . . . effete, maybe,' is how George Shaw describes Lawrence and Paul Morel (and him-self) as adolescents and young men. 'Everybody else would be torturing dogs. Killing each other. So you would hide your aspirational/pretentious things under your snorkel parka, lit-erally. When I think of all the bands I missed seeing when I was growing up because I was stupidly looking at Matisse.'

As *The Catcher in the Rye* was to become a kind of life-manual for half a century of American adolescents, so Paul Morel became a kind of Holden Caulfield figure for several generations of British working-class 'scholarship boys'. *Sons and Lovers* was one of the first (and remains one of the best) novels of British proletarian life. Its main preoccupation – the miner's son exiled from his own class by a powerful self-education but excluded from any other class by his own social and intellectual uncertainty – was still being revisited by nov-elists and film-makers of the 'kitchen sink' school, thirty years after Lawrence's death.

The weekend before I visited him in Eastwood, George Shaw had taken his father on a pub crawl in Nottingham. But it wasn't just a crawl round any pubs: it was all the pubs used by Arthur Seaton in Alan Sillitoe's 1958 novel *Saturday Night and Sunday Morning*, and later in Karel Reisz's film starring Albert

Finney as the truculent young lathe operator (motto: 'All I want is a good time, the rest is propaganda') who refuses to be browbeaten by either his bosses or his family. In his first year at Sheffield Art School, probably under the influence of Cindy Sherman, he produced grainy, black-and-white stills of himself as a skinhead out of an Alan Clarke made-for-television movie (*Made in Britain*, *Scum*), and a fifties Ted in the mould of Seaton, and Vic in John Schlesinger's 1962 version of Stan Barstow's *A Kind of Loving*.

Shaw grew up in Tile Hill, a sixties council estate on the south side of Coventry, where his parents still live. (He showed me a recent newspaper article his father had sent him in which Tile Hill was described as the seventh poorest of Coventry's 230 parishes. 'Abuse, vandalism and the threat of violence', the article said, were part of everyday life.) George Shaw senior worked for British Leyland until he was made redundant in 1979. Being laid off brought on a kind of breakdown and he hasn't worked since, although by all accounts he is a fierce autodidact and a dogged reader. George junior's fetishising of an industrial North which was just beginning to be dismantled as he was being born in 1966 can no doubt be traced back to the crude sidelining of his father. George, along with his sisters and younger brother, would be pulled out of bed to watch early Ken Loach and Dennis Potter reruns, particularly the Nigel Barton plays, Potter's sequence about a displaced working-class boy turned disillusioned Labour politico, and be urged to 'Watch this. This is your education.'

George's father has a brother, Mick, a self-taught painter, who has been doing portraits of the same mid-century icons for forty years: Dean, Brando, Monroe, Buddy Holly, these same faces, over and over. 'My dad and my uncle associated themselves with certain figures, certain films and literature, to build up a picture of themselves,' George says. 'In my dad's case, something like Dennis Potter, something like Nigel Barton, something like Albert Finney, something like Arthur Seaton, then by extension something like Alan Sillitoe. And then we would watch *If . . .*'

George also has a personal pantheon or set of lodestones; a sort of museum of himself. Last year in a London gallery he showed drawings of some of them: Ian Curtis of Joy Division; Peter Sutcliffe; Bob and Terry from *The Likely Lads*; characters from *Dad's Army*; James Joyce; Samuel Beckett; Morrissey; Dai Bradley, the boy actor from *Kes*; the Specials were there; all the children that Hindley and Brady killed . . . 'It wasn't a celebration of them in their place, which was how Pop art might be. It was about how they could be used in a personal narrative. How they were sucked into my drama. These characters stand in for characters that I knew at school, or certain sensations I had as a child.'

As an adolescent, he developed an obsession with Francis Bacon. He drew Bacon's studio from photographs found in books and magazines. Then, when he was sixteen, he started to stalk him. He'd use the school holidays and any other opportunity to travel to London. He'd take the milk train from Coventry to Euston, and loiter in Reece Mews in South Kensington where, by taking a magnifying glass to a picture of the back of one of the canvases, he had discovered Bacon lived. In one end of the mews and out the other, guiltily, shiftily, round and round. This went on for a year before he got his first sighting of his prey. 'I thought, Fuck! This is fucking incredible! He could be in there, working on something now. And I was just absolutely transfixed.' So what did he do? 'As is usual with me, I found my body doing my thinking for me and I found myself banging on the door. I don't know what I thought was going to happen. I just thought something would happen. I think it's the hope that you might uncover something that hasn't been uncovered before. That there would be something hidden, or something dark, or something that has never been explored before. It's actually you standing in the real world on a bit of concrete or a bit of grass, finding something out for the first time. And it's also, I suppose, the avoidance of dealing with your own life. And the sash window went up and "Fuck off!" . . .

'I thought it was great. I remember once asking Malcolm McLaren for an autograph in Old Compton Street in the early nineties. And he just went, "Why don't you fuck off?" I think I quite liked all that. It reinforced what an artist did; that separation, and that exile. And it all becomes suffused then with this working-class romanticism.'

George had made up his mind to be an artist while he was still at school. He was a competitive drawer. As a fourteen-year-old he'd take minicabs from life-drawing class to life-drawing class. It was 1980. The Specials were singing 'Hope the chip shop isn't closed, 'cos their pies are really nice; I'll stand in the taxi queue, stand in someone else's spew, wish I had lipstick on my shirt, instead of piss stains on my shoes,' but he was a budding Paul Morel. 'I could draw naked women from *Penthouse*. I could draw Marilyn Monroe. I could do a kettle so that it looked really shiny.'

But when he started at Sheffield Art School in the mid-eighties, it was soon made clear to him that that kind of skill was about as useful as a chocolate teapot: 'For me, it was the equivalent of learning the violin to grade nine, then arriving to study music and they give you a biscuit tin and say, "Bang on that for three years and be done with it." What's the fucking point?'

When he finished at Sheffield he gave up art completely. He worked at Charing Cross hospital in London, as a technician in the mortuary, and in surgery, making dissection videos for students, taking identification photographs for the police. He drifted back to Sheffield and taught in a special-needs school for four years. Making excuses, as he sees it now. Fiddling about. 'I thought every aspiration I'd had as a kid was fucked. I hadn't made it; I was just another reject. Making really bad paintings; drinking too much. I did that for years.' It was only after being accepted at the Royal College of Art in 1996 that he started doing what he does now: quiet, modestly proportioned paintings in household Humbrol paint of the flats and pubs and recreational spaces of the Tile Hill estate that show, as Philip Larkin famously wrote of Coventry, that 'nothing, like something, happens anywhere'.

Every morning George walks from Brinsley past the mummified winding gear of the pit where Lawrence's father worked; past the cottage where Lawrence's grandparents lived; on past the former colliery company offices, now a Lawrence heritage centre available for 'D. H. Lawrence' weddings, to the former lace factory in the heart of Eastwood where he has his studio. There, much as Lawrence mentally revisited the ash pits and backstreets of his early years from the safe distance of Sardinia, New Mexico and Australia, Shaw paints the flashers' coppices and pissy alleys, the deserted precincts and all the drab fabric of his estate. He works from snapshots that he takes furtively when he hopes nobody's looking. There is evidence, though, that he is watched. Not long ago, on a damp day, he distributed pages of pornography around the floor of a wood whose hidden places and informal paths he often paints. The idea was to let it mulch for an hour before photographing it. But inside half an hour it was all gone. 'It's funny,' he said, 'you never find pornography like that in London. But here you do. Kathryn always finds it quite remarkable. She says I can spot it out the car window. "There it is!"'

It has become a truism in recent years, in art and elsewhere, that anything banal can be transformed into horror; anything familiar into something terrifying. Although nothing sinister has ever happened, as far as he knows, in any of the places he paints, Shaw has this kind of implacable, refrigerated David Lynch take on cheapened urban experience.

It is no more than a coincidence that the narrow miners' back-to-backs that Lawrence immortalised in his early novels find their modern equivalent in the gimcrack, Plexiglas-panelled, low-cost workers' housing of Tile Hill that George Shaw has decided to make his subject. But it is odd nevertheless that he has ended up putting his own singular stamp on the neighbourhood where he grew up – appropriating it, in a way – in a place that is so powerfully inhabited by the ghost of a single person. Drinking in the Sun Inn, not much changed in eighty years, George is never not aware that Lawrence drank there; the blue-line Lawrence trail dogs his days. It is as if Eastwood only ever existed in the novels of D. H. Lawrence.

'He is quickly becoming – I am allowing him to become,' George said, 'a heavy monkey on my back, always in the corner of my eye when I'm out on the streets or in the pub. He's there sitting in the corner making notes, taking the piss, rubbing his ginger beard and looking down his nose at the shit on his shoes.'

Lawrence was an elitist. He was anti-democratic. He considered himself separate from, and above, the mob; an aristocratic spirit. He was Nietzsche's most devoted British disciple. 'My great religion', Lawrence wrote in a famous letter of

1913, 'is a belief in the blood, the flesh, as being wiser than intellect. We can go wrong in our minds. But what our blood feels and believes and says, is always true.' Bertrand Russell claimed that it was these ideas of blood consciousness that led straight to Auschwitz.

In his book *The Intellectuals and the Masses* John Carey makes a powerful case for Lawrence being a racist. And in a biography, *The Married Man*, Brenda Maddox writes about his affinity with far-right political groups. Of *Kangaroo* (1923), a political thriller about a secret fascist army, she writes, 'he was unhappy about the dark anarchic races waiting to pour into Australia and sensed behind them the yellow Japanese waiting to descend on Australia "like a ripe pear"'. He did not like the races to mix.

'To understand D. H. Lawrence,' Frieda Lawrence once wrote of her husband, 'one must know that he belongs to the Midlands, that navel of England. It is a strange black country with an underworld quality that is rather frightening.' It was in order to get the measure of the community he has joined that, a few weeks ago, George Shaw went to a British Movement recruitment meeting in a pub in Heanor, visible from Eastwood, on the other side of Langley Mill. Racism is once more on the agenda in British politics. The anti-fascist magazine *Searchlight* has identified the East Midlands – Mansfield and Nottingham in particular – as being especially active.

Violence has been a hallmark of the British far right, and George had noticed that, shortly after it opened in Langley Mill, the window of Khan's late-night convenience store had been put in. At the meeting in Heanor he found the usual rabble of skinhead neo-fascists, misfits and thugs. 'Imagine if I'm walking around looking pretty much like the person who's going to beat me up, how much more uncomfortable you'd feel with a big turban on and loads of kids. Imagine if you look completely different, and an outsider. One of the things you get from Lawrence is this threatening atmosphere.' 'Keep England English', the rallying-cry at Heanor, had a distinctly Lawrentian ring.

One afternoon I left George doing a painting of the back of the Social Club in Tile Hill, a subject which he treats with all the seriousness of Monet painting Rouen Cathedral, and walked down to Langley Mill. Khan's convenience store had been reglazed. But there was a sign now on a piece of cardboard with a ragged, corrugated edge, which said: 'Moving premises – shop closed'.

A light was on in the shop. Behind the closed blinds, one of the upstairs rooms was lit. The Khans' van was parked in the car park opposite, adjacent to the Railway Tavern, a few yards from the 'En Memoriam' slogan and Hitler face. The lettering on the van was new, and in bright primary colours: 'Cheap Cigarettes – Sandwiches – Asian Food'.

I went to the side door and pressed the bell. The door was painted blue and like a fortress. The outside of the shop and the upstairs windows had all been painted blue. I could smell the fresh paint. There was a number on the side of the van, but when I called it I got a machine with a pre-set English voice. I pressed the bell again. I could sense some movement behind the blind, but nobody came.

'English culture has a flavour of its own,' George Orwell wrote in a much-anthologised essay, 'England, Your England'. 'Moreover, it is continuous, and stretches into the future and into the past, there is something in it that persists, as in a living creature. What can the England of 1940 have in common with the England of 1840? But then, what have you in common with the child of five whose photograph your mother keeps on the mantelpiece? Nothing, except that you happen to be the same person.'

Many years ago, perhaps even before he was born, Mick Shaw, George's uncle, painted a picture especially for George's dad. His dad put it on the fireplace wall of their house in Coventry and it has hung there ever since: a triangular face, bright eyes, fiery red hair like George's own. He says his sister grew up assuming it was the devil. It wasn't, of course: it was D. H. Lawrence. George says he never knew why. 'My dad and my uncle Mick aren't the type to talk about things like that,' he said. 'They'd rather talk about the colour of a jacket in *Rebel Without a Cause*.'

2001

Like Patrick Caulfield, another saloon-bar romantic whose subject has long been the hypnotic allure of the cheap and disregarded and the blissful, occasionally transcending melancholy of human absence, George Shaw makes paintings with drinking places as their titles. But where Caulfield, in sumptuous reveries such as *The Blue Posts*, *Paradise Bar*, *Happy Hour* and *After Lunch* is all burgundied and blood-red interiority, Shaw keeps strictly to the outside and the margins, painting the poor brick-and-plastic fabric of the pubs and social clubs on the sixties council estate in Coventry where he grew up.

Over a period of just a few years he has marked out Tile Hill as his territory as single-mindedly as any roaming mongrel or butcher's dog and, in the continuing series of paintings he calls Scenes From the Passion, has painted the precincts and playgrounds and litter-strewn alleys and copses of his childhood using the kind of Humbrol paint usually applied to Airfix models of toy boats and aeroplanes. Knowing that the infant James Bulger was daubed in Humbrol model paint by his schoolboy killers – and knowing, further, that George Shaw also obviously knows this (he has drawn portraits of Peter Sutcliffe, the Yorkshire Ripper, and pictures of all the children that Myra Hindley and Ian Brady killed) – glosses the paintings with a light even more sickly sinister than the light leaking from their characteristically bruised-looking and leaden skies.

As a landscape painter of nondescript but concretely real places invaded by a sense of their own haunting, time-shifted unreality, Shaw shares a clear affinity with Peter Doig, who was one of his teachers at the Royal College of Art in London. But Doig grew up in rural Canada and his paintings are alt-country and kind of trippy; Buffalo Springfield or the Byrds to Shaw's sarkier Smiths and the Fall. With their snowy pixellation and psychedelic colours, they hark back to the loved-up generation of Ecstasy crunchers and (even earlier) the Summer of Love.

Shaw is a drinker; the product of a drinking culture. Tile Hill was built to house the families of motorcar workers at British Leyland. When they started being laid off in their thousands after the Thatcher government came to power in 1979 there wasn't a lot for many of them to do except drink. The centrepiece of Shaw's touring show, What I Did This Summer, is a bold triptych of pubs; man-made islands floating on slicks of greasy asphalt under dirty, glooming, confectionery-coloured skies. *The Unicorn* – foursquare, Tudorbethan – is the sort of place the members of the Rotary Club are likely to meet for lunch. *The Hawthorn Tree* is dingy art deco, decaying. *The New Star* – jerry-built, bodged, added-on to, fifties impermanent – is the place where it all kicks off, half-gram deals bagged up and waiting, shooters stowed under the seats. Like all Shaw's work, these are paintings devoid of human presence;

creepily unpeopled. There are car parks but no cars; sign-boards but no discernible signs. No 'Specials' boards, no satellite dishes, no helpful pointers or narrative clues.

Like the buildings and street furniture in all Shaw's paintings, all three pubs seem imperilled by the physical fact of the trees and bushes which crowd around them, the land they are standing on appearing to be in the process of being reclaimed by the monster with a million worm-like heads – spiky, implacable nature. The toxic yellow sycamores in *The New Star*, the industrial spruce and bullying, sun-blocking leylandii lay sole claim to the strong vital instinct of health in this environment. In picture after picture, skeins and black webs of naked branches claw their way across the mirror surface like matted hairs or blood vessels or swarming, disfiguring thread veins.

If the predatory nature in his paintings is reminiscent of the natural world as it appears in the poems of D. H. Lawrence, that is because Shaw has spent the past few years living in Lawrence's home village of Eastwood, and has familiarised himself with books by and about Lawrence. He is that most unfashionable thing: a literary painter. He did his MA dissertation on James Joyce. ('In Ellmann's biography of Joyce,' he told me once, 'he mentions that one of the reasons Joyce got totally dissatisfied with Catholicism and favoured art as a new kind of religious focus was because art celebrated faults, whereas the religion went for purity.') While he was a student at Sheffield Art School in the mid-eighties, he wrote a paper called 'Working-Class Masculinity in British Social-Realist Cinema' . . .

Shaw also writes. As an ancillary activity, a breakout from the close-worked, brick-by-brick and leaf-by-leaf rendering of the armpits of Tile Hill, he sits alone in pubs getting sozzled and writing notes to himself. 'I can remember the locations of where things were said . . . The lower field outside the classrooms, a conversation with Father Devaney about going into the priesthood by the bushes in the church and the social club car park . . . That piece of dumped, hardened tarmac at the entrance to Pigwood that marked a long way from home. Further than I could imagine. That stump in the woods next to the crab-apple trees where dad rolled his cigarettes with his little machine on his knee . . . If I worked as long as I drank. If I drank as long as I worked. If I didn't drink at all. If I didn't work at all.'

Unfashionability, of course, is now established as the quickest route to becoming the latest thing. 'You see so much modern art that looks like modern art,' Peter Doig once said. I was reminded of this by a comment that appeared in the visitors' book the day after George Shaw's show opened at Newlyn Art Gallery in October: 'Fantastic! Some modern art at last that we oldies can enjoy!'

It was a curious experience seeing his paintings of derelict garages and porn-littered copses, his evocations of ugliness, banality and boredom, hanging in the home of British abstraction; soaking up the light in the place where personal 'expression' in art has almost been established as a religion. And there was an inescapable impression at the private viewing that a number of those present (it was an elderly crowd) felt they were having their noses rubbed in what Lawrence, in a famous passage, referred to as 'the utter negation of natural beauty, the utter negation of the gladness of life, the utter absence of the instinct for shapely beauty which every bird and beast has'. They were being challenged to acknowledge that there could be a kind of beauty in the cheapened urban experience many of them had packed up and fled the cities to escape.

The irony is that, while appearing to be a social-realist

painter, and while admitting to the sense of ominousness and air of foreboding that wreathe his paintings like a miasma, Shaw shares the belief of the abstractionists that painting is fundamentally a translation into visual language of invisible states of mind.

He quotes the German poet Novalis: '"The world must become romanticised, and in that way we find again its original meaning for us."' And then, word perfect, he quotes 'this nice little line from Camus': '"A man's work is nothing but the slow trek to rediscover, through the detours of art, the two or three great and simple images in whose presence his heart first opened."'

'I virtually operate like a paedophile or a serial killer, I think,' Shaw said. 'Just skulking about with the camera hidden. I'll whip it out very quickly, take the image and then put it back in. I feel like I'm a kind of heritage industry on my own background.'

2003

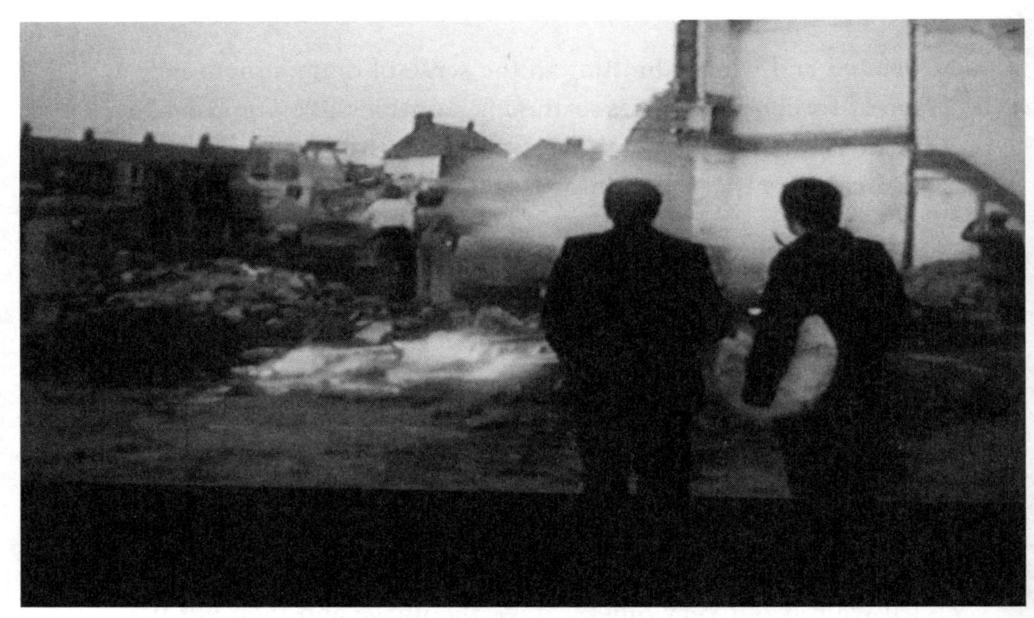

GORDON
BOB AND TERRY
WATCH AS THEIR
LOCAL IS
DEMOLISHED
GEORGE

ANGELA DE LA CRUZ

It is hard to find a language for unfortunates. Don DeLillo made this observation some years ago in a novel called *Mao II* which took its title from a Warhol painting and spent many pages digressing on the condition of the urban dispossessed, specifically the rag-pickers and tent-dwellers who squatted New York's Tomkins Square Park in the late eighties.

I was recently reminded of the *Mao II* passages by some of the photographs reproduced in Lucy Lippard's book *The Lure of the Local*, a meditation on the magic of place. One of them shows the makeshift hutment occupied by Nathaniel, the man regarded for a time as the 'Mayor' of Tomkins Square Park: built around a park bench and lashed together from tatters of tarpaulin and bin liners and plastic potato sacks, it flaps and billows and is clearly the product of thousands of impulse decisions and Bacofoil-and-chewing-gum emergency repairs.

Another picture in Lippard's book carries the caption, 'Highway Camp, Encinitas, California' and shows three brothers and their friends from a small town in Guatemala asleep on a terrace over Interstate 5 near San Diego, high above the neon-crazy street corner where they await drive-by offers of daily work. The contours of the children's bodies under their thin blankets – a sharp knee, the blade of a hip – echo the huddled lumpiness of Nathaniel's tent. The photograph is accompanied by some lines from a poem by Miguel Algarin:

> I am not the garbage, the booze, the guns, the dirt,
> I am the song, the baptism, the wedding.
> I am the newborn child that grows among rank weeds.

The paintings of Angela de la Cruz have no deliberate documentary intention, and they do not allude to any obvious social engagement on the part of the artist. They are abstractions, for a start – square or rectilinear monochrome canvases daubed blood red, curdled white, thick cloacal brown – with no discernible figurative content. Neither do titles such as *Vertical IV*, *Minimum X* or *Loose Fit VII* provide any useful pointers.

And yet *Clutter VI (with White Blanket)*, one of the central pieces in de la Cruz's recent show at Lisson Gallery in London, immediately evoked images of the derelict, the roughly dossed-down and debased, and other 'unfortunates' whose place is the street. Like many of her most successful paintings, *Clutter VI* flirts with the idea of being a sculpture. It sprawls on the floor – a large, pristinely painted, bathroom-white, unstretched canvas thrown over a kind of ghat of . . . well, large, mankily painted, dirty canvases and their stretchers. And not just dirty, but broken – systematically smashed and kicked about a bit and discarded in the yard outside de la Cruz's Islington studio to take whatever the world and the weather chose to throw at them; failed paintings, wastes of space and so (until their crappiness was confirmed by their wretched appearance, which in de la Cruz's eyes made them recyclable) surplus to requirements.

In addition to Nathaniel's tent and the child workers from Guatemala huddled together on their ledge above the busy Interstate, *Clutter VI* reminded me of a set of pictures from that morning's *Guardian* – photographs of the wreckage of Palestinian homes after Israeli troops swept into the Rafah refugee camp in Gaza and laid waste to it with bulldozers. Something to do with the juxtaposition of ruinated cinder block and decimated stone and the fresh bedlinen and tablecloths that the once-again homeless refugees had put up over their heads for protection.

Such a burden of reference for so unbombastic (indeed so fastidiously self-effacing, almost pathetic) a work to labour under! But when I spoke to her, it was with yet another human tragedy that de la Cruz said she had come to associate many of the pieces in her new show.

Although she has been based in London for the last fifteen years, she was born and grew up in La Coruña in Spain, where her mother and the other members of her immediate family still live. And the terrorist bombing of three commuter trains in Madrid in March this year, in which more than two hundred people died, is the event she believes resonates most profoundly in much of the work that she has brought to completion since then. 'When I was reading an article about the bombs in Madrid, people were covering all the bodies with black and white. White was an unidentified body. So I was thinking very much in terms of death. And then I became really obsessed with blankets. Blankets and body bags.'

Like British contemporaries such as Rachel Whiteread, Sarah Lucas and Damien Hirst, de la Cruz has studiously avoided the human body, but her work is nevertheless aggressive in its referencing of it. Unlike Hirst and the others, she actively encourages an anthropomorphic reading of her paintings. 'All my work', she has said, 'is activated by human experience. My paintings are figurative objects.' Out of all the duffing-up of stretchers, and heavy-duty ripping and pummelling of canvases, she hopes to achieve a metaphoric human anatomy. The English critic Adrian Searle once watched de la

Cruz moving studios: 'As she carried two smallish paintings across the yard, . . . skittering their bottom edges along the ground, she said, "See how I treat my babies! Don't tell any-one!"'

Ashamed was the title she gave to the first painting she cut. *Homeless* is what she called the first painting she broke. She was in her studio in London. Her father had just died unexpectedly in Spain. 'One day I just broke the painting. Not in anger,' she once said, 'but in sadness. It was at that moment I realised I had in my hands the possibility of another kind of relationship with my work.'

Ashamed (1995) was a small painting which hung abjectly in a corner. *Homeless* (1996) was a big painting which stood abjectly on the floor. Both paintings were white and had clearly started life as some kind of bastard offspring of Robert Ryman, whose retrospective de la Cruz had seen at the Tate and which, for reasons she still finds problematical putting into words, had made something in her flip or click. 'I saw it so quickly. Maybe ten minutes. And yet I remember all the paint-ings afterwards. Everything.'

As Georges Braque said, in the end the problem with art is that you can explain everything about it except the bit that matters. The important thing here is that it was a painter who turned her round. Because she is unshiftable on one point: that, as close as they appear to come to the condition of sculp-ture, painting is what her work remains. 'Even though the paintings have got this object-like quality they still remain paintings. It's very important that painting is stationed within the parameters of tradition, otherwise it has no meaning. I am trying to research the language of painting.'

De la Cruz is pursuing her practice in brave and continually unconventional ways. If drawing for Paul Klee was taking a line for a walk, painting for de la Cruz is taking a canvas for a larging-it night on the tiles that will most likely involve a quick bunk-up (see *Torso*, 2004), a chuck-up (see *Vomit Painting*, 1996) and a bit of a rumble (*Bully*, 1997; *Broken into Pieces*, 1999) followed by a chance to sleep it off in the cells (*Knackered*, 1998; *Ripped*, 1999). 'Dishevelled' and 'hung-over' are the adjectives that apply across the board. Paintings might tangle with a chair or a table or a set of metal shelves, as in the Still-Life series. They might get stuck in a door, as in *Stuck* (2001). Or they might end up humiliatingly scrunched in a ball and sidefooted into a corner, as in the series called Nothing. De la Cruz has very cleverly short-circuited the eons-old 'problem' with painting by incorporating its very destruction into the work itself.

At the beginning of this year she embarked on a new series called Clutter. In the Clutter paintings, old failed 'paintings-in-waiting' are not cannibalised or grafted onto other paintings as previously, but restretched, broken up and tidied away inside deep, aluminium-reinforced paintings that she refers to as 'clutter bags'. These are some of her most realised works and they took me straight back to *Mao II*, and in particular this passage:

She talked to the woman who lived in a plastic bag half a block from [her] building. This person knew some things about bundling and tying. Survival means . . . you hide what you own inside something else so that you may seem to possess one chief thing when it is really many things bundled and tied and placed inside each other, a secret universe of things, unwhisperable, plastic bags inside plastic bags, and the woman is somewhere in there too, bagged with her possessions.

If there is a suggestion of the bag-lady aesthetic about de la Cruz both in her work and in person, it is perhaps in some way a reaction to her respectable Catholic Spanish roots. There is a Spanish word, *cursi*, which the 1984 edition of the *Diccionario de la Real Academia Española* defines as: '1. Said of a person with pretensions to refinement and elegance. 2. Applied to that which, appearing to be elegant or luxurious, is ridiculous or in bad taste. 3. Said of artists and writers, or of their works, when they vainly attempt to show excessive refinement or elevated feelings.'

Even the briefest acquaintance is enough to know that the culture of *cursileria*, dominant in Spain throughout the last century and at least the one before, is something de la Cruz would go a very long way out of her way to avoid. When she was a child, the girls' version of 'tinker, tailor, soldier, sailor' in games in Galicia was '*viuda, casada, soltera, monja*' (widow, wife, spinster, nun). She is, on her own admission, drawn to the orphaned, the pathetic, the discarded and 'the down below'. She explains that the colours of her paintings are colours of the body: the red of blood, the brown of shit.

The notion of disgust intrigues her and is linked to the raw, *art brut* ruses that characterise her work. *Viuda, casada, soltera, monja*. Blood, piss, semen, shit. 'All my work', she has said, 'has got this element, a certain abjectness, a sense of dirt. Things sagging, dripping. They are all about pushing, pulling, putting in and out, opening the body. Pleasure, the visceral, the body, eroticism, these are all important ideas in my work.'

'American abstract art is a lie, a sham, a cover-up for a poverty of spirit,' Philip Guston wrote in an angry note to himself that was found in his desk after his death. 'A mask to mask the fear of revealing oneself. A lie to cover up how bad one can be. Unwilling to show this badness, this rawness. It is laughable, this lie. Anything but this! What a sham! Abstract art hides this, hides the lie. Don't! Let it show! It is an escape from the true feelings we have, from the "raw" primitive feelings about the world – and us in it.'

Guston, you feel, would have been in sympathy with de la Cruz's further adventures in painterly abstraction. She is taking it to places it has never been, and perhaps never thought it would go.

2004

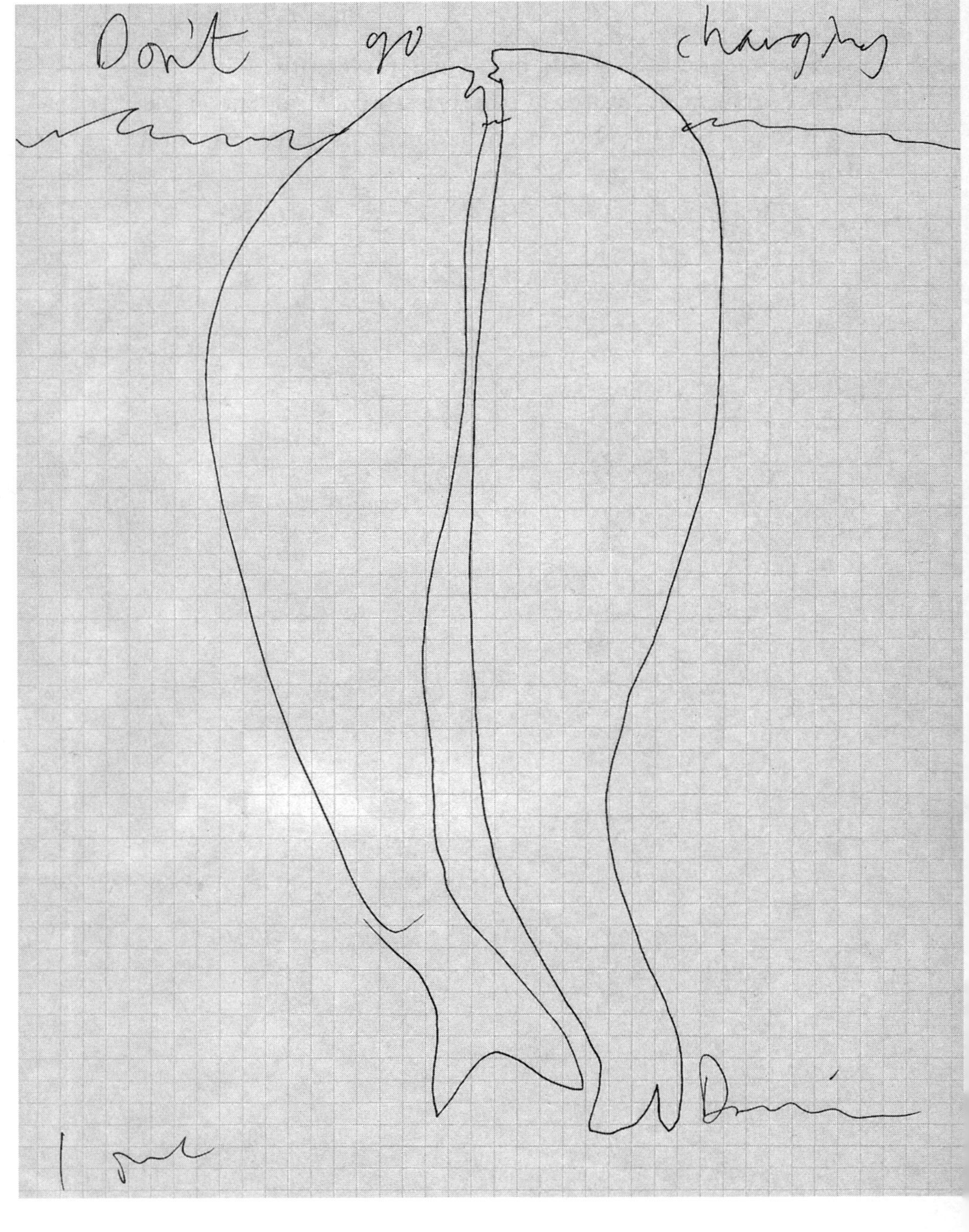

Don't go changing
I don't

CHANTAL JOFFE

According to his most recent biographer John Richardson (who has made himself to Picasso studies what Richard Ellmann is to James Joyce, say, or David Sylvester became to Francis Bacon), Picasso singled out the physicality of Degas's 'pig-faced whores' for admiration. 'You can smell them,' he said.

In his eighties, Picasso described to his friend Hélène Parmelin how he had once, as a young man in his twenties, shown his great cubist painting *Woman in a Chemise in an Armchair* of 1913 to Braque. 'Is this woman real?' Picasso had asked. 'Do her armpits smell?' And the two artists proceeded to use the armpit quotient as a test of real painting. 'This one smells a bit but not that one . . .'

This physicality is what so much of Picasso's art is about. It is partly what Bacon was referring to when he once said that he admired 'the brutality of fact' in Picasso's painting, compared to the lyrical and decorative qualities associated with Matisse. Matisse, Bacon believed, was guilty of 'turning fact into lyricism'. Picasso, on the other hand, was an artist who throughout his career (for virtually the entire course of the twentieth century, in fact) stood accused of promoting 'the cult of ugliness' – an extreme form of the realist refusal of beauty and harmony in favour of an unideal bodiliness. (*Woman in an Armchair* was a ribald, sexually explicit cubist deconstruction of an elegant portrait Matisse had made of his wife, Amélie, dating from the same year.)

The key to cubism is the recognition that it dissolves traditional representation. 'Picasso shatters forms,' Matisse once said. 'I am their servant.' In cubism, Donald Kuspit has written, the body – 'all bodies, the very bodiliness of the world' – is shown in the process of disintegration. *Les Demoiselles d'Avignon* (1907), the giant step of Picasso's early days and the most crucial single work in the development of cubism, was initially experienced by many artists of the period as more 'pointlessly' ugly than anything they had previously seen.

People were shocked. The *Demoiselles* was regarded as profoundly disturbing, and for many of the same reasons that Manet's *Olympia* (1863) had been experienced as scandalous when it was first shown over a generation earlier. The 'superreal' (Picasso's word) women in both paintings – prostitutes, as it happens – were seen as threatening both in their regal nakedness and in the unflinching gaze they return to the spectator. (This direct address – the cold, come-on stare; the pretty, brutal smile; the painted visage, blank and blatant – is the characteristic look of the porno starlets and catwalk models who, isolated in their narrow cage-frames, populate Chantal Joffe's paintings.)

According to Richardson, the beginnings of Picasso's confrontational whorehouse painting can probably be traced back to an essay that the poet Charles Baudelaire published in 1863, coincident with *Olympia*. In 'The Painter of Modern Life', Baudelaire addressed the same issues that Picasso addresses in the *Demoiselles*, namely his notion of whoredom as an ideal subject for an artist. The prostitute, Baudelaire writes,

is a perfect image of savagery in the midst of civilisation. She has a kind of beauty which comes to her from sin . . . Sometimes they effortlessly adopt poses that would be the joy of the most fastidious sculptor, if only the sculptor of today had the courage and the wit to seize hold of nobility everywhere, even in the mire . . . In this foggy chaos, bathed in golden light, undreamed of by indigent chastity, gruesome nymphs and living dolls, whose childlike eyes have sinister flashes, move and contort themselves.

It was Picasso's intention to contaminate the pristine air of the salon and the academy by opening them up to the plebeian facts of daily life in the modern city, and in this he succeeded. Joffe's practice of incorporating in her collage 'drawings' pages clipped from magazines at both the glossy and the trashy ends of the spectrum is a clear continuation of the tradition started by Picasso and Braque and their cubist contemporaries, who delighted in bringing cheap catalogues, posters, newspapers, street signs and other eyesores of the new urban environment into their work.

But before turning to these instantly recognisable symbols of admass vulgarity and superficiality, Picasso first launched his assault on conventional turn-of-the-century sensibilities and notions of 'beauty' by grafting Egyptian masks and African tribal scarifications onto the five nude figures in the *Demoiselles d'Avignon*. Picasso took his deforming, aggressive, caricatural drawings of fright-masks directly from his sketchbooks and transferred them unabridged to the canvas of the *Demoiselles*. In the process, Adam Gopnik has demonstrated, he elevated satiric imagery into the realm of art, where it was changed by its new context and in turn changed that context, radically transforming the language of modern art. 'It was Picasso's discovery of archaic and primitive art that allowed him to release the energy of his notebooks into the world of his big finished portraits,' Gopnik concludes.

It had been Joffe's original intention (quite quickly abandoned) to offer her own transcription of the big, peculiarly proportioned *Demoiselles*. She made photographic self-portraits posing as all five women (shown in the current show as a small collage). She made a drawing of herself as the crouching figure in the painting's bottom right-hand corner. (Picasso had based this on sketches of his mistress of the time, Fernande Olivier, astride a bidet.) Picasso is, of course, a colossus: 'Picasso is the issue, Picasso is the one to beat, Picasso is the fastest gun in the West,' as Sylvester once wrote. Joffe says she concentrated on the *Demoiselles* period 'as a way of trying to limit the vastness of his output for myself'.

Like Georges Braque, whom Picasso more than once described as his 'wife', and whose work Picasso always made their shared dealer, Kahnweiler, sell at one-fifth the price of his own, Joffe came to feel increasingly that in getting close to Picasso, 'one risked coming under his domination'; that his is an influence – enlivening and deadening; inescapable and yet crucial to escape – which extends beyond the grave.

2006

NEO RAUCH

'The history of modern Germany is, in part, a history of silences,' Neal Ascherson wrote recently. 'First there were things one learned not to say, soon followed by questions one learned not to ask, leading to sights one learned not to see.' The silences, as Günter Grass has made clear in his autobiography, held on both sides. In the West, the decision not to speak about the past was, in some sense, voluntary; in the East, these silences and others were enforced. If the painters of the communist GDR wanted to register a protest against the oppressive state, they had to do it slyly, mock classically, in code: Icarus tumbling to earth after flying too close to the sun, like members of the dictatoriat deformed by power, was a popular symbol.

But then the wall came down in 1989 and the pupils of the old painters of the GDR were free to interpret the new world as it was revealed to them. Neo Rauch, a recent graduate of the art academy in Leipzig, in the heavily industrial far east of the former East Germany, started painting large canvases that hovered somewhere between socialist realism and Pop art. In her book *Stasiland*, Anna Funder writes about the elaborate system of signs the 'internal army' of agents used to communicate with each other in the street: 'agents signalling to each other from corner to corner, stroking noses, tummies, backs and hair . . . lifting their hats to strangers — a choreography for very nasty scouts'.

It could be a description of the semi-surreal figures in a typical Rauch painting: his best-known works are peopled by blank-looking figures from the fifties performing enigmatic tasks of physical labour, and are reminiscent of Soviet-era instruction manuals and illustrations. They quickly earned Rauch a reputation as the next great German painter, following an earlier generation that includes Richter, Baselitz, Kippenberger and Kiefer. The New Leipzig School, with Rauch as its acknowledged leader, became a collecting phenomenon: a Rauch painting called *Losung* (Password) sold at Sotheby's in London in June for £456,000. Leipzig – run-down, depressed, increasingly depopulated – has acquired some of the art-world cachet of New York in the fifties or London in the nineties.

The New Leipzig School – Rauch and some of his former pupils, who include Tilo Baumgartel, Matthias Weischer, Christoph Ruckhaberle and Martin Kobe – have coalesced into what Joachim Pissarro of the Museum of Modern Art described to the *New York Times* as 'suddenly the hottest thing on earth'. Significantly, perhaps, having witnessed the failure of two bright new dawns – those of postwar communism and post-Cold War capitalism – the New Leipzig painters are seen as having 'a distinctively Leipziger air of unease and disillusionment' in common; their work is imbued with a deep melancholy. They are also a reminder of bygone eras when most artists were painters and most painters were men.

The Leipziger Baumwollspinnerei – a former cotton mill in a far-flung, dismal suburb – was in full fête for the start of the city's annual art weekend, a recently invented tradition. The *Spinnerei* used to accommodate 4,000 people in a complex of nineteenth-century factories and workers' tenements so vast and self-sufficient it was known as 'a city in the city'. The mills started to be run down after the fall of the wall, and had ceased production completely by the mid-nineties. Now half of the factory buildings are rented out again to around a hundred artists who have settled into the red-brick tenements on Spinnereistrasse, with the galleries representing the cream of them – the stars of the New Leipzig School – settled into high, white, top-lit spaces at street level. There's a shop selling artists' materials, a fine-wine supplier and a top-notch restaurant with a pretty garden in what used to be the clocking-in shop by the factory gates.

Café Mule was overflowing with visitors in the opening, early-evening hours of Leipzig's art weekend, and the half-mile strip of cobbled street between the tracks which used to carry the factory wagons had turned into a kind of runway for the well-heeled locals with their late-summer tans and designer glasses, and the fly-ins from Seoul and Cologne and Manhattan, unsteady in their Jimmy Choos and Manolos on the uneven street.

Rauch had a new show, and traffic on the opening night was all one-way. The Rubell family of Miami, and the Michael Ovitzes of Hollywood, were among the first to start collecting Rauch's work. The Rubells showed two dozen of their Leipzig canvases at the Massachusetts Museum of Contemporary Art earlier this year at the same time as the Cleveland Museum was showing the Ovitz family's From Leipzig, a show it described as 'the twenty-first century's first bona fide artistic phenomenon'.

Both shows were well received and – ironically, given the current, much-touted American 'renaissance' – welcomed for being refreshingly non-American. 'Razzle-dazzle effects, willful trashiness and breezy pop culture signifiers are all shunned,' *Art In America*'s reviewer wrote. The Leipzig painters shared a commitment to images more appropriate to 'probing issues of belonging and alienation in a reunified Germany'.

Neo Rauch makes a point of always talking about his 'workshop' rather than his studio. Rauch (it means 'smoke' in German) is seen as the bridge between the older painters of the GDR and the young artists of a unified Germany. He keeps the hours of a factory worker, nine to six every day, with a midday break to prepare lunch for his wife, the painter Rosa Loy. He is now a professor of painting at the art academy in Leipzig, where he was himself a student. During the thirties, a whole generation of artists had been forced to emigrate, comply or stay without work under the Nazis. After the war, Soviet socialist realism demanded the kitsch depiction of worthy workers, jolly tractor drivers and smiling peasants.

The Leipzig academy functions as both a training camp and a kind of moral institute. There is an unfashionable commitment to the traditional techniques of life drawing, draughtsmanship and painting. Although new media were integrated into the curriculum in the nineties, experimentation is not expected in finished work by students in the painting school and any tendency towards extreme stylisation or abstraction is discouraged. 'The disadvantages of the wall are well known,' Rauch's tutor at the Leipzig academy, its former director Arno Rink, has said. 'If you want to talk of an advantage, you can say it allowed us to continue in the tradition of Cranach and Beckmann. It protected the art against the influence of Joseph Beuys.'

Rauch's parents were killed when he was six weeks old in a train crash just outside the Leipzig station, and so he has never known why he was given the unusual first name. But he strongly dislikes its connection with newness and innovation, because he considers himself to be a 'very conservative' person, anti-progressive and resistant to change. 'In the last decade, my painting contemporaries were literally pushed into the underground,' he has said, 'and they had to fit into the role of cultural pariah, according to the will of a clique of curators addicted to progress.'

Rauch is tall and gaunt and, like his paintings, exudes a kind of chaffing and intimidating, rather unfriendly wit. For the private view of his show he wore a dark suit and a white shirt and a brand-new pair of boat-sized, bespoke, black leather oxfords. He was the cool centre of a room aquiver with the purchasing power of many of those on *Art Review*'s about-to-be-announced 2006 list of art's hot and heavy one hundred. Rauch himself was in at sixty-six. Gerd Harry Lybke, his dealer, was one place behind at sixty-seven, a disappointment, no doubt, for a man who is unabashed at declaring himself the powerhouse and kingmaker of the whole Leipzig scene.

Later, during a lavish reception at the Museum der Bildenden Künste, while Rauch lurked where he feels an artist belongs, in the shadows ('an artist's workshop should always be installed on the fringe'), Lybke, known to one and all as 'Judy', clambered onto the seat of a velvet chair and did a comic turn. Judy Lybke was a life model for many years, sitting for Rauch and a number of the other artists he now represents through his Berlin and Leipzig galleries, Eigen + Art. He was thinner in those days, with Jimi Hendrix hair; now he is florid-faced and rotund and likes the kind of clothes Ronnie Corbett is famous for wearing, with an added Bavarian twist.

For the big night he turned out in pink pinstripes with red suspenders and cinching buckles. This was in stark contrast to the head-to-toe black of the elderly couple he buzzed around busily. Donald and Mera Rubell (twenty-nine on *Art Review*'s list) started collecting work by the Leipzig artists for their private

Miami museum in 2003. 'What happened to us in Leipzig was very unique,' Mrs Rubell said. 'Discovering five artists in one day had never happened to us in forty years of collecting.' *Vorfuhrung*, a twelve-by-sixteen-foot canvas from the present show, was the latest giant Neo Rauch jewel in their collection.

'Very much pink,' the Danish collector Ole Faarup said of the Rubells' million-dollar purchase. 'Too much pink. I don't think Mr and Mrs Rubell have chosen well.' Faarup, a furniture millionaire from Copenhagen, is a grandfatherly figure who considers himself the 'godfather' of the Leipzig School. He had made a visit to Rauch's studio long before the Rubells jetted in and made his selection there. It consolidated his holdings in a group he first stumbled across five years ago by chance: frustrated in his objective of bagging a major Sarah Lucas at her Berlin show in 2001, he had been redirected to an artist-run co-operative called Liga, where Tilo Baumgartel and a number of his Leipzig contemporaries were on show. 'In charge was this girl who looked like she was aged about fifteen,' Faarup remembers. 'She gave me Tilo's number but he didn't want to sell. "I've promised them to friends." I was travelling with the director of the Copenhagen Modern Museum, who was as stunned by this work as me. "Don't you understand? We're talking about bringing your work into a museum collection here!"'

Acting on a tip-off from Faarup, Anthony Wilkinson became the first London dealer to make the trip east. It was while he was hanging his show at Wilkinson's gallery in Hackney that Baumgartel opened the door to what he took to be 'a Pizza Hut driver — rather untidy-looking all in blue'. It was, of course, Charles Saatchi on the prowl.

Of all Leipzig artists, Baumgartel probably has the closest personal and working relationship with Neo Rauch. They paint in adjacent spaces in the *Spinnerei* and have lunch in the studio together every day. Baumgartel follows the same orderly work habits and is imbued with the same self-discipline as his former teacher who, at the age of twenty-nine, was twelve years older than Baumgartel when the wall came down.

They came across the cotton mill while riding around on their bikes one day and moved in just as the last of the mill workers were moving out. 'Now the old factory has developed into a new one,' Baumgartel says. 'Raw materials in the art supplies shop on the ground floor, production areas in the studios upstairs, distribution by the dealers. In the beginning it was silent, romantic, a little bit tragic/romantic. Now it is the opposite. A factory without bosses.'

Saturday saw Judy Lybke, hung-over but still in paunchy Teutonic demigod mode, glad-handing the crowd that was eddying through his gallery. 'A question!' he commanded. 'C'mon, ask me a question! Not one of your tired ones. One that I haven't been asked.' OK. What did he think about during the eight years that he spent eight hours a day being a nude model? 'Sex!'

Not Soviet oppression? Not the all-hearing, all-seeing Stasi? It was still the era of the GDR. 'Sex! I had three one-night stands a day, every day! Women were the same. This free-sex thing is over since the wall falling down. A woman has three men now, you call her a bitch!' He grabbed the arm of a young woman who happened to have wandered within reach. 'Is true, *ja*? Women fuck three men a day in the DDR?' She blushed and pushed him away.

Later the woman told me her name was Mrs Ondrej. She was the wife of Vlado Ondrej, a Leipzig academy-trained print-maker with a studio on staircase-3. They had been among the first into the old *Spinnerei* buildings when the area was still considered a dangerous place to be: 'full of alcoholics, drug-takers, people on the street'. These had all been tidied away into 'Gropius buildings' – high-rises – in west Leipzig. We were being jostled by gallery-goers carrying glasses of wine, gallery hopping in the international style, as we talked. 'We said,' Mrs Ondrej said, 'when the beer at the corner shop is replaced by champagne, it is time to move on.'

2006

ACKNOWLEDGEMENTS

Among many commissioning editors and art directors, past and present, I'd like to thank:

Hugh Allan, Lisa Allardice, Moyra Ashford, Tom Baker, Jonathan Barnbrook, Jason Beard, Bruce Bernard, Gunn Brinson, Mark Boxer, Susan Boyd, Geoffrey Cannon, Maddie Costa, Hunter Davies, Melissa Denes, David Driver, Charlie English, Ron Hall, Suzanne Hodgart, Liz Jobey, Ian Katz, Simon Kelner, Magnus Linklater, Nick Logan, Ulrich Loock, Annelena McAfee, Patrick Nicholson, Deborah Orr, Paul Rambali, Michael Rand, Susan Raven, David Robson, Susanna Rustin, Sarah Spankie, John Tennant, Rebecca Wilson.

At Faber:
Stephen Page, Lee Brackstone, Angus Cargill.
Dave Watkins; Donna Payne, Alex Kirby; Anna Pallai, Kate Burton; John Grindrod; Helen Francis; Trevor Horwood for his copy-editing.

INDEX